MW00790369

Studies in Theology

Studies in Theology

by
LORAINE BOETTNER

Author of

The Reformed Doctrine of Predestination
Immortality
The Millennium
Roman Catholicism
A Harmony of the Gospels
The Christian Attitude Toward War
The Reformed Faith

THE PRESBYTERIAN AND
REFORMED PUBLISHING COMPANY

STUDIES IN THEOLOGY
by Loraine Boettner

Copyright, 1947, by
Loraine Boettner

Any one is at liberty to use material from this book with or without credit. In preparing this book the writer has received help from many sources, some acknowledged and many unacknowledged. He believes the material herein contained to be a true statement of Scripture truth, and his desire is to further, not to restrict, its use.

Nineteenth Printing, February 1989

*56th thousand
including translations*

ISBN: 0-87552-115-0

PRINTED IN THE UNITED STATES OF AMERICA

CONTENTS

Chapter I.
The Inspiration of the Scriptures

Chapter II.
Christian Supernaturalism

Chapter III.
The Trinity

Chapter IV.
The Person of Christ

Chapter V.
The Atonement

FOREWORD

The different chapters of this book were originally written as independent books or magazine articles. *The Inspiration of the Scriptures* was first published as a series of articles in the magazine CHRISTIANITY TODAY in 1936, then in book form in 1937 and reprinted in 1940. *Christian Supernaturalism* appeared as a series of articles in the same magazine in 1937. *The Trinity* was printed in two parts in THE EVANGELICAL QUARTERLY, London, England, in 1938 and 1939. *The Atonement* was published in book form in 1941. *The Person of Christ* was published in book form in 1943.

In order that these may be made more readily available and presented in systematic order, it has been decided to combine them in one volume under the general title *Studies in Theology*. Incidentally, the fact that these were written at different times and independently of each other accounts in part for a small amount of repetition where the subjects over-lap.

LORAINE BOETTNER.

WASHINGTON, D. C.

Chapter I

THE INSPIRATION OF THE SCRIPTURES

1. The Nature of Scripture Inspiration

The answer that we are to give to the question, "What is Christianity?" depends quite largely on the view we take of Scripture. If we believe that the Bible is the very word of God and infallible, we will develop one conception of Christianity. If we believe that it is only a collection of human writings, perhaps considerably above the average in its spiritual and moral teachings but nevertheless containing many errors, we will develop a radically different conception of Christianity, if, indeed, what we then have can legitimately be called Christianity. Hence we can hardly over-estimate the importance of a correct doctrine concerning the inspiration of the Scriptures.

In all matters of controversy between Christians the Scriptures are accepted as the highest court of appeal. Historically they have been the common authority of Christendom. We believe that they contain one harmonious and sufficiently complete system of doctrine; that all of their parts are consistent with each other; and that it is our duty to trace out this consistency by a careful investigation of the meaning of particular passages. We have committed ourselves to this Book without reserve, and have based our creeds upon it. We have not made our appeal to an infallible Church, nor to a scholastic hierarchy, but to a trustworthy Bible, and have maintained that it is the word of God, that by His providential care it has been kept pure in all ages, and that it is the only inspired, infallible rule of faith and practice.

That the question of inspiration is of vital importance for the Christian Church is easily seen. If she has a definite and authoritative body of Scripture to which she can go, it is a comparatively easy task to formulate her doctrines. All she has to do is to search out the teachings of Scripture and embody them in her creed. But if the Scriptures are not authoritative, if they are to be corrected and edited and some parts are to be openly rejected, the Church has a much more difficult task, and there can be no end of conflicting opinions concerning either the purpose of the Church or the system of doctrine which she is to set forth. It is small wonder that determined controversy rages around this question today when Christianity is in a life and death struggle with unbelief.

It should be noted that the Church has not held all of her other doctrines with such tenacity, nor taught them with such clearness, as she has this doctrine of inspiration. For instance, there has been considerable difference of opinion between denominations as to what the Bible teaches concerning baptism, the Lord's Supper, predestination, inability of the sinner to do good works, election, atonement, grace, perseverance, etc.; but in the Scriptures we find this doctrine taught with such consistency and clearness that all branches of the Church, Protestant and Roman Catholic alike, have agreed with instinctive judgment that the Bible is trustworthy and that its pronouncements are final.

But while this has been the historic doctrine of Christendom, and while today it remains embedded in the official creeds of the churches, it is apparent on every side that unbelief has made serious inroads. Perhaps no event in recent Church History has been more amazing than the swing away from faith in the authority of the Scriptures. Even Protestants, who at the time of the Reformation took as their basic principle an authoritative Bible rather than an authoritative Church, have shown a great tendency to neglect the Bible. While numerous books and articles have been written on this subject in recent times, it must be admitted that most of these have been designed to explain away or to tone down the doctrines which the Church has held from the beginning.

The indifference which the Church has manifested toward sound Scripture doctrine in recent days is probably the chief cause of the uncertainty and of the internal dissension with which she is faced. Ignorance concerning the nature of the doctrine of inspiration, or want of clear views concerning it, can only result in confusion. Millions of Christians today are like men whose feet are on quicksand and whose heads are in a fog. They do not know what they believe concerning the inspiration and authority of the Bible.

Much of this uncertainty has arisen because of the searching critical investigation which has been carried on during the past century, and we often hear the claim made that the historic Church doctrine of the inspiration of the Scriptures must be given up. Hence the burning question today is, Can we still trust the Bible as a doctrinal guide, as an authoritative teacher of truth, or must we find a new basis for doctrine, and, consequently, develop a whole new system of theology?

The marvelous unity of the Bible can be explained on no other ground than that of divine authorship. It is confessedly one book, yet it is made up of sixty-six different books, composed by not less than forty writers, spread over a period of not less than sixteen hundred years. The writers moved in widely separated spheres of life. Some were kings and scholars with the best education that their day afforded;

others were herdsmen and fishermen with no formal education. It is impossible that there should have been collusion between the writers. Yet there is but one type of doctrine and morality unfolded. The Messianic spirit and outlook pervades the Old Testament, beginning early in Genesis where we are told that the seed of the woman is to bruise the head of the serpent, and continuing through the ritual of the sacrificial system, the Psalms, the major and minor prophets until Malachi closes the Old Testament canon with the promise that "the Lord, whom ye seek, will suddenly come to his temple." And "Christ crucified" is the theme of the New Testament. The marvelous system of truth that is begun by Moses in the book of Genesis is brought to completion by John in the book of Revelation. In the development of no other book in the history of the world has there ever been anything that even remotely approaches this phenomenon that we find in the Bible.

That there is a wide and impassable gulf between the Bible and all other books is apparent to even the casual observer. "Holy, holy, holy" seems to be written on its every page. As we read, it speaks to us with authority and we instinctively feel ourselves under obligation to heed its warnings. It is certainly furnished with an influence which is possessed by no other book, and we are forced to ask the question, Whence comes it? And since it is so unique in the power which it exerts, so lofty in the moral and spiritual principles which it sets forth, and since it so repeatedly claims to be of divine origin, are we not justified in believing that claim to be true, that it is in fact the very word of God?

The terms "plenary inspiration" and "verbal inspiration" as used here are practically synonymous. By "plenary inspiration" we mean that a full and sufficient influence of the Holy Spirit extended to all parts of Scripture, rendering it an authoritative revelation from God, so that while the revelations come to us through the minds and wills of men they are nevertheless in the strictest sense the word of God. By "verbal inspiration" we mean that the Divine influence which surrounded the sacred writers extended not only to the general thoughts, but also to the very words they employed, so that the thoughts which God intended to reveal to us have been conveyed with infallible accuracy — that the writers were the organs of God in such a sense that what they said God said.

Inspiration Necessary to Secure Accuracy

That this inspiration should extend to the very words seems most natural since the purpose of inspiration is to secure an infallible record of truth. Thoughts and words are so inseparably connected that as a rule a change in words means a change in thought.

In human affairs, for instance, the man of business dictates his letters to his secretary in his own words in order that they may contain his exact meaning. He does not assume that his secretary will correctly express important, delicate, and complicated matters which might be given him in general terms. Much less would the Holy Spirit say to His penman, "Write to this effect." The Bible assumes to speak concerning a number of things which are absolutely beyond the reach of man's wisdom — the nature and attributes of God, the origin and purpose of man and of the world, man's fall into sin and his present helpless condition, the plan of redemption including our Lord's substitutionary life and death, the glories of heaven, and the torments of hell. More than a general supervision is necessary if the truth concerning these great and sublime subjects is to be given without error and without prejudice. Inerrancy requires that God shall choose His own words. All men who have tried to explain these deep things without supernatural revelation have done little more than show their own ignorance. They grope like the blind, they speculate and guess and generally leave us in greater uncertainty than before. In the nature of the case these things are beyond man's wisdom. We have only to look at the pagan systems or at the arrogant and speculative theories of our own philosophers to find what the limits of our spiritual wisdom would be apart from the Bible. Whether we turn to the philosophers among the Greeks, to the Mystics of the East or to the intellectuals among the Germans, the story is the same. In fact many of the world's supposedly advanced thinkers have even doubted the existence of God and the immortality of the soul. God alone is capable of speaking authoritatively on these subjects; and of all the world's books we find that the Bible alone gives us on the one hand an adequate account of the majesty of God, and on the other hand an adequate account of the sinful state of the human heart and a satisfactory remedy for that sin. It shows us that neither laws nor education can change the human heart, that nothing short of the redemptive power of Christ can make man what he ought to be.

A mere human report of divine things would naturally contain more or less error, both in regard to the words chosen to express the ideas and in the proportionate emphasis given the different parts of the revelation. Since particular thoughts are inseparably connected with particular words, the wording must be exact or the thoughts conveyed will be defective. If it be admitted, for instance, that the words, ransom, atonement, resurrection, immortality, etc., as used in Scripture have no definite authority or meaning behind them, then it follows that the doctrines based on them have no definite authority. In Scripture's own use of Scripture we are taught the stress which it lays upon the very words which it employs, the exact meaning depending upon the use of a particular word, as when our Lord says that "the Scripture cannot be broken" (John 10:35); or when He answered the Sadducees by referring them to the words spoken to Moses at the burning bush where the whole point of the argument depended on the tense of the verb, "I am the God of Abraham, and the God of Isaac, and the God of Jacob" (Mark 12::26); or when Paul stresses the fact that in the promise made to Abraham the word used is singular and not plural — "seed," "as of one," and not "seeds, as of many;" "And to thy seed, which is Christ" (Gal. 3:16). In each of these cases the argument turns on the use of one particular word, and in each case that word was decisive because it had divine authority behind it. Oftentimes the exact shade of meaning of the original words is of the utmost importance in deciding questions of doctrine and life.

A Definite System of Theology

For any serious study of Christian doctrines we must first of all have the assurance that the Bible is true. If it is a fully authoritative and trustworthy guide, then we will accept the doctrines which it sets forth. We may not be able to grasp the full meaning of all of these things, there may in fact be many difficulties in our minds concerning them; but that they are true we shall never doubt. We acknowledge our limitations, but we shall believe in so far as the truth has been revealed to us. The fortunes of distinctive Christianity are in a very real sense bound up with those of the Biblical doctrine of inspiration, for unless that stands we have nothing stable.

If we have a trustworthy Scripture as our guide, we shall have an evangelical, as distinguished from a naturalistic, humanistic or Unitarian system of theology; for we find the evangelical system clearly taught in the Bible. But if the Bible is not a trustworthy guide, we shall then have to seek a different basis for our theology, and the probability is that we shall have but little more than a philosophical system left. To undermine confidence in the Bible as an inspired Book is to undermine confidence in the whole Christian system. This truth is rather painfully impressed upon us when we attempt to read some of the recent religious books, even systematic theologies, in which the writers appeal not to Scripture but to the teachings of various philosophers to prove their points. If the Bible is not trustworthy we might as well save ourselves the labor of "revising" our creeds. We might as well throw them away and make a fresh start, for we shall then have to develop a whole new theology. To date we have accepted the distinctive doctrines of the Christian system because we found them taught in the Bible. But apart from the Bible we have no authoritative standard.

Unless the Bible can be quoted as an inspired book its authority and usefulness for public preaching, for comfort in sickness or death, and for instruction in every perplexity, have been seriously impoverished. Its "Thus saith the Lord" has then been reduced to a mere human supposition, and it can no longer be considered our perfect rule of faith and practice. If it cannot be quoted as an inspired book, its value as a weapon in controversy has been greatly weakened, perhaps entirely destroyed; for what good will it do to quote it to an opponent if he can reply that it is not authoritative? Today, as in every past age, the destructive critics, skeptics, and modernists of whatever kind center their attacks on the Bible. They must first be rid of its authority or their systems amount only to foolishness.

The inspiration for which we contend is, of course, that of the original Hebrew and Greek words as written by the prophets and apostles. We believe that if these are understood in their intended sense — plain statements of fact, figures of speech, idioms and poetry as such — the Bible is without an error from Genesis to Revelation. While it leaves much unsaid, we believe that all that it does say is true in the sense in which it is intended. We do not claim infallibility for the various versions and translations, such as the American Standard or King James versions, and much less do we claim infallibility for the rather free one man translations which have attained some vogue in recent years. Translations will naturally vary with each individual translator, and are to be considered accurate only in so far as they reproduce the original autographs. Furthermore, some of the Hebrew and Greek words have no full equivalent in the English language, and sometimes even the best scholars differ as to the exact meaning of certain words. And further still, we must acknowledge that we have none of the original autographs, but that our oldest manuscripts are copies of copies. Yet the best of the present day Hebrew and Greek scholars assert that in probably nine hundred and ninety-nine cases out of a thousand we have either positive knowledge or reasonable assurance as to what the original words were, so accurately have the copyists reproduced them and so faithfully have the translators done their work. Hence he who reads our English Bible as set forth in the American Standard or King James version has before him what is, for all practical purposes, the very word of God as it was originally given to the prophets and apostles. Certainly we have reason to thank God that the Bible has come down to us in such pure form.

This has been the historic Protestant position concerning the authority of Scripture. It was held by Luther and Calvin, and was written into the creeds of the post-Reformation period. The Lutheran doctrine of inspiration was set forth in the Form of Concord, which reads: "We believe, confess, and teach that the only rule and norm, according to which all dogmas and all doctors ought to be esteemed and judged, is no other whatever than the prophetic and apostolic writings of the Old and New Testament." The doctrine of the Reformed Church was stated in the Second Helvetic Confession as follows: "We believe and confess, that the canonical Scriptures of the holy prophets and apostles of each Testament are the true word of God, and that they possess sufficient authority from themselves alone and not from man. For God Himself spoke to the fathers, to the prophets, and to the apostles, and continues to speak to us through the Holy Scriptures." And in the Westminster Confession of Faith the Presbyterian Church declared that "It pleased the Lord, at sundry times and in divers manners, to reveal Himself and to declare His will unto His Church; and afterward . . . to commit the same wholly unto writing." "The authority of the Holy Scripture, for which it ought to be believed and obeyed, dependeth not upon the testimony of any man or church, but wholly upon God (who is truth itself) the author thereof; and therefore it is to be received because it is the word of God." And further that both the Old and New Testament have been "immediately inspired by God and by His singular care and providence kept pure in all ages." In more recent times it has been reasserted by Hodge, Warfield and Kuyper. That these men have been the lights and ornaments of the highest type of Christianity will be admitted by practically all Protestants. They have held that the Bible does not merely *contain* the word of God, as a pile of chaff contains some wheat, but that the Bible in all its parts *is* the word of God.

2. The Writers Claim Inspiration

Our primary reasons for holding that the Bible is the inspired Word of God are that the writers themselves claim this inspiration, and that the contents of their messages bear out that claim. The uniformity with which the prophets insisted that the messages which they spoke were not theirs but the Lord's — that their messages were the pure and unmixed Word of God, spoken out by them just as they had received them — is a striking phenomenon of Scripture. "Thus saith the Lord" was the prophet's constant reminder to the people that the words which he spoke were not his own, but God's. Paul and the other apostles claimed to speak not in the words which man's wisdom taught, but in words which the Spirit taught (I Cor. 2:13). Not only the substance of their teaching, but also its form of expression, was asserted to be of Divine origin.

Although the claim that they spoke with Divine authority is characteristic of the writers throughout the entire Bible, they never once base that authority on their own wisdom or dignity. They speak as the Lord's messengers or witnesses, and their words are to be obeyed only because His authority is behind them. Those who heard them heard God, and those who refused to hear them refused to hear God (Ezek. 2:5; Matt. 10:40; John 13:20).

And since the writers so repeatedly claimed inspiration, it is evident that they were either inspired or that they acted with fanatical presumption. We are shut up to the conclusion that the Bible is the Word of God, or that it is a lie. But how could a lie have exerted the uniquely beneficial and morally uplifting influence that the Bible has exerted everywhere it has gone? To ask such a question is to answer it.

Let us also notice that the contemporaries of the New Testament writers, as well as the early church fathers — men who were in the best position to judge whether or not such claims were true — accepted these claims without question. They acknowledged that a great gulf existed between those writings and their own. As to the dying Sir Walter Scott there was but one "Book," so to these early church fathers there was but one authoritative Divine word. They based doctrines and precepts on it. The Gospels and Epistles contain an abundance of internal evidence showing that they were expected to be received and that they were received with reverence and humility. And as we follow the course of history down through the centuries the evidence becomes all the more abundant. Even the heretics bear witness to this fact, anxious as they are to be rid of such authority. Furthermore, the writings themselves contain no contradictions or inconsistencies which would destroy their claims. With perfect harmony they present the same plan of salvation and the same exalted moral principles. If, then, in the first place, sober and honest writers claim that their words were inspired by God; and if, in the second place, these claims not only went unchallenged but were humbly accepted by their contemporaries; and if, in the third place, the writings contain no contradictory evidence, then certainly we have a phenomenon which must be accounted for.

Objection is sometimes made to the New Testament books on the ground that they are not the writings of Jesus but only of His followers, and that they were not written until some time after His death. But it is hardly to be expected that Jesus would have given a full account of the way of salvation during His earthly ministry, for that could not have been understood until after His death and resurrection. He could, indeed, have set it forth by way of prophecy even in the days of His flesh, and in fact He announced to His disciples the general nature of the plan. But even His most intimate disciples appear to have been unable to understand the nature of His work until their minds were enlightened by the Holy Spirit on the day of Pentecost. All things considered, the most natural method was that which He chose—the fulfillment of the events, and then their explanation through inspired writers. That, also, was in accordance with the Lord's procedure throughout Old Testament times.

Scripture Teaching Concerning Inspiration

The Biblical doctrine of the true purpose and function of the prophets and their manner of delivering the message is clearly set forth in the Lord's words to Moses: "I will raise them up a prophet from among their brethren, like unto thee; *and I will put my words in his mouth, and he shall speak unto them all that I shall command him*" (Deut. 18:18). Jehovah would speak not so much to the prophets as through them. They were to speak precisely the words given them, but no others. "I have put my words in thy mouth," the Lord said to Jeremiah in appointing him a prophet to the nations (Jer. 1:9). Identically the same words were spoken to Isaiah (51:16; 59:21), and the formula, "Thus saith Jehovah," is repeated some eighty times in the book of Isaiah alone. Even the false prophet Balaam could speak only that which Jehovah gave him to speak — "And the angel of Jehovah said unto Balaam, Go with the men; but only the word that I shall speak unto thee, that thou shalt speak" (Nu. 22:35; 23:5, 12, 16). In many Old Testament passages it is nothing other than a process of "dictation" which is described, although we are not told what the method was by which this dictation was accomplished. In others we are simply given to understand that Jehovah spoke through chosen men as His organs, supervising them in such a manner that their spoken or written words were His words and were a distinctly superhuman product. The uniform teaching of the Old Testament is that the prophets spoke when, and only when, the word of Jehovah came unto them: Hosea 1:1; Amos 1:3; Micah 1:1; Malachi 1:1, etc.

The characteristic Hebrew word for prophet is *nabhi,* "spokesman," not merely spokesman in general, but by way of eminence, that is, God's spokesman. In no case does the prophet presume to speak on his own authority. That he is a prophet in the first place is not of his own choosing, but in response to a call from God, oftentimes a call which was obeyed only with reluctance: and he speaks or forbears to speak as the Lord gives him utterance.

And in strong contrast with this high calling of the true prophets we should notice the stern warnings and denunciations against those who presume to speak without having received a Divine call. "But the prophet that shall speak a word presumptuously in my name, which I have not commanded him to speak, or that shall speak in the name of other gods, that same prophet shall die" (Deut. 18:20); "Woe unto the foolish prophets, that follow their own spirit, and have seen nothing" (Ezek. 13:3). It is a serious thing for mere men, with unwashen hands, to presume to speak for the Most High. Yet how common it is for the destructive critics of our day to deny this or that statement in the Bible, or to tell us that we need a shorter Bible, or perhaps even a new Bible composed of modern writings! And the error committed by men in adding to God's word, as the Roman Catholics do with their "Apocrypha" and church traditions, the Christian Scientists with their "Science and Health With Key to the Scriptures," and the Mormons with their "Book of Mormon," is fully as bad as to take from it.

Testimony of Jesus to the Old Testament

That Jesus considered the Old Testament fully inspired is abundantly clear. He quoted it as such, and based His teachings upon it. One of His clearest statements is found in John 10:35, where, in controversy with the Jews, His defense takes the form of an appeal to Scripture, and after quoting a statement He adds the significant words, "And the Scripture cannot be broken." The reason that it was worth while for Him, or that it is worth while for us, to appeal to Scripture, is that it "cannot be broken." And the word here translated "broken" is the common one for breaking the law, or the Sabbath, meaning to annul, or deny, or withstand its authority. In this statement Jesus declares that it is impossible to annul, or withstand, or deny the Scripture. For Him and for the Jews alike, an appeal to Scripture was an appeal to an authority whose determination was final even to its minute details.

That Jesus considered all Scripture as the very word of God is shown in such a passage as Matt. 19:4. When some of the Pharisees questioned Him on the subject of divorce His reply was: "Have ye not read, that he who made them from the beginning made them male and female, and said, 'For this cause shall a man leave his father and mother, and shall cleave to his wife; and the two shall become one flesh. . . . What therefore God hath joined together, let not man put asunder." Here He explicitly declares that God is the author of the words of Gen. 2:24: *"He who made them . . . said,"* "A man shall leave his father and mother, and shall cleave to his wife." And yet as we read these words in the Old Testament there is nothing to tell us that they are the words of God. They are presented only as the words of Scripture itself or of Moses, and can be assigned to God as their Author only on the basis that all Scripture is His word. Mark 10:5-9 and I Cor. 6:16 present the same teaching. Wherever Christ and the Apostles quote Scripture, they think of it as the living voice of God and therefore divinely authoritative. They have not the slightest hesitation in assigning to God the words of the human authors, or in assigning to the human authors the most express words of God (Matt. 15:7; Mark 7:6, 10; Rom. 10:5, 19, 20).

In His stinging rebuke to the Sadducees, "Ye do err, not knowing the Scriptures" (Matt. 22:29), the very thing which He points out is that their error comes, not because they have followed the Scriptures, but precisely because they have not followed them. He who founds his doctrine and practice on Scripture does not err. So common was its use, and so unquestionable was its authority, that in the fiercest conflict He needed no other weapon than the final "It is written"! (Matt. 4:4, 7, 10; Luke 4:4, 8; 24:26). His last words before His Ascension contained a rebuke to the disciples because they had not understood that all things which were written in the entire Scriptures "must needs be fulfilled" (Luke 24:44). If it was written that the Christ should suffer these things, then all doubt concerning Him was rendered absurd. The disciples were to rest securely on that word as on a sure foundation. Hence we receive the Old Testament on the authority of Christ. He hands it to us and tells us that it is the Word of God, that the prophets spoke by the Spirit, and that the Scriptures cannot be broken. By His numerous quotations He has welded it to the New Testament so that they now form one unified Bible. The two Testaments have but one voice. They must stand or fall together.

New Testament Manner of Quoting the Old Testament

If Jesus held that the entire Old Testament was infallible, the idea is no less clearly set forth by the Apostles. The familiar way in which they quote any part of the Scriptures as the word of God, regardless of whether the original words are assigned to Him or not, shows that He was considered as speaking all through the Old Testament. In Heb. 3:7 the words of the psalmist are quoted as the direct words of the Holy Spirit, "Wherefore, even as the Holy Spirit saith, Today if ye shall hear his voice, Harden not your hearts, as in the provocation" (Ps. 95:7). In Acts 13:35 the words of David (Ps. 16:10) are said to have been the words of God, "He (God) saith in another psalm, Thou wilt not give thy Holy One to see corruption." In Romans 15:11 the words of the psalmist are ascribed to God, "And again (He saith), Praise the Lord, all ye Gentiles; And let all the peoples praise Him" (Ps. 117:1). In Acts 4:24, 25 the Apostles ascribe to God the words spoken by David in the second psalm, "God . . . who by the Holy Spirit, by the mouth of our father David thy servant, didst say, Why do the Gentiles rage, And the peoples imagine vain things?" In Hebrews 1:7, 8 the same teaching is found concerning two other psalms. In Romans 15:10 the words of Moses are ascribed to God, "And again He saith, Rejoice, ye Gentiles, with His people" (Deut. 32:43).

These quotations show clearly that in the minds of Christ and the Apostles there was an absolute identification between the text of the Old Testament and the voice of the living God. And it is, of course, not to be inferred that the inspiration of the New Testament is in any way inferior to that of the Old. In fact the tendency has been to assign a lower position to the Old Testament. When the Old Testament is shown to be inspired there is usually no question about the New.

CLAIMS OF THE NEW TESTAMENT WRITERS FOR THEIR OWN WRITINGS

When we examine the claims which the New Testament writers make for their own works we find that they claim full inspiration for them and place them on the same level with the Scriptures of the Old Testament. All schools of present-day Biblical criticism acknowledge that these claims were repeatedly made, even though they deny that they are true. We find, for instance, that when the Apostles began their ministry they received from Christ Himself a promise of supernatural guidance: "But when they deliver you up, be not anxious how or what ye shall speak: for it shall be given you in that hour what ye shall speak. For it is not ye that speak, but the Spirit of your Father that speaketh in you" (Matt. 10:19, 20; Mark 13:11; Luke 12:11, 12). This same promise was repeated at the close of His ministry (Luke 21:12-15). Perhaps the most important promise is found in the Gospel of John: "When He, the Spirit of truth, is come, He shall guide you into all the truth" (16:13). The Apostles later claimed this guidance. They have not the least shadow of doubt as to the exact truth of their words, whether on historical or doctrinal matters,—a rather striking phenomenon, since accurate and truth-loving historians commonly express less, and not greater, assurance when they descend to details. So authoritative does Paul claim his gospel to be that he pronounces wrong and accursed any one who teaches differently, even though it be an angel from heaven. ". . . But though we, or an angel from heaven, should preach unto you any gospel other than that which we preached unto you, let him be anathema . . ." (Gal. 1:6-9). Their commands are from the Lord, and are given with binding authority, ". . . the things which I write unto you, that they are the commandment of the Lord" (I Cor. 14:37,; II Thess. 3:6, 12). In writing to the Corinthians Paul distinguishes between the commands which Christ gave, and the commands which he gives, but places his own alongside those of Christ's as of equal authority (I Cor. 7:10, 12, 40). He asserts that what they preached was in truth "the word of God" (I Thess. 2:13). Such things were to be immediately and unquestionably received. We should also notice his easy way of combining the book of Deuteronomy and the Gospel of Luke under the common head of "Scripture," as if that were a most natural thing to do (I Tim. 5:18): "For the Scripture saith, Thou shalt not muzzle the ox when he treadeth out the corn. And, the laborer is worthy of his hire" (Deut. 25:4; Luke 10:7). This same practice was common among the early church fathers.

In II Tim. 3:16 (translating the Greek in its most natural sense) Paul tells us that "All scripture is given by inspiration of God, and is profitable for doctrine, for reproof, for correction, for instruction in righteousness." This marginal translation, which has behind it the. authority of Archbishop Trench, Bishop Wordsworth, and others of the Revised Version Committee, as well as the authority of that prince of exegetes and theologians, Dr. Benjamin B. Warfield, is much to be preferred to the rendering of the Revised Version, which reads, "Every scripture inspired of God is profitable," etc. This latter translation has been repudiated by numerous scholars as a calamitous and hopelessly condemned blunder, and even by some of the critics as false criticism. As Dr. Warfield has pointed out, the very term in the Greek, *theopneustos,* means not that a product of human origin is breathed into by God, but that a Divine product is breathed out by God. It means "God breathed," "produced by the creative breath of the Almighty," "God-given." There is no other term in the Greek language which would have asserted more emphatically the Divine origin of the product.

In the writings of Peter we find the same high estimate of New Testament Scripture. He declares, for instance, that "No prophecy ever came by the will of man: but men spake from God, being moved (or literally, *borne, carried along*) by the Holy Spirit" (II Peter 1:21).

He declares that the Apostles "preached the Gospel . . . by the Holy Spirit sent forth from heaven" (I Peter 1:12). He places Paul's writings on the same high plane with "the other scriptures"—"Our beloved brother Paul also, according to the wisdom given to him, wrote unto you; in all his epistles . . . as also the other scriptures" (II Peter 3:15, 16). More dignity and reverence and authority than that could not be ascribed to any writing.

Luke declares that on the day of Pentecost the disciples spoke "as the Spirit gave them utterance" (Acts 2:4). And John, the beloved disciple, even pronounces a curse on any one who dares to take from or add to his writing (Rev. 22:18, 19). Such claims as these, if based only on human authority, would exhibit only the most astounding impudence.

It is, of course, impossible to explain away the innumerable texts which teach plenary inspiration, and the idea that they might be explained away is based on the odd notion that this doctrine is taught only in isolated texts here and there. It is true that some texts teach it with exceptional clearness, and those are the ones which skeptics would most like to be rid of. But these passages are simply the climax of a progressive and pervasive testimony to the divine origin and infallibility of these writings, a testimony equally strong in the two Testaments. "The effort to explain away the Bible's witness to its plenary inspiration," says Dr. Warfield, "reminds one of a man standing safely in his laboratory and elaborately explaining—possibly with the aid of diagrams and mathematical *formulae*—how every stone in an avalanche has a defined pathway and may easily be dodged by one with some presence of mind. We may fancy such an elaborate trifler's triumph as he would analyze the avalanche into its constituent stones, and demonstrate of stone after stone that its pathway is definite, limited, and may easily be avoided. But avalanches, unfortunately, do not come upon us stone by stone, one at a time, courteously leaving us opportunity to withdraw from the pathway of each in turn: but all at once, in a roaring mass of destruction. Just so we may explain away a text or two which teach plenary inspiration, to our own closest satisfaction, dealing with them each without reference to its relation to the others: but these texts of ours, again, unfortunately do not come upon us in this artificial isolation; neither are they few in number. There are scores, hundreds, of them; and they come bursting upon us in one solid mass. Explain them away? We should have to explain away the whole New Testament. What a pity it is that we cannot see and feel the avalanche of texts beneath which we lie hopelessly buried, as clearly as we may see and feel the avalanche of stones! Let us, however, but open our eyes to the variety and pervasiveness of the New Testament witness to its high estimate of Scripture, and we shall no longer wonder that modern scholarship finds itself compelled to allow that the Christian Church has read her records correctly, and that the church-doctrine of inspiration is simply a transcript of the biblical doctrine; nor shall we any longer wonder that the church, receiving these Scriptures as her authoritative teacher of doctrine, adopted in the very beginning of her life the doctrine of plenary inspiration, and has held it with a tenacity that knows no wavering, until the present hour."

3. The Nature of the Influence by Which Inspiration is Accomplished

The evangelical Christian churches have never held what has been stigmatized the "mechanical" theory of inspiration, despite the charges often made to the contrary. Instead of reducing the writers of Scripture to the level of machines or typewriters we have insisted that, while they wrote or spoke as they were moved by the Holy Spirit, they nevertheless remained thinking, willing, self-conscious beings whose peculiar styles and mannerisms are clearly traceable in their writings. If their native tongue was Hebrew, they wrote Hebrew; if it was Greek, they wrote Greek; if they were educated, they wrote as men of culture; if uneducated, they wrote as such men would write. We do not separate the divine and human elements, but insist that the two are united in perfect harmony so that every word of Scripture is at one and the same time the word of God and also the word of man. The writers themselves make it plain that in this process the divine influence is primary and the human secondary, so that they are not so much the originators but rather the receivers and announcers of these messages. Hence what they wrote or spoke was not to be looked upon as merely their own product, but as the pure Word of God, and for that reason it was to be received and implicitly obeyed.

The fact that we can so easily trace the peculiar style or manner of expression through the writings of Paul or John or Moses shows that the Scriptures were given in a way which made allowance for human personalities. If it were otherwise the Scriptures would then be reduced to a .dead level of monotony, and we would indeed have a mechanical theory of inspiration in which the writers were little more than automatons. It lies in the very idea of inspiration that God would use the agents which He employs according to their individual natures. One type of man would be chosen to write history, another type to write poetry, and still another type to set forth doctrines, although these functions might overlap in some writers. And back of that we are to remember that throughout the entire life of the prophet God's providential control had been preparing him with the particular talents, education and experience which would be needed for the message which he was to give. This providential preparation of the prophets, which gave them the proper spiritual, intellectual and physical background, must, indeed have had its beginning in their remote ancestors. The result was that the right men were brought to the right places at the right times, and wrote the particular books or gave the particular messages which were designed for them. When God wanted to give His people a history of their early beginnings, He prepared a Moses to write it When He wanted to give them the lofty and worshipful poetry of the psalms, He prepared a David with poetic imagination. And since Christianity in its very nature would demand logical statement, He prepared a Paul, giving him a logical mind and the appropriate religious background which would enable him to set it forth in that manner. In this natural way God so prepared the various writers of Scripture that with the appropriate assistance of His directing and illuminating Spirit they freely and spontaneously wrote what He wished as He wished and when He wished. Thus the prophet was fitted to the message, and the message was suited to the prophet. Thus also the distinctive literary style of each writer was preserved, and each writer did a work which no one else was equipped to do.

On some occasions inspiration amounted to little if anything more than a process of dictation. God spoke and man recorded the words: Gen. 22:15-18; Ex. 20:1-17; Is. 43:1-28, etc. On other occasions the writers functioned as thinkers and composers with all of their native energy coming into play as they deliberated, recollected and poured out their hearts to God, the Holy Spirit exercising only a general supervision which led them to write what was needful and to keep their writings free from error, e.g., Luke 1:1-4; Rom. 1:1-32; Eph. 1:1-23, etc. In narrating simple historical facts and in copying lists of names or numbers from reliable sources this superintendence was at a minimum. Perhaps in some instances they were not even conscious of the Spirit's directing influence as they wrote.

In the main, however, we can say that the words of the prophets express not merely something which has been thought out, inferred, hoped or feared by them, but something conveyed to them,—sometimes an unwelcome message forced upon them by the revealing Spirit. They naturally shrank from giving messages which foretold destruction for the people or for the nation. Yet they were not at liberty to say either more or less than what had been given to them, for he who is entrusted with a message from the King is not at liberty to omit or change any part of it but must give it out just as he has received it. Isaiah, for instance, immediately after his glorious vision and official appointment, was sent with an unwelcome message to his countrymen, and was even told beforehand that the people would not hear, that the effect of his preaching would be further rebellion and further hardening of their hearts. Yet he was not able to change the message, but could only inquire, "Lord, how long?" (Is. 6:9-13). Ezekiel likewise was sent to a rebellious people and was told that they would not hear (3:4-11) But whether they would hear or whether they would forbear, they were to know that a prophet of the Lord had been among them (Ezek. 2:5). Much as the prophet might like to speak otherwise, he could only give the message which had been given to him. If the people failed to heed the warning the responsibility rested on themselves (Ezek. 33:1-11). The objectivity of the message is further shown in that sometimes the prophets themselves did not understand the revelations which were given through them (Daniel 12:8, 9; Rev. 5:1-4).

Nor is the work of the Holy Spirit in inspiration to be considered any more mysterious than His work in the spheres of grace and providence. The first exercise of saving faith in the regenerated soul, for instance, is at one and the same time a work induced by the Holy Spirit and a freely chosen act of the person. And throughout the Bible the laws of nature, the course of history, and the varying fortunes of individuals are ever attributed to God's providential control. "Jehovah hath His way in the whirlwind and in the storm, and the clouds are the dust of His feet," Nahum 1:3. "He maketh His sun to rise on the evil and the good, and sendeth rain on the just and the unjust," Matt. 5:45. "The Most High ruleth in the kingdom of men, and giveth it to whomsoever He will, and setteth up over it the lowest of men," Dan. 4:17. "It is God who worketh in you both to will and to work, for His good pleasure," Phil. 2:13. "The king's heart is in the hand of Jehovah as the watercourses: He turneth it whithersoever He will," Prov. 21:1.

Inspiration must have been somewhat like the touch of the driver on the reins of the racing steeds. The preservation of the individual styles and mannerisms indicates as much. Under this providential control the prophets were so governed that while their humanity was not superseded their words to the people were God's words and have been accepted as such by the Church in all ages.

That the writers of Scripture often used other documents or sources in the composition of their books is apparent to even the casual reader.

For instance, the thirty-seventh chapter of Isaiah and the nineteenth chapter of II Kings are exactly alike. Hence Isaiah and the writer of II Kings must have had access to the same source materials. Many of the accounts in the different Gospels are told in almost identical language. If it be definitely proven, for instance, that the Pentateuch consists of different parts which in turn are based on older documents, our doctrine of inspiration can accept that view. In dealing with historical or legal data especially the writers of Scripture may have used sources as naturally as do present-day writers, with this difference: that the Holy Spirit supervised their work in such a way that they selected out only the material which God wanted given to the people, and set forth that material in such a way that it was free from error. We are not so much concerned with the method by which they wrote as we are about the value and authority of their final product. The more naturally and the less mechanically this writing took place, the better.

It is not to be expected that we should give a full explanation as to how the divine and human agents co-operated in the production of Scripture. Suffice it to say that in most cases it was something much more intimate than what is commonly known as "dictation." The trouble with us is that oftentimes we seek full explanations for those things which in their deeper aspects should only be adored as mysteries, such as the Trinity, the atonement, the relationship between the sovereignty of God and the freedom of man, and the inspiration of the Scriptures. The modernist with his naturalistic basis easily solves these problems by ignoring the Divine, but is unaware how superficial he is. Evangelicals have truly grappled with these problems. They have acknowledged both the Divine and human elements and have brought about a partial solution while confessing that the human mind cannot fully comprehend the deep things of God.

It is, of course, not to be assumed that inspiration rendered the prophets omniscient. Their inspiration extended only to the contents of the particular messages which were given through them. In matters of science, philosophy or history which were outside their immediate purpose they stood on the same level with their contemporaries. They were preserved from error when speaking the Lord's message, but inspiration in itself no more made them astronomers or chemists than it made them agriculturists. Many of them may have believed with their contemporaries that the sun moved around the earth, but nowhere in their writings do they teach that it does. Paul could not err in his teachings, although he could not remember how many people he had baptized at Corinth (I Cor. 1:16). We have already observed that

Daniel and John did not fully understand all the revelations given through them. Isaac unwittingly pronounced the prophetic blessing on Jacob instead of his favorite son Esau, and when he later discovered that he had been deceived he was utterly unable to change it. When Moses recorded the promise that Abraham was to be the father of many nations, he little realized that in the later era all of the Gentile Christians were to be included in that promise and that eventually it would embrace the whole world (Gal. 3:29; Eph. 2:13, 14; Rom. 4:13; Acts 13:17).

Nor does the doctrine of inspiration imply that the writers were free from error in their personal conduct. Moses wrote voluminously concerning the early history of Israel and is commonly considered the greatest of the Old Testament prophets; yet at the waters of Meribah he took to himself the glory which belonged only to Jehovah, and for that offense he was not permitted to enter the promised land (Nu. 20:7-13). Balaam spoke certain great truths, and Saul was among the prophets. Peter likewise was infallible as a spokesman of the Lord, and yet on at least one occasion he fell into serious error in his personal conduct and it was necessary for Paul to resist him to the face, for he stood condemned (Gal. 2:11-14).

Furthermore, we find that inspiration was flexible enough to allow for some personal matters, as when Paul asked Timothy to come to him shortly and to bring his coat and certain books which he had left at Troas (II Tim. 4:13). It includes personal advice in regard to Timothy's health, I Tim. 5:23), and personal concern for the treatment accorded to the returned slave Onesimus (Philemon 1:10-16).

Hence we see that the Christian doctrine of inspiration is not the mechanical lifeless process which unfriendly critics have often represented it to be. Rather it calls the whole personality of the prophet into action, giving full play to his own literary style and mannerisms, taking into consideration the preparation given the prophet in order that he might deliver a particular kind of message, and allowing for the use of other documents or sources of information as these were needed. If these facts were kept more clearly in mind the doctrine of inspiration would not be so summarily set aside nor so unreasonably attacked by otherwise cautious and reverent scholars.

4. The Alleged Errors in Scripture

One of the most distressing things in present-day churches is that whereas in the religious debates of earlier days they used to argue about what the Bible said, never for a moment doubting that what it said was true, groups within the various churches are now arguing as to whether or not the Bible is trustworthy. A short time ago the writer heard a sermon by a professor from a well-known theological institution in which he declared that the Bible contained historical, moral and literary errors. This is a serious charge and if it could be proved it certainly would destroy the Christian doctrine of inspiration.

That the Bible contains some statements which we in our present state of knowledge are not able to explain fully, is readily admitted. Our knowledge of the Hebrew and Greek languages is by no means perfect. There are a number of words or idioms, for instance, which occur only once or only a few times in Scripture, and it sometimes happens that even the best scholars are not in full agreement as to their exact meaning.

It gives us no little satisfaction, however, to know that as scholarship and archaeological discovery have advanced the great majority of the supposed "Biblical errors" which were so confidently paraded by skeptics and atheists a few decades ago have been cleared up. Today scarcely a shred of the old list remains. It gives us even greater satisfaction to know that despite all of the merciless attacks which through the ages have been made on the Bible, and despite all of the fierce light of criticism which so long has been beating upon its open pages, *not so much as one single error has been definitely proved to exist anywhere in the Bible.* Without exception up to the present time where the conflict has been joined and the verdict rendered the skeptic has been proved wrong and the Bible right. Those supposed discrepancies remain today as only too readily forgotten warnings against those who in their eagerness to do violence to the Scripture doctrine of inerrancy throw historical and literary caution to the winds.

It is to be noted further that the alleged errors have been for the most part trivial. In no cases have important doctrines or important historical events been in question. When fuller light is turned on them most of them, like ghosts, melt away from sight. Few if any of them are anything more than mistakes on the part of copyists or translators; and certainly no one has a right to say there are errors in the Bible unless he can show beyond reasonable doubt that they were in the original manuscripts.

The few difficulties which still remain are so trivial that no one should be seriously troubled by them. There is every reason for believing that with additional knowledge they too will be cleared up. It is little exaggeration to say that on the whole they bear about the same relation to the Bible that a few grains of sandstone detected here and there in the marble of the Parthenon bear to that building. In view of past experience it is important to keep in mind that there is a strong presumption against any of them being real errors, a presumption which can be measured only by the whole weight of evidence which can be brought forward to prove that the Bible is a fully trustworthy guide in moral and spiritual matters.

When we remember that the Bible was in process of being written over a period of about fifteen hundred years, that some forty authors living in different ages with different points of view in life and with diverse literary talents had a part in its production, that the religious and political history of the country was hopelessly complicated, and that confessedly accurate Roman historians have sometimes fallen into error in narrating contemporary events, the marvel is, not that there are a few things recorded in the Bible which are difficult to understand, but that the number is so few.

Even though it be admitted that the Bible contains some few statements which we in our present state of knowledge are not able to harmonize, that should afford no rational ground for denying the general doctrine of Scripture infallibility. We have the word of Christ Himself that "the Scripture cannot be broken" (John 10:35); and more than that we should not ask. In the material universe we see evidences of design so manifold, and diverse, and wonderful, that the mind is driven to the conclusion that it has an intelligent Author. And yet here and there we find monstrosities. The fact that in our present state of knowledge we are not able to explain fully why snakes and mosquitoes and malaria germs were created does not prevent us from believing that the world had an intelligent and benevolent Creator. Neither should the Christian give up his faith in a fully inspired Bible just because he is unable to harmonize every detail with all of the remainder.

Perhaps no other science in recent times has done so much to confirm the Bible as has archaeology. The patient work of explorers and excavators in Egypt, Babylonia, Assyria and Palestine, with their picks and shovels, has opened volumes of ancient history for us, giving us graphic accounts of the languages, literature, institutions and religions of peoples who had long since been forgotten except as they were incidentally mentioned in the Bible. Here we have the records chiseled in stone, burnt into the clay brick tablets, recorded in one way or another on the monuments, tombs, buildings, papyrus and pottery. Without exceptions these discoveries confirm the truthfulness of the Bible, and time after time the theories and guesses of the destructive critics have been proved wrong. In fact the enemies of the Bible have met no more relentless foe than the science of archaeology. The evidence presented from this source is so impartial, unimpeachable and conclusive that it compels acceptance by friend and foe alike.

EXAMPLES OF ALLEGED ERRORS

Space forbids us giving a detailed list of the "errors" which have been pointed out in Scripture, yet our discussion would be incomplete if we did not give a few examples. At first sight there seems to be a contradiction between Acts 9:7 and Acts 22:9 concerning the conversion of Saul. In the former it is said that the men who traveled with Saul heard the voice which spoke to him, while in the latter it is said they did not hear the voice. The difficulty is solved, however, by the fact that the Greek word translated "voice" may also mean "sound" and is so translated in the marginal reference given with Acts 9:7. We conclude that the men who were traveling with Saul heard the sound, but did not understand the words.

It has been only a few years since the destructive critics had nothing but scorn for any one who accepted Luke's statements that the island of Cyprus was ruled by a "pro-consul" (Acts 13:7), and that Lysanias was a contemporary tetrarch with the Herodian rulers (Luke 3:1). Yet how quickly the scorn was forgotten when archaeological discovery vindicated the Biblical statements.

Whether in the healing of the centurion's servant the centurion himself went to Jesus and asked that his servant be healed, as Matthew leads us to believe (8:5), or whether he sent unto Him elders of the Jews as Luke says (7:3), is all the same so far as the point of the story is concerned. In our everyday language we ascribe to the person the thing which his agents or servants do at his command.

The accusation which Pilate wrote on the cross is given with slight variations by the different Gospel writers: It appears, however, that the explanation for this is to be found mainly in the fact that the accusation was written in three languages, in Latin, Greek and Hebrew, that there were variations in the originals, and that at least one of the writers may have given a free translation, there being no substantial difference for instance between Mark's statement, "The King of the Jews," and Luke's statement, "This is the King of the Jews."

Whether on the resurrection morning the stone was rolled away from the tomb by human hands, as we might infer from the accounts given by Mark, Luke and John (although they are careful not to say that it was by human hands, but only that the stone was rolled away), or whether an earthquake was used to serve the purpose as Matthew more specifically tells us (28:2), makes no difference in regard to the essential point of the story that Christ arose and came forth from the tomb on that morning. Matthew has given the account in greater detail at this point, telling us that the Lord used the forces of nature to accomplish His purpose, while the other writers have simply recorded the important religious truth that the tomb was opened. It often happens that the sacred writers, like secular writers, describe events from different points of view or with different points of emphasis. In cases of this kind there is no more contradiction between the narratives than there is, for instance, between four photographs of the same house, one of which is taken from the west, another from the north, another from the east, and another from the south, although they may present quite different views.

Matt. 27:5 says that Judas brought his money back to the priests, then went out and hanged himself, while Acts 1:18 says that he obtained a field with his money. But weaving together the two fuller accounts it appears that what really happened was that when the priests rejected the money Judas threw it down in the temple and then went out and hanged himself. But after his treachery and suicide such disgrace attached to him that no friends or relatives came to care for the body and that it had to be buried at public expense. The priests remembered that his money had been brought back, that it could not be put into the treasury since it was blood money; and now that his body needed burial they very appropriately decided to use the money to buy a burial ground, perhaps the very field in which he had committed suicide. Hence he is said to have obtained a field with the reward of his iniquity,—not that he personally bought it, but that it was purchased with his money and he was buried in it.

Many critics claim that the reference to Jeremiah in Matt. 27:9 is an error, and that the reference should have been to Zechariah (11:12, 13). This, however, seems to be a case of "Subsequent Mention," such as Acts 20:35 and Jude 14. Matthew says that Jeremiah "spoke" these words, and certainly no one can prove otherwise. Apparently Jeremiah spoke them, Zechariah wrote them down, and Matthew, under the guidance of the Holy Spirit, quoted them and assigned them to Jeremiah. Perhaps Matthew had other books which assigned them to Jeremiah but which have since been lost. The fact that Matthew's quotation is not quite the same as that found in Zechariah may also indicate that he possessed other books.

It is sometimes said that in Gen. 36:31 the reference to the "king" (or kings) who ruled over the children of Israel proves that the book of Genesis was not written by Moses but by some later person. We are to remember however, that Moses was a prophet, that long before this the promise had been given to Abraham that kings would arise

(Gen. 17:6; 35:11), that Moses himself predicted the rise of kings in Israel (Deut. 17:14-20), and that in Gen. 36:31 he simply says that kings were reigning in Edom before any had yet arisen in Israel.

In regard to Ex. 9:19 it is sometimes asked how the Egyptians could have had any cattle left to be killed by the hail, which was the seventh plague, when Ex. 9:6 declares that all of them had been killed by the murrain, which was the fifth plague. This is explained, however, by the fact that the fifth plague did not kill the cattle which belonged to the Israelites, and that during the time which had elapsed between the fifth and seventh plagues the Egyptians doubtless had taken possession of many of those.

The fact that the Ten Commandments as given in Exodus 20:3-17 and Deut. 5:7-21 shows some variation in wording, or that in a number of instances where the New Testament writers have quoted from the Old Testament they have not given the exact words but only the general meaning, is no argument against verbal inspiration unless it can be proved that they intended to quote *verbatim*. A writer or speaker is entirely within his rights if he chooses to repeat his thoughts in a somewhat different form, and this is what the Holy Spirit has done. Human language at its best is too imperfect to express the fullness of the Divine Mind, and we should not limit the Holy Spirit to a sterotyped form of speech. The New Testament writers are often more concerned to give the basic truth, setting it fortn with variety and richness, than they are to follow a stereotyped form. This consideration sets aside a large number of the contradictions which some critics profess to find in the Bible. Furthermore, if we find a passage which is capable of two interpretations, one of which harmonizes with the rest of Scripture while the other does not, we are duty bound to accept the former. Whether the statement in question be in Scripture, in historical records, or in legal documents, the accepted principle of interpretation is that the meaning which assumes the document to be self-consistent and reasonable is to be preferred to the one which makes it inconsistent and unreasonable. To act on any other basis is to act with prejudice and to assure error rather than to prove it. The critics of the Bible, however, have often been only too glad to neglect this rule.

Many of the so-called "moral difficulties" of the Old Testament arise only because people fail to take into consideration the progressive nature of revelation. Much more, of course, is expected of us who live in the Christian era and who have the full light of the New Testament than was expected of those who lived in the former ages. Here too there is "first the blade, then the ear, then the full corn in the ear." Sometimes misunderstanding arises because of failure to distinguish between what the Scriptures record and what they sanction.

Probably the most serious problems arise in regard to matters such as the destruction of the Canaanites, the imprecatory Psalms, the substitutionary doctrine of the atonement, and the doctrine of eternal punishments. We may not be able to solve all the difficulties connected with these, but the objection that they are morally wrong proceeds on the assumption that there can be no such thing as retributive justice. We must remember, however, that while God is good and rewards righteousness, He is also just and most certainly punishes sin, and that the punishment of sin is as obligatory on Him and reflects His glory as truly as does the rewarding of righteousness. This is taught in the New Testament as clearly as in the Old, and it is at the basis of the doctrine that the punishment for our sins could not simply be cancelled but had to be laid on Christ if we were to be saved. Furthermore, the Old Testament teaches that not only certain individuals but sometimes whole towns and tribes were so degraded that they were a curse to society and unfit to live. Even the religion of some tribes was desperately corrupt, that of Baal and Ashtaroth, for instance, being accompanied by lascivious rites, the sacrifice of newborn children in the fire by their parents, and the kissing of the images of these heathen gods.

The Old Testament attitude toward polygamy, divorce, slavery, intoxicants, and kindred themes, is often ridiculed by present-day critics, but if seen in its proper setting is itself an argument for the divine origin of the Bible. In regard to almost all such questions we find that the design of the Bible is to set forth basic principles which shall be applicable to all peoples and races and in all ages rather than to give specific laws which while suited to one type of people under certain social conditions might not be equally suited to others. The making of specific laws governing social and civil affairs and suited to local conditions is left largely to later legislative bodies. Consequently the laws of the Bible are not as specific as many people would like them to be. In regard to the use of intoxicants, for instance, we certainly are told that "Wine is a mocker, strong drink a brawler; And whosoever erreth thereby is not wise," Prov. 20:1; that no drunkard shall inherit the kingdom of God I Cor. 6:10; that we are not to spend our money for that which is not bread, Is. 55:2; and many other similar statements. On the basis of these we should be able to frame suitable legislation dealing with the liquor traffic. The wisdom which the Bible showed in dealing with those evils in a primitive age—giving laws and

principles which regulated them, and in regulating destroyed them—
is strong evidence in itself that the law is of superhuman origin.

THE BIBLE AND SCIENCE

The Bible, of course, was not written from the scientific point of
view, and the person who attempts to deal with it as if it were a text-
book on science will be badly disappointed. Written long before the
rise of modern science, it was intended primarily not for scientists and
intellectuals but for the common people. Its language is that of the
common people, and its subject matter is primarily religious and
spiritual. Had it been written in the language of modern science or
philosophy it would have been unintelligible to the people of earlier
ages, and in fact would also be unintelligible to multitudes in our
own day. Moreover, while we certainly have no desire to disparage
the scientific accomplishments of our day but wish rather to accept them
and use them to the full, we must point out that textbooks on science
have to be rewritten at least once every generation and that so rapidly
is scientific research progressing in our day that most books on scientific subjects are obsolete within ten years. But in the Bible we have
a Book which has had no revision for multiplied centuries and which
appeals to the heart and intelligence of people today as strongly as it
has ever done in the past. Those who go to the Bible for spiritual
and intellectual inspiration find it as fresh and inspiring as if it had
been written but yesterday.

One of the most marvelous things about the Bible is that although
it was written in a day of ancient ignorance and superstition it does
not contain the popular errors and fallacies of that day. Moses as the
Crown Prince of Egypt attended the best of their schools and "was
instructed in all the wisdom of the Egyptians" — most of which is
considered pure nonsense today — but he did not write that in his
books. The weird and fantastic theories held by the Egyptians concerning the origin of the world and of man were passed over completely; and in the first chapter of Genesis in majestic language which
has never been surpassed to this day he gives an account of God's creation of the world and of man, no statement of which is disproved by
modern science. Other prophets who were in contact with the Chaldean
and Babylonian science were equally guided so that while personally
they may have believed many things which were erroneous they wrote
only what was in harmony with the truth.

Some of the prophets may have believed, for instance, that the
world was flat. But nowhere in their writings do they teach us that
it is flat. When they speak of the sun rising and setting, or of the

four corners of the earth, or of the ends of the earth, we are not to take those expressions literally. We use the same expressions today, but we do not mean to affirm that the sun goes around the earth, or that the earth is flat or rectangular. In our everyday speech we often describe things as they appear, rather than as they are known to be. And while skeptics as a class are ever ready to affirm that the Bible teaches that the world is flat, hardly one can be found who is honest enough to quote the one particular verse in which the Bible *does* make a statement about the shape of the earth. In describing the greatness and majesty of God Isaiah says that "He sitteth above the circle of the earth,"— the Hebrew word translated "circle" literally means "roundness" (40:22). Nor are the skeptics any more anxious to quote Job's statement when in contrast with the popular ideas of his day he wrote, "He stretcheth out the north over the empty space, And hangeth the earth upon nothing" (26:7).

In the year 1861 the French Academy of Science published a list of fifty-one so-called scientific facts, each of which, it was alleged, disproved some statement in the Bible. Today the Bible remains as it was then, but not one of those fifty-one so-called facts is held by men of science.

Distinction should always be made between the speculations in the realm of science and its clearly proven facts. The speculations of science are like the shifting currents of the sea, while the Scriptures have breasted them like the rock of Gibralter for two thousand years. The Bible has not been shown to contradict so much as one proven fact of science; on the contrary the account which it presents of the origin and order of the world, as contrasted with that found in other ancient books, corresponds with the findings of modern science to a degree that is perfectly marvelous. The conflict which some people suppose to exist between the Bible and science simply does not exist.

Perhaps the primary reason there has been so much confusion regarding the relationship between religion and science is the failure on the part of so many people to discriminate between facts and opinions. True science deals only with established facts; opinions may be as varied as the people who express them. Organic evolution, for instance, as it is usually set forth rules out the supernatural and contradicts the Bible. But it must be remembered that organic evolution is not science, but only a theory, an hypothesis. Not one of the five arguments usually advanced to support it is sound, and many distinguished scientists do not believe in the theory of organic evolution but in fiat creation as taught in the Bible. A minister who has not studied science has no right to invade the domain of science and speak freely about

it. Neither does a scientist who has had no experience in the moti-
vating and regenerating power of the Holy Spirit have any right to
invade the field of religion and speak freely about that. There have been
numerous instances in recent years where outstanding scientists, with
no special religious training, have presumed to write or speak their
minds quite freely on religious subjects. But their opinions concerning religion are worth no more than are those of any other person—
for the simple reason that they are assuming to speak concerning
things outside of their legitimate field. The mere fact that a man is
an authority within his own field does not entitle him to speak authoritatively on subjects outside of that field. True religion and true science
never contradict each other but individual ministers and individual
scientists will differ endlessly. Science has indeed done many marvelous
things. But its domain is strictly limited to the material side of life.
It has no authority to speak concerning spiritual things. Where it
has been made a substitute for religion it has invariably turned out to
be a false Messiah.

The relationship between the Bible and science has been quite clearly
set forth by Dr. Samuel G. Craig in the following paragraph:

"It is one thing to say that the Scriptures contain statements out
of harmony with the teachings of modern science and philosophy and
a distinctly different thing to say that they contain proved errors.
Strictly speaking there is no modern science and philosophy but only
modern scientists and philosophers — who differ endlessly among
themselves. It is only on the assumption that the discordant voices of
present-day scientists and philosophers are to be identified with the
voice of Science and Philosophy that we are warranted in saying that
the Bible contains errors because its teachings do not always agree
with the teachings of these scientists and philosophers. Does any one
really believe that Science and Philosophy have yet reached, even approximately, their final form? May it not rather be contended that they
are so far removed from their ultimate form that if the teachings of
the Bible were in complete harmony with present-day science and
philosophy it is altogether certain that they would be out of harmony
with the science and philosophy of the future? If, for example, the
anti-supernaturalism of the dominant science and philosophy of today
is to be characteristic of science and philosophy in their final forms,
then, unquestionably the Bible contains many errors. Who, however, is
competent to assert that this will be the case? But unless it is certain
that the science and philosophy of the future will be essentially one
with the dominant science and philosophy of today, we go beyond
the evidence when we say that the Bible contains proved errors on

the ground that its teachings contradict the teachings of present-day scientists and philosophers" (*Christianity Rightly So Called*, p. 217).

5. The Trustworthiness of the Bible

After a survey of the alleged errors and discrepancies, including not only the typical ones just mentioned, but also many others, we assert, without fear of successful contradiction, that no one of these is real. As Christians we call this book the "Holy Bible." But if it were only a relatively good book, setting forth many valuable moral and spiritual truths, but also containing many things which are not true, we would then have no right to apply to it the adjective "holy." It would then be on a level with other books, and would differ from them not in kind but only in degree.

But how different is our attitude toward it when we approach it as the very word of God, an inspired, infallible rule of faith and practice! How readily we accept its statements of fact and bow before its enunciations of duty! How instinctively we tremble before its threatenings, and rest upon its promises! As we proclaim the word of life from the pulpit, or in the classroom; as we attempt to give comfort at some bed of sickness, or in a bereaved home; or as we see our fellowmen struggling against temptation or weighed down with care, and would give them encouragement and hope for this world and the next, how thankful we then are for a fully trustworthy Bible! In such cases we want to know that we have not merely something that is probable or plausible, but something that is sure.

What might be called The Law of Ancient Documents, generally accepted by scholars in the study of either religious or secular books, is that "Documents apparently ancient, not bearing upon their face the marks of forgery, and found in proper custody, are presumed to be genuine until sufficient evidence is brought to the contrary." Now we submit that judged by this principle the books of both the Old and the New Testament are what they profess to be and that they should be accepted at face value. We are confident that when the critics are through, when the battle is over and the smoke has all been cleared away, the books of the Bible, if they could but speak, would say to us what Paul said to the Philippian jailor: "Do thyself no harm: for *we are all here.*"

It seems rather difficult at first to understand why so many persons have busied themselves to point out errors in the Bible. But when we look a little more closely we find that this is a book which judges men and points out the sin of the heart. Unconverted man does not like this, and would much prefer to read a newspaper or a sensational novel. An account of a trial in one of our criminal courts interests him a great deal more than does a chapter in the New Testament. And since he does not like to have the truth told about himself and the world in which he lives, he tries to pick flaws in the blessed Book. The reason that he cannot leave it alone is that it does not leave him alone. Infidels in every age and from every class have labored hard to find out some errors which would convict the Scriptures of falsehood. They find no pleasure in pointing out errors in Virgil, or Cicero, or Shakespeare; but the Bible they cannot endure. And, sad to say, the determined enemies of the Word are to be found not only in the ranks of the vulgar and coarse, but also among the refined and cultured. Time and again those who have nothing else in common will, nevertheless, agree in their determined opposition to the Bible.

Testimony of Outstanding Scholars

In modern times there are, of course, many scholars who for various reasons attempt to discredit the written word. They usually begin by attacking the Old Testament and then carry their attack over into the New Testament. We are glad to say, however, that there are many other scholars of at least equal learning and skill who declare that the Bible is fully reliable. The late Dr. Benjamin B. Warfield, who for thirty-three years was Professor of Systematic Theology in Princeton Theological Seminary, was, we believe, the greatest systematic theologian and Greek scholar that America has produced. After having examined the evidence on which the destructive critics base their conclusions he had no hesitation whatever in pronouncing that evidence utterly worthless, and in declaring that the Bible from Genesis to Revelation is what it claims to be, the very word of God. His recently published book, *Revelation and Inspiration,* is undoubtedly the best book on the subject.[1] *The Sunday School Times* had abundant reason for pronouncing it "the most learned, exhaustive and convincing defense of the verbal inspiration of the Bible which has appeared in modern times," and in adding that "Dr. Warfield's acquaintance with sources, and his pointing out errors of opponents in quoting sources, seems fairly uncanny. If this book were widely read it would serve as a decisive check upon the many vagaries of 'inspiration' with which the believer is now confronted."

---

1. Reprinted, 1948, under the title, *The Inspiration and Authority of the Bible.*

In regard to the Old Testament we feel reasonably safe in asserting that no greater authority has arisen in modern times than Dr. Robert D. Wilson. Possessed of a working knowledge of forty-five languages and dialects, and probably knowing more about the Old Testament than did any other man, his conclusion was set forth in the following words: "For forty-five years continuously I have devoted myself to the one great study of the Old Testament in all its languages, in all its archaeology, in all its translations, and, so far as possible, everything bearing upon its text and history . . . The evidence in our possession has convinced me that 'at sundry times and in divers manners God spake unto our fathers through the prophets,' and that the Old Testament in Hebrew, 'being immediately inspired by God,' has 'by His singular care and providence been kept pure in all ages'." Dr. Wilson's book, *A Scientific Investigation of the Old Testament,* in which his evidence and conclusions are set forth in simple and convincing language, and a more recent book, *The Five Books of Moses,* by Dr. Oswald T. Allis, who probably is the outstanding Old Testament scholar of the present day, should be read by every person who would be well informed concerning these matters.

The world still awaits a theory which will render an adequate account of the origin and authority of the Bible on any other hypothesis than that it came from God. One after another of the theories which have been advanced have fallen of their own weight or have been disproved by other destructive schemes. Up to date no hypothesis except that of divine origin has been able to maintain itself for as much as half a century. This in itself is a confession that the origin of the book cannot be accounted for by any other means than that given by the prophets themselves. Nor have we reason to believe that any more successful theory will arise in the future. Hence the only rational course for us to follow is to accept the Bible for what it professes to be until we can account for it by some other means.

It is interesting to note that down through the ages the orthodox Christian faith has been developed and set forth through the reverent and patient and anxious care of the Origens and Augustines, the Luthers and Calvins, the Hodges and Warfields, who believed the Bible to be fully inspired, and not by the Pelagians and Socinians, the Wellhausens and Fosdicks, with their superficial doubts as to whether Moses or Paul or even Christ and the apostles meant very much by what they said. May there never be occasion for people to say of us what was said of those of old time, that we received the word of God as it was ordained by angels, and kept it not.

Grounds for Our Belief That the Bible Is Infallible

When we assert that the Bible is completely trustworthy whether as regards its factual, doctrinal or ethical representations, we do not mean that we have personally examined each and every statement of the Bible with such care that we feel justified in asserting that they are all true, nor do we imply that we are possessed of omniscience. We reach that conclusion by first noting the claims which the Bible makes for its own inspiration and trustworthiness, and then testing those claims by the facts which are given us through Biblical criticism and exegesis. In view of the many evidences which substantiate this claim, such as the lofty moral and spiritual level which is maintained throughout the book, the promised guidance of the Holy Spirit, the many prophecies which were made in certain ages and fulfilled in detail in later ages, the inherent unity of the book, the simple and unprejudiced manner in which the accounts are given, etc., and in the absence of any proved errors, we conclude that the Bible is what it claims to be, a fully inspired book. This seems to be the only logical and proper way to approach the problem. If we reject this method, then, in order to arrive at a conclusion, we must make a comprehensive examination of every part of Scripture, taking it verse by verse, statement by statement, and prove its truth or falsity. But if we attempt this method it is not long until we come up against things hard to understand, statements concerning which we do not have adequate information, and prophecies which are as yet unfulfilled. We soon find ourselves, like certain persons of old, wresting the Scriptures to our own intellectual destruction.

The position of Conservative scholarship concerning this question has been presented clearly and convincingly by Dr. Samuel G. Craig. After stating that "the Bible bears witness to its own complete trustworthiness," he adds: "If that were not the case, the most we could possibly say would be that the Bible is without proved errors. That is obvious when it is remembered that even the latest parts of the Bible were written nearly two thousand years ago, that the Bible as a whole deals with periods of history with which at best we are imperfectly informed, that it relates the beliefs and experiences of many individuals of whom we know but little, that it contains representations alleged to have been supernaturally revealed, including many predictions not yet fulfilled—not to mention other matters. No one, not even the greatest scholar, has even a fraction of that knowledge that would be required to warrant him in affirming, on the basis of his knowledge alone, that the Bible is free from error. The case, however, is quite different, it seems to us, if testimony of their own complete trustworthiness is itself a part of the phenomena of Scripture. Then the way is open to assert their complete trustworthiness without first proving a universal negative. We would not be understood as implying that the mere fact that the Bible claims infallibility relieves us of the responsibility of examining its passages to ascertain whether its contents accord with the claim. However, if the Bible makes this claim and if even the most careful examination of its contents discloses nothing that contradicts it, it is at least possible that the claim is a valid claim. If on examining the Bible we find that all its statements that we are able to verify are trustworthy we will be more and more disposed to believe that the statements that are incapable of verification are also trustworthy. Our warrant, in brief, for asserting the inerrancy of the Bible is (1) *the absence of proved errors* and (2) *the witness which the Bible bears to its own complete trustworthiness.* (Italics ours.) Our confidence in the trustworthiness of the writers of the Bible is such that we feel fully warranted in accepting their statements as true even when we have no means of verifying them." And again, "We are dependent on the Scriptures for our knowledge of all the distinctive facts and doctrines of Christianity. If we cannot trust them when they tell us about themselves, how can we trust them when they tell us about the deity of Christ, redemption in His blood, justification by faith, regeneration by the Holy Spirit, the resurrection of the body and life everlasting?" (*Christianity Rightly So Called*, p. 226).

Furthermore, the importance of the testimony of the Scriptures to their own trustworthiness is not fully realized unless we keep in mind the fact that the trustworthiness of Christ is equally involved. In the words, "The Scripture cannot be broken," and "Till heaven and earth pass away, one jot or one tittle shall in no wise pass away from the law until all things be accomplished," He ascribed absolute authority to the Scriptures of the Old Testament as an organic whole and made them the rule of life. At these points there is no question about the purity of the Greek text. Repeatedly He quoted the Scripture as final. Hence the authority of Scripture and the authority of Christ are inseparably connected. There are some, of course, who bow before Him and rejoice in Him as their Lord and Master while at the same time they ascribe not only historical but moral faults to the Scriptures. But such an inconsistent attitude cannot long be maintained. It seems absurd that we should be at the same time His worshippers and His critics. Only ignorance or lack of thought makes it possible for any person to suppose that he can remain orthodox in his conception of

Jesus while accepting many of the views set forth by the destructive critics. When we reach the place where we say, "Jesus taught so and so, but the real truth of the matter is thus and thus," we simply cannot any longer worship Him as Lord and Master. Hence the question, "What think ye of Christ? whose son is He?" is closely parallel to the question, What think ye of the Bible? whose book is it? Investigation convinces us that the Bible, like the Christ which it sets forth, is truly human and truly divine. As He was true man, in all points tempted like as we are, yet without sin, because also divine, so the Bible is a truly human book, written by men like ourselves, yet without error, because also divine.

When we say that inspiration extends to all parts of the Bible we do not mean to say that all parts are equally important. It is readily admitted that Genesis, or Matthew, or Revelation, for instance, is of much greater importance than Second Chronicles, or Haggai, or Jude. As Paul tells us, "One star differeth from another star in glory," — yet God made them all. In the human body some organs are of vastly greater value than others, the eyes or heart, for instance, as compared with the fingers, or toes, or hair. In fact, we can even do without certain organs if necessary, although a whole body is much more normal, healthy and desirable. And so it is with the Bible; not all parts are equally valuable, but all parts are equally true.

And further, we do not mean to say that had there been no inspiration there could have been no Christianity. We readily admit that had the writers of Scripture been shut up to their unaided faculties, as ordinary historians and teachers, they might, nevertheless, have given us fairly true and accurate accounts of the messages they received and of the events which took place, and that Christianity might have continued, although no doubt in a greatly impoverished form. Even if the Bible as a book had become completely lost the essential truths concerning the way of salvation might have been handed down to us with some degree of purity. But to what uncertainties, and doubts, and errors constantly begetting worse errors, we would then have been exposed! That we would then have had only a very weak and diluted form of Christianity will hardly be denied. To see what our fate would have been we need only look at such groups as the Roman Catholic or Greek Catholic Church, or at the Nestorian or Coptic churches, yes, and at present day Modernism with its untrustworthy Bible and its endless confusion. In the first two of these churches the people have been denied access to the Scriptures; in the other two they have had the Scriptures but with a large mixture of error. Without the Bible, then, we might still have had a form of Christianity;

but, O, how much poorer we should have been! What a privilege it is to have in our hands a book every line of which was given by inspiration of God! — to have a divinely given history of the past, the present, and the future! Who can estimate aright such a privilege as this? As a matter of practical experience the strongest single factor making for the persistence of true Christianity and of righteousness in general down through the ages has been a fully trustworthy Bible in the hands of the common people.

We believe that the Bible as we now have it is complete, and that no new books are ever to be added. We believe this because the Bible gives us a sufficiently clear account of the relationship which exists between God and men, and of God's plan of redemption as it has been worked out by Christ and as it is now being applied to His people by the Holy Spirit. This is the view set forth in the Westminster Confession: "The whole counsel of God, concerning all things necessary for His own glory, man's salvation, faith, and life, is either expressly set down in Scripture, or by good and necessary consequence may be deduced from Scripture: unto which nothing at any time is to be added, whether by new revelations of the Spirit or traditions of men."

It should be kept in mind that the Protestant doctrine concerning the inspiration and authority of Scripture differs considerably from that held by the Roman Catholic Church. The Council of Trent, which met in the Italian city by that name and which concluded its sessions in the year 1653, set standards that the Roman Catholic Church has held quite consistently ever since. It affirmed the divine inspiration and authority of Scripture, but with some reservations. It declared that the Vulgate, which was St. Jerome's Latin translation of the Bible, and which was completed in the year 405, was the "authentic" text of Scripture, and that "no one is to dare or to presume to reject it under any pretext whatever." Furthermore, and more important, it introduced a fundamentally different estimate of the place of authority in religion, and of religion itself, when it put alongside of the Scriptures as of equal authority certain traditions of the church, consisting mainly of decrees issued by the popes and by church councils, and declared that the church alone was to be acknowledged as "the judge of the true sense and interpretation of the Holy Scriptures." This, of course, puts the final authority for the interpretation of Scripture in the hands of fallible and sinful men, and opens wide the floodgate to all kinds of error.

6. The Plenary Inspiration of the Bible

INCONSISTENT POSITION OF THE MODERNISTS

We have already said that so-called Modernists or Liberals have no consistent stopping place. They must either go clear over to rationalism and barren negation, or they must turn back again to an authoritative Scripture. The history of Protestant Liberalism shows us very clearly that it has had extreme difficulty in maintaining itself even on the platform of theism, to say nothing of that of Christianity. Its tendency has been constantly downgrade, a progressive repudiation of all the fundamentals of the Christian faith. The Modernist, if he proceeds logically in the direction which his premises carry him, denies, first, the inspiration of the Scriptures, then the miracles, then the deity of Christ, then the atonement, then the resurrection, and finally, if he goes to the end of his road, he ends up in absolute skepticism. New England Unitarianism affords an example of this very thing. Strange as the words may sound in our ears, it is not uncommon in some places in America today to hear the "atheistic shade" of modern theology spoken of. There is, unfortunately for some, a happy consistency in the processes of reason which drives the various philosophical and religious systems to their logical conclusions.

Practically all evangelical churches require those who are ordained to the ministry to take a public vow that they accept the Bible as the Word of God. In the Presbyterian Church, U.S.A., for instance, every minister and elder at his ordination solemnly vows before God and men that he "believes the Scriptures of the Old and New Testaments to be the *Word of God,* the only *infallible* rule of faith and practice." (Italics ours.) (Form of Government, XIII:IV; XV:XII.) Since this confession is thoroughly evangelical it means that none but evangelicals can honestly and intelligently accept this ordination. A Modernist has not the slightest right to be a minister or elder in an evangelical church, and any Modernist who does become such lacks good morality as well as good theology. To declare one thing while believing the contrary is hardly consistent with the character of an honest man. And yet while our ordination vows are so thoroughly evangelical, how many there are even among the ministers of our churches who either deny or pass lightly over this basic Christian truth, the infallibility of the Scriptures!

Sometimes those who hold a low view of inspiration attempt to evade the issue by merely saying that the Bible *contains* the word of

God. This loose formula, however, means practically nothing. A river in India, "rolling down its golden sands," certainly *contains* gold. But just what the relative proportion is between the sand and the gold may be very hard to determine. If the Bible only *contains* the Word of God, as even the Modernist is willing to admit, then certainly it may lack a great deal of being infallible, and we are then left to the mercies of "Higher Criticism," or to our own individual opinions, as to just which elements are the words of God and which are only the words of man.

As Dr. Clarence E. Macartney has recently said, "Those who have departed from faith in an infallible Bible have made desperate, but utterly vain efforts, to secure a suitable substitute and other standing ground. But as time goes by, the pathetic hopelessness of this effort is more and more manifest. Such catchwords as 'progressive revelation,' 'personal experience,' 'devotion to the truth,' etc., are one by one being cast into the discard. Modernism and Liberalism, by the confession of their own adherents, are terribly bankrupt, nothing but 'cracked cisterns,' into which men lower in vain their vessels for the water of life. There is no plausible substitute for an inspired Bible. No one can preach with the power and influence of him who draws a sword bathed in heaven, and who goes into the pulpit with a 'Thus saith the Lord' back of him . . . When man faces the overwhelming facts of sin, passion, pain, sorrow, death, and the beyond-death, the glib and easy phrases of current Modernism and flippant Liberalism are found to be nothing but a broken reed. Therefore, he who preaches historic Christianity and takes his stand upon a divine revelation has, amid the storms and confusions and darkness of our present day, an incomparable position. . . . There are not wanting signs today that men will return to the Holy Scripture, to drink again of the Water of Life and strengthen their souls with the Bread of Life, and that a prodigal Church, sick of the husks of the far country, will return to its Father's house."

Those who reject the Church doctrine of inspiration in favor of some lowered form have never been able to agree among themselves as to which parts of the Bible are inspired and which are not, or to what extent any part is inspired. If this high doctrine of verbal inspiration is rejected, there is no consistent stopping place short of saying that the Scripture writers were inspired only as was Shakespeare, or Milton, or Tennyson; and in fact some of the critics have consistently followed out their premises and have reached that conclusion. We submit, however, that if the other miracles recorded in Scripture be accepted there is no logical reason for rejecting the miracle of inspiration, for inspiration is simply a miracle in the realm of speaking or writing. Most of the objections which are brought against the doctrine today can be traced more or less clearly to the assumption that the supernatural is impossible.

Assurance That the Bible Is the Word of God

The question naturally arises, How are we to *know* that the Bible is the Word of God? We reply: *By the witness of the Holy Spirit within our hearts as we read.* As the Christian reads the Bible he instinctively feels that God is speaking to him. The Holy Spirit bears witness with his spirit that these things are so, the primary and decisive grounds for his conviction being not external but internal. To the spiritually illuminated the word is self-authenticating. He does, indeed, find much additional assurance to be had in noting the many incomparable excellencies of the writings, such as the lofty spiritual and moral truths set forth, the unity of all the parts, the majesty of the style, the uniformly uplifting influence of the Bible wherever it has gone, its appeal at one and the same time to the learned philosopher and to the poor black man of the jungle, its statement of truth in such simple language that even a child can grasp its meaning while even the most learned man cannot exhaust its depths, the minute fulfillment of prophecies centuries after they were spoken, etc. These are, indeed, proofs which should compel acceptance, and they can be effectively used to stop the mouths of objectors; but in the final analysis they are of subordinate value only. Apart from the inner illumination of the Holy Spirit they will not convince the unbeliever, no matter how logically and skillfully they may be presented.

The attempt to prove the divine origin of the Bible from these external criteria is similar to that of proving the existence of God from the external world. We may cite the ontological, the teleological, the cosmological, and the moral arguments, and the evidence seems convincing enough to the believer. Yet none of these arguments are demonstrative and coercive, and they usually leave the skeptics unconvinced. When we consent to stake the authority of Scripture on external arguments we are consenting to fight the battle on the field of our opponents' choosing, and we then simply have to make the best of a vulnerable position. These arguments in themselves are of such a nature as to invite doubt in the unregenerate mind, and they can never permanently settle the question. When we consent to fight the battle on these grounds we are making a concession to Rationalism, a system which assumes that the human reason is capable of sitting in judgment upon and evaluating all human experiences, and which denies the necessity of any divine revelation whatsoever.

In our deepest selves we are either regenerate or unregenerate. Paul tells us that "the natural (unregenerate) man receiveth not the things of the Spirit of God: for they are foolishness unto him; and he cannot know them, because they are spiritually judged" (I Cor. 2:14); and again he says that the gospel of Christ crucified is "unto Jews a stumbling block, and unto Gentiles foolishness"; but unto them that are called, both Jews and Greeks, it is "the power of God, and the wisdom of God" unto salvation (I Cor. 1:23, 24). Consequently the unregenerate man assumes an antagonistic attitude, and will not be convinced by any amount of external testimony. Ultimately every person has to make a choice between the *vox Dei* and the *vox mundi,* the voice of God and the voice of the world; and the question as to which of these he acknowledges to be the more authoritative is determined by whether the soul is regenerate or unregenerate. It is as impossible for the unaided human reason to understand the deep things of the Spirit as it is for the ordinary psychologist to give an adequate explanation of the process of conversion. Every attempt to convince the unregenerate soul of the divine origin of the Bible by means of scholarly and historical proof can only result in failure, and must be given up as completely as when Jesus forebore to convince the members of the Sanhedrin that he was not guilty of blasphemy when they had made up their minds to the contrary. This was the principle for which the Protestant Church stood at the time of the Reformation. While the Roman Catholics acknowledged the Church as the source of authority, and the Humanists acknowledged the human reason, the Protestant principle, as it was given typical expression for instance in the Westminster Confession, was the voice of God speaking in the soul. "The authority of the Holy Scripture, for which it ought to be believed and obeyed, dependeth not upon the testimony of any man or church, but wholly upon God (who is truth itself), the author thereof; and therefore it is to be received, because it is the Word of God . . . Our full persuasion and assurance of the infallible truth, and divine authority thereof, is from the inward work of the Holy Spirit, bearing witness by and with the word in our hearts" (I:IV, V). We would doubtless make better progress in our present day discussions if we kept that principle in mind.

In the final analysis, then, the Christian's faith does not depend upon external proofs, but upon an inner experience. He lives by the Scripture and enjoys its light. He has an inner conscious assurance —

call it mysticism or whatever you will — that he is a child of God, and that the Scriptures are the word of God. The external proofs help to clarify and strengthen his faith, but his absolute and inescapable proof that the Christian system in general is the true system is found in the witness of the Holy Spirit in his heart as he reads and in his experience as a Christian. Although he may not be possessed of scholarly and scientific evidence which would enable him to meet the destructive critics on their own ground, he repels all their doubts in the same manner as did the blind man who was healed by the Saviour, and who replied to every argument of the Pharisees with the immovable conviction of certainty: "Whether he is a sinner, I know not: one thing I know, that, whereas I was blind, now I see." He no more asks permission of the critic to believe than he asks permission of the scientist to breathe, but finds both most natural and spontaneous. He does, indeed, find that truly scientific and scholarly study gives clearer direction to the word, and that it enables him to systematize and understand it better. But his authority for belief is from the heart rather than from the reasoning processes of the head.

This does not mean that we deprecate scholarship. Nowhere has the principle of sound scholarship and scientific investigation existed in a healthier state than in the loyal sons of the Evangelical churches. In fact, we are persuaded that except for the service which scholarship has rendered, the Christian faith would have been well-nigh helpless against the attacks of unbelief. We desire a solid historical foundation for our faith, and our investigation shows that we have such. We acknowledge that the external proofs, when presented to unbelievers in a reasonable way, point the way to God and often prepare the heart for the gracious work of the Holy Spirit. But we simply wish to point out that these proofs which are relied upon so heavily by some are ineffective unless supplemented by the work of the Holy Spirit in the heart.

Our opponents will probably complain that this method of procedure gives a strong dogmatic cast to the discussion. They forget, however, that they proceed in exactly the same way: they too proceed from premises which are as axiomatic, even though they profess to be particularly subject to reason. Their axiom is that the human reason is competent to judge all things, even the deep things of God. While we acknowledge that theirs is also a dogmatic procedure, we do not complain about it, since they *cannot* do otherwise — the mind which has not been enlightened by the Spirit is not able to discern the things of the Spirit. As Thornwall has fittingly said, "the reality of evidence is one thing, the power to perceive it, is quite another. It is no objection to the brilliancy of the sun if it fails to illuminate the blind." We each have our fixed method of procedure. All we can ask is that these principles be put to a practical test, and that we be given opportunity to see which best squares with the experiences of life and reality.

CONCLUSION

In conclusion, then, we would say that it is of the utmost importance that the Lord's people be thoroughly rooted and grounded in this great doctrine of the plenary inspiration of Holy Scripture, and that having examined the evidence they be convinced that the Bible is the very Word of God. Since all of the other Christian doctrines are derived from the Bible and rest upon it for their authority, this doctrine is, as it were, the mother and guardian of all the others. We believe that the foregoing statements are facts which will stand the test of scholarship and of historical investigation, and that they will not be denied by any informed and honest-minded person.

While in our day the Bible has been sadly neglected even in many of the churches, we believe that the time is coming when the Bible shall have its rightful and honored place in the Church and in the affairs of men. At any rate we look forward confident that when the tumult is over, when the present storm of unbelief has subsided, the sacred heights of Sinai and Calvary will again stand forth, and that amid the wreck of thrones, extinct nations, and shattered moral principles, mankind, tried by so many sorrows, purified by so much suffering, and wise with so much unprecedented experience, will again bow before an omnipotent and merciful God as He is revealed in an infallible Bible.

CHAPTER II

CHRISTIAN SUPERNATURALISM

1. The Place of the Supernatural in Religion

Every thinking person sooner or later reaches the position where he must make some decision concerning the relationship which exists between the natural world in which he lives and the supernatural world which lies above and beyond him. Where do the natural and the supernatural meet, and how are they related to each other? As far back as we can go in human history we find that man has been vitally interested in the origin and purpose of the world and of humanity. Where shall he find the key to the mystery of being? What is the final truth and explanation of all this marvelous system? Man's intellect as well as his moral and religious nature drives him on until he reaches some settled conclusion regarding these matters.

Today, even in religious circles, there seems to be a strong drift away from a frank recognition of the supernatural as a factor in our daily lives. A subtle pantheistic philosophy is abroad, which tends to deny that there is any distinction between the natural and the supernatural. Even the phenomena of life and mind are explained away on materialistic principles. The mainstay of this movement is, of course, the theory of "evolution," according to which we are told that all development, including that of plants, animals, and even man, has been due to an urge inherent in matter as such, by which higher forms are developed from lower. Specifically we may define evolution as *a continuous, progressive change, according to certain laws, and by means of resident forces.* This movement is anti-supernaturalistic to the core, and in many cases has developed into an atheistic naturalism which will know nothing beyond what is given through the five senses.

Since the thinking of the world is to such a great extent actuated by this naturalistic philosophy it is impossible but that Christian thinking should also be influenced in that direction. We find many of the supposedly Christian teachers and writers ruling out as much of the supernatural as they dare; and in some circles the question seems to be not how much of the supernatural was accepted by Christ and the Apostles, but, How little of the supernatural can we have and still call ourselves Christians?

Consequently, the fundamental conflict in which Christianity is engaged today in the intellectual sphere is a conflict between the *Supernaturalism* of the Bible and the *Naturalism* of other systems. Beneath all the attacks lies an undercurrent of Naturalism, sometimes openly advocated, but more often cleverly concealed, depending on whether the person making the attack is outside of or within the ranks of professing Christians.

In regard to the present conflict in the Church those who accept the supernatural are commonly known as "Evangelicals" or "Conservatives," while those who reject the supernatural are known as "Modernists" or "Liberals." The terminology, however, would have been much more accurate had the terms "Supernaturalists" and "Anti-Supernaturalists" been used to designate the two groups, for *Modernism or Liberalism is essentially a denial of the supernatural* more or less consistently carried out. The term "Modernist" is especially misleading since it implies that the formative principle of that system is modern, while the fact of the matter is that the anti-supernaturalistic principle has been held by some groups in every age of Church history.

The more thoroughgoing Modernists start out with the assumption that the supernatural is impossible. Consequently they refuse to recognize anything in nature, life or history outside the lines of natural development, all evidence to the contrary being ruled out of court without examination. The less consistent Modernists retain elements of the supernatural, although there is little agreement among them as to which parts are to be rejected and which are to be kept. Since the system is essentially one of denial, Modernists find it practically impossible to formulate their beliefs in creedal statements. Between such a view of the world and Christianity, it is perfectly correct to say there can be no agreement. Possibly the Modernists may claim that theirs is an improved and purified form of Christianity, but certainly no one can claim that it is the Christianity of Christ and His Apostles.

Modernism, then, offers us a "non-miraculous" Christianity. We are prepared to say, however, that a "non-miraculous" Christianity is simply a contradiction of terms. In order to make our position clear we may define a miracle as *an event in the external world, wrought by the immediate power of God, and designed to accredit a message or a messenger.* Dozens of miracles in this sense are recorded in Scripture. They distinctly were not merely results caused by the application of supposedly "higher laws" which are unknown to us, as some would have us believe. Most of them were works of mercy and healing, although on rare occasions they were used for punishment. We accept them not merely on the report of a credulous and unscientific people, but on the clear testimony of Scripture which we believe to be the Word of God Himself. That the doctrine of miracles is firmly grounded in Scripture is admitted even by those who deny the truth of the doctrine.

Miracle, in the sense of a direct entrance of God in word and deed into human history for gracious ends, is of the very essence of Christianity. The entire New Testament is based on the conception of Jesus as a supernatural Person. Modernism, however, denies not only His miracles, but His deity, His incarnation, His vicarious suffering and death, His resurrection and His claim to be the final Judge of all men. Modernism also rejects an external authority, represents sin as a necessity of development, and nullifies the true conception of sin by starting man off at a state but little removed from that of the brute, while Christianity asserts most emphatically that man has an external Ruler and Judge, and that sin is not something which belongs to the Divine idea of the human race but rather something which entered the race when man deliberately turned aside from his allegiance to his Creator and from the path of his normal development. In other words Christianity involves the idea of a Fall as the presupposition of its doctrine of Redemption, whereas Modernism asserts that the so-called Fall was in a reality a *rise,* and in effect denies the need of any redemption in the Scriptural sense. When anti-supernaturalistic Modernism attacks the Christian doctrine of redemption, and seeks to evaporate it away with a set of platitudes about the guiding hand of God in history, it has assaulted Christianity in the very citadel of its life. With Dr. Warfield we assert that "Supernaturalism is the very breath of Christianity's nostrils, and an anti-supernaturalistic atmosphere is to it the deadliest miasma." Christianity, by its very nature, is committed unreservedly to a belief in the supernatural; and where it has given up that belief it may still exist as a philosophical system, but it has forfeited every right to be called historic Christianity. As Christian men we must assert with all possible emphasis the purity and absoluteness of the supernatural in redemption and revelation.

Belief in Theism and Belief in the Miraculous

We wish to call special attention to the fact that if we are theists as opposed to atheists, if we believe in a personal, self-existent God who created and who rules the heavens and the earth, we have admitted belief in the great basic principle of the supernatural, which in turn should make belief in miracles, visions, inspiration and revelation a very easy matter. Once the existence of God is admitted the possibility of the supernatural cannot be denied, for God is then the great *super-natural* Fact. The atheist cannot believe in miracle, for he has no God to work miracles. Neither can the pantheist nor the deist believe in miracle, for the former identifies God with nature while the latter has separated God and the universe so far that they can never be brought together again. But if God exists as the theist believes, if He created and rules the heavens and the earth, no rational person can deny that He has both the power and the knowledge to intervene in the universe which He has made. As Dr. Floyd E. Hamilton has said, "Unless the created is above the Creator, unless the designed thing is greater than the Designer, unless the law is above the Law-Maker, there is no escaping the conclusion that God can, if He wishes, intervene in the universe to carry out His Divine purposes." And as Dr. James Orr has told us, "Many speak glibly of the denial of the supernatural, who never realize how much of the supernatural they have already admitted in affirming the existence of a personal, wise, holy, and beneficent Author of the universe. They may deny supernatural actions in the sense of miracles, but they have affirmed supernatural Being on a scale and in a degree which casts supernatural action quite into the shade. If God is a reality, the whole universe rests on a supernatural basis. A supernatural presence pervades it; a supernatural power sustains it; a supernatural will operates in its forces; a supernatural wisdom appoints its ends. The whole visible order of things rests on another,—an unseen, spiritual, supernatural order,—and is the symbol, the manifestation, the revelation of it."

For the theist the occurrence of any particular miracle becomes simply a matter of evidence. If the existence of natural law in the world proves that miracles are impossible, they also prove that God cannot exercise a providential control over the world and that prayer cannot be answered. Furthermore, the logical corollary to this is that if opposition to the supernatural is consistently carried out, it cannot stop with the denial of miracles, but must carry the person straight over into agnosticism or atheism. It is the height of inconsistency for the Modernist to admit the existence of God, and yet to deny the miracles recorded in Scripture on the ground that they are opposed to natural law. A little reflection should convince any one that the whole theistic conception of the universe is at stake in the denial of miracles.

The Person of Christ and the Doctrine of Miracles

The basic assumption of the Christian system is that Jesus Christ was and is a truly Divine Person, the second Person of the trinity, who at a certain period in history came to earth and took upon Himself our humanity, in whom dwells the fulness of the Godhead bodily, and who, therefore, is to be honored, worshipped and trusted even as God is. If Christ was, as the Scriptures teach, a Divine Person, the miracles recorded of Him are only what we would normally expect of such a Person, so that, as Dr. Warfield has so beautifully expressed it, "When our Lord came down to earth He drew heaven with Him. The signs which accompanied His ministry were but the trailing clouds of glory which He brought from heaven which is His home."

The miracles are not mere appendages to the story but are so bound up with the life and teachings of Christ, so woven into the very warp and woof of New Testament Christianity, that their removal would not only destroy the credibility of the Gospels, but would leave Christ Himself a personage as mythical as Hercules. They were the normal expression of the powers resident in His nature,—sparks, as it were, which revealed the mighty fires within. They stand or fall with the supernatural Person of Christ and with the nature of the work He is said to have accomplished by His suffering and death. If He was a truly supernatural person who vicariously suffered and died in behalf of others, and who arose in a resurrection, they are to be accepted as genuine. If on the other hand we take the view of present-day Modernism that Jesus was only an ideal man, the fairest flower of humanity but nothing more, they must be rejected as incredible. The difference between a Divine Christ with genuine miracles working out a supernatural redemption, and a merely human Christ who is a remarkable teacher and example but who has no power to work miracles, is the difference between two totally diverse religions. It is high time that we do some clear thinking and that we accept the Christ of the New Testament as our Lord and Saviour, or that we reject Him and His miracles as does present-day Modernism.

Ways in Which God Reveals Himself

If, as the Scriptures tell us, God is a personal Being and has created man in His own image, it seems most reasonable to believe that He would have communion and fellowship with the being which He had created. That He should isolate Himself from man would seem most unnatural. Since man was created a free agent and was given a choice between good and evil, it would certainly have seemed strange for God not to have revealed to him the purpose He had in placing him here. Furthermore, if it is true that every man has an immortal soul which is to spend eternity either in heaven or in hell it would seem most unnatural and unreasonable for God to have left him in ignorance of those momentous facts. If man's eternal weal or woe is determined by the course he charts for himself during a short lifetime upon this earth with no further chance after death to correct his mistakes, he must know something of the issues which are being decided. And most of all, if after man has fallen into sin God plans to redeem him and to bring him to salvation through a crucified and risen Lord—through a redemption which was purchased only at an infinite cost to Himself— then a direct intervention of the heavenly Father in behalf of His bewildered and helpless children is in the highest degree probable.

Since it is, therefore, not only possible but highly probable that God would have revealed Himself to man, we next ask, In what ways could that revelation have been given? We find that there are at least five ways in which such a revelation might have been given, and in which, in fact, the Scriptures declare that God has revealed Himself. In the first place He might have revealed Himself directly, appearing in what is called a *theophany,* in which He would have been personally visible and would have talked with man face to face. This is probably the way God spoke to Adam in the Garden of Eden, and would probably have been the most natural and ordinary way for Him to have spoken in later times had it not been for the fact of sin. But when man corrupted himself he destroyed that intimate companionship and erected a barrier between himself and God which has been broken through only on very rare occasions. Since the Fall man has been afraid of God. He has instinctively felt that he could not look upon the face of God and live. Consequently we would not expect that many revelations would have been given in that manner.

In the second place revelations might have been given through dreams, in which case the revelation would have been placed in the mind while man was in an unconscious state; or through visions, in which case the revelation was external to man and was seen or heard through the ordinary faculties. This method, the Scriptures tell us, was very commonly used.

In the third place God might have supernaturally enlightened the minds of chosen men, causing them to perceive clearly the spiritual truths which they in turn were to speak to the people. This method was used in practically every period of the Old Testament era, as well as at the beginnning of the Christian era. Time and again the prophets repeated the words, "Thus saith the Lord," and then proceeded to give forth the messages which God had given to them.

In the fourth place, it was possible for God to so influence certain prophets and apostles that they would write the messages which He wished given to the people. This influence was exerted through the superintending power of the Holy Spirit, and is known as "inspiration." On some occasions this practically amounted to dictation. On other occasions the writers made full use of their native talents as they deliberated, recollected and poured out their hearts to God, the Holy Spirit exercising only a general influence which led them to write what was needful and to keep their writings from error.

The fifth and most important way God revealed Himself was through His only begotten Son, who was both God and man, and who while existing in human form came into very intimate personal relations with His fellow men. This was, beyond all others, the clearest, fullest and most advanced revelation that man has received.

2. Assurance that a Revelation is Genuine

Granted that any person has received a revelation, it would also follow that he should be able to give some proof to his fellow men that he does possess such a revelation. Otherwise he would not be believed. In our human relations whenever some one comes to us claiming to represent another person or institution we demand that he present his credentials. We have a right to demand credentials, and they must be of such a nature that they cannot be duplicated by any other person. Likewise, the prophet who comes with a message from God must be able to show his credentials, and they must be of such a nature that they cannot be duplicated. They must accredit him as a true representative of the court of heaven. Hence it seems very reasonable to expect that in the course of God's dealings with the human race certain men would have been accredited as His messengers and would have been given power to do works of a supernatural order.

These unique works of the prophets and apostles bear the same relation to the works of later ministers and missionaries that the Apostolic office bears to the pastoral office. The extraordinary gifts belonged to the extraordinary office. The prophets and apostles not only worked miracles but possessed the gift of inspiration and wrote books which we acknowledge to be the Lord's word to the people; but this gift is not possessed by present-day ministers. Revelation and miracles go together While the former remained in the Church, the latter remained also; but when the process of revelation had been completed with the work of Christ and the explanation of that work by the apostles, miracles also ceased. A new era of miracles would indicate a new era of revelation. We believe, however, that with the closing of the New Testament Canon revelation was completed and that we are to expect no more such works until the end of the world.

We have said that the chief purpose of a miracle is to accredit a message or a messenger. This is also clearly stated in Scripture by the Apostle John who wrote, "Many other signs therefore did Jesus in the presence of the disciples, which are not written in this book; but these are written, that ye may believe that Jesus is the Christ, the Son of God; and that believing ye may have life in His name" (John 20:30, 31); and again by the writer of the epistle to the Hebrews, who tells us that the message of salvation which was first "spoken through the Lord, was confirmed unto us by them that heard; God also bearing witness with them, both by signs and wonders, and by manifold powers, and by gifts of the Holy Spirit" (2:3, 4).

Miracles are not to be put on a level with the tricks of a magician or of a wonderworking fakir. Yet it is probably no exaggeration to say that nine-tenths of the opposition to the Christian doctrine of miracles is due to the fact that this distinction is not kept in mind. It is not the bare possibility of miracles which may happen at any time and in the hands of any kind of people, that we contend for, but miracles as an integral part of God's plan of redemption as that plan was made known to a lost and unbelieving race. That, we hold, was a sufficient cause for setting aside the ordinary laws of nature on certain occasions. We readily grant that uninspired men cannot work miracles, and that the age of miracles ceased when the Apostles had given their last message to the world. Consequently we insist that when men discuss the miracles of Scripture they must not beg the question by putting those miracles in an environment foreign to that in which the Scriptures put them. They must not be considered in an abstract manner, but as an integral part of the Christian system of redemption.

MIRACLES AND THE SUBSTANCE OF CHRISTIANITY

It is important to point out that apart from their evidential value certain of the miracles such as the incarnation and resurrection enter into the very substance of Christianity to such a degree that apart from them there is no such thing as Christianity. We know, for instance, that many miracles were wrought which have not been recorded in the Bible, and we readily acknowledge that some of those recorded might have been left unrecorded without seriously impairing the Christian system; but such miracles as the incarnation and resurrection are.so vital to the system that their omission would leave us with a radically different religion. For by the incarnation God was enabled to enter personally into the human race, and as the God-man, Jesus Christ, in His capacity as the federal head and representative of His people He took upon Himself the penalty due to us for sin, suffered and died for us on the cross and thus redeemed us; and also as the God-man, in His capacity as the federal head and representative of His people, subject to all of the trials which befall human nature, He overcame all temptation and perfectly kept the moral law (which our former head and representative, Adam, failed to keep) and thus earned for us eternal life. And by the resurrection He as federal head and representative of His people triumphed over death, came forth from the grave with a glorious body, and calls His people to a life of eternal happiness and joy. Paul spoke only the solemn truth when he declared, "If Christ hath not been raised, then is our preaching vain, your faith also is vain. . . . If Christ hath not been raised, your faith is vain; ye are yet in your sins"; and again, "If we have only hoped in Christ in this life, we are of all men most pitiable" (I Cor. 15:14, 17, 19). Hence the miracles of incarnation and resurrection are such vitally important parts of the Christian system that if they are omitted what we have left cannot rightly be called historic Christianity.

The Purpose of Prophecy

Another way in which God can accredit a revelation to man is through the foretelling of events, or predictive prophecy. This, in reality, is a miracle in the realm of knowledge, a supernatural unfolding of future events. The principal value of a miracle worked in the physical world is to accredit a revelation immediately to the people to whom it is given, while the principal value of prophecy is to accredit the revelation to people who live years later and who see its fulfillment. The Lord alone is able to declare the end from the beginning, and to make known the things which are yet to come. After the prediction has been fulfilled we look back and realize that only a person with supernatural knowledge could have made the prediction, and consequently we accept the remainder of his message as also true.

By prophecy, in the sense of foretelling events, we mean not mere general statements or shrewd guesses such as a person might make by closely observing present tendencies. In every-day conversation the term is sometimes used in that sense, but not properly so. We mean rather the foretelling of events in such detail that only the hypothesis of supernatural knowledge can adequately account for their fulfillment. Today in America, for instance, the political observers with best intellect and keenest insight are not able to predict with any accuracy what the political fortunes of this country will be during the next four years, much less can they predict what these fortunes will be during the next four hundred years. What person forty years ago could have predicted in detail the two world wars, or the rise of Bolshevism, Fascism, or Nazism? Or who today would dare to prophesy in detail the political conditions of Europe twenty-five years from now? And yet we find that the Old Testament prophets did this time after time. Some of the events which they prophesied were not to be fulfilled until centuries after the prophecies were written, and they were set forth in such detail that they cannot be accounted for by anything less than supernatural revelation. We know, for instance, that the Scriptures of the Old Testament were written centuries before the time of Christ. Consequently when we find prophecies foretelling the very town in which He should be born, the virgin birth, the sojourn in Egypt, numerous things about His manner of life and public ministry, and some fifty prophecies which were fulfilled in detail at the time of His crucifixion and resurrection, we have convincing proof that the Scripture writers had supernatural knowledge and that the messages which they gave really came from God. Dr. Floyd E. Hamilton, in his admirable book, "The Basis of Christian Faith", quotes authority for the statement that "there are in the Old Testament three hundred and thirty-two distinct predictions which were literally fulfilled in Christ." He goes on to say, "The mathematical probability that these would all be fulfilled would be represented by a fraction having one for the numerator and eighty-four followed by ninety-seven ciphers as the denominator!" Fulfillment of the many Scripture prophecies, with never so much as one case of error, is the strongest possible evidence that the Bible is the word of God.

"I declare the end from the beginning, and from ancient times things that are not yet done," says the Lord (Is. 46:10). Listen to Jehovah's challenge to the idol-gods of Babylon to predict future events: "Produce your cause, saith Jehovah; bring forth your strong reasons, saith the King of Jacob. Let them bring them forth, and declare unto us what shall happen: declare ye the former things what they are, that we may consider them, and know the things that are to come hereafter, that we may know ye are gods" (Is. 41:21-23). The dumb idols of the heathen of course know nothing concerning the future, nor can man of himself predict what is going to happen except through a vague and indefinite system of guesswork. But Jehovah, who made this challenge, has fully demonstrated His power to predict the future. He has done so in His holy word, the Bible. Several other nations and sects possess books of a religious nature which they call "sacred books." Not one of them, however, dares make predictions concerning the future. Had the writers of any of those books dared predict the future they would by that very thing have furnished the strongest evidence of their deceptions. Among all of the world's thousands of books, sacred or otherwise, the Bible is the *only* book which contains predictions, and it is preeminently what no other is or can be, a book of prophecy. The fulfillment of these prophecies has shown it to be a supernatural book, a revelation from God. In view of this fact it is a great misfortune that the professing Church of our day almost completely neglects and ignores the study of prophecy. The result is that the Church has lost one of its most powerful weapons against infidelity, and that the denial of the inspiration of the Bible has become very widespread. Such denial could not flourish if the facts were presented. We may also add that this neglect has given occasion for the rise of perverted sects such as Russellism and extreme dispensationalism, whose strength is found mostly in their appeal to prophecy.

Miracles and the Laws of Nature

Perhaps the chief reason that so many men of our day reject the supernaturalism of the Bible is because of a common and widespread belief that the "laws of nature" render miracles impossible. Everywhere about us we see the uniformity of natural law. That the laws of nature do exist is acknowledged as definitely in the Bible as in science. In general such uniformity is necessary in order that we may plan for the future and have the assurance that industry and thrift will be rewarded. Unless nature was thus steady and reliable the world would not be a place in which we could live and work, but rather a crazy system of chance in which anything might happen at any time. The laws of nature are, in the final analysis, merely God's will as to how the material universe should behave. They were established by the creative power of Him who has given to every creature its nature and has appointed its bounds and limits, who established the earth, and by whose ordinances it is governed (Ps. 119:90, 91). The reason they are so uniform is because God is a rational, omniscient, all-powerful Being, whose plan for the universe was worked out in eternity and is caused to move steadily toward its goal. They reflect His power and wisdom. They also are symbols of His constancy and faithfulness.

We hold that nature is neither self-existent nor self-made, but that it is a manufactured article. As Christians we maintain that God *created* the heavens and the earth, and that the work of creation was in the strictest sense a *super*natural work. Consequently we believe that God is not only immanent in matter but that He is transcendent over matter, and that the great sphere of His life and activity lies above and beyond this world. We hold that it is inconceivable that His dealings with the human race should be confined to the limits of the laws which He has ordained for the regulation of material substance, and we affirm that it is His prerogative to set aside or supersede these laws whenever He sees fit to do so.

And when we come to investigate more carefully the character of these "laws" we soon discover that they are not themselves forces in nature, but are merely general statements of the way in which these forces act so far as we have been able to observe them. They are not powers which rule all nature and force obedience to themselves, but rather mere abstractions which have no concrete existence in the external world. They are not eternal and absolute, but were brought into existence and implanted on nature at the time of the original creation. Furthermore, God is under no compulsion to keep them forever uniform, but may set them aside whenever it better serves His purpose to do so. As Dr. Shedd has well said, we must remember that "the order of the universe is a means, not an end, and like other means must give way when the end can be best promoted without it. It is the mark of a weak mind to make an idol of order and method, to cling to established forms of business when they clog instead of advancing it." Granted that we have a personal God and that He has implanted these laws upon the universe which He has created, there is no reason why He may not alter these laws on occasions if He so desires. It is utterly derogatory to the character of God to assume that He is subject to external laws, especially to the laws of matter. He has not imprisoned Himself within His own material creation.

Spiritual Values Superior to Material Values

As Christians we believe that the redemption of the human race from sin was a sufficient cause for God on occasion to set aside the ordinary laws of nature and to work above or contrary to them. We believe that in the Bible we have evidence which proves that He has intervened and that miracles have occurred. We hold that when the human race, which was the thing of primary value in this whole creation, had fallen into sin and was to be redeemed from sin, the laws of nature were not to be considered such fixed and sacred things that God could not move except within their limits, that the moral and spiritual development of human souls was of more importance in His sight than was the uniformity of nature.

The Scriptures tell us of the disastrous fall of the human race into sin; and since we believe not merely in a God of physical order but primarily in a God of holiness, we regard it as most becoming for Him to intervene. Consequently, the incarnation, the atonement, the resurrection and such other revelations and confirmatory signs as He sees fit to give not only commend themselves to us as satisfying our human needs but as most worthy of a God of moral perfection. In such a situation the presumption against miracles is changed into a presumption in their favor, and we are prepared to find the Scriptures setting forth a redemptive process which is supernatural to the core.

We are not then, considering miracles and the supernatural in the abstract, as random or chance happenings, but in relation to a loving heavenly Father and His plan of redemption for a sinful race. We readily grant that sporadic, inconsequent miracles would prove nothing, and would themselves be hard to prove. If we were to hear a report that a miracle had recently been performed in England or Argentina, we would have very serious doubts about the truth of that report; and further investigation would most likely prove that our doubts were well founded. The bare possibility of a leper having been immediately healed, or of a dead man restored to life, viewed simply from the standpoint of present-day physical science, is not an adequate or correct statement of the issue which has been raised by Christianity. But given a supernatural crisis, a supernatural Teacher and a supernatural revelation, miracles are found to be in order like jewels on the state robes of a king. In fact their absence would be unaccountable. To tear miracles out of the great moral and spiritual framework set forth in the Christian system and to treat them as isolated events is as unreasonable as to attempt to study a comet apart from the general system of astronomical laws and forces to which it belongs. Miracles need give no offense to any persons except those who would place the mechanical order of nature above the moral and spiritual order.

It should be clearly understood that there is no conflict between true religion and true science. Religion and science operate in different spheres,—or perhaps it would be more accurate to say that the spiritual and the physical are the opposite poles of the sphere of truth. The task of science is the observation and classification of facts in the *material* realm. True science confines itself strictly to the realm of material things and expresses no opinion whatever as to the reality of the supernatural, as to whether or not miracles have happened or can happen. It is not science but *philosophy* which passes behind the scenes of our material existence and expresses opinions about the causes which are at work there. Science may, indeed, furnish part of the data which the philosopher uses in constructing his system, but there its authority ceases. The scientist may also be a philosopher, but the two roles must not be confused. We insist that the authority of science must not be claimed for statements which in reality are only philosophical deductions. True science neither confirms nor opposes the Christian view of the world which underlies the doctrine of miracles.

Those who advocate the Christian doctrine of miracles, then, are not champions of chaos in an ordered world. Rather they are zealous for law and order of a higher type, that of the spiritual realm, which they hold has been thrown into chaos by man's choice of evil. They point out that sin, disease, sorrow and death are unnatural and abnormal in an ideal world, and that the great majority of the Scripture miracles had as one of their purposes the restoration of order in those regards. In the highest sense they were not violations but restorations of order. They show that the God of spirits is also the God of nature, that spirit and personality are superior to matter, and that the world is held together not merely by physical or mechanical force but by love and holiness.

The tendency of present-day Modernism, of course, is to merge everything into nature and to admit of no other causes. What the Modernist needs to prove, therefore, is not simply that natural causes operate uniformly, but that every physical effect must have a physical cause. That, however, he is unable to do, and that, we hold further, no one except an atheist has a right to assert. In our own natures we find that mind influences matter,—we will to walk or run, to play a piano or to lift a weight, and the effect of mind on matter is clearly seen. We do not understand how the result is accomplished, but we know that it is very real. And if God has so arranged it that our wills produce these physical effects, certainly there is no reason for denying that His omnipotent will may produce infinitely greater effects.

To the objection that we cannot be sure that any particular event is a miracle since we cannot determine with certainty the boundary between the natural and the supernatural, we reply that there are some classes of events about which no person can really doubt, e.g., the raising of Lazarus from the dead, the cleansing of the leper by a touch of the hand, the multiplying of the loaves and fishes, and Jesus' walking on the waters of the sea of Galilee. We may not know the exact boundaries of the natural, but no one can doubt that these events far transcend those boundaries.

Some people are in the habit of using the word "miracle" in a very loose sense, meaning any unusual event such as a remarkable surgical operation, the working of a new chemical or of a new electrical appliance. These, however, are not real miracles, but events which can be explained by the ordinary laws of nature if we are familiar with them.

3. Extraordinary Providences

There is another class of events recorded in Scripture which may be more accurately referred to not as miracles but as "extraordinary providences." In these cases the Lord simply directs the forces which are already at work in nature so that they serve His purposes. Examples are: most of the plagues which came on the Egyptians, the flight of quails which brought meat to the Israelites in the wilderness, the fall of the walls of Jericho if by an earthquake, the great draught of fishes recorded in the Gospels, the rolling away of the stone from the mouth of the tomb of Jesus on the resurrection morning which Matthew specifically tells us was caused by an earthquake, etc. The importance of these events is not lessened by their being put in a separate class, for while not strictly miraculous they do give clear evidence of Divine intervention. There was nothing miraculous, for instance, in the locust plague considered in itself, for such plagues have continued to visit Egypt even to the present day; but when the plague came at the exact time that Moses as the Lord's spokesman had said that it would come, and departed at the appointed time, or when the quails came in great numbers to the right place and at the very time Moses had promised, or when the walls of Jericho fell at the appointed time, then, these events, taken in connection with the words of the prophet, became as clear evidence of Divine intervention as if they had been pure miracles. They proved the prophet to be the messenger of Him who controls the laws of nature and uses them to serve His purposes.

Throughout the Bible the laws of nature, the course of nations, the varying fortunes of individuals, are ever attributed to God's providential control. All things, both in heaven and earth, from the seraphim down to the tiny atom, are ordered by His never-failing providence. So intimate is His relationship with the whole creation that a careless reader might be led toward pantheistic conclusions. Yet individual personalities and second causes are fully recognized—not as independent of God, but as having their proper place in His plan. "To suppose that anything is too great to be comprehended in His control," says Dr. Charles Hodge, "or anything so minute as to escape His notice; or that the infinitude of particulars can distract His attention, is to forget that God is infinite. . . . The sun diffuses its light through all space as easily as upon any one point. God is as much present everywhere, and with everything, as though He were only in one place, and had but one object of attention." And again, "He is present in every blade of grass, yet guiding Arcturus in his course, marshalling the stars as a host, calling them by their names; present also in every human soul, giving it understanding, endowing it with gifts, working in it both to will and to do. The human heart is in His hands; and He turneth it even as the rivers of water are turned." And with this agree the Scriptures, for we read, "Jehovah doeth His will in the whirlwind and in the storm, and the clouds are the dust of His feet," Nahum 1:3. "He maketh His sun to shine on the evil and the good, and sendeth rain on the just and the unjust," Matt. 5:45. The famine in Egypt appeared to men to be only the result of natural causes; yet Joseph could say, "The thing is established of God, and God will shortly bring it to pass." The Lord sent His angel to shut the mouths of the lions so that they should not hurt Daniel, Daniel 6:22. "Behold the nations are as a drop in the bucket, and are accounted as the small dust of the balance; behold, He taketh up the isles as a very little thing," Is. 40:15. "He changeth the times and the seasons; He removeth kings, and setteth up kings," Daniel 2:21. "A man's heart deviseth his way, but the Lord directeth his steps," Prov. 16:9. "It is God who worketh in you both to will and to work, for His good pleasure," Phil. 2:13.

Miracles Are Not Worked Today

We should say further that we believe the age of miracles is past. They do not simply appear at random on the pages of Scripture, but are inseparably connected with periods in which God is revealing His will and plan to His people. When any are reported today we are inclined to reject them outright. We believe that the revelation of the plan of salvation for the world was a fully sufficient cause for miracles in order that that infinitely important revelation might be adequately accredited. Since New Testament times, however, it has been God's purpose not to introduce new and unneeded revelations but to spread this one completed revelation, which is the Christian Gospel, throughout the world, and to bring mankind to a saving knowledge of this truth. Having received the Christian Gospel, the world is not in need of newer and fuller revelations, but needs only to be brought to a saving knowledge of the truth which has already been given. The abundant display of miracles during the public ministry of Jesus and in the Apostolic Church is a mark of the richness and fulness of revelation in that age; and when that period closed, miracle working passed away as a matter of course.

This is also the view of miracles taught by John Calvin. When at the time of the Reformation the Roman Catholics pointed to their alleged miracles and demanded that the Protestants produce works of a similar kind, Calvin replied that the Protestants set forth no new

Gospel, but retained the very same truths which had been confirmed by all the miracles of Christ and the Apostles. It is important to keep in mind that the Scriptures teach that the completed revelation of God is given in Christ, and that in the dispensation of the Holy Spirit that one completed revelation is to be diffused to all mankind. If we keep clearly in mind the truly Biblical purpose for which miracles were given—to accredit a new and divinely given message—we shall find that we have a guiding principle which makes it easy to distinguish between genuine and spurious miracles in Church history.

Many people seem inclined to think that miracles were constantly being performed by the prophets. As a matter of fact they were rare occurrnces. As Dr. John D. Davis, in *A Dictionary of the Bible*, says, "The miracles of the Bible are confined almost exclusively to four periods, separated from each other by centuries: (1) The time of the redemption of God's people from Egypt and their establishment in Canaan under Moses and Joshua. (2) The life and death struggle of the true religion with heathenism under Elijah and Elisha. (3) The exile, when Jehovah afforded proof of His power and supremacy over the gods of the heathen, although His people were in captivity (Daniel and his companions). (4) The introduction of Christianity, when miracles, dreams and visions are elementary aids to faith and belong to the kindergarten stage of revelation. They are like the Law, which, Paul tells us, was the instrument of an earlier age and served as "a schoolmaster to bring us to Christ." God speaks to us through the

And while God does not use miracles in speaking to us who live in the twenthieth century, He does speak to us as clearly, even much more clearly, than He ever spoke to people in olden times. We have His completed revelation given to us in a miracle Book, the Bible. This Book is available for all people at a cheap price, whereas most of the former revelations were given to comparatively small groups, most of whom could neither read nor write. The fact of the matter is that miracles, dreams and visions are elementary aids to faith and belong to the kindergarden stage of revelation. They are like the Law, which, Paul tells us, was the instrument of an earlier age and served as "a schoolmaster to bring us to Christ." God speaks to us through the developments of Church History which we have seen take place during the past nineteen centuries, in which we have witnessed the transformation of individuals and of whole nations through the power of the Gospel, a marvelously rich proof of His guidance of His people. He speaks to us through fulfilled prophecy, which is far more abundant for us than it has ever been for any preceding generation. He also speaks to us through the general intellectual enlightenment which characterizes our age, and through the discoveries which have been made in such sciences as Biology, Chemistry, Physics, Astronomy, etc. There is truth in Thomas Fuller's statement that "Miracles are the swaddling-clothes of the infant Church," and in John Foster's comment that "Miracles are the great bell of the universe, which draws men to God's sermon." It is a greater honor which God bestows on us in that He does not speak to us through those elementary means, but that He appeals to our reason and intellect. Those persons do not display much wisdom who insist that He should still speak to us as in primitive times. For Him to do so would be to address us not as men and women but as children.

Lying Wonders

We are not to receive credulously every sign or wonder which is put forth as a miracle, but must test their genuineness, first, by making sure that they reveal something of the character of God and teach truth concerning Him; and secondly, they must be in harmony with the established truths of religion. Some events are reported today, apparently on good authority, which we can ascribe to no other cause than that they are worked by forces of evil.

Not only do the Scriptures teach that the holy angels have access to this world, that they are "ministering spirits sent forth to do service for the sake of them that shall inherit salvation," and that they guard and keep the Lord's people (Heb. 1:14; Ps. 91:11, 12; Matt. 2:13, 19; 28:2-7; Luke 1:11, 26; 2:10-15; 22:43; Acts 1:10; 5:19; 12:7-10; Gen. 19:1-16). They also teach that the Devil and other fallen spirits or demons have access to this world and that they tempt and corrupt human beings so far as they are able (Gen. 3:1-15; Job 1:6-2:7; Matt. 8:28-32; 10:8; 12:22; Mark 1:23. 24; 7:25-30; Luke 8:12; Acts 10:38; 16:16-18). Although invisible to our eyes, good and bad spirits are constantly about us.

Sometimes the evil spirits work wonders in the realm of nature or in revealing the future. Paul tells us that the coming of the man of sin will be "according to the working of Satan with all power and signs and lying wonders," II Thess. 2:9. Our Lord said, "There shall arise false Christs, and false prophets, and shall show great signs and wonders; so as to lead astray, if possible, even the elect," Matt. 24:24; and in the book of Revelation John refers to the "spirits of demons, working signs" (16:14). The Egyptian magicians produced snakes from their rods (Ex. 7:11, 12). They also turned water into blood and produced frogs (Ex. 7:22; 8:7), but could not bring forth lice (Ex. 8:18, 19).

False prophets and sorcerers who attempted to mislead the people of God with their delusions were to be put to death (Deut. 13:1-5; Ex. 22:18), and strict commands were given against consulting those who practiced fortune telling or those who had familiar spirits (Lev. 20:6; Deut. 18:10, 11; II Kings 21:6; II Chr. 33:6, Is. 8:19). To encourage such things was *sin*, because it led the people away from the true God. Those who consulted them did so in direct violation of God's command, and almost invariably turned out bad, e.g., Saul (I Sam. 28:8-19); Ahaziah (II Kings 1:14); Manasseh (II Kings 21:1-15). The sorcerer Simon was misleading the people and was severely condemned by Peter, Acts 8:9-24). Another sorcerer, Elymas, was condemned by Paul, Acts 13:8-12. The works of such persons were not simply pronounced frauds, although there was doubtless much fraud connected with them; they were pronounced works of the Devil or of evil spirits, and the people were told to have nothing to do with them. Every age has produced its crop of fortune tellers, mind readers, mesmerists and spiritualistic mediums, dangers from which we should flee as from an East India cobra.

These signs, whether wrought in heathen lands or by modern sorcerers, are almost invariably mere wonders, exhibitions of strange powers, wanton violations of the natural order. By contrast the miracles of Scripture are preeminently works of mercy and healing, the whole bearing of which implies the restoration and confirmation, not the violation, of natural or spiritual law. Some of the people engaged in those works have been frank enough to say that their works were wrought through the power of the Devil. We do not acknowledge such signs or wonders as true miracles, for (1) they are not performed by the power of God, (2) their moral character is bad, and (3) they are not designed to prove that the person who works them is the Lord's prophet.

4. The Alleged Roman Catholic Miracles

In contrast with the doctrine of the Protestant churches that miracles were given to attest revelation and that when revelation ceased miracles also ceased, the Roman Catholic Church claims that the spread of the Church is also a primary cause for miracles and that in every age God has been pleased to work a multitude of miracles for that purpose. Consequently it points to a body of miracles wrought in these later times as large and imposing as that of any period in Biblical history. Protestants insist, however, that nowhere in Scripture are we told that miracles are wrought for the spread of the Church.

Protestants acknowledge that incidentally the spread of the Church, as well as the relief of suffering and distress, were aided by the miracles wrought; but they insist that since New Testament times those objectives are to be accomplished by natural means.

We should hardly think it possible that the superstitions and miracle-tales which flourished so luxuriantly during the Middle Ages could maintain themselves in the light of the twentieth century. We find, however, that the Church of Rome, while existing in the twentieth century, is not a part of it. The fact of the matter is that it is a Medieval church which has survived into the twentieth century, and that isolating its people as much as possible from present day progress and enlightenment, it has continued to live in much the same atmosphere of superstition and credulence as that in which it found itself surrounded a thousand years ago.

We must remember that the Church, in coming into the world, came into a heathen world. After the decrees of Emperor Constantine, first legalizing Christianity and then making it the preferred religion of the empire, Church membership became a popular thing and the people flocked into the Church in great numbers. Some came because they were true Christians, but most of the new adherents came because of the social, political or financial advantages which were to be gained. In many cases they were little more than baptized heathen, and they brought their heathen conceptions into the Church with them little changed except in those things which were plainly contradicted by their Christian confession. In a real sense the Church was in turn conquered by the world which it had conquered. As it made its way ever more deeply into the world, enjoying the favors and privileges which came from governmental approval, it was ever more deeply immersed in a heathen atmosphere — an atmosphere surcharged with belief in supernatural powers and influences. Some of the heathen gods and goddesses were taken over into the Church and worshipped as Christian saints. Those who were superstitious remained superstitious, and there was no end to the wild and fantastic miracles which were supposed to have occurred in connection with the pagan idols and temples. This background made it extremely easy for the people to believe the miracle stories which were told concerning the saints and their relics.

A strange phenomenon in regard to these miracles is that, whereas up until the early part of the fourth century (the time at which the Church was legalized) we find not so much as one single writer among the church fathers who claims to have seen a miracle worked, nor one who names any of his predecessors since the time of the

Apostles as having wrought miracles, after we reach the fourth century we have a veritable deluge of miracles. And further, these miracles are not only ascribed to the foremost missionaries and saints of the Church, but are recorded by those missionaries and saints as miracles which they themselves have seen or know of. It is claimed, for instance, that the bones of Stephen were found in Jerusalem in the year 415, that certain parts of them were brought into Northern Africa and Italy, and that everywhere they were taken miracles were worked. At different periods in Church history we find Chrysostom, Gregory the Great, Bernard of Clairvaux, and even the great Augustine declaring in parts of their writings that miracle working had ceased, then in later writings they relate a considerable number of miracles. Augustine, for instance, tells us that he was an eye witness to a miracle in Milan in which sight was restored to a blind man. The interesting thing about the case, however, is that he did not seem to have recognized the miraculous character of the event until several years afterward, and had in the meantime expressed it as his conviction that miracles were no longer being performed.

The church fathers do not claim to have performed miracles themselves, yet they report miracles of every conceivable sort which were supposed to have been worked by saints of earlier times, and then it has usually happened that writers of the next generation or later record miracles which were supposed to have been worked by these men. In regard to Thomas à Becket, of Canterbury (England), we have very full accounts of his life and have many letters which were written by him. In none of these does either he or his contemporaries claim that he could work miracles. The stories of miraculous happenings are confined almost entirely to miracles believed to have been wrought by the power of his dead body or at his tomb. Most of the miracle workers of this period appear to have become so posthumously, the honor being thrust upon them rather than claimed by them, so that there seems to be good ground for the taunt of the unbelieving Gibbon in his *History of the Decline and Fall of the Roman Empire:* "It may seem somewhat remarkable that Bernard of Clairvaux, who records so many miracles of his friend, St. Malachi, never takes any notice of his own, which in their turn, however, are carefully related by his companions and disciples. In the long line of ecclesiastical history, does there exist a single instance of a saint asserting that he himself possessed the gift of miracles?"

Perhaps the greatest shrine of miraculous healings in the entire world is at Lourdes, France, where an apparition of the Virgin Mary is supposed to have been seen in 1858, and where numberless supernatural favors are supposed to have been shown by her to pilgrims who have gone there. Literally hundreds of thousands of persons, we are told, have made that pilgrimage, although most of those have gone because of religious motives rather than because of sickness. The whole atmosphere of the place is said to be surcharged with Mary worship. Lourdes does not register her failures, yet it is known that the proportion is very great. One Roman authority tells us rather apologetically that "Hardly one in a thousand of these come to be cured of any sickness." It is generally understood that only about ten per cent of those seeking cures go away benefited. As with most such shrines, very little is said about the enormous mass of disappointment and despair of those who go away unbenefited.

That some cures have been worked at these shrines can hardly be denied, although to all appearances they are the same in kind and are products of the same forces as those wrought today by Christian Scientists, mesmerists, faith-healers. Some medical schools today, recognizing the power of "suggestion" and of proper mental states, are putting courses in psychiatry into their curriculum. There have been many cases where patients have worried themselves sick because of wrong mental attitudes, or after suffering from neurotic or rheumatic afflictions have failed to note the recovery which the body has made, and when as a result of the right kind of thoughts having been powerfully suggested to their minds suddenly discover themselves in a practically normal condition. Some persons who make pilgrimages to shrines approach them with a mind eminently receptive to suggestion, believing implicitly that a cure will be worked ; and then, further aided by the ecstasy produced by solemn religious rites, a most fervent prayer, or an immersion in holy water, have found that faith produced the desired results.

We do not attempt to give a full explanation of these cures ; certainly we cannot claim to have complete knowledge of all the forces which may assist in bringing about a cure in such conditions as are usually present at these shrines. There are many other things in our daily lives which we cannot explain, but which nobody supposes to be miraculous. The fact that a thing is inscrutable to us is no sufficient reason for allowing ourselves to be stampeded into acknowledging it as miraculous. There may be, and doubtless are, forces at work in nature which are very improperly understood as yet. These can apply to mind as well as to matter. Their existence is strongly suggested by such things as hypnotism, mind reading, mental telepathy, clairvoyance, etc.

We believe that God alone can work miracles, and that He alone is to receive religious veneration. Consequently when the Christian Scientists claim miracles through the application of a foolish philosophy which denies the reality of sin, disease and pain, or when the Roman Catholics claim miracles as the product of an atmosphere surcharged with the idolatrous worship of the Virgin Mary or with veneration for relics such as dead men's bones, teeth or hair, we deny that true miracles are possible under such conditions. For the infinitely wise and just and holy God whom we worship to perform miracles under such conditions, and not in the congregations of His true saints, would be for Him to contradict His very nature. The fact that these cures are reported not only from Roman Catholic shrines, but from faith-healers in all kinds of cults, even from Mohammedan lands, is proof sufficient that the power which each of them claims is no private possession but is the common property of the whole world, and that it is to be had by men of all religions·calling upon their various gods.

Furthermore, most of the reputed cures, when investigated, are found to be false. Hardly one in a hundred of them will stand the test of investigation. There is a great contrast between the simplicity and majesty of the Scripture miracles and the trivial, fantastic, and even repellent nature of so many of the ecclesiastical miracles. Most of this latter type, usually alleged to have been performed at the grave or with the "rotten bones" of some saint — together with alleged pieces of wood from the true cross, a sample of the blood of Saint Januarius which is preserved in the cathedral at Naples and which liquifies once every year, samples of the milk of the Virgin Mary which are claimed by several churches in Italy and France, etc., — have been barefaced impostures openly justified by the priests on the ground of pious frauds. The fact that they are claimed on behalf of a system which contains so much deceit and evil, and that they are propagated to spread the influence of a church which has been guilty of such inhuman and anti-Christian persecutions down through the centuries is in itself a sufficient reason for rejecting them outright.

5. Cures Wrought by the Faith-Healers

Another class of people who claim to work cures in our day are the faith-healers, Christian Scientists and mind-cure specialists. When a serious attempt is made to investigate these cases most of them, like those of the Roman Catholics, are found to be false. We must acknowledge, however, that some of them have been real. Practically all these latter cases have to do with nervous or mental disorders, rheumatic pains, or afflictions which are little if anything more than imaginary. Occasionally those who have been incapacitated for some time have made greater recovery than they realize, and when in connection with a faith-healer's suggestion they suddenly discover their regained strength they sincerely believe that a miracle has been wrought.

It is common knowledge that many people who think themselves to be seriously sick do by that very means make themselves sick. Every physician can testify that he has been called upon to treat dozens of such cases, and that in treating them his primary task is to get his patients into a different state of mind. In such cases the power of suggestion is much more effective than medicine. The cures of the Christian Scientists are in reality not Mind-cures but mind-cures, wrought by the patient's own change of thought — which, indeed, is the substance of what is asserted scores of times by Mrs. Eddy herself in her book, "Science and Health."

What finally emerges in these cases is a definite boundary which separates that class of cures which can be wrought by mental reactions, and those which cannot. In no cases have broken bones, cancer, spinal meningitis, scarlet fever, etc., been cured, nor have amputated limbs, fingers, or even such things as lost teeth or lost hair been restored. The inability of faith-healers to work cures of this kind is in itself an admission that their cures are not truly supernatural.

Another point to be kept in mind is that comparatively few physicians are good diagnosticians, even though they may have practiced medicine all their lives. Perhaps there is no physician who has not been badly deceived more than once in regard to the nature of the disease he was trying to treat — as the autopsy has shown. This is only natural, since the human body is such a highly complicated organism. Doctors often pronounce a case hopeless, only to be surprised by the patient's recovery. Yet faith-healers never tire of telling how this or that doctor gave up a particular case as hopeless. Few contrasts are more remarkable than the scorn which the average faith-healer has for physicians as healers, and the unbounded confidence which he reposes in them as diagnosticians. If he can say that on the testimony of this or that doctor the case was hopeless, he considers that the end of all argument.

The question before us is not as to whether or not God hears and answers prayer, for we believe firmly that He does — we disagree with the faith-healers, however, in that we believe He answers prayer not by miracles, but in accordance with His general providential control; nor is it a question as to whether or not He heals the sick, for this we also believe. The question is: Does God heal the sick in ways which are truly miraculous, without the use of means? And does that healing take place in such a manner that the use of means is unnecessary, or a mark of a lack of faith, or even of sinful distrust on the part of Christians?

In the first place we would point out that the Scriptures contain no promises of such miraculous healings. The passage in Mark 16: 17, 18, which is the chief one relied upon by faith-healers, is now recognized as spurious by practically all scholars.[1] The evidence is that those verses were not in the original, but were added by later copyists. The second most quoted passage is James 5:14, 15: "Is any among you sick? let him call for the elders of the church; and let them pray over him, anointing him with oil in the name of the Lord; and the prayer of faith shall save him that is sick, and the Lord shall raise him up; and if he have committed sins, it shall be forgiven him." As Dr. Warfield has well said, "Here we have nothing but a very earnest exhortation to sick people to turn to the Lord in their extremity, and a very precious promise to those who thus call upon Him, that the Lord will surely hearken to their cry." The thing emphasized is that the sick man should get himself prayed for officially by the elders of the church, which prayer, offered in faith, shall surely be heard. The Lord always answers a sincere prayer, perhaps not in the way we ask, but in the way that is best for us. And in answer to the prayer for the sick, the Lord will raise him up, perhaps physically, but at any rate spiritually, which is more important. In this passage the anointing oil is a secondary thing. Certainly there is nothing here which would exclude the ordinary medical means. Oil was a well-nigh universal remedy in the medical practice of the day, and the passage means that the sick man is to be given his medicine in the name of the Lord. The resources of civilization are ours, and we should avail ourselves of all that science knows, remembering that God is the real physician who takes away sin, sickness and death, and that it is He who gives righteousness, healing and life.

Furthermore, we would point out that we have no more reason to believe that our sicknesses and diseases will be cured without means than we have to believe that if we fail to plow and plant we will nevertheless be given food. As well might we expect to live without eating as to recover from sickness without medicine. Surely faith-feeding is quite as rational as faith-healing. And if diseases are to be

---

1 A marginal reference in the American Standard Version reads: "The two oldest Greek manuscripts, and some other authorities, omit from verse 9 to the end. Some other authorities have a different ending to the Gospel."

cured by faith, then why may not death, which is simply the result of disease or injury, also be eliminated in the same way? If cures are to be had by faith, then each successive cure, each successive victory, should be easier than the last, and the body should become immortal. The Scriptures, however, tell us that "It is appointed unto man once to die" (Heb. 9:27); and not even the most zealous of the faith-healers have been able to overcome that affliction. The Bible knows nothing of the redemption of the body in this life. That, it teaches, is to be accomplished in the next life, at the time of the resurrection. After the most careful study we are convinced that the claims of the faith-healers are false.

To neglect the laws of nature which God has ordained, and to refuse to use means, is to act with presumption and to cast disrespect upon God Himself. We believe that the same laws which we depend upon to bring the harvest of corn and wheat may be equally depended upon to bring the harvest of disease and death which we reap every year. No matter how righteous and holy a person may become, if he violates the laws of nature he must suffer for it. If he walks out of the tenth-story window in defiance of the law of gravity he falls with the same certainty and with the same rate of accelerating velocity as other men. The law of gravity is not suspended because of his good moral character.

While faith-healers denounce the calling of a physician and the use of medicine as "un-Scriptural," "dishonouring to God," and as a certain mark of unbelief, almost every one of them in times especially of their last sickness has done that very thing. This was true of Mrs. Eddy, A. B. Simpson, A. J. Gordon, and others. Mrs. Eddy used eye-glasses instead of overcoming the defects of her eyesight by mind, and is reported to have been considerably annoyed when asked why she did not employ the mind-cure in that regard. She also employed the good offices of a dentist to obtain relief from an aching tooth, and even availed herself of his "painless method" to guard herself against unnecessary suffering. Yet according to her own teaching, the decayed tooth, the jumping nerves and the cruel forceps were only illusions.

A great contrast betweeen the Scripture miracles of healing and the reputed cures of the faith-healers is that so many of the latter are only partial cures, or cures which require a considerable period of time to become effective. But when Jesus healed the result followed immediately and was complete. He did not stop half way. He had only to say, "I will; be thou made clean," and the leper was healed. He opened the eyes of the blind by a touch, and commanded the palsied man to take up his bed and walk. The man's withered hand was restored whole. The blind man saw clearly. The lame man leaped up and walked. Jesus healed all who came to Him; yet it is acknowledged even by faith-healers themselves that the great majority of those who come seeking cures today go away not cured. They usually claim that those who go away uncured do so because of weak faith; yet Jesus healed all who came regardless of whether their faith was weak or strong. Furthermore, if miracles were to be considered common, every-day experiences, normal and not extraordinary, they would attract no particular attention and could not be considered the credentials of the Lord's spokesmen, which was their chief purpose in Biblical times.

Faith-healers are very emphatic in their contention that sickness is always contrary to the will of God, and that only a lack of faith keeps any person from being immediately healed. These claims, however, fail to take into consideration certain Scripture statements which declare that on various occasions God Himself has inflicted the disease or the suffering for wise and beneficent purposes. Miriam was smitten with leprosy in order that she and Aaron might be turned from their sinful course (Nu. 12:10). The Lord struck the illegitimate son of David because of the sin which had been committed (II Sam. 12:15). The psalmist said, "It is good for me that I have been afflicted; That I may learn thy statutes" (Ps. 119:71.) When Jesus was asked, "Rabbi, who sinned, this man or his parents, that he should be born blind?" He replied, "Neither did this man sin, nor his parents; but that the works of God should be made manifest in him" (John 9:3). The sickness of Lazarus was "for the glory of God, that the Son of God may be glorified thereby" (John 11:4).

Paul was *given* "a thorn in the flesh, a messenger from Satan to buffet him, that he should not be exalted over-much" (II Cor. 12:7)— a physical handicap which we find was intended for a good purpose, namely, that his eminence and success beyond that of the other disciples should not fill him with pride and arrogance. Though he earnestly "besought the Lord thrice, that it might depart from him," it was not removed. We venture to say that in all the world today there is not a Christian mightier in prayer, more devoted, more Spirit-filled and enlightened than was the Apostle Paul. If God would not remove this affliction, though He was besought so earnestly to do so, certainly the faith-healers should hesitate a bit before censoring the suffering saint of today for a lack of faith which they claim would, if he had it, bring relief to his body. When Paul was told by the

Lord that it was better for him to endure this suffering, that the Lord's grace would be sufficient for him, he answered, "Most gladly therefore will I rather glory in my weakness, that the power of Christ may rest upon me" (II Cor. 12:9). In such cases where God is working out some great and good purpose (which probably is unknown to the person who suffers), no amount of prayer will bring healing. Further, we find Paul leaving Trophimus sick at Miletus (II Tim. 4:20), and in the realm of practical medicine urging Timothy to "use a little wine for thy stomach's sake, and thine often infirmities" (I Tim. 5:23).

Even Christ Himself, we are told, "learned obedience by the things which He suffered" (Heb. 5:8); and in bringing many sons into glory it was God's purpose also "to make the Author of their salvation perfect through sufferings" (Heb. 2:10). The writer of the epistle to the Hebrews tells us that "Whom the Lord loveth He chasteneth, and scourgeth every son whom he receiveth" (12:6); and again, "God dealeth with you as with sons; for what son is there whom his father chasteneth not? But if ye are without chastening, whereof all have been made partakers, then are ye bastards, and not sons" (12:7, 8). Instead of sickness being an evidence of God's displeasure, it is oftentimes the mark of His favor. The plain fact of the matter is that there is not so much as one verse in all the Bible which states that God wills that His children should be kept from all suffering and affliction. There are many verses which teach that God chastises His children for their spiritual enlightenment. It often happens that the best saints in the Church, those whose spiritual life is truest and deepest, are called upon to endure the greatest pain, while persons of immoral character often have relatively little suffering.

Health is, of course, the general rule for God's people. In each particular instance we are to pray for healing until it becomes clear that it is not God's will to heal the person; and then we are to pray for grace to bear it, that we may be able to say with Jesus in Gethsemane, "Not my will, but thine, be done." We are to remember further that no affliction can come to the children of God except as it is filtered through the sands of His love, and that it will not continue one moment longer than necessary to serve the wise and good purposes which He has in view. "To them that love God all things work together for good." (Rom. 8:28).

There is a sense in which the Devil is the author of disease and suffering, although he can inflict a penalty only as he receives permission from God. God often temporarily delivers a person over to

Satan, that his bodily and mental sufferings may react for his salvation (I Cor. 5:5). One essential lesson in the book of Job is that the child of God is hedged about by protecting love and infinite power, and that Satan cannot touch him without first obtaining permission. In the New Testament accounts the Devil and the demons were immediately subject to the commands of Jesus.

In conclusion we would say that the chief error of the faith-healers lies in the fact that they confuse redemption itself (which is objective to us and takes place outside of us) with the effects of redemption (which are subjective to us and take place within us). Redemption was worked out for us by Christ, and was completed when He died on the cross. The application of that redemption to our souls and bodies by the Holy Spirit, however, is a long process which is carried forward throughout all of our lives here, and which is not completed until we stand with sanctified souls and glorious resurrection bodies before the throne of God. We are no longer under the curse of sin, but so long as we remain in this world we are subjected to temptations and innumerable times we fall into sin. We are enabled, however, more and more to die unto sin and to live unto righteousness. Likewise, in our physical nature we continue weak, subject to disease and certain to die — death being the last enemy to be conquered. The error of the faith-healers is that they set forth a thoroughly un-Scriptural idea of sickness and pain, and try to appropriate here and now those blessings which are not to be conferred until the process is completed.

Again we say that the question is not whether God hears and answers prayer, for we believe that He does. On numerous occasions the present writer has received unmistakable answers to prayer, in the realm of health and in other affairs. But those answers have come not as immediate miracles, but through means, and in the course of God's providential control of events over periods of time. We have definite promises in Scripture that true prayer will be answered, that what we ask *in Christ's name* will be given (John 14:13, 14; Matt. 7:7, 8; James 5:16). Hence we are not to ask for selfish and vainglorious purposes but rather for such things as we have reason to believe are in accord with His will and for His glory, or for such things as we can qualify with the phrase, "If it be thy will"—remembering that Jesus Himself in His most intense and urgent prayer in the Garden of Gethsemane added, "Not my will, but thine, be done" (Luke 22:42). It often happens that what we ask for and want most would not be good for us, in which cases God answers our prayers in the highest form by giving us not what we ask but what He in His wisdom sees will be best for us.

Chapter III

THE TRINITY

1. Introduction

In this chapter we shall attempt to set forth in as clear language as possible the basic truths which the Church holds concerning the doctrine of the Trinity. We shall first present the Scripture evidence on which the doctrine rests and then we shall present the credal statements and formulations that have been set forth by church councils and by individual thinkers as they have applied themselves to the interpretation of that evidence through the two thousand years of the Christian era.

The doctrine of the Trinity is perhaps the most mysterious and difficult doctrine that is presented to us in the entire range of Scripture. Consequently we do not presume to give a full explanation of it. In the nature of the case we can know only as much concerning the inner nature of the Godhead as has been revealed to us in the Scriptures. The tri-personality of God is exclusively a truth of revelation, and one which lies outside the realm of natural reason. Its height and depth and length and breadth are immeasurable by reason of the fact that the finite is dealing with the Infinite. As well might we expect to confine the ocean within a tea-cup as to place a full explanation of the nature of God within the limits of our feeble human minds. It is not our purpose to engage in metaphysical subtleties, nor to speculate on the implications which may be drawn from this doctrine. We do hope, however, that under the guidance of the Holy Spirit we shall be enabled to set forth in a plain simple way, yet as fully as the limitations of our finite minds and language will permit, the truth concerning it, and to guard it against the errors and heresies which have prevailed at one time or another in the history of the Church. While we are not able fully to comprehend the Divine mind, we nevertheless have been created in the image of God and therefore have the right, within limits, to conceive of God according to the analogy of our own nature, and we should be able to grasp enough of this sublime revelation which God has been pleased to give concerning Himself to make a considerable advance in our spiritual growth. Since in the study of this doctrine we are absolutely dependent on revelation (there being nothing else quite similar to or analogous with it in our own consciousness or in the material world), and since the subject of our study is transcendently sacred, that subject being the innermost nature of the infinitely righteous and transcendent God, our attitude should be that of disciples who, with true humility and reverence, are ready to receive implicity whatever God has seen fit to reveal.

Since God is the Creator, Preserver and final Disposer of all things, the One in whom we live and move and have our being, our knowledge of Him must be basic and fundamental to all our knowledge. In answer to the question, "What is God?", the Scriptures reveal Him to us, in the first place, as a rational and righteous Spirit, infinite in His attributes of wisdom, being, power, holiness, justice, goodness, and truth; and in the second place they reveal Him to us as One who exists eternally as three "Persons", these three Persons, however, being one in substance and existing in the most perfect unity of thought and purpose. It is evident, moreover, that if God does thus exist in three Persons, each of whom has His distinctive part in the works of creation, providence, redemption and grace, that fact governs His activity in all spheres of His work and, consequently, the doctrine which treats of the nature of His Person must seriously affect all true theology and philosophy. Doctrines vital to the Christian system, such as those of the Deity and Person of Christ, the Incarnation, the Atonement, etc., are so inextricably interwoven with that of the Tri-unity of God that they cannot be properly understood apart from it.

We should notice that the doctrine of the Trinity is the distinctive mark of the Christian religion, setting it apart from all the other religions of the world. Working without the benefit of the revelations made in Scripture, men have, it is true, arrived at some limited truths concerning the nature and Person of God. The pagan religions, as well as all philosophical speculations, are based on natural religion and can, therefore, rise to no higher conception than that of the unity of God. In some systems we find monotheism with its belief in only one God. In others we find polytheism with its belief in many separate gods. But none of the pagan religions, nor any of the systems of speculative philosophy have ever arrived at a trinitarian conception of God. The fact of the matter is that apart from supernatural revelation there is nothing in human consciousness or experience which can give man the slightest clue to the distinctive God of the Christian faith, the tri-une, incarnate, redeeming, sanctifying God. Some of the pagan religions have set forth triads of divinities, such as, for instance, the Egyptian triad of Osiris, Isis and Horus, which is somewhat analogous to the human family with father, mother and child; or the Hindu triad of Brahma, Vishnu and Schiva, which in the cycle of pantheistic evolution personifies the creative, preservative and destructive powers of nature; or the triad set forth by Plato, of goodness, intellect and will,—which are not examples of true and proper tri-personality, not real persons who can be addressed and worshipped, but only personifications of the faculties or attributes of God. None of these systems have anything in common with the Christian doctrine of the Trinity except the notion of "threeness".

Before undertaking the more detailed study of the doctrine of the Trinity it may be well to remind ourselves that man's knowledge of God has been progressive. The most general revelation of the existence of God has been given through nature and is therefore common to all men. The existence of God is an intuitive truth universally accepted by the unprejudiced mind. Man knows himself to be dependent and responsible, and therefore posits the One on whom he is dependent and to whom he is responsible. He attributes to this One in an eminent degree all of the good qualities which he finds in himself, and thus comes to know God as a personal Spirit, infinite, eternal, and perfect in His attributes.

The Second stage in the revelation concerning the nature and attributes of God was that given through the Old Testament period. There a great advance is made over the revelation given through man's intuition and through nature, and God is disclosed as particularly the God of grace and the redeemer of sinners. The third stage, the one in which at present we are particularly interested, is that given in the New Testament in which God is represented as existing in a trinity of Persons, each of whom performs a distinctive part in the works of creation, providence, and redemption. As Dr. Warfield has pointed out:

"The elements of the plan of salvation are rooted in the mysterious nature of the Godhead, in which there coexists a trinal distinction of persons with absolute unity of essence; and the revelation of the Trinity was accordingly incidental to the execution of this plan of salvation, in which the Father sent the Son to be the propitiation for sin, and the Son, when He returned to the glory which He had with the Father before the world was, sent the Spirit to apply His redemption to men. The disclosure of this fundamental fact of the divine nature, therefore, lagged until the time had arrived for the actual working out of the long-promised redemption; and it was accomplished, first of all in fact rather than in word, by the actual appearance of God the Son on earth and the subsequent manifestations of the Spirit, who was sent forth to act as His representative in His absence." (*Studies in Theology*, p. 113)

We believe that the cosmological, teleological, ontological, and moral arguments for the existence of God are valid for any one with an open and unprejudiced mind. Perhaps they will not convince a rationalist or an atheist, but at present we are not particularly concerned with that class of persons. That theism alone is capable of solving the riddle of the universe is the firm conviction of present day scientific and philosophical thought as we have it set forth in the writings of the most outstanding leaders in these fields, such as Eddington, Jeans, Millikan, Whitehead, Hocking, Brightman, etc. The materialistic concept which held almost undisputed sway a few decades ago has been replaced with the idea that behind all that we see there is a personal God who is the Creator and Sustainer of the universe.

The present writer assumes that his readers are convinced theists. Others could hardly be expected to have an interest in theology, much less to be concerned about the doctrine of the Trinity. The psalmist gave the divine appraisal of Atheism in the words, "The fool hath said in his heart, There is no God" (xiv. 1). As a recent writer has pointed out, Atheism is "the very quintessence of absurdity, folly raised to the *nth* degree. In view of the manifold proofs of His power and wisdom on every hand, it is hard to see how any open mind can deny the existence of a Supreme Being who rules over all. To maintain that this far-flung universe is the result of an accidental juxtaposition of atoms, a fortuitous confluence of cosmic forces, is a hypothesis too nonsensical for refutation. As has been pointed out more than once, as well expect a million monkeys banging away on typewriters accidentally to produce a *Paradise Lost*. An atheistic explanation of the origin of the world (the sum total of all that is) calls for an immeasurably greater credulity than the tenets of Theism. If there be no God the cosmos is a hopeless riddle" (Dr. C. Norman Bartlett, *The Triune God*, p. 36).

But while it is so widely recognized that Theism alone offers an adequate explanation of the universe, the fact remains that many theists who firmly believe in the existence of a personal God deny just as strongly that there is a plurality of persons in the Godhead as is set forth in the trinitarian faith. In the Christian doctrine of the Trinity they see only tritheism, or some one of the myriad varieties of polytheism which have been so common in both ancient and modern times. They look upon it as an absurdity or as a contradiction of terms, and are never tired of asserting that if God is one He cannot be three. But when we give more careful thought to the theistic problem we find that the absurdity and irrationality lie on their side of the fence, and that the conception of God as an eternally lonely, solitary person is utterly out of the question. And while we do not go so far as to say that the personality of God necessarily implies the doctrine of the Trinity, we do believe that the personal traits of love, honour, fellowship, trust, sympathy, etc., cannot flower forth in their full beauty and fragrance unless there are objective personal relationships, and that this is true of Deity as well as of humanity.

The theory that God is superpersonal is, of course, an absurdity. In the nature of the case Divine personality is an infinitely greater thing than human personality; but the only alternative to a personal God is an impersonal God. And when we assert that God is impersonal we assert the primary tenet of atheism. If God exists, He must be personal. We cannot worship the Principle of the Absolute, nor hold communion with a Cosmic Power; and to assert that God is super-personal is but to deceive ourselves with a high-sounding phrase.

2. Statement of the Doctrine

Assuming that Theism is the accepted form of belief. and that God is personal, we would state the doctrine of the Trinity under the following heads:

1. THERE IS BUT ONE LIVING AND TRUE GOD

One of the most common objections alleged against the doctrine of the Trinity is that it involves tritheism, or a belief in three Gods. The fact of the matter, however, is that it stands unalterably opposed to tritheism as well as to every other form of polytheism. Scripture, reason and conscience are in perfect agreement that there is but one self-existent. eternal, supreme Being in whom all of the divine attributes or perfections inhere and from whom they cannot be separated. That both the Old and the New Testament do teach the unity of God is clearly set forth in the following verses:

"Hear, O Israel: Jehovah our God is one Jehovah" (Deut. 6:4). "Thus saith Jehovah, the King of Israel, and his Redeemer, Jehovah of hosts: I am the first, and I am the last; and beside me there is no God" (Isa. 44:6). The Decalogue, which is the foundation of the moral and religious code of Christianity, as well as of Judaism, has as its first and greatest commandment, "Thou shalt have no other gods before me" (Exod. 20:3). "I and the Father are one," said Jesus (John 10:30). "Thou believest that God is one; thou doest well" (Jas. 2:19). "We know that no idol is anything in the world, and that there is no God but one" (I Cor. 8:4). There is but "one Lord, one faith, one baptism, one God and Father of all, who is over all, and through all, and in all" (Eph. 4:5,6). "I am the Alpha and the Omega, the first and the last, the beginning and the end" (Rev. 22: 13). From Genesis to Revelation God is declared to be one.

That the universe is a unit is the settled conclusion of modern science and philosophy; and with this, of course, goes the corollary that the God who created it and who rules it is One. Astronomers tell us, for instance, that the same principles which govern in our solar system are also found in the millions of stars which are trillions of miles away. Physicists analyze the light that comes from the sun and from the distant stars and tell us that not only are the same elements, such as iron, carbon, oxygen, etc., which are found on the earth also found on them, but that these elements are found in practically the same proportion as here. From the law of gravitation we learn that every material object in the universe attracts every other material object with a force which is directly proportional to their masses and inversely proportional to the square of the distance between their centers. Hence every grain of sand in the desert and on the sea-shore is linked up with every sun in the universe. The sluggish earth mounts upward to meet the falling snowflake. The microscope reveals marvels just as wonderful as those revealed by the telescope, and everywhere it is the same unified system.

Certainly the Unitarians have no monopoly on the doctrine of the unity of God. Trinitarians hold this just as definitely. The unity of God is one of the basic postulates of theism, and no system can possibly be true which teaches otherwise.

II. WHILE GOD IN HIS INNERMOST NATURE IS ONE, HE, NEVERTHELESS, EXISTS AS THREE PERSONS

The best concise definition of the doctrine of the Trinity, so far as we are aware, is that found in the Westminster Shorter Catechism: "There are three persons within the Godhead; the Father, the Son and the Holy Ghost; and these three are one God, the same in substance, equal in power and glory." We would prefer, however, to use the term "Spirit" rather than "Ghost," since a ghost is commonly understood to be a spirit that once had a body but lost it, and the Holy Spirit has never possessed a body of any kind.

We have seen that the Scriptures teach that there is but one true and living God. They teach with equal clearness that this one God exists as three distinct Persons, as Father, Son, and Holy Spirit:

(a) The Father is God: "To us there is one God, the Father, of whom are all things" (I Cor. 8:6). "Paul, an apostle . . . through

Jesus Christ, and God the Father" (Gal. 1:1). "There is . . . one God and Father of all" (Eph. 4:6). "At that season Jesus answered and said, I thank thee, O Father, Lord of heaven and earth . . ." (Matt. 11:25). "For him (the Son) the Father, even God, hath sealed" (John 6:27). "According to the foreknowledge of God the Father" (I Pet. 1:2). "That every tongue should confess that Jesus Christ is Lord, to the glory of God the Father" (Phil. 2:11). "I ascend unto my Father and your Father, and my God and your God" (John 20:17). "But the hour cometh, and now is, when the true worshippers shall worship the Father in spirit and truth" (John 4:23). Jesus prayed to God the Father (Mark 14:36; John 11:41; 17:11, etc.).

(b) The Son is God: "Christ . . . who is over all, God blessed for ever" (Rom. 9:5). "For in Him (Christ) dwelleth all the fulness of the Godhead bodily" (Col. 2:9). "Thomas answered and said unto him, My Lord and my God" (John 20:28). "I and the Father are one" (John 10:30). "Looking for the blessed hope and appearing of the glory of the great God and our Saviour Jesus Christ" (Titus 2:13). "Thou art the Christ, the Son of the living God" (Matt. 16:16). Christ assumed power over the Sabbath, and "called God His own Father, making Himself equal with God" (John 5:18). He assumed the prerogatives of God in forgiving sins (Mark 2:5). "In the beginning was the Word, and the Word was with God, and the Word was God" (John 1:1).

The attributes which can be ascribed only to God are ascribed to Christ: Holiness—"Thou art the Holy One of God" (John 6:69); "Him who knew no sin," (II Cor. 5:21); "Which of you convicteth me of sin?" (John 8:46); "Holy, guileless, undefiled, separate from sinners" (Heb. 7:26). Eternity—"In the beginning was the Word" (John 1:1); "Before Abraham was born, I am" (John 8:58); "But of the Son he saith, Thy throne, O God, is for ever and ever" (Heb. 1:8); "The glory which I had with thee before the world was" (John 17:5). Life — "In Him was life" (John 1:4); "I am the way, and the truth, and the life: no one cometh unto the Father but by me" (John 14:6); "I am the resurrection and the life" (John 11:25). Immutability—"Jesus Christ is the same yesterday and to-day, yea and for ever" (Heb. 13:8), "They (the heavens) shall perish; but thou continuest. . . . They shall be changed: but thou art the same" (Heb. 1:11, 12). Omnipotence—"All authority hath been given unto me in heaven and on earth" (Matt. 28:18); "The Lord God, who is and who was and who is to come, the Almighty" (Rev. 1:8). Omniscience—"Thou knowest all things" (John 16:30); "Jesus knowing their thoughts" (Matt. 9:4); "Jesus knew from the beginning who they were that believed not, and who it was that should betray Him"

(John 6:64); "In whom are all the treasures of wisdom and knowledge hidden" (Col. 2:3). Omnipresence—"I am with you always" (Matt. 28:20); "The fulness of him that filleth all in all" (Eph. 1:23). Creation—"All things were made through him; and without him was not anything made that hath been made" (John 1:3); "The world was made through him" (John 1:10); "For in him were all things created, in the heavens and upon the earth, things visible and things invisible, whether thrones or dominions or principalities or powers; all things have been created through him, and unto him; and he is before all things, and in him all things consist" (Col. 1:16, 17); "Upholding all things by the word of his power" (Heb. 1:3). Raising the dead—"And he (God the Father) gave him (Christ the Son) authority to execute judgment . . . for the hour cometh in which all that are in the tombs shall hear his voice, and shall come forth; they that have done good, unto the resurrection of life; and they that have done evil, unto the resurrection of judgment" (John 5:27-29). Judgment of all men—"But when the Son of man shall come in his glory, and all the angels with him, then shall he sit on the throne of his glory: and before him shall be gathered all the nations: and he shall separate them one from another, as the shepherd separateth the sheep from the goats; and he shall set the sheep on his right hand, and the goats on the left. Then shall the King say unto them on his right hand, Come, ye blessed of my Father, inherit the kingdom prepared for you from the foundation of the world. . . . And he shall say also unto them on the left hand, Depart from me, ye cursed, into the eternal fire, which is prepared for the devil and his angels. . . . And these shall go away into eternal punishment: but the righteous into eternal life" (Matt. 25:31-46). Prayer and worship are to be directed to Christ—"If ye shall ask anything in my name, that will I do" (John 14:14); "He was parted from them, and was carried up into heaven. And they worshipped him" (Luke 24:51, 52); "Stephen, calling upon the Lord, and saying, Lord Jesus, receive my spirit" (Acts 7:59); all are to "honor the Son, even as they honor the Father. He that honoreth not the Son honoreth not the Father that sent him" (John 5:23); Believe on the Lord Jesus, and thou shalt be saved" (Acts 16:31); "Let all the angels of God worship him" (Heb. 1:6); "That in the name of Jesus every knee should bow . . . and that every tongue should confess that Jesus Christ is Lord, to the glory of God the Father" (Phil. 2:10, 11); "Our Lord and Saviour Jesus Christ" (II Pet. 3:18); "Jesus Christ, to whom be the glory for ever and ever" (Heb. 13:21;—and when we compare these verses with statements such as we have in Isaiah, "Look unto me and be ye saved, all the ends of the earth; for I am God, and there is none else" (45:22), and Jeremiah, "Thus saith Jehovah, Cursed is the man that trusteth in man and maketh flesh his arm" (17:5), we are faced with this dilemma: either the Christian doctrine of the Trinity must be true, or the Scriptures are self-contradictory; either the Scriptures recognize more Gods than one, or Christ, together with the Father and the Holy Spirit is that one God.

All of these ascriptions of holiness, eternity, life, immutability, omnipotence, omniscience, omnipresence, creation, providence, raising the dead, judgment of all men, prayer and worship due to Christ, most clearly teach His Deity. Such attitudes of mind if directed toward a creature would be idolatrous.

(c) The Holy Spirit is God: "Peter said, Ananias, why hath Satan filled thy heart to lie to the Holy Spirit? . . . Thou has not lied unto men, but unto God" (Acts 5:3, 4); "For who among men knoweth the things of a man, save the spirit of the man, which is in him? even so the things of God none knoweth, save the Spirit of God" (I Cor. 2:11); "But when the Comforter is come, whom I will send unto you from the Father, even the Spirit of truth, which proceedeth from the Father, he shall bear witness of me" (John 15:26). In the Baptismal Formula, "Go ye therefore, and make disciples of all the nations, baptizing them in the name of the Father, and of the Son, and of the Holy Spirit" (Matt. 28:19), and in the Apostolic Benediction, "The grace of the Lord Jesus Christ, and the love of God, and the communion of the Holy Spirit, be with you all" (II Cor. 13:14), the Holy Spirit is placed on a plane of absolute equality with the Father and the Son as Deity and is regarded equally with them as the source of all power and blessing.

There are many, even among professedly Christian people, who have no higher conception of the Holy Spirit than that of an impersonal, mysterious, supernatural power or influence of God. It is true that in the Old Testament, where the emphasis was upon the unity of God, the references to the Spirit, while not incapable of being applied to a distinct person, were more generally understood to designate simply God's power or influence. But in the more advanced revelation of the New Testament the distinct personality of the Holy Spirit is clearly seen. No longer can He be looked upon as merely a divine power or influence, but as a divine Person. Some people, even among those in the Christian Churches, because they are very thoughtless, speak of the Holy Spirit as *it,* when a little reflection would show them that the proper term is *He* or *Him.*

That the Holy Spirit is a Person is clearly taught in the following verses: "The Spirit said unto Philip, Go near, and join thyself to this chariot" (Acts 8:29). "The Spirit said unto him (Peter), Behold, three men seek thee. But arise, and get thee down, go with them, nothing doubting: for I have sent them" (Acts 10:19, 20). "The Holy Spirit said, separate me Barnabas and Saul for the work whereunto I have called them" (Acts 13:2). "The Holy Spirit shall teach you in that very hour what ye ought to say" (Luke 12:12). "When he, the Spirit of truth, is come, he shall guide you into all the truth: for he shall not speak from himself; but what things soever he shall hear, these shall he speak: and he shall declare unto you the things that are to come. He shall glorify me: for he shall take of mine, and shall declare it unto you" (John 16:13, 14). "And I will pray the Father, and he shall give you another Comforter, that he may be with you for ever, even the Spirit of truth: whom the world cannot receive; for it beholdeth him not, neither knoweth him: ye know him; for he abideth with you, and shall be in you" (John 14:16, 17),—here the Holy Spirit is called a "Comforter" (marginal reference Advocate), that is, one called to stand by our side as our Guide, Teacher, Instructor, Sponsor; and in the nature of the case, therefore, He must be a Person. In a parallel passage Christ is similarly spoken of,—"We have an Advocate with the Father, Jesus Christ the righteous" (I John 2:1) "The spirit Himself maketh intercession for us with groanings which cannot be uttered" (Rom. 8:26). "Grieve not the Holy Spirit of God" (Eph. 4:30). "He that hath an ear, let him hear what the Spirit saith to the churches" (Rev. 2:17). "Every sin and blasphemy shall be forgiven unto men; but the blasphemy against the Spirit shall not be forgiven. And whosoever shall speak a word against the Son of man, it shall be forgiven him; but whosoever shall speak against the Holy Spirit, it shall not be forgiven him, neither in this world, nor in that which is to come" (Matt. 12:31, 32)—the language here used implies that it is impossible to commit a sin against a more divine personage than the Holy Spirit, that of all possible sins the sin against the Holy Spirit is the worst, both in its nature and consequences, and thus implies His eternal dignity and Deity.

Words which in the Old Testament are ascribed to God are in the New Testament more specifically said to have been spoken by the Holy Spirit,—compare Jer. 31:33, 34 with Heb. 10:15-17; Ps. 95:7-11 with Heb. 3:7-11; Isa. 6:9, 10 with Acts 28:25-28. In the Old Testament we read that the Holy Spirit brought order out of the primeval chaos (Gen. 1:2); and He strove to lead the ante-diluvians in the ways of righteousness (Gen. 6:3); He equipped certain men to become prophets (Num. 11:26, 29); He instructed the Israelites as a people (Neh. 9:20); He came upon Isaiah and equipped him to be a prophet (61:1), and caused Ezekiel to go and preach to those of the captivity

(3:12, 15). In the New Testament the miracle of the virgin birth of Christ was wrought through His power (Luke 1:35); He descended on Jesus at the baptism and equipped Him for the public ministry (Matt. 3:16); He was promised as a Comforter and Teacher to the disciples (John 16:7-13); He came upon the disciples on the day of Pentecost and equipped them to be world missionaries (Acts 2:1-42); He kept Paul from going in one direction and sent him in another (Acts 16:6-10); He equips different individuals with different gifts and talents (I Cor. 12:4-31); He performs the supernatural work of regenerating the souls of men (Titus 3:5, John 3:5); He inspired the prophets and apostles so that what they spoke or wrote in God's name was truly His word to the people (II Pet. 1:20, 21); in the works of regeneration and sanctification He applies to the heart of each of the Lord's people the objective redemption which was wrought out by Christ, and in general He directs the affairs of the advancing Church. He is thus set forth as the Author of order and beauty in the physical world, and of faith and holiness in the spiritual world.

Throughout the Scriptures the Holy Spirit is thus set forth as a distinct Person, with a mind, will and power of His own. Baptism is administered in His name. He is constantly associated with two other Persons, the Father and the Son, whose distinct personalities are recognized,—a phenomenon which could lead only to confusion if He too were not a distinct Person. The personal pronouns, "He," "Him," "I," and "Me," are applied to Him, pronouns which can be used intelligently only when applied to a person. They occur so repeatedly through the prose narratives and cannot be set aside as a tendency to personify an impersonal force. That two and two make four does not appear more clear and conclusive than that the Holy Spirit is a living Agent, working with consciousness, will and power.

After the personality of the Holy Spirit is established there are but few who will deny His Deity. It is certain that He is not a creature, and consequently those who admit His personality accept His Deity readily enough. Most of the heretical sects that have maintained that Christ was a mere man have, in accordance with that, maintained that the Spirit was only a power or influence. This was the opinion held by the Gnostics and Socinians, as well as that held by present-day Unitarians and rationalists.

That there should be any doubt at all concerning the personality of the Spirit may seem strange; and yet, as Dr. A. H. Strong has pointed out:

"It is noticeable that in Scripture there is no obtrusion of the Holy Spirit's personality, as if He (the One who inspired the prophets as they wrote) desired to draw attention to Himself. The Holy Spirit shows not Himself, but Christ. Like John the Baptist, He is a mere voice, and so an example to Christian preachers, who are themselves 'made . . . sufficient as ministers . . . of the spirit' (II Cor. 3:6). His leading is therefore often unperceived; He so joins Himself to us that we infer His presence only from the new and holy exercises of our own minds; He continues to work in us even when His presence is ignored and His purity is outraged by our sins" (*Systematic Theology*, p. 324).

III. THE TERMS "FATHER," "SON" AND "HOLY SPIRIT" DESIGNATE DISTINCT PERSONS WHO ARE OBJECTIVE TO EACH OTHER

The terms Father, Son and Spirit do not merely designate the different relations which God assumes toward His creatures. They are not analogous to the terms Creator, Preserver and Benefactor, which do express such relations, but are the proper names of different subjects who are distinct from one another as one person is distinct from another. That this is true is clear from the following personal relations which they bear toward each other:

(*a*) They mutually use the pronouns I, thou, he and him when speaking to or of each other. "This is my beloved Son, in whom I am well pleased; hear ye him" (Matt. 17:5). "Father, the hour is come; glorify thy Son, that the Son may glorify thee" (John 17:1). "I came out from the Father, and am come into the world: again, I leave the world, and go unto the Father" (John 16:28). "When he, the Spirit of truth, is come, he shall guide you into all the truth: for he shall not speak from himself: but what things soever he shall hear, these shall he speak: and he shall declare unto you the things that are to come" (John 16:13).

(*b*) The Father loves the Son, and the Son loves the Father. The Spirit glorifies the Son. "The Father loveth the Son, and hath given all things into his hand" (John 3:35). "I have kept my Father's commandments, and abide in his love" (John 15:10). "He (the Holy Spirit) shall glorify me; for he shall take of mine, and shall declare it unto you" (John 16:14).

(*c*) The Son prays to the Father. "And now, Father, glorify thou me with thine own self with the glory which I had with thee before the world was" (John 17:5). "And I will pray the Father, and he shall give you another Comforter, that he may be with you for ever" (John 14:16).

(*d*) The Father sends the Son, and the Father and the Son send the Holy Spirit who acts as their Agent. "He that receiveth you receiveth me, and he that receiveth me receiveth him that sent me" (Matt. 10:40). "As thou didst send me into the world" (John 17:18). "And this is life eternal, that they should know thee the only true

God, and him whom thou didst send, even Jesus Christ" (John 17:3). "But the Comforter, even the Holy Spirit, whom the Father will send in my name, he shall teach you all things, and bring to your remembrance all that I said unto you" (John 14:26). "It is expedient for you that I go away; for if I go not away, the Comforter will not come unto you; but if I go, I will send him unto you" (John 16:7).

Thus we see that the Persons within the Godhead are so distinct that each can address the others, each can love the others, the Father sends the Son, the Father and the Son send the Spirit, the Son prays to the Father, and we can pray to each of them. They act and are acted upon as subject and object, and each has a particular work to perform. We say they are distinct persons, for a person is one who can say I, who can be addressed as thou, and who can act and be the object of action.

The doctrine of the Trinity, then, is but the synthesis of these facts. When we have said these three things,—that there is but one God, that the Father and the Son and the Spirit is each God, and that the Father and the Son and the Spirit is each a distinct Person,—we have enunciated the doctrine of the Trinity in its fulness. This is the form in which it is found in the Scriptures, and it is also the form in which it has entered into the faith of the Church.

3. Further Scripture Proof

While there is no single passage in Scripture which sets forth the doctrine of the Trinity in formal, credal statement, there are numerous passages in which the three Persons are mentioned in such a manner as to exhibit at once their unity and their distinctness. Most important of these is the Great Commission given in Matthew 28:19, in which baptism is commanded "in the name of the Father and of the Son and of the Holy Spirit." In this, the initiatory rite of the Christian religion, the doctrine of the Trinity is purposely set forth in such a manner as to keep it before the minds of the people as a cardinal doctrine of the faith. "What we witness here," says Dr. Warfield, "is the authoritative announcement of the Trinity as the God of Christianity by its Founder, in one of the most solemn of His recorded declarations. Israel had worshipped the one only true God under the Name of Jehovah; Christians are to worship the same one only and true God under the Name of 'the Father, and the Son, and the Holy Spirit.' This is the distinguishing characteristic of Christians; and that is as much as to say that the doctrine of the Trinity is, according to our Lord's own apprehension of it, the distinctive mark of the religion which He founded." (*Biblical Doctrines,* p. 155).

The Apostolic Benediction — "The grace of the Lord Jesus Christ, and the love of God, and the communion of the Holy Spirit, be with you all" (II Cor. 13:14), which is a prayer addressed to Christ for His grace, to the Father for His love, and to the Holy Spirit for His fellowship — is designed to serve the same purpose. In this formula, as in that of baptism, the divinity, and consequently the equality, of each of the persons in the Godhead is taken for granted; and no other interpretation is rationally possible except that which the Church has held down through the ages, namely, that God exists in three Persons and that these three are one in substance, equal in power and glory.

In the account of our Lord's baptism we find as clear teaching concerning the reality of the Trinity as any one can reasonably ask for, — Christ the Son stood there in human form and was visible to all the people, the voice of God the Father spoke from heaven, saying, "This is my beloved Son, in whom I am well pleased," and the descent of the Holy Spirit upon Christ was seen as that of a dove (Matt. 3:16, 17).

In the announcement of the birth of Jesus three divine Persons came into view: "And the angel answered and said unto her, The Holy Spirit shall come upon thee, and the power of the Most High shall overshadow thee: wherefore also the holy thing which is begotten shall be called the Son of God" (Luke 1:35). Here we read of the coming of the Holy Spirit, of the power of the Most High, and are told that the Child is to be known as the Son of God. Also, in the parallel account of Matthew 1:18-23 the three persons of the Trinity are named.

The distinction between the Father and the Son and the Holy Spirit is announced by Jesus when He says: "But when the Comforter is come, whom I will send unto you from the Father, He shall bear witness of me" (John 15:26).

In the final discourse and prayer (John, chs. 14-17), Christ spoke to and of the Father and promised to send another Comforter, the Holy Spirit, who would guide, teach, and inspire the· disciples. Here again the personality and Deity of the Father, Son and Holy Spirit are recognized with special clearness.

The teaching of Jesus is, of course, trinitarian throughout. In accordance with the Hebrew idea of sonship,—that whatever the father is, that the son is also,—He claimed to be the Son of God Matt. 9:27; 24:36; Mark 8:31; Luke 10:22; John 9:35-37; 11:4); and the Jews, with exact appreciation of His meaning, understood

Him to claim that He was "equal with God" (John 5:18), o
put it more briefly, they understood Him to claim that He was "C
(John 10:33). He claims that He knows the Father and that
Father knows Him with perfect mutual knowledge: "All thin
have been delivered unto me of my Father: and no one knoweth wh
the Son is, save the Father; and who the Father is, save the Son
and he to whomsoever the Son willeth to reveal him" (Luke 10:22;
also Matt. 11:27). The title, "Son of God," in such a sense that
it involves absolute community with God the Father in knowledge and
power, is attributed to Him and accepted by Him (Matt. 8:29; 14:33;
27:40, 43, 54; Mark 3:11; Luke 4:41; 22:70; John 1:34, 49; 11:27).
But while He thus asserts that His eternal home is in the depths of the
Divine Being, He sets forth in equally clear language His distinctness
from the Father: "Jesus said unto them, If God were your Father,
ye would love me: for I came forth and am come from God; for
neither have I come of myself, but he sent me" (John 8:42). And to
His disciples He said: "In that day ye shall ask in my name: and
I say not unto you, that I will pray the Father for you; for the
Father himself loveth you, because ye have loved me, and have
believed that I came forth from the Father. I came out from the
Father, and am come into the world; again, I leave the world,
and go unto the Father" (John 16:26-28).

Hence our primary reason for believing the doctrine of the Trinity
is, as we have stated elsewhere, not because of any general tendency
of human thinking to go in that direction, nor because of any analogies
in nature, but only because it is a clearly revealed doctrine of the Bible.
For those who accept the authority of the Scriptures the evidence is
conclusive. We do not here attempt to argue with those who deny
that authority, but refer them to the Christian doctrine of the Inspiration of the Scriptures. Unless we are agreed that the Scriptures are an
authoritative revelation from God, it is useless to argue over the
doctrine of the Trinity. The Christian finds the proofs for the trustworthiness of the Bible so convincing that he is compelled to accept its
teaching concerning the Trinity even though his finite mind is not
able to comprehend its full meaning.

Yet while it is true that the evidence for the doctrine of the Trinity
is found in the Bible, it is also true that, as in the case of the other
doctrines in the Christian system, there is no place where this doctrine
is set forth in a complete and systematic form. The different elements
of the doctrine, such as the unity of God, the true and equal Deity
of the Father, Son and Holy Spirit, their distinct personality, the
relationship which they bear to each other, to the Church, and to

the world, etc., while expressed most clearly in the New Testament are found scattered through all parts of the Bible from the first chapter of Genesis to the last of Revelation. It is only by proving these elements separately, as we have attempted to do, that the truth of the whole doctrine is most satisfactorily brought out. The doctrine is given in Scripture, not in formulated definition, but in fragmentary allusions; and it is only as we assemble the *disjecta membra* into their organic unity that we are able to grasp its true meaning. It lies in Scripture as it were in solution, and comes into clear view only when it is crystallized out from its solvent. The Bible is not a work on Systematic Theology, but only the quarry out of which the stone for such a temple can be obtained. Instead of giving us a formal statement of a theological system it gives us a mass of raw materials which are to be organized and systematized and worked up into their organic relations. Nowhere, for instance, do we find a formal statement of the doctrine of the Inspiration of the Scriptures, or of the sovereignty of God, or of the Person of Christ. The Bible gives us an account of the creation of the world and of man, of the entrance of sin, and of God's purpose to redeeem man from sin. It tells particularly of God's merciful dealings with one group of people, the Israelites, and of the founding of Christianity; and the doctrinal facts are given with but little regard to their logical relations. These doctrinal facts therefore need to be classified and arranged into a logical system and thus transformed into theology. That the material in the Bible is not arranged in a theological system is in accordance with God's proceaure in other realms. He has not given us a fully developed system of biology, astronomy, economics, or politics. We simply find the unorganized facts in nature and experience, and are left to develop them into a system as best we may. And since the doctrines are not thus presented in a systematic and formal way it is, of course, much easier for varied and false interpretations to arise.

That even in the New Testament the doctrine of the Trinity is not set forth with anything even approaching systematic treatment, but rather in the form of incidental allusions, may occasion some surprise. But while not presenting the doctrine with argumentative reasoning, nor in creedal statements, the New Testament everywhere assumes it; and the unstudied naturalness and simplicity with which it is given makes it all the more impressive and illuminating. We find not merely a text here and there, but such a wealth of trinitarian implications that, as Dr. Bartlett says:

"They blossom forth everywhere in such profusion that the reverent and unprejudiced reader seeking light upon this subject is troubled, not by a paucity of proof texts, but by an embarrassment of riches." (*The Triune God,* p. 22).

Dr. Warfield points out that the whole book is saturated with Trinitarianism:

"Jesus Christ and the Holy Spirit are the fundamental proof of the doctrine of the Trinity. This is as much as to say that all the evidence of whatever kind, and from whatever source derived, that Jesus Christ is God manifested in the flesh, and that the Holy Spirit is a Divine Person, is just so much evidence for the doctrine of the Trinity; and when we go to the New Testament for evidence of the Trinity we are to seek it, not merely in the scattered illusions to the Trinity as such, numerous and instructive as they are, but primarily in the whole mass of evidence which the New Testament provides of the Deity of Christ and the Divine personality of the Holy Spirit. When we have said this, we have said in effect that the whole mass of the New Testament is evidence for the Trinity. For the New Testament is saturated with evidence of the Deity of Christ and the Divine personality of the Holy Spirit" (*Biblical Doctrines,* p. 146).

That a doctrine which to us is so difficult should, even in the hands of a people who had become fiercely monotheistic, take its place silently and imperceptibly among accepted Christian truths without struggle and without controversy, is certainly one of the most remarkable phenomena in the history of human thought. We have not far to seek, however, for the explanation. Marvellous developments had taken place between the closing of the Old Testament and the opening of the New. To quote Dr. Warfield again:

"It may carry us a little way to remark, as it has been customary to remark since the time of Gregory of Nazianzus, that it was the task of the Old Testament revelation to fix firmly in the minds and hearts of the people of God the great fundamental truth of the unity of the Godhead; and it would have been dangerous to speak to them of the plurality within this unity until this task had been fully accomplished. The real reason for the delay in the revelation of the Trinity, however, is grounded in the secular development of the redemptive purpose of God; the times were not ripe for the revelation of the Trinity in the unity of the Godhead until the fulness of the time had come for God to send forth His Son unto redemption, and His Spirit unto sanctification. The revelation in word must needs wait upon the revelation in fact, to which it brings its necessary explanation, no doubt, but from which it derives its own entire significance and value. The revelation of a Trinity in the Divine unity as a mere abstract truth without relation to manifested fact, and without significance to the development of the kingdom of God, would have been foreign to the whole method of the Divine procedure as it lies exposed to us in the pages of Scripture" (*Biblical Doctrines,* p. 145).

The revelation that God exists in three Persons, as Father, Son and Holy Spirit, is, in fact, the only basis on which the Christian doctrine of redemption can be intelligently set forth. Hence the revelation concerning the plurality of Persons in the Godhead is not given for the mere purpose of presenting something which shall be puzzling and inscrutable to human minds, but as a necessary step in the much fuller revelation concerning the plan of salvation. The incarnation of God the Son and the outpouring of God the Holy Spirit at Pentecost marked two tremendous advances in the divine plan. The revelation of the Trinity was incidental to the fuller development of the plan of salvation, and at the time of the writing of the New Testament books the doctrine was already the common property of Christian believers. Hence in speaking and writing to one another they assumed this common trinitarian consciousness rather than instructed one another about something concerning which there was no disagreement, and the result is that we find the doctrine everywhere pre-supposed, presented in the form of allusion rather than in express teaching.

4. The Trinity in the Old Testament

In regard to all of the great doctrines of the Bible we find that revelation has been progressive. What is only intimated at first is set forth clearly and fully as time goes on. The obscure hint in the Old Testament is found to coincide perfectly with the fuller revelations in the New. As with our physical eyesight God does not cause the sun to rise with a sudden flash, lest such strong and glorious light should blind us, so He has also borne with our immature spiritual eyesight; He did not at first manifest Himself in the wonderful personality of the Messiah, the sun of Righteousness, and in the personality of the Holy Spirit, but revealed Himself gradually, precept upon precept, line upon line, here a little, there a little, until our understanding was prepared to receive the whole truth. Since the doctrine of the Trinity is one which arises out of the completed redemption as it is presented to us in the New Testament and cannot be intelligently comprehended apart from that redemption, we should not expect to find it set forth with any clearness in the Old Testament. And yet, if the doctrine is a vital and necessary part of the Christian system we would expect that at least some foregleams or intimations of it might be given. And this we find actually to be the case.

"The Old Testament," says Dr. Warfield, "may be likened to a chamber richly furnished but dimly lighted; the introduction of light brings into it nothing which was not in it before; but it brings out into clearer view much of what is in it but only dimly or even not at all perceived before. The mystery of the Trinity is not revealed in the Old Testament; but the mystery of the Trinity underlies the Old Testament revelation, and here and there almost comes into view. Thus the Old Testament revelation of God is not corrected by the fuller revelation which follows it, but only perfected, extended and enlarged" (*Biblical Doctrines*, p. 142).

The orderly, progressive way in which these doctrines are revealed, through the successive writings in the sixty-six books and over a period of approximately fifteen hundred years, is one of the strongest arguments for the Divine origin of the Bible. As all that is in the full grown tree was potentially in the seed, so we find that the clearly revealed doctrines of the New Testament were given in rudimentary form in the earliest chapters of Genesis. This is true of doctrines such as those of redemption, the Person and work of the Messiah, the nature of the Holy Spirit, and the future life. But in regard to no other doctrine is this more true than in regard to that of the Trinity. Indirect allusions to the Trinity were permitted by the Holy Spirit who presided over the writing of the books, but there is no reason to believe that the truth was apprehended in any adequate way even by the prophets themselves. The doctrine itself was veiled and held in reserve until the accompanying work of Christ in redemption made it intelligible to the human mind.

Hence the Old Testament emphasizes the unity of God and special care is taken not to aggravate the constant tendency of Israel toward polytheism. A premature revelation of the Trinity might have been a hindrance to religious progress; for the race then, like the child now, needed to learn the unity of God before it could profitably be taught the Trinity. Otherwise it might have fallen into tritheism. Abraham in Chaldea, and the Israelites in Egypt and later in Palestine, needed to be guarded against the almost universal urge toward polytheism. The first and greatest commandment of the Decalogue was directed against polytheism, and the second and next most important was directed against idolatry with its strong tendency toward polytheism. For centuries this was drilled into the consciousness of Israel and established as a primal truth; then at long last a new day dawned, the Messiah came personally to live among and instruct His people, and the Holy Spirit was manifested in power in the early Church. The Church was then ready for the further truth that while God is One, He, nevertheless, exists as three Persons. Even after the New Testament revelation men have found it extremely difficult to state the doctrine of the Trinity without verging on Tritheism on the one hand, or Modalism or Unitarianism on the other.

PLURAL NAMES AND PRONOUNS

In the very first chapter of Genesis, as well as in many other places, we find that the names of God are in the plural, *Elohim,* also *Adonai;* and with these plural forms of the divine name singular verbs and adjectives are usually joined,—a remarkable phenomenon in view of the fact that the Hebrew language also contained the singular term *El,* meaning God. Along with the plural name, God sometimes uses plural pronouns in referring to Himself: "Let us make man in our image, after our likeness" (Gen. 1:26, 27); "And Jehovah God said, Behold, the man is become as one of us, to know good and evil" (spoken of Adam after the fall) (Gen. 3:22); "Come, let us go down, and there confound their language" (at the tower of Babel) (Gen. 11:7); "And I heard the voice of the Lord, saying, Whom shall I send, and who will go for us?" (Isa. 6:8). In these verses we have counsel within the Trinity, God speaking with Himself. He is not taking counsel with, nor asking advice of, the angels, as some have suggested; for the angels are not His counsellors, but His servants, and, like man, infinitely below Him in knowledge. In the Divine nature itself, the Bible teaches us, is to be found that plurality of personal powers which polytheism separated and sought to worship in isolation.

The words of Moses which are so often quoted by the Jews today, "Hear, O Israel: Jehovah our God is one Jehovah" (Deut. 6:4), are in the English translation an unmeaning repetition of words, but in the original Hebrew they contain much sound instruction. "Jehovah our Elohim is one Jehovah" the word Elohim being plural shows that God the Lord, in covenant engagement and manner of existence, is more than one, yet is "one Jehovah" as regards essence of being.

THE ANGEL OF JEHOVAH

Very important is the fact that, beginning with the book of Genesis and continuing with ever-increasing clearness throughout the remainder of the Old Testament, we find a distinction made between Jehovah and the Angel of Jehovah who presents Himself as one in essence with Jehovah yet distinct from Him. Such an event, in which God assumes the form of an angel or of a man in order to speak visibly and audibly to man, is commonly known as a "theophany." As the revelation is unfolded by the procession of the prophets we find that divine titles and divine worship are given to this Angel and accepted by Him, that He is revealed as an eternal Being, the Mighty God, the Prince of peace, the Adonai, the Lord of David, that He is to be born of a virgin, that He will be despised and rejected of men, a man of sorrows and acquainted with grief, that He will bear the sin of many, and that he will, above all, set up the kingdom of righteousness which is to increase until it fills the whole earth. These prophecies, as the New Testament makes clear, were fulfilled in Christ, the second Person of the Trinity, who in His Divine-human capacity wrought redemption for His people and who is to rule until all enemies have been placed under His feet.

In Genesis 16:7-13 we have an account of a theophany in which the Angel of Jehovah appeared to Hagar out in the wilderness, commanded her to return to her mistress, and promised that He would multiply her seed exceedingly. Now it is clear that no created angel, speaking in his own name, could have claimed such authority. Here we are face to face with God Himself under a different manifestation; and Hagar, realizing this great truth, "called the name of Jehovah that spake unto her, Thou art a God that seeth: for she said, Have I even here looked after him that seeth me?"

In Genesis 18:1—19:29 we have a remarkable revelation of God to Abraham with the idea of the Trinity in the background. There we read: "And Jehovah appeared unto him by the oaks of Mamre . . . and he looked, and, lo, three men stood over against him . . . and when he saw them . . . he bowed himself to the earth, and said, My Lord (not lords), If now I have found favour in thy sight . . . And they said unto him, Where is Sarah thy wife? And he said, Behold, in the tent. And he (Jehovah) said, I will certainly return unto thee when the season cometh round; and, lo, Sarah thy wife shall have a son. And Sarah heard in the tent door, which was behind him. Now Abraham and Sarah were old, and well stricken in age. . . . And Sarah laughed within herself. . . . And Jehovah said unto Abraham, Wherefore did Sarah laugh? . . . Is anything too hard for Jehovah?" Although the visitors appear as three men, that is, three persons, Abraham addresses them in the singular, and throughout this passage the singular references to Jehovah and the plural references to the three men are used interchangeably. And after the two "men" had gone on toward Sodom, Jehovah still stands before Abraham who pleads with Him to spare the city. Yet when the two men appear before Lot in Sodom it is Jehovah who speaks to him. "And he (Jehovah) said, Escape for thy life . . . And Lot said unto them (plural) . . . Let me escape thither (to Zoar). . . . And he (Jehovah) said, See, I have accepted thee concerning this thing also, that I will not overthrow the city of which thou hast spoken." In other words, Jehovah who appeared to Abraham and the three men that Abraham saw apparently were the same, and Jehovah who appeared to Lot and the two men that Lot saw apparently were the same.

In Genesis 22:1-19 we have references to God and also to one who is "the angel of Jehovah." In verse 2 God commands Abraham: "Take now thy son . . . and offer him there for a burnt offering," while in verse 12 the Angel of Jehovah retracts and nulllifies the command of God, with the words: "Lay not thy hand upon the lad." In verses 15-18 this angel of Jehovah swears by Himself as Jehovah, saying that He is Jehovah, and gives Abraham the promise of three-fold blessing.

In Genesis 32:22-32 Jehovah appeared to Jacob under the guise of a mysterious person who wrestled with him all the night. In the morning Jacob realized that he had been face to face with God, and asked for His blessing. He called the name of the place "Peniel," "for," said he, "I have seeen God face to face."

The Angel of Jehovah appeared to Moses in the burning bush and commissioned him to go back to Egypt and deliver the Israelites. He gave Moses the promise that He would be with them and that He would lead them out (Exod. 3:1-22). In this passage the terms "God" and "Angel of Jehovah" are used interchangeably. A little later God talked with Moses on Mount Sinai and gave him the Ten Commandments. In the New Testament Stephen tells us that it was the Angel who spoke to Moses on the Mount (Acts 7:38), and Paul tells us specifically that Christ was the spiritual "rock" which followed the Israelites throughout their wilderness journey (I Cor. 10:4).

In Ex. 23:20-23 God, speaking through Moses, promises to send His Angel before the children of Israel to keep them and to bring them into the promised land. In regard to this Angel they were especially warned: "Take ye heed before him, and hearken unto his voice; provoke him not; for he will not pardon your transgression: for my name is in him." Here we find that the Angel of Jehovah has power to forgive sins; and this in itself identifies Him with Jehovah, for we are taught that only God can forgive sins. In the New Testament we find that this power and authority belongs to the Lord Jesus Christ.

In Deuteronomy 18:18, 19 we find a most wonderful prophecy given through Moses. "I will raise them up a prophet from among their brethren, like unto thee; and I will put my words in his mouth, and he shall speak unto them all that I shall command him. And it shall come to pass, that whosoever will not hearken unto my words which he shall speak in my name, I will require it of him." Concerning this prophecy ex-Rabbi Leopold Cohn says:

"Every Jewish scholar will admit that there has not been any other prophet like unto Moses outside of the Lord Jesus, who was even greater than Moses. That this promised future prophet is identical with the Angel of Exodus 23:21 is proven by God's command to obey Him. In addition to all these previous names and characteristics God calls Him here prophet and tells us that He will be born of a woman and be like one of our brethren. (And) notice, please, the particular punishment for disobeying this wonderful Person. 'I will require it of him.' That means that in case of Israel's disobedience to the Messiah, God is going to punish continually until they will repent and obey" (Pamphlet, *The Trinity in the Old Testament,* p. 8).

In Joshua 5:13—6:3 another strange appearance is recorded. "And it came to pass, when Joshua was by Jericho, that he lifted up his eyes and looked, and behold, there stood a man over against him with his sword drawn in his hand: and Joshua went unto him, and said unto him, Art thou for us, or for our adversaries? But he said, Nay; but as prince of the host of Jehovah am I now come. And Joshua fell on his face to the earth, and did worship, and said unto him, What saith my lord unto his servant? And the prince of Jehovah's host said unto Joshua, Put off thy shoe from off thy foot; for the place whereon thou standest is holy. . . . And Jehovah said unto Joshua, See, I have given into thy hand Jericho, and the king thereof, and the mighty men of valour. . . ." This "man," this "prince of Jehovah's host," whom Joshua discovered to be Jehovah Himself, is quite plainly the promised Angel who was to go before the children of Israel and lead them into the land.

In the light of the New Testament this Angel of Jehovah who appeared in Old Testament times, who spoke as Jehovah, exercised His power, received worship and had the authority to forgive sins, can be none other than the Lord Jesus Christ, who comes from the Father (John 16:28), speaks for Him (John 3:34; 14:24), exercises His power (Matt. 28:18), forgives sin (Matt. 9:2), and receives worship (Matt. 14:33; John 9:38). God the Father has not been seen by any man (John 1:18), neither could He be sent by any other; but God the Son has been seen (I John 1:1,2), and has been sent (John

5:36). Apart from Christ the puzzling question would be, Who can this mysterious personality be?

Indirect allusions to a complexity of persons within the Godhead are found in numerous other places. Examples are: "Jehovah saith unto my Lord, Sit thou at my right hand, Until I make thine enemies thy footstool" (Ps. 110:1), a passage which in the New Testament Christ applies to Himself (Mark 12:35-37). "Jehovah said unto me, Thou art my son; This day have I begotten thee" (Ps. 2:7), which Paul tells us was fulfilled in Christ (Acts 13:33). "Thy throne, O God, is for ever and ever" (Ps. 45:6); and the writer of the book of Hebrews tells us that this relates to Christ and His kingdom (1:8).

The fact of the matter is that the Old Testament predictions of the coming Messiah,—such as that He should be born of a virgin (Isa. 7:14), born in Bethlehem of Judea (Mic. 5:2), the son of David and heir to his throne (II Sam. 7:12-16; Isa. 9:7), that the government should be upon His shoulder, and His name should be called Wonderful, Counsellor, the Mighty God, the Everlasting Father, the Prince of Peace (Isa. 9:6), that He should work miracles in opening the eyes of the blind, unstopping the ears of the deaf, healing the lame, and causing the dumb to speak (Isa. 35:5, 6), that He should be a man of sorrows, acquainted with grief, having no special beauty, that He should be a suffering Messiah, wounded for our transgressions and bruised for our iniquities, our substitute as a sacrifice to God (Isa. 53:1-12), that He should suddenly come to His temple (Mal. 3:1), that in His official entry into Jerusalem He should come in meekness, riding upon an ass (Zech. 9:9), etc.,—taken in connection with the descriptions of the One known as the Angel of Jehovah, were designed to make it possible for the people to recognize the Lord Jesus Christ at once by comparing these descriptions with His works, and, accepting Him, to receive forgiveness for sins.

THE HOLY SPIRIT IN THE OLD TESTAMENT

Ordinarily the Old Testament references to the Spirit were so indistinct that they were understood to refer only to an energy or influence which proceeded from God. Nowhere is the Spirit specifically called a person; yet when He is spoken of it is in terms that may properly be applied to a person. As read in the light of the New Testament, however, there are a number of places in which He is seen to be a distinct Person. Examples are: "Who hath directed the Spirit of Jehovah, or being his counsellor hath taught him?" (Isa. 40:13); "Thou gavest also thy good Spirit to instruct them" (Neh. 9:20); "My Spirit shall not strive with man for ever" (Gen. 6:3); "Take not thy

holy Spirit from me" (Ps. 51 :11) ;"Whither shall I go from thy Spirit?"
(Ps. 139 :7) ; and in Isaiah 63 :7-11 we may say that the Trinity actually
comes into view, for here we have a reference to "Jehovah" who is
the God of Israel and who bestows great blessings upon His people,
to the "angel of his presence" who "was their Saviour," and to the
"holy Spirit" who was in their midst and who was "grieved" at their
rebellion. Three times He is called the "holy Spirit" (Ps. 51 :11 ; Isa.
63 :10, 11). Some theologians have understood the threefold ascription of praise in the seraphim's song, "Holy, holy, holy, is Jehovah
of hosts; the whole earth is full of his glory" (Isa. 6 :3), with its
close parallel in the angelic chorus of Revelation 4 :8, "Holy, holy, holy,
is the Lord God, the Almighty, who was and who is and who is to
come," as having reference to the Trinity. Certainly the divinely given
formula which the priests were to use in blessing the people, "Jehovah
bless thee, and keep thee : Jehovah make his face to shine upon thee,
and be gracious unto thee : Jehovah lift up his countenance upon thee,
and give thee peace" (Num. 6 :24-26), finds its counterpart with explicit reference to the Trinity in the Apostolic Benediction of the New
Testament Church : "The grace of the Lord Jesus Christ, and the
love of God, and the communion of the Holy Spirit, be with you all"
(II Cor. 13 :14).

Yet it is beyond question that, apart from the New Testament
revelation, these intimations of the distinct personalities of the Son
and of the Spirit were obscure,—and purposely so, we may say, since
the people were not then ready to grasp the meaning of such a revelation. No scholars using the Old Testament alone have ever arrived
at a trinitarian conception of God. In fact Jews unite with Mohammedans in accusing Trinitarians of polytheism. At New Testament times
those who had been trained under the law, the Pharisees, for instance,
appear to have thought of the Spirit of God and the power of God
as equivalent terms.

But while not fully revealed and not recognized until Pentecost,
the Holy Spirit as the executive of the Trinity was from the beginning the sustainer and moulder of the laws of nature, the One who
inspired the prophets and who could be sinned against and grieved.
In the second verse of the very first chapter in Genesis we read that
"The Spirit of God moved upon the face of the waters,"—the marginal reading says, "was brooding upon."

"Amid the darkness that surrounded the primeval chaos," says
Dr. J. Ritchie Smith, "the Spirit of God is discovered, brooding upon
the face of the waters, like a bird upon its nest" (*The Holy Spirit in
the Gospels,* p. 34).

Just as electricity was present in nature and played a vitally important part in the lives of men long before they discovered it and learned to make it serve so many wonderful purposes, so the Holy Spirit was living and active as a distinct Person in the Godhead from eternity and moulded the affairs of men without His distinct personality being known to them.

"Even in the first chapter of Genesis," says Dr. Charles Hodge, "the Spirit of God is represented as the source of all intelligence, order, and life in the created universe; and in the following books of the Old Testament He is represented as inspiring the prophets, giving wisdom, strength, and goodness to statesmen and warriors, and to the people of God. This Spirit is not an agency, but an agent, who teaches and selects; who can be sinned against and grieved; and who, in the New Testament, is unmistakably revealed as a distinct person. When John the Baptist appeared, we find him speaking of the Holy Spirit as of a person with whom his countrymen were familiar, as an object of divine worship and the giver of saving blessings. Our Divine Lord also takes this truth for granted, and promises to send the Spirit, as a Paraclete, to take His place; to instruct, comfort, and strengthen them, whom they were to receive and obey. Thus, without any violent transition, the earliest revelations of this mystery were gradually unfolded, until the Triune God, Father, Son, and Spirit, appear in the New Testament as the universally recognized God of all believers" (*Systematic Theology*, I, p. 447).

JEWISH MISUNDERSTANDING OF THE DOCTRINE

The Christian doctrine of the Trinity has been generally misunderstood among the Jewish people, with the result that they believe we worship three Gods. To set forth this idea and the reason for its strong hold on the Jewish people to-day we propose to quote rather extensively from the writings of one who is in a position to understand the problem,—from the writings of Ex-Rabbi Leopold Cohn. Says he:

"The reason that the Jews have become estranged from the doctrine of the Triune God is found in the teachings of Moses Maimonides. He compiled thirteen articles of faith which the Jews accepted and incorporated into their liturgy. One of them is 'I believe with a perfect faith that the Creator, blessed be His name, is an *absolute one*' (Hebrew, 'Yachid'). This has been repeated daily by Jews in their prayers, ever since the twelfth century, when Moses Maimonides lived. This expression of an *'absolute one'* is diametrically opposed to the word of God which teaches with great emphasis that God is not a

'Yachid,' which means an only one, or an *absolute one,* but 'achid,' which means a *united* one. In Deuteronomy 6:4 God laid down for His people a principle of faith, which is certainly superior to that of Moses Maimonides, inasmuch as it comes from God Himself. We read, 'Hear O Israel, the Lord our God, the Lord is ONE,' stressing the sense of the phrase 'one' by using not 'yachid,' which Moses Maimonides does, but 'achid,' which means a *united* one.

"We want now to trace where these two words, 'yachid' and 'achid,' occur in the Old Testament and in what connection and sense they are used, and thus ascertain their true meaning.

"In Genesis I we read, 'And there was evening and there was morning, *one* day.' Here the word 'achid' is used, which implies that the evening and the morning—two separate objects—are called *one,* thus showing plainly that the word 'achid' does not mean an *'absolute* one,' but a *united* one. Then in Genesis 2:24 we read, 'Therefore shall a man leave his father and his mother and shall cleave unto his wife, and they shall be *one* flesh.' Here too the word 'achid' is used, furnishing another proof that it means a *united* one, referring, as it does in this case, to two separate persons.

"Now let us see in the Word of God where that expression 'yachid,' an *'absolute* one,' is found. In Genesis 22:2 God says to Abraham, 'Take now thy son, thine *only* son.' Here we read the word 'yachid.' The same identical word, 'yachid,' is repeated in the 12th verse of the same chapter. In Psalm 25:16 it is again applied to a single person as also in Jeremiah 6:26, where we read, 'Make thee mourning as for an *only* son.' The same word, conveying the sense of one only, occurs in Zechariah 12:10, 'And they shall look upon me whom they have pierced, and they shall mourn for Him as one mourneth for his *only* son.'

"Thus we see that Moses Maimonides, with all his great wisdom and much learning, made a serious mistake in prescribing for the Jews that confession of faith in which it is stated that God is a 'yachid,' a statement which is absolutely opposed to the Word of God. And the Jews, in blindly following the so-called 'second Moses' have once more given evidence of their old proclivities of perverting the Word of the living God. The Holy Spirit made that serious complaint against them through Jeremiah the prophet, saying, 'For ye have perverted the words of the living God, of the Lord of hosts our God' (Jer. 23:36).

"This is therefore the belief of the true Christian. He does not have three gods, but 'one,' a Scriptural one, which is in Hebrew 'achid,' and which consists of three personal revelations of God as we shall see in the following Scriptures.

"In the very first verse of the Bible we find two manifestations of the Godhead. 'In the beginning *God* created . . . and the *Spirit of God* moved.' Here we see plainly that God taught us to believe that He is the creator of all things and that His Spirit is moving upon this world of ours to *lead, guide* and *instruct* us in the way He wants us to walk. So here in the first chapter of the Bible are *two* manifestations of God.

"It will interest the reader to know that the most sacred Jewish book, the Zohar, comments on Deuteronomy 6:4—'Hear O Israel, Jehovah our God, Jehovah is one,' saying, 'Why is there need of mentioning the name of God three times in this verse?' Then follows the answer. 'The first Jehovah is the Father above. The second is the stem of Jesse, the Messiah who is to come from the family of Jesse through David. And the third is the way which is below (meaning the Holy Spirit who shows us the way) and these three are one.' According to the Zohar the Messiah is not only called Jehovah but is a very part of the Triune Jehovah." (*The Trinity in the Old Testament,* pp. 3, 4).

5. One Substance, Three Persons

Much of the opposition to the doctrine of the Trinity has arisen because of a misunderstanding of what it really is. We do not assert that one God is three Gods, nor that one person is three persons, nor that three Gods are one God. God is not three in the same sense in which He is one. To assert that He is would, indeed, make the doctrine what the Unitarians are ever fond of declaring it to be, mathematical absurdity. We assert rather that within the one Divine "substance" or "essence" there are three mutually related yet distinct centers of knowledge, consciousness, love and will. "Substance" or "essence" is that which the different members of the Godhead have in common, that in which the attributes and powers of Deity inhere; "person" is that in which they differ.

Yet while there are three centers of knowledge, consciousness, love and will, each of the Persons possesses *in toto* the one indivisible, incorporeal substance of Deity in which the attributes and powers inhere, and therefore possesses the same infinite knowledge, wisdom, power, holiness, justice, goodness and truth. They work together or co-operate with such perfect harmony and unity that we are justified in saying that the Triune God works with one mind and one will. What the one knows, the others know; what the one desires, the others desire; and what the one wills, the others will. Independence and self-existence are not attributes of the individual persons, but of the Triune God;

hence there are not three independent wills, but three dependent wills, if we may so speak, each of which is exercised for the honour and glory and happiness of the other two.

We can illustrate the nature of the Trinity partially as follows: a bank or railroad, for instance, is owned and operated not by an individual but by many officials, stock-holders, and workers, who have a community of interests; yet we have no hesitation in speaking of the corporation in the singular and saying that the First National Bank desires to make this investment, or that the Pennsylvania Railroad is opposed to the passage of a certain piece of legislation by Congress. The decisions reached by the board of directors express the desires and purposes of the corporation as a whole. Similarly, although we believe there are three distinct Persons in the Godhead, we speak of God in the singular and apply to Him the pronouns He, Him and His.

In thinking of this mystery we are to remember that the processes of our own thinking, feeling and willing in our purely human personalities remain a complete mystery to us. It is also to be pointed out that since the incarnation Christ has also thought and felt and willed in a human manner, although the union of the Divine and the human psychological activity within the Divine-human Person, like the unity of the Persons within the Godhead, is uncomprehensible to us.

The error of the Unitarians is that while they construct a doctrine of the Divine unity they do so at the expense of the Divine personality. They look upon the Father, Son and Holy Spirit as but three successive aspects or modes in which God reveals Himself, comparable to that of a man who is known in his own family as father, in the business world as a banker, and in the Church as an elder. Such a view gives us only a modal Trinity. Any statement of the doctrine which fails to set forth both the unity and the tri-personality of the Godhead falls short of the Scripture teaching.

Since the three Persons of the Trinity possess the same identical, numerical substance or essence, and since the attributes are inherent in and inseparable from the substance or essence, it follows that all of the Divine attributes must be possessed alike by each of the three Persons and that the three Persons must be consubstantial, co-equal and co-eternal. Each is truly God, exercising the same power, partaking equally of the Divine glory, and entitled to the same worship. When the word "Father" is used in our prayers, as for example in the Lord's prayer, it does not refer exclusively to the first person of the Trinity, but to the three Persons as one God. The Triune God is our Father.

The doctrine of the Trinity cannot lead to Tritheism; for while there are three Persons in the Godhead, there is but one substance or essence, and therefore but one God. It is rather a case of the one life substance, Deity, existing consciously as three Persons. The three Persons are related to the divine substance not as three individuals to their species, as Abraham, Isaac and Jacob to human nature; they are only one God,—not a triad, but a Trinity. In the inmost depths of their being they are inherently and inescapably one.

That each of the Persons of the Trinity does possess *in toto* the numerically same substance is proved by such Scripture verses as the following: "For in him dwelleth all the fulness of the Godhead bodily" (Col. 2:9). "I and the Father are one" (John 10:30). "Believe me that I am in the Father, and the Father in me" (John 14:11). "God was in Christ reconciling the world unto Himself" (II Cor. 5:19).

It need not surprise us that in the Godhead we find a form of personality entirely unique and different from that found in man. In the ascending scale of life as we know it in this world there are numerous modes of existence as we pass from the simpler to the more complex forms. In the plants we find what is truly called life, although it is so elementary that it does not even come to consciousness. In the insects we find sensitiveness and instinct, two particulars in which they far surpass the plant life. In the birds and animals we find affection between parent and offspring, which in some cases is very strong, together with a much higher type of instinct than is found among the insects. Man in his turn makes a tremendous advance over the animals in that he possesses reasoning power, a deep moral consciousness, and an immortal soul. These higher stages in man's nature are of course absolutely incomprehensible to the animals, birds and insects, which can, at best, have only a very vague understanding of his nature, although they fear him and recognize him as their master. Consequently we need not be surprised that the nature of God surpasses our comprehension,—that the one divine substance is conscious in three Persons, in Father, Son and Holy Spirit,—and that no attempt is made to explain that mystery to us, probably for the very reason that our little minds are utterly incapable of grasping such truth. Doubtless we are as incapable of understanding God's nature as the animals and birds are of understanding ours.

Hence it is admitted that our knowledge of the relationships which subsist between the three Persons of the Trinity extends only to the surface. There must be infinite depths in the conscious being of God to which human thought can never penetrate. We are told clearly, however, that God has existed from eternity as three self-conscious persons. Certainly we are not prepared to say that this tri-personality which has been revealed to us exhausts the mystery of the Godhead. As Dr. A. A. Hodge has well said:

"For aught we can know, in the depths of the Infinite Being there may be a common consciousness which includes the whole Godhead, and a common personality. This may all be true; but what belongs to us to deal with is the sure and obvious fact of revelation, that God exists from eternity as three self-conscious Persons, the Father, Son and Holy Spirit."

How shall we define the term "person"? As it is used in modern Psychology it means an intelligent, free, moral agent. But in setting forth the doctrine of the Trinity the Church has used the term in a sense different from that in which it is used anywhere else. The word "Person" as it is applied to the three subsistences within the Godhead, like the more important word "Trinity," is not found in Scripture itself; yet the idea which it expresses is Scriptural, and we do not know any other word that expresses so well the idea we have in mind. In the science of Theology, as in all other sciences, some technical terms are an absolute necessity. When we say there are three distinct persons in the Godhead we do not mean that each one is as separate from the others as one human being is from every other. While they are said to love, to hear, to pray to, to send, and to testify of each other, they are, nevertheless, not independent of each other; for as we have already said, self-existence and independence are properties, not of the individual persons, but of the Triune God. The singular pronouns I, Thou, He and Him are applied to each of the three Persons; yet these same singular pronoun's are applied to the Triune God who is composed of these three Persons. Hence too much stress must not be laid on the mere term. The Father, Son and Holy Spirit can be distinguished, but they cannot be separated; for they each possess the same identical numerical substance or essence. They do not merely exist alongside of each other, as did Washington, Jefferson and Franklin, but they permeate and interpenetrate each other, are in and through each other.

Consequently, in theological language we would define a person as a mode of subsistence which is marked by intelligence, will, and individual existence. The Church fathers realized, of course, that they were dealing with a doctrine which was far above the comprehension of the human mind, and, in developing the creeds, they did not attempt to explain the mystery of the Trinity, but only to state it as well as they were able with the language at their disposal. We can hope to do no more.

A Plurality of Persons Within the Godhead is in Harmony with Reason

Instead of the doctrine of the Trinity being contrary to reason as charged by Unitarians, a little considered thought should convince us that a plurality of Persons within the Godhead is eminently agreeable to reason. That there should be specifically three Persons does not necessarily follow, but that God might be more than One seems very probable. We shrink from the thought of an eternally lonely God, and take refuge in the Christian doctrine of the Trinity. This doctrine, we find, is of such a nature that, on the one hand, it avoids the hard monotheism of the Jews and Mohammedans, and on the other, the crass polytheism of the Greeks and Romans. Through the truth which it presents we are enabled to see that God has always been independent of the entire creation, that within His own nature there is to be found that absolute perfection and self-sufficiency which we instinctively ascribe to Him. Unless there is to be found that plurality of Persons within His own nature, time as well as eternity would seem to be unbearably monotonous to Him. For where among the creatures are there to be found personalities capable of responding fully to His own personality? Men and angels, while created in His image, are infinitely below Him; even the nations, Isaiah tells us, are as a drop in the bucket, and as the small dust of the balance (40:15). Only within the fellowship of the Father, Son and Holy Spirit is there to be found that full interplay of personality which the nature of God demands. And when once we have conceived of God as Trinity we can never again be satisfied with a modalistic or Unitarian conception of Him.

It has long been customary to say that the attribute of love in God proves a plurality of Persons within the Godhead,—that love is necessarily self-communicative, and that with a unitary God it could have existed only as a craving, unsatisfied, under the category of the possible rather than of the actual. This reasoning further asserts that since God is infinite His love must be infinite, and that it therefore demands an infinite object. It is usually further asserted that these two infinite Persons demand a third through whom their love is communicated and to whom it is also given. This line of reasoning, however, does not seem fully conclusive. It at least seems possible that God's own all-perfect Being could have supplied a satisfying object for His love. To say that love, in its very nature, is self-communicative, and that it therefore demands an object other than itself, seems to be merely a play on words. If we may imagine a lonely Robinson Crusoe, for instance, shipwrecked on an island for the remainder of his life, and imagine further that the storm which shipwrecked him also killed all the other persons with whom he was acquainted, would that, even as regards a limited human being, mean that the remainder of his life would be abnormal in the sense that he would be destitute of the attribute of love? Might there not be, even within his own limited nature, a kind of love based on good conscience and moral uprightness? The attribute of love need not disappear just because a person is alone. But while love in itself does not prove that there must be a plurality of Persons in the Godhead, yet what added richness, fulness and force is given to this love in either God or man when there is fellowship with others! Only thus is personality seen at its best. Hence while reason does not give us the doctrine of the Trinity in the first place, i.e., apart from revelation, it does render the negative service of showing that the doctrine is not inconsistent with other known truth, and also the positive service of showing that only on the basis of the Trinity do we have a fully adequate conception of God as self-conscious Spirit and living love.

There are, of course, elements of truth even in polytheism, distorted and perverted though they may be, and present-day men of letters, as well as philosophers in all ages and the pagan people in all nations, have found relief in speaking of "the gods."

"The most widely diffused of all religious systems," says Dr. J. Ritchie Smith, "polytheism is the perversion of a great truth, the truth of the variety and fulness of the divine nature. Lacking the conception of a God everywhere present and active, men were forced to assume a host of divinities, betweeen whom the attributes and energies of the Deity may be distributed, and who in virtue of their numbers may accomplish the works of creation and providence. . . . It is the distinctive mark of polytheism that it sacrifices the unity to the variety of the divine nature. Against this error the Old Testament everywhere contends. Not until it was extirpated from the minds of the chosen people, and the taint of idolatry purged away in the furnace of affliction, was the truth revealed in its fulness that polytheism strove so vainly to express. The Old Testament overthrows the error, the New Testament brings to light the truth, of polytheism. . . . The fulness and variety that men seek in many gods are found in one. The doctrine of the Trinity at once preserves the unity and discloses the fulness of the divine nature. God is one, is the message of the Old Testament; God is one in three Persons, is the message of the New; and the revelation is complete" (*The Holy Spirit in the Gospels,* p. 19).

6. Meaning of the Terms "Father", "Son", and "Spirit"

To our occidental type of mind the terms "Father" and "Son"
carry with them, on the one hand, the ideas of source of being and
superiority, and on the other, subordination and dependence. In theological language, however, they are used in the Semitic or Oriental
sense of *sameness of nature.* It is, of course, the Semitic consciousness
which underlies the phraseology of Scripture, and wherever the Scriptures call Christ the "Son" of God they assert His true and proper
Deity. The term "Son" is applied to Christ, not merely as an official
title in connection with the work of redemption, nor because of His
incarnation or supernatural birth, nor because of His resurrection,—
although in these regards He is preeminently the Son of God,—but
primarily to designate an inherent trinitarian relationship. In the economy of redemption, and for the accomplishment of a specific purpose, He
temporarily accepted a position subordinate to that of the Father. In its
deepest sense it is a unique sonship which cannot be predicated of,
nor shared with, any creature. Father and Son are co-eternal and
co-equal in power and glory, partaking of the same nature and substance, and have always existed as distinct Persons. The Father is,
and always has been, as much dependent on the Son as the Son is
on the Father, for, as we need to keep in mind, self-existence and
independence are properties not of the Persons within the Godhead,
but of the Triune God.

In Hebrews 1:5-8, for instance, the writer sets forth the superiority
of Christ as a Divine Person. Being Divine, or Deity, the express
image of the invisible God, He is called the "Son" of God, which
means precisely the same thing. He came into the world as the Son,
and had existed from eternity as such. Being the Son, the One
through whom the worlds were created and the heir of all things,
He is declared by the writer to be God and to reign upon an everlasting throne. During the public ministry the Jews, in accordance
with the Hebrew usage of the term, correctly understood Jesus' claim
to be the "Son" of God as equivalent to asserting that He was "equal
with God," or, simply "God" (John 5:18; 10:33); and it was for
claiming to be "the Christ, the Son of God," that He was accused of
blasphemy by the high priest and sentenced by the Sanhedrin to be
crucified (Matt. 26:63-66).

This idea has perhaps been more clearly expressed by Dr. Warfield
than by any other. Says he:

"What underlies the conception of sonship in Scriptural speech is
just 'likeness'; whatever the father is that the Son is also. The emphatic

application of the term 'Son' to one of the Trinitarian Persons, accordingly, asserts rather His equality with the Father than His subordination to the Father; and if there is any implication of derivation in it, it would appear to be very distant. The adjunction of the adjective 'only begotten' (John 1:14; 3:16-18; I John 4:9) need add only the idea of uniqueness, not of derivation (Ps. 22:20; 25;16; 35;17) ; and even such a phrase as 'God only begotten' (John 1:18) may contain no implication of derivation, but only of absolutely unique consubstantiality; as also such a phrase as 'the first-begotten of all creation' (Col. 1:15) may convey no intimation of coming into being, but merely assert priority of existence. In like manner, the designation 'Spirit of God' or 'Spirit of Jehovah,' which meets us frequently in the Old Testament, certainly does not convey the idea there either of derivation or of subordination, but is just the executive name of God— the designation of God from the point of view of His activity—and imports accordingly identity with God; and there is no reason to suppose that, in passing from the Old Testament to the New Testament, the term has taken on an essentially different meaning. It happens, oddly enough, moreover, that we have in the New Testament itself what amounts almost to formal definitions of the two terms 'Son' and 'Spirit,' and in both cases the stress is laid on the notion of equality or sameness. In John 5:18 we read: 'On this account, therefore, the Jews sought the more to kill him, because, not only did he break the Sabbath, but also called God his own Father, making himself equal with God.' The point lies, of course, in the adjective 'own.' Jesus was, rightly, understood to call God 'his own Father,' that is, to use the terms 'Father' and 'Son' not in a merely figurative sense, as when Israel was called God's son, but in the real sense. And this was understood to be claiming to be all that God is. To be the Son of God in any sense was to be like God in that sense; and to be God's *own* Son was to be exactly like God, to be 'equal with God.' Similarly, we read in I Corinthians 2:10, 11: 'For the Spirit searcheth all things, yea, the deep things of God. For who of men knoweth the things of a man, save the spirit of man which is in him? Even so the things of God none knoweth, save the Spirit of God.' Here the Spirit appears as the substrate of the Divine self-consciousness, the principle of God's knowledge of Himself: He is, in a word, just God Himself in the innermost essence of His Being. As the spirit of man is the seat of human life, the very life of man itself, so the Spirit of God is His very life-element. How can He be supposed, then, to be subordinate to God, or to derive His being from God?" (*Biblical Doctrines*, p. 163).

Thus we find that the divine and original idea of fatherhood and sonship in *sameness of nature*. In the Godhead this is, of course, a purely spiritual relationship, and is in accordance with the transcendence of Deity. In the finite human sphere, where man is but a faint and imperfect pattern of God, the ideas of fatherhood and sonship, besides implying sameness of nature, imply also the ideas of origination and subordination, as well as a material nature which is mediated by sex. In the divine sphere sonship is absolute, while in the human it is relative, very much as the attributes of wisdom, power, holiness, justice and love are absolute in God but relative in man. Hence while the limitations of human language are such that we are not able to express these ideas fully, the relationship which subsists between the first and second Persons of the Trinity finds its closest analogy in the relationship which an earthly father bears to his son.

And in like manner the third Person of the Trinity, partaking of the same life substance and equal with the Father and the Son in power and glory, is called the Spirit. As the everywhere-present executive of the Trinity, immaterial and invisible, He is Spirit in the truest sense of the word. He is called the "Holy" Spirit because He is absolutely holy in His own nature, and is the source and cause of holiness in the creatures.

We have seen that the terms "Father" and "Son" are not at all adequate to express the full relationship which exists between the first and second Persons of the Godhead. They are, however, the best that we have. They are the terms used in Scripture, and besides expressing the idea of sameness of nature, they are found to be reciprocal, expressing the ideas of love, affection, trust, honour, unity and harmony, — ideas of endearment and preciousness. When we are told that God "gave" His Son for the redemption of the world we are led to understand that the situation was in some ways analogous to that of a human father who gives his son for missionary service or for the defense of his country. It is something which involves sacrifice on the part of the father as well as privation and suffering on the part of the son. And, similarly, when the term "Spirit" is applied to the third Person of the Trinity it is not implied that His nature is in any way different from theirs, for they each partake of the numerically same substance, and are all equally spirit. He is so called, however, because He is the very life element of Deity, and because so far as our relation to God is concerned God comes to us in a spiritual way pre-eminently through this Person, His Spirit communes with our spirits, speaks to our consciences, cleanses our hearts, and leads us in right paths.

That the terms "Father" and "Son" are used in a peculiar sense as applied to the first and second Persons of the Trinity might easily be inferred from their varied usage in other parts of Scripture and in everyday speech. We read, for instance, that Jabal was the father of such as dwell in tents and have cattle, and that Jubal was the father of all such as handle the harp and the pipe (Gen. 4:20, 21). Abraham was given the promise that he should be the father of a multitude of nations (Gen. 17:4) ; and today every Jew regards himself as a son of Abraham. Jehovah said of the nation, "Israel is my son, my first-born" (Exod. 4:22). Of a king whose position before God is one of special honour and authority, as was that of Solomon, the Lord could say, "I will be his father, and he shall be my son" (II Sam. 7:14). Judas was a "son of perdition" (John 17:12). We are familiar with the early Church "fathers," and we speak of one who has shown us the way of righteousness as our father in the faith. George Washington is said to have been the father of his country. The Germans speak of the fatherland, and the English of the mother country. We say that Mr. So-and-so is a loyal son of Calvin, or Luther or Wesley, and we have groups of people who call themselves Daughters of the American Revolution, or Sons of the American Legion. Hence it is quite clear that in religious as well as in secular affairs the terms father and son are used in a variety of senses.

And beyond this, although in perfect harmony with it, we find that much Scripture teaching is given in figurative language. Christ is called the Lamb of God (John 1:29; Rev. 7:14) ; the good shepherd (John 10:11) ; the door (John 10:7). He is the true vine, and His disciples are the branches (John 15:1-5) ; He is the true light (John 1:9) ; His disciples are the light of the world (Matt. 5:14), and the salt of the earth (Matt. 5:13). Similarly, God is declared to be love (I John 4:8) ; light (I John 1:5) ; a consuming fire (Heb. 12:29). The psalmist declares that Jehovah is his rock, his fortress, his shield and high tower (18:2), and that the righteous take refuge under His wings (91:4). When we are told that God is angry, or that He repents, or forgets, or laughs, the writer is, of course, using figurative language. Such expressions are known as anthropomorphisms, instances in which the divine action as seen from the human viewpoint is likened to that of a man who is actuated by these states of mind. These are instances in which God adjusts Himself to human language, "talking down" to us, in much the same way that human parents find it necessary to talk down to their children. We know that as a matter of fact God is altogether free from the passions and failings of human nature.

Hence in accordance with this general method of procedure it was only most fitting that the terms "Father," "Son" and "Spirit" should have been chosen to express the relationship which the first and second Persons of the Trinity bear to each other, which the third bears to the first and second, and which the first bears to us. Our language contains no terms better fitted to convey the desired meaning.

Similarly, the term "person," as we have indicated before, is but an imperfect and inadequate expression of a truth that transcends our experience and comprehension. When applied to the different members of the Godhead it only approximates the truth. It is, if you please, a make-shift, and is employed in Scripture in this sense. Yet it expresses more clearly than any other word we know the conception which the Scriptures give of the Father, Son and Holy Spirit. It is used to express an idea of personality within the Godhead which lies, we may say, approximately half-way between that of a mere form of manifestation, or personification, which would lead to Unitarianism, and the idea of fully separate, independent personalities such as is found in human beings, which would lead to Tritheism. It expresses a distinction not identical with, but in some respects analogous to, that subsisting between three different men. If there were three Gods, they would, of course, limit each other and deprive each other of Deity, since it would be impossible for each to be infinite. There is room for many finite beings, but room for only one infinite Being. The merit of the statement of this doctrine in the Athanasian Creed was that it preserved the distinct personalities and also the unity of the Godhead: "The Father is God, the Son is God, the Holy Ghost is God; and yet there are not three Gods but one God. So likewise the Father is Lord, the Son is Lord, the Holy Ghost is Lord; yet there are not three Lords but one Lord. For as we are compelled by Christian truth to acknowledge each person by Himself to be God and Lord, so we are forbidden by the same truth to say that there are three Gods or three Lords." Hence in view of the defects of human language, the very limited revelation which God has seen fit to give us concerning this subject, and the fact that the nature of this distinction must be incomprehensible to us, we are ready not only to admit, but to point out precisely, the imperfection of the language which we are obliged to employ in setting forth this doctrine.

7. Subordination of the Son and Spirit to the Father

In discussing the doctrine of the Trinity we must distinguish between what is technically known as the "immanent" and the "economic" Trinity. By the "immanent" Trinity we mean the Trinity as it has subsisted in the Godhead from all eternity. In their essential, innate life we say that the Father, Son and Holy Spirit are the same in substance, possessing identical attributes and powers, and therefore equal in glory. This relates to God's essential existence apart from the creation. By the "economic" Trinity we mean the Trinity as manifested in the world, particularly in the redemption of sinful men. There are three *opera ad extra,* additional works, if we may so describe them, which are ascribed to the Trinity, namely, Creation, Redemption and Sanctification. These are works which are outside of the necessary activities of the Trinity, works which God was under no obligation or compulsion to perform.

In the Scriptures we find that the plan of redemption takes the form of a covenant, not merely between God and His people but between the different Persons within the Trinity, so that there is, as it were, a division of labour, each Person voluntarily assuming a particular part of the work. 1st,—To the Father is ascribed primarily the work of Creation, together with the election of a certain number of individuals whom He has given to the Son. The Father is in general the Author of the plan of redemption. 2nd,—To the Son is ascribed the work of redemption, to accomplish which He became incarnate, assuming human nature in order that, as the federal head and representative of His people, He might, as their substitute, assume the guilt of their sin and suffer a full equivalent for the penalty of eternal death which rested upon them. He thus made full satisfaction to the demands of justice, which demands are expressed in the words, "The soul that sinneth, it shall die," and, "The wages of sin is death." Also, in His capacity as the federal head and representative of His people, He covenanted to keep the law of perfect obedience which was originally given to their forefather Adam in his representative capacity, which law Adam had broken and had thereby plunged the race into a state of guilt and ruin. Identifying Himself thus with His people, He paid the penalty which rested on them and earned their salvation. Acting as their King and Saviour, and also as Head of the Church which He thus forms, He directs the advancing kingdom and is ever present with His people. 3rd,—To the Holy Spirit is ascribed the works of Regeneration and Sanctification, or the application to the hearts of individuals of the objective atonement which has been wrought out by Christ. This He does by spiritually renewing their hearts, working in them faith and repentance, cleansing them of every taint of sin, and eventually glorifying them in heaven. Redemption, in the broad sense, is thus a matter of *pure grace,* being planned by the Father, purchased by the Son, and applied by the Holy Spirit.

If we may be so bold as to draw an analogy with our federal government where, when it functions normally, we have three equal and co-ordinated branches, we may say that the Father, in planning and creating the world, in ordaining its laws, and in giving to the Son a people to be redeemed by Him, corresponds to the Legislative branch; the Holy Spirit, through His regenerating and cleansing power and through His control of the minds of men and of the forces of nature, corresponds to the Executive branch; and the Son, giving Himself in the satisfaction of divine justice, and then acting as Judge of the entire world, corresponds to the Judicial branch.

Yet while particular works are ascribed pre-eminently to each of the Persons, so intimate is the unity which exists within the Trinity, there being but one substance and "one God," that each of the Persons participates to some extent in the work of the others. "I am in the Father, and the Father in me," said Jesus (John 14:11). "He that hath seen me hath seen the Father" (John 14:9). "God was in Christ reconciling the world to himself" (II Cor. 5:19). "I will not leave you desolate: I come unto you" (through the Holy Spirit) (John 14:18). As Dr. Charles Hodge says:

"According to the Scriptures, the Father created the world, the Son created the world, and the Spirit created the world. The Father preserves all things: the Son upholds all things; and the Spirit is the source of all life. These facts are expressed by saying that the persons of the Trinity concur in all acts *ad extra*. Nevertheless there are some acts which are predominantly referred to the Father, others to the Son, and others to the Spirit. The Father creates, elects, and calls; the Son redeems; and the Spirit sanctifies." (*Systematic Theology,* I, p. 445).

Hence we say that while the spheres and functions of the three persons of the Trinity are different, they are not exclusive. That which is done by one is participated in by the others with varying degrees of prominence. The fact of the matter is that there have been three great epochs or dispensations is the history of redemption, corresponding to and successively manifesting the three Persons of the Godhead. That of the Father began at the creation and continued until the beginning of the public ministry of Jesus; that of the Son, embracing a comparatively short period of time, but the important period in which redemption was worked out objectively, began with the public ministry of Jesus and continued until the day of Pentecost; and that of the Holy Spirit began with the descent of the Holy Spirit on the disciples on the day of Pentecost and continues until the end of the age.

In regard to the work of the economic Trinity we find there is a definite procedure in the work of redemption and also in the government of the world in general, the work of the Father in creation and in the general plan for the world being primary, that of the Son in redeeming the world being subordinate to and dependent on that of the Father, and that of the Holy Spirit in applying redemption coming later in time and being subordinate to and dependent on that of the Father and of the Son. Hence in regard to the work of redemption particularly, which is the great and all-important work that God does for man in this world, there is a logical order, that of the Father being first, that of the Son second, and that of the Spirit third. And when the Persons of the Trinity are mentioned in our theological statements it is always in this order.

The Father sends the Son and works through Him (John 17:8; Rom. 8:3; I Thess. 5:9; Rom. 5:1), and the Father and Son work through the Holy Spirit (Rom. 5:5; Gal. 5:22, 23; Titus 3:5; Acts 15:8, 9). In Christ's own words He that is sent is not greater than he that hath sent him (John 13:16); and in His state of humiliation, speaking from the standpoint of His human nature, He could say, "The Father is greater than I" (John 14:28). Paul tells us that we are Christ's, and that Christ is God's (I Cor. 3:23); also, that as Christ is the head of every man, so God is the head of Christ (I Cor. 11:3). Numerous things are predicated of the incarnate Son which cannot be predicated of the second Person of the Trinity as such,— Jesus, in His human nature, advanced in wisdom (Luke 2:52), and even late in His public ministry did not know when the end of the world was to come (Matt. 24:36). In the work of redemption, which we may term a work of supererogation since it is undertaken through pure grace and love and not through obligation, the Son who is equal with the Father becomes as it were officially subject to Him. And in turn the Spirit is sent by, acts for, and reveals both the Father and the Son, glorifies not Himself but Christ, and works in the hearts of His people faith, love, holiness and spiritual enlightenment. This subordination of the Son to the Father, and of the Spirit to the Father and the Son, relates not to their essential life within the Godhead, but only to their modes of operation or their division of labour in creation and redemption.

This subordination of the Son to the Father, and of the Spirit to the Father and the Son, is not in any way inconsistent with true equality. We have an analogy of such priority and subordination, for instance, in the relationship which exists between husband and wife in the human family. Paul tells us that that relationship is one of equality in Christ Jesus, in whom "there can be no male and female" (Gal. 3:28),—woman's soul being of as much value as man's,—yet one of personal priority and subordination in which in the home and the State the husband is the acknowledged spokesman and leader. As Dr. W. Brenton Greene says:

"In the sight of God husband and wife are, and in the eye of the law ought to be, halves of one whole and neither better than the other. But while this is so and cannot be emphasized too strongly, the relationship of husband and wife, nevertheless, is such that the position of the wife is distinct from and dependent on that of the husband. This does not imply that the wife as a person is of inferior worth to her husband: in this respect there is neither male nor female; for they are both 'one in Christ Jesus.' Neither does it mean that the mission of the wife is of less importance than that of the husband. There are certain functions, moral and intellectual as well as physical, which she fulfills far better than her husband; and there are certain other functions of supreme necessity which only she can fulfill at all. What is meant, however, is that as there are some things of primary importance that only the wife can do; so there are other indispensable functions that only the husband ought to discharge, and chief among these is the direction of their *common* life. He, therefore, should be the 'head' of the 'one body' that husband and wife together form. Whether we can understand it or not, such a relationship is not inconsistent with perfect equality. It is not in the case of the Trinity. Father, Son and Spirit are equal in power and glory. Yet the Son is second to the Father, and the Spirit is second to both the Father and the Son, as to their 'mode of subsistence and operation.' Whatever, therefore, the secondary position of the wife as regards her husband may imply, it need not imply even the least inferiority" (Notes on *Christian Sociology*).

In the political realm we may say that the president of the United States is officially first, the governor of a state officially second, and the private citizen officially third. Yet they are each equally possessed of human nature, and in fact the private citizen may be a better man morally and spiritually than either the governor or the president. Also, two men of equal rank in private life may join the army, one to become a captain, the other to become a private soldier in the ranks of this captain. Officially, and for a limited time, one becomes subordinate to the other, yet during that time they may be equals in the sight of God. In the work of redemption the situation is somewhat analogous to this,—through a covenant voluntarily entered into, the Father, Son and Holy Spirit each undertake a specific work in such a manner that, during the time this work is in progress, the Father becomes officially first, the Son officially second, and the Spirit officially third. Yet within the essential and inherent life of the Trinity the full equality of the persons is preserved.

8. The Generation of the Son and the Procession of the Holy Spirit

The kindred doctrines of the Eternal Generation of the Son and of the Eternal Procession of the Holy Spirit are admittedly doctrines which are but very obscurely understood by the best of theologians. Certainly the present writer, with his limited study and experience, is not under the delusion that he shall be able to give a fully satisfactory explanation of them. He proposes only to define the doctrines and to offer a few brief comments.

The Eternal Generation of the Son, as stated by a representative theologian, is defined as: "an eternal personal act of the Father, wherein, by necessity of nature, not by choice of will, He generates the person (not the essence) of the Son, by communicating to Him the whole indivisible substance of the Godhead, without division, alienation, or change, so that the Son is the express image of His Father's person, and eternally continues, not from the Father, but in the Father, and the Father in the Son" (Dr. A. A. Hodge, *Outlines of Theology,* p. 182).

The following Scripture verses are commonly given as the principal support of this doctrine: "For as the Father hath life in Himself, even so gave He to the Son also to have life in Himself" (John 5:26); "Believe me that I am in the Father, and the Father in me" (John 14:11); "Even as thou, Father, art in me, and I in thee" (John 17:21); "That ye may know and understand that the Father is in me, and I in the Father" (John 10:38); Christ is declared to be "the effulgence of his glory, and the very image of his substance" (Heb. 1:3); "For God so loved the world, that He gave his only begotten Son, that whosoever believeth on Him should not perish, but have eternal life" (John 3:16).

The present writer feels constrained to say, however, that in his opinion the verses quoted do not teach the doctrine in question. He feels that the primary purpose of these and similar verses is to teach that Christ is intimately associated with the Father, that He is equal with the Father in power and glory, that He is, in fact, full Deity, rather than to teach that His Person is generated by or originates in an eternal process which is going on within the Godhead. Even though the attempt is made to safeguard the essential equality of the Son by saying that the process by which the Son is generated is eternal and necessary, he does not feel that the attempt is successful. If, as even

Augustine, for instance, asserts, the Father is the *Fons Trinitatis*—
the fountain or source of the Trinity—from whom both the Son and
the Spirit are derived, it seems that in spite of all else we may say
we have made the Son and the Spirit dependent upon another as their
principal cause, and have destroyed the true and essential equality
between the Persons of the Trinity. As we have stated before, when
the Scriptures tell us that one Person within the Trinity is known as the
"Father," and another as the "Son," they intend to teach, not that
the Son is originated by the Father, nor that the Father existed prior
to the Son, but that they are the same in nature.

This, apparently, was also the position held by Calvin, for at the
conclusion of his chapter on the Trinity he says:

"But, studying the edification of the Church, I have thought it
better not to touch upon many things, which would be unnecessarily
burdensome to the reader, without yielding him any profit. For to
what purpose is it to dispute, whether the Father is always begetting?
For it is foolish to imagine a continual act of generation, since it is
evident that three Persons have subsisted in God from all eternity"
(*Institutes,* Book I, Chap. 13).

PROCESSION OF THE HOLY SPIRIT

The Procession of the Holy Spirit has commonly been understood
to designate "the relation which the third person sustains to the first
and second, wherein by an eternal and necessary, i.e., not voluntary,
act of the Father and the Son, their whole identical divine essence,
without alienation, division, or change, is communicated to the Holy
Ghost" (Dr. A. A. Hodge, *Outlines in Theology,* p. 189).

"Procession" is a more general term than "Generation," although
in each case the process is admittedly inscrutable. Procession is said
to differ from Generation in that the Son is generated by the Father
only, while the Spirit proceeds from both the Father and the Son at
the same time,—or as some have put it, proceeds from the Father,
through the Son.

What we have said concerning the alleged Scripture proof for the
doctrine of the generation of the Son is even more applicable to that
which is advanced to prove the procession of the Spirit. There is, in
fact, only one verse in Scripture which is commonly put forward to
prove this doctrine, and it is found in John 15:26: "But when the
Comforter is come, whom I will send unto you from the Father, even
the Spirit of truth, which proceedeth from the Father, he shall bear
witness of me." Again, the best Bible scholars are divided as to whether
or not this verse teaches the "procession" of the Spirit in the sense that

His Person originates as the result of an inscrutable although eternal and necessary process within the Godhead, or whether the verse merely has reference to His mission in this world as He comes to apply the redemption which Christ purchased. Jesus uses a similar form of expression when of His own redemptive mission He says, "I came out from the Father, and am come into the world: again, I leave the world, and go unto the Father" (John 16:28). In the original Greek the phrase, "came out from," which is here used of Jesus, is stronger than the "proceedeth from," which is used of the Spirit; yet the context of John 16:28 makes it perfectly clear that what Jesus said of Himself had reference to His mission and not to what is commonly termed His eternal generation; for His coming forth from the Father into the world is contrasted with His leaving the world and going back to the Father. We are, of course, told that the Holy Spirit is sent by the Father and by the Son; but the mission as He comes to apply redemption is an entirely different thing from the procession. It seems much more natural to assume that the words of John 15:26, which were a part of the Farewell Discourse, and which were, therefore, spoken within the very shadow of the cross, were not philosophical but practical, designed to meet a present and urgent need, namely, to comfort and strengthen the disciples for the ordeal through which they too were soon to pass. This was His method of teaching on other occasions, and it is at least difficult to see why He would have departed from it on this occasion. He was soon to leave the disciples, and He simply gave them the promise that another Helper, who likewise comes from the Father, shall take His place and be to them what He has been and do for them what He has done. It would seem that, since they hardly knew of the Spirit as yet, this would not at all have been an appropriate occasion to instruct them concerning the metaphysical relation which subsists between the Father and the Spirit. They are taught rather that the Spirit comes with divine authority, and that He is continually going forth from the Father to fulfill His purposes of Grace.

Hence John 15:26, at best, carries no decisive weight concerning the doctrine of the procession of the Spirit, if, indeed, it is not quite clearly designed to serve an entirely different purpose. We prefer to say, as previously stated, that within the essential life of the Trinity no one Person is prior to, nor generated by, nor proceeds from, another, and that such priority and subordination as we find revealed in the works of creation, redemption and sanctification, relate not to the immanent but to the economic Trinity.

Historically, the doctrine of the Procession of the Holy Spirit, which supposedly is of lesser consequence than that of the Generation of the Son, has been perverted and exaggerated out of all proportion to its real importance, and has been made the object of bitter and prolonged controversy between the Eastern and Western churches. It was, in fact, the immediate occasion of the split in Christendom in the eleventh century, and to this day it constitutes the main difference in doctrine between the Greek Orthodox and the Roman Catholic churches. The Greek church has maintained that the Spirit proceeds from the Father only, while the Latin church, and also the Protestant churches generally, have maintained that He proceeds from both the Father and the Son. But certainly the evidence for the doctrine is too scanty, and its meaning too obscure, to justify the hard feeling and the ecclesiastical division which has resulted from it.

9. The Trinity Presents a Mystery but not a Contradiction

To expect that we who do not understand ourselves nor the forces of nature about us should understand the deep mysteries of the Godhead would certainly be to the last degree unreasonable. Of all the Christian doctrines this is perhaps the most difficult to understand or to explain. That God exists as a Trinity has been clearly revealed in Scripture; but the particular mode in which the three Persons exist has not been revealed. When we behold the Triune God we feel like one who gazes upon the midday sun. The finite is not able to comprehend the infinite; and the marvelous personality of the Father, Son and Holy Spirit remains and must ever remain a profound mystery regardless of all the study that the greatest theologians of the Church have expended upon it. When we try to grasp its meaning the words in Job come to mind, "Canst thou by searching find out God? Canst thou find out the Almighty unto perfection?" The question answers itself.

In every sphere we are called upon to believe many truths which we cannot explain. What, for instance, is light? What gives the force of gravity its pull, and through what medium does it act? How does the mind make contact with the physical brain?

"There are many things in the world which are true but which cannot be understood," says Dr. Floyd E. Hamilton. "What is the real nature of electricity? What is life? What enables a human body to turn the same food into bone, teeth, flesh, and hair? These are but a few of the questions which man has never been able to answer, and probably never will, but that fact does not affect their truth. They exist, and their existence does not depend upon our understanding them. In the same way, the Triune God exists and His existence does not depend upon our understanding the mysteries of His nature" (*The Basis of Christian Faith,* p. 278).

And Dr. David S. Clark remarks:

"We must distinguish between apprehension and comprehension. We can know what God is, without knowing all He is. We can touch the earth while not able to embrace it in our arms. The child can know God while the philosopher cannot find out the Almighty unto perfection." (*A Syllabus of Systematic Theology,* p. 59).

"It is a mystery indeed," says Professor Flint, "yet one which explains many other mysteries, and which sheds a marvelous light on God, on nature, and on man" (*Anti-Theistic Theories,* p. 439).

Most people will admit, for instance, that they do not understand Einstein's theory of relativity; yet few will be so bold as to declare it irrational. We do not understand how such a vast amount of energy can be locked up within the atom; but the recently developed atomic bomb proves beyond doubt that it is there. Unless God were too great for our full intellectual comprehension, He would surely be too small to satisfy our spiritual needs.

But while the doctrine of the Trinity presents a mystery, it does not present a contradiction. It asserts that God is one in one respect— in substance or essence—and that He is three in an entirely different respect—in personal distinctions; and the charge of anti-trinitarians, that there is no middle ground between the Unitarian position (which asserts the unity of God but denies the Deity of Christ and the personality of the Holy Spirit) and Tritheism (which asserts that there are three Gods) is easily refuted by this fact. The doctrine of the Trinity is above reason, and could never have been discovered by man apart from divine revelation; yet it cannot be proved contrary to reason, nor inconsistent with any other truth which we know concerning God.

Furthermore, we hardly see how any one can insist that the doctrine of the Trinity strikes the average person as unreasonable when as a matter of fact Pantheism (which holds that every person and every thing which exists is but one of the innumerable forms in which God exists) is the form of philosophy which has been the most widely diffused and the most persistently held by the various peoples down through the ages. If the human mind has been able to conceive of God as existing in such an infinite number of forms, surely the statement that He exists in three Persons should not be hard to believe. The fact is that the doctrine as presented in Scripture is found to be eminently agreeable to reason. The historic Christian Church in all its branches has held tenaciously to this doctrine; and on the part of individuals the deepest and truest and most fruitful Christian faith has been found in those who have had an experimental knowledge and fellowship not only with God the Father, but also with Christ the Son and with the Holy Spirit,—that is, in Evangelicals as distinguished from Unitarians and Modernists.

Let it be remembered that we are under no obligation to explain all the mysteries connected with this doctrine. We are only under obligation to set forth what the Scriptures teach concerning it, and to vindicate the teaching as far as possible from the objections that are alleged against it. It is a doctrine which should never be presented to an unbeliever as a subject for argumentative proof, for it can be accepted only by faith, and that only after the person is convinced that God has spoken and that He has revealed this as a truth concerning Himself. With the Psalmist we are compelled to say, "Such knowledge is too wonderful for me; it is high, I cannot attain unto it" (139:6); and with Athanasius, "Man can perceive only the hem of the garment of God; the cherubim cover the rest with their wings." But though we are not able to give a full explanation of our faith we may know, and should know, what we believe and what we do not believe, and should be acquainted with the facts and truth on which our faith rests.

Many analogies have been given down through the ages to illustrate this doctrine, but we had as well admit that none of them have been of any special value and that some of them have been positively misleading. Some of the more common are: body, soul and spirit; intellect, emotion and will in man; stem, flower and seed in the plant; egg, larva and butterfly in the insect; solid, liquid and gas in matter; light, heat and radiance in the sun, etc. None of these, however, are true analogies. All of them fail to do justice to the personal element, particularly to the tri-personal element, in the Godhead. The best of them, that of intellect, emotion and will in man, presents three functions in one person, but not three persons in one substance. Those of the solid, liquid and gas, or of the egg, larva and butterfly, are not Christian, but Unitarian; for they represent the same substance as going through three successive stages.

Since there is none like God,—for "to whom will ye liken God, or what likeness will ye compare unto Him,"—we shall look in vain for any explanation of the Trinity either in the structure of our own minds or in nature about us. As the Trinity is not discoverable by reason in the first place, so it is not capable of proof by reason in the second place. We receive it only because it is taught in Scripture, and just as it is taught there. As Luther said concerning this doctrine:

"We should, like the little children, stammer out what the Scriptures teach: that the Father is truly God, that Christ is truly God, that the Holy Ghost is truly God, and yet that here are not three Gods, or three Beings, as there are three men, three angels, or three windows."

10. Historical Aspects of the Doctrine

During the first three centuries of the Christian era, theological discussion was centered almost entirely on the relationship subsisting between the Father and the Son, to the almost complete neglect of the doctrine of the Holy Spirit. In the nature of the case the development of a formal statement of the doctrine of the Trinity was a slow process. During the second and third centuries the influence of Stoic and Platonic thought caused some to deny the full Deity of Christ and to attempt to reduce Him to such dimensions as were considered commensurate with a world of time and space. Then against this tendency there arose a reaction, known as Monarchianism, which identified the Father, Son and Holy Spirit so completely that they were held to be only one Person who manifested Himself in different capacities.

We are not to infer that the doctrine of the Deity of Christ was a deduction from that of the Trinity, but rather the reverse. Because of the claims which Christ made, the authority which He assumed, the miracles which He worked, and the glory which He displayed, particularly in His resurrection, the early Christians were practically unanimous in their recognition of Him as truly God. This conviction, together with the inferential statement of the doctrine of the Trinity in the Baptismal Formula and in the Apostolic Benediction, served as their basis in the formulation of the doctrine. But since they were equally convinced that there was but one true God, the difficulty arose as to how to reconcile these two fundamental articles of the faith. There were some who attempted to solve the difficulty by denying the Deity of Christ, but their numbers were so few during the first two centuries that they had little influence.

This controversy was settled for the early Church by the Council of Nicaea, in Asia Minor, which met in the year 325. Under the influence of Athanasius, who later became Bishop of Alexandria, the Council declared for the full and eternal Deity of Christ, who was declared to be "God of God, Light of Light, Very God of Very God, being of one substance with the Father."

But so absorbed had the Council been in working out the doctrine concerning the Person of Christ that it omitted to make any definite statement concerning the Holy Spirit. Athanasius had taught the true Deity of the Holy Spirit, but many of the writers of the period identified Him with the Logos or Son, while others regarded Him as but the impersonal power or efficacy of God. It was but natural that until the question concerning the Person and nature of the Son was settled not much progress could be made in the development of the doctrine of the Holy Spirit. The defect of the Nicene Creed was remedied, however, by the Second Ecumenical Council, which met at Constantinople in 381, and included in its creed the statement: "We believe in the Holy Ghost, who is the Lord and Giver of life, who proceedeth from the Father, who, with the Father and Son, together is worshipped and glorified, who spake by the prophets."

Another heresy which arose was that of Sabellianism. This view held that there was but one Person in the Godhead, and that the terms Father, Son and Holy Spirit simply denoted this one Person in different capacities. As Creator of the world He was known as Father; as Redeemer of the race He was known as the Son; and when working in the hearts of men He was known as the Holy Spirit. Some chose to say that it was the same God who in Old Testament times was known as Father, who afterward became incarnate as the Son, and who reveals Himself in the Church as the Holy Spirit. These different manifestations of the same Person were considered analogous to that of a man who is known in his home as father, in the Church as an elder, and in the community as a doctor.

But this view satisfied the religious consciousness of Christians in only one regard, namely, in recognizing the true Deity of Christ. Its defects were glaring; for if the phases were successive, then God ceased to be the Father when He became the Son, and ceased to be the Son when He became the Holy Spirit. The incarnation was reduced to a temporary union of the Divine and the human nature in the man Jesus Christ. This view was so out of harmony with the Scriptures that it was soon rejected, and the Church doctrine, which is neither Tritheism nor Sabellianism but the true mean between these errors, was maintained.

One other trinitarian heresy that we should notice was that of the Socinians. They held that Christ was only a man, a very good man to be sure, in fact the best of men because more fully animated and controlled by the power of God than any other had ever been, but who had no existence until he was born by ordinary generation of Joseph and Mary. They acknowledged that he possessed a more advanced revelation from God than had been given to any of the earlier prophets or teachers. They perceived the impropriety of worshipping a creature as the Arians had done, regardless of how high he might be exalted; and while less orthodox than the Arians, they were at this point more consistent. This view was, of course, condemned by the Church, but it has continued as a heresy on the outskirts of true religion down through the ages. Present-day Modernism, which is essentially a denial of the supernatural in religion, also carries on the Socinian tradition with more or less consistency.

To Augustine belongs the credit for having made a considerable advance in the development of the doctrine, and for centuries his book, *On The Trinity,* remained the standard work on the subject. While Athanasius had secured the acceptance by the Church of the true personality and Deity of the Father, Son and Holy Spirit, he did allow that the Son and the Holy Spirit were subordinate to the Father in order and dignity. Augustine did away with the idea of subordination by stressing the numerical unity of their essence, and through his powerful influence the doctrine was accepted by the Church in fact as well as in theory. Although the Reformation was a time of great advances in the development of doctrine, that of the Trinity has been wrought out so clearly at the earlier period that there was no tendency to enter into speculation concerning it. Both Luther and Calvin refused to go beyond the simple statements of Scripture, although it did fall to Calvin to reassert the self-existence and the full equality of the Son and the Holy Spirit with the Father against those who taught that the generation of the Son and the procession of the Holy Spirit denoted perpetual communication of essence from the Father and therefore dependence. In Calvin's statement the idea of the equalization of the persons took the place of the ideas of generation and procession.

The Church of the Scriptures and of the creeds is, of course, Trinitarian, not Unitarian. Up until a century ago every denomination and practically every local church taught the doctrine of the Trinity as a matter of course. But with the passing of the years a change has taken place, and even in many of the so-called evangelical churches this doctrine, which sets forth eternal and unchanging truth, is scarcely mentioned, while in others it, like many other essential truths, is challenged, doubted or denied. The truth has not changed, but the attitude of many in our generation toward that truth has changed; and today the controversy rages with new vigour, not only against the foe without, but also against the fleece-clad foe within.

In an excellent article on *The Doctrine of the Trinity,* Dr. Clarence E. Macartney has the following to say about the present-day controversy.

"What Athanasius contended against in his day was the effort to give the world a damaged Christ. He knew that a damaged Christ was no Christ. He knew that a redemption wrought out by any other save the God of redemption, God the Father, God the Son, and God the Holy Spirit, was no redemption at all. Under different names and forms there appears from time to time that same subtle effort of unbelief to persuade the world to accept a damaged Christ instead of the Christ who is the eternal Son of God. Not since the days of Arius has there been so widespread and warmly propagated a movement to substitute for the New Testament Christ, the Christ of redemption, a lesser Christ, a damaged Christ. The leaders of this movement either openly deny the New Testament accounts of the miraculous entry of Christ into the world, or hold the acceptance or the rejection of those accounts of how Christ came has nothing to do with Christianity. This new Christ probably did not work miracles. He did not die on the cross as a substitute for man, taking his place, and bearing his sins before the law of God. He did not rise from the dead with the same body in which He was entombed in Joseph's sepulchre, nor in that body did He ascend into the heavens to intercede at the right hand of God the Father Almighty; and the repeated statements of the New Testament about His glorious and triumphant return to the earth mean only that truth and right are at length to prevail upon the earth. Yet the men who hold these views still talk, and some of them still preach, about Christ. What Christ? 'Who is this?' the people exclaimed when Jesus rode into Jerusalem amid the plaudits of the multitude. Today the Christian Church may well exclaim concerning this new, this damaged Christ, 'Who is this?' "

It may be of interest to give a brief summary of the creedal statements of the Church concerning this doctrine. We have said that during the first three centuries there were no important councils and that the formulation of a creedal statement was a slow process. The early Christians held the doctrine, as it were, in solution; time and controversy were destined to precipitate it out. Because of the bitterness of the Jews, the mockery of the pagans, and the inevitable confusion and contradiction in the mode of statement even by those within the Church who honestly intended to hold what the Scriptures taught concerning it, the Church was compelled to analyse the doctrine and to set it forth in clear-cut, formal statements.

The best summary of the teaching of the various creeds, so far as we know, is found in the above-mentioned article by Dr. Macartney, and is prefaced by the following remarks:

"As we read these statements let us remember that they represent no idle and airy speculations, but a noble effort of trained minds to define and explain the truth of the Trinity as they had found it in the pages of the Bible and in the traditions of believing Christians. Let us remember, too, that these statements, especially the earlier ones, were formulated in times when Christianity was being fiercely assailed by unbelief. At Pittsburgh, St. Louis, Chicago, Detroit, and other cities of the United States, the visitor is taken to see an old fort, or the site of an old fort, where the first settlers established themselves and defended themselves. These log forts, with loophole and outlook, standing now in the midst of great cities, mark the growth and progress of the nation, for without the enterprise, heroism and sacrifice which are associated with these forts, there would not have been a nation. These ancient confessions are like venerable fortresses. They mark the crises in the history of Christianity and recall the heroism and daring of men who refused to have their Christian heritage taken from them, and in the face of a world of unbelief cried out, 'Credo! I believe!' There is no cant so ignorant, so wretched, so worthy of immeasurable scorn, as that so popular today, which belittles creeds and the men who gave them to us, and the men who defend them, and say that they have nothing to do with practical Christianity. Without these creeds, and the courage and love and faith which they represent, Christianity would long ago have perished from off the face of the earth."

1. The Nicene Creed (325) :

"We believe in one God—And in one Lord Jesus Christ, the Son of God, begotten of the Father, light of light, very God of very God, begotten, not made, being of one substance with the Father—And in the Holy Ghost."

2. The Niceno-Constantinopolitan Creed (381).

In this creed the clauses concerning the Father and the Son are practically the same as in the Nicene Creed. But the article concerning the Holy Ghost is changed to the following: "And in the Holy Ghost, who is the Lord and giver of life, who proceedeth from the Father, who, with the Father and Son, is worshipped and glorified, who spake by the prophets."

3. The Athanasian Creed (origin and time uncertain, but the most logical and elaborate of the creeds) :

"And the Catholic Faith is this: that we worship one God in Trinity and Trinity in Unity, neither confounding the Persons nor dividing the Substance; for there is one Person of the Father, another of the

Son, and another of the Holy Ghost. But the Godhead of the Father, of the Son, and of the Holy Ghost is all one; the glory equal, the majesty co-eternal. For like as we are compelled by the Christian verity to acknowledge every Person by Himself to be God and Lord, so we are forbidden by the Catholic Religion to say, There are three Gods, or three Lords."

4. The Augsburg Confession (1530),—the oldest Protestant creed and the accepted standard of Lutheranism:

"There is one Divine essence which is called and is God, eternal, without body, indivisible, of infinite power, wisdom, goodness, the Creator and Preserver of all things, visible and invisible. And yet there are three Persons of the same essence and power, who also are co-eternal, the Father, the Son, and the Holy Ghost."

5. The Thirty-Nine Articles (1571),—the creed of the Church of England and of the Protestant Episcopal Church in the United States:

"There is but one living and true God. And in the unity of this Godhead there are three Persons, of one substance, power and eternity, the Father, the Son, and the Holy Ghost."

6. The Westminster Confession (1647),—the creed of the Presbyterian Church, with which the Canon of the Synod of Dort, the symbol of the Reformed Church, agrees quite closely:

"There is but one living and true God. In the unity of the Godhead there are three Persons, of one substance, power, and eternity—God the Father, God the Son, and God the Holy Ghost. The Father is one, neither begotten not proceeding; the Son is eternally begotten of the Father; the Holy Ghost eternally proceeding from the Father and the Son."

11. Practical Importance of the Doctrine

The doctrine of the Trinity is not to be looked upon as an abstract metaphysical speculation, nor as an unnatural theory which has no bearing on the practical affairs of life. It is rather a most important revelation concerning the nature of the only living and true God, and of His works in the salvation of men. The very purpose of the Gospel is, of course, to bring us to the knowledge of God precisely in the way in which He has revealed Himself. And as Calvin tells us in the introductory sentence in his *Institutes:*

"True and substantial wisdom principally consists of two parts, the knowledge of God, and the knowledge of ourselves."

And then he adds that "no man can take a survey of himself but he must immediately turn to the contemplation of God in whom he lives and moves: since it is evident that our very existence is nothing but a subsistence in God alone."

The knowledge of God the Father who is the source of redemption, of God the Son who achieves redemption, and of God the Holy Spirit who applies redemption, is declared in Scripture to be eternal life. Every other conception of God presents a false god to the mind and conscience. So different is the system of theology developed, and the manner of life which flows from it, that for all practical purposes we may say that Unitarians and Trinitarians worship different Gods.

This is an advanced doctrine which was not made known in Old Testament times, and that for the very reason that it could not be understood until the objective work of redemption had been completed. But in the New Testament it is interwoven with the whole Christian economy, not in terms of speculative philosophy but in those of practical religion.

"The doctrine of the Trinity," says Dr. Bartlett, "lies in the very heart of Christian truth. It is the centre from which all other tenets of our faith radiate. If we entertain wrong views of the nature of the Supreme Being our entire theology is imperiled" (*The Triune God,* p. 13).

Inscrutable, yet not self-contradictory, this doctrine furnishes the key to all of the other doctrines which have to do with the redemption of man. Apart from it doctrines such as the Deity of Christ, the incarnation, the personality of the Holy Spirit, regeneration, justification, sanctification, the meaning of the crucifixion and the resurrection, etc., cannot be understood. It thus underlies the whole plan of salvation. As Dr. Henry B. Smith tells us:

"For the Trinity there is a strong, preliminary argument in the fact that in some form it has always been confessed by the Christian Church, and that all that has opposed it has been thrown off. When it has been abandoned, other chief articles, as the atonement, regeneration, etc., have almost always followed it, by logical necessity; as when one draws the wire from a necklace of gems, the gems all fall asunder" (*System of Christian Theology,* p. 49.)

"The idea of the Trinity," says Dr. Warfield, "illuminates, enriches and elevates all our thoughts of God. It has become a commonplace to say that Christian theism is the only stable theism. That is as much as to say that theism requires the enriching conception of the Trinity to give it permanent hold upon the human mind—the mind finds it difficult to rest in the idea of an abstract unity for its God: and that the human heart cries out for the living God in whose Being there is that fulness of life for which the conception of the Trinity alone provides."

And again:

"If he (the believer) could not construct the doctrine of the Trinity out of his consciousness of salvation, yet the elements of his consciousness of salvation are interpreted to him and reduced to order only by the doctrine of the Trinity which he finds underlying and giving their significance and consistency to the teaching of the Scriptures as to the processes of salvation. By means of this doctrine he is able to think clearly and consequently of his threefold relation to the saving God, experienced by him as fatherly love sending a Redeemer, as redeeming love executing redemption, as saving love applying redemption. . . . Without the doctrine of the Trinity, his conscious Christian life would be thrown into confusion and left in disorganization if not, indeed, given an air of unreality; with the doctrine of the Trinity, order, significance and reality are brought to every element of it. Accordingly, the doctrine of the Trinity and the doctrine of redemption, historically, stand or fall together. A unitarian theology is commonly associated with a Pelagian anthropology and a Socinian soteriology. It is a striking testimony which is borne by F. E. Koenig: 'I have learned that many cast off the whole history of redemption for no other reason than because they have not attained to a conception of the Triune God' " (*Biblical Doctrines,* pp. 139, 167).

The doctrine of the Trinity gives us a *theocentric* system of theology, and thus places in true proportion the work of God the Father. God the Son, and God the Holy Spirit. This system alone gives us the proper approach to the study of theology, showing that it must be from the standpoint of the triune God rather than from that of the second or third Person of the Trinity, or from man,—that is, theocentric rather than Christocentric or anthropocentric. It should be unnecessary for us to have to say that theocentric theology (by which we mean that which is generally known as the Reformed or Calvinistic faith) gives Christ a very high place in the system. He is the God-man, the center and course of salvation; but while soteriology has a prominent place, it is not made the organizing principle, but rather one of the subdivisions in the theological system. The history of doctrine shows quite clearly that those who have attempted to organize the system of theology around the person of Christ, regardless of their good intentions, have tended to slight other vital truths and to drift into a superficial system. Their system is unstable and tends to gravitate downward, relinquishing one doctrine after another until it becomes anthropocentric.

The third system, quite common in our day and generally known as Modernism or Humanism, is anthropocentric,—that is, it attempts to understand the nature of God by reconstructing Him from what we know of man. This system allows man to cast his own shadow over God, limiting His Lordship. It means that Christ is to be looked upon primarily as a man, and that, as expressed by an outstanding Modernist of our day, nobody should go to Jesus "to his manger and his cross to find the omnipotence that swings Orion and the Pleiades." All such errors are to be avoided by placing God in His triune nature at the center of our theological system. Only thus shall we arrive at a true knowledge of Him. This is the Biblical order: first, the Father, who is the Creator and the Author of salvation; then the Son, who provides redemption objectively; and then the Holy Spirit, who applies redemption.

One cause of the strength of the Trinitarian theology has been the appeal which it makes to the inward sense of sin,—that sad weight which rests so heavily upon every serious soul,—while the great weakness of Unitarianism has been its insensibility to the reality and consequences of sin. Trinitarians have seen sin not merely as misfortune or incomplete development, but as awful and heinous crime, repulsive to God, and deserving His just wrath and punishment. They have held that it could not merely be pardoned without an atonement (that is, without any one suffering the consequences), but that God is under as much obligation to punish sin as He is to reward righteousness. On the other hand Pelagians, Socinians, and present-day Modernists and Unitarians have taken a superficial and minimizing view of sin, with the inevitable result that their faith has been superficial, their religious feelings have been deadened, and the sinews of all evangelistic and missionary effort have been cut. Having given up the doctrine of the Trinity, they naturally take a low view of the person of Christ. Even according to their own admission the great literature to which a Christian would turn for faith, hope, love and inspiration has been almost exclusively the product of trinitarian writers. Hence the best method to use in dealing with Modernists and Unitarians is to arouse in them the sense of sin; for once a person realizes the hideous and ghastly nature of his sin he also realizes that none other than a Divine Redeemer can save him from it.

And that brings us to another point: If there were no trinity, there could be no incarnation, no objective redemption, and therefore no salvation; for there would then be no one capable of acting as Mediator between God and man. In his fallen condition man has neither the inclination nor the ability to redeem himself. All merely human works are defective and incapable of redeeming a single soul. Between the Holy God and sinful man there is an infinite gulf; and only through One who is Deity, who takes man's nature upon Himself and suffers and dies in his stead, thus giving infinite value and dignity to that suffering and death, can man's debt be paid. Nor could a Holy Spirit who comes short of Deity apply that redemption to human souls. Hence if salvation is to be had at all it must be of divine origin. If God were only unity, but not plurality, He might be our Judge, but, so far as we can see, could not be our Saviour and sanctifier. The fact of the matter is that God is the way back to Himself, and that all of the hopes of our fallen race are centred in the truth of the Trinity.

It is difficult to maintain in the independence and self-sufficiency of God on any other than the Trinitarian basis. Those who believe in a uni-personal God almost instinctively posit the eternity of matter or an eternal and necessary creation in order to preserve a subjective-objective relationship. Even many Trinitarian theologians have held—whether correctly or not there is difference of opinion—that the Divine nature demands either an eternal Christ or an eternal creation. It is felt that apart from a creation a unitary God would be a most lonely and solitary Being, limited in companionship, love, mercy, justice, etc., and hence not self-sufficient. The Unitarian conception of God is unstable, and these considerations to quite a large extent account for its distinct tendency toward Pantheism. In the New England theology, for instance, we find that the high Unitarianism of Channing degenerated into the half-fledged Pantheism of Theodore Parker, and then into the full-fledged Pantheism of Ralph Waldo Emerson. As Trinitarians we feel that a God who is necessarily bound to the universe is not truly infinite, independent and free.

"A Unitarian, one-personed God," says Dr. Charles Hodge, "might possibly have existed, and if revealed as such, it would have been our duty to have acknowledged His lordship. But, nevertheless, He would have always remained utterly inconceivable to us—one lone, fellowless conscious being; subject without object; conscious person without environment; righteous being without fellowship or moral relation or sphere of right action. Where would there be to Him a sphere of love, truth, trust, or sympathetic feeling? Before creation, eternal darkness; after creation, only an endless game of solitaire, with worlds for pawns." (*Systematic Theology*, I, p. 127).

This Unitarian idea of God over-emphasizes His power at the expense of His other attributes, and tends to identify Him with abstract cause and thought. On the other hand the doctrine of the Trinity shows us that in His relations with us His love is primary, and that

His power is exercised in the interests of His love rather than that His love is exercised in the interests of His power. The words, "God is love" (I John 4:8) are not a rhetorical exaggeration, but an expression of truth concerning the Divine nature. We are convinced that the trinitarian conception of God, as judged by its piety and morality at home and its missionary zeal abroad, is by all odds the highest: and once we have thus conceived of God and felt the new fullness, richness and force given through the divine fellowship we can never again be satisfied with a modalistic or Unitarian conception.

Something of the invaluable service rendered by the doctrine of the Trinity is brought out when we see how it embraces, combines and reconciles in itself all the half-truths of the various religions and heresies that have held sway over the minds of men. There have been in the main three outstanding false systems, namely, Polytheism, Pantheism, and Deism. That these systems embrace elements of important truth cannot be denied; yet upon the whole they are false and injurious.

The truth in Polytheism, which is that God exists in a plurality of persons and powers, abundantly sufficient within His own nature to allow free play to all of the moral and social qualities or personality, is embraced in the doctrine of the Trinity; but its errors, that it destroys the unity of God, and that it separates and personifies these various powers and worships them in isolation or under some visible manifestation such as the sun, moon, rivers, trees, animals, images, etc., is rejected.

The truth of Pantheism, which is that God is everywhere present and active, the irresistible current of force which flows through all movements and all life,—a truth which, as Dr. A. A. Hodge says, "is realized in the Holy Ghost, who, while of the same substance as the Father, is revealed to us as immanent in all things, the basis of all existence, the tide of all life, springing up like a well of water from within us, giving form to chaos and inspiration to reason, the ever-present executive of God, the Author of all beauty in the physical world, of all true philosophy, science and theology in the world of thought, and of holiness in the world of the Spirit",—is embraced in the doctrine of the Trinity; but the errors of Pantheism, which are that God has no personal existence except as He comes to consciousness in man, that His only life is the sum of all creature life, and that His immediate participation in every thought and act of the creatures makes Him the author of sin, is rejected. Furthermore, in the incarnation of Christ the eternal Son God has stooped to a real and permanent incarnation, and has done sublimely what the incarnations of the heathen mythology have only caricatured.

The truth of Deism, which is that God is the Creator of the universe, the ultimate source of all power, enthroned in the highest heaven, and that His power is manifested through second causes, namely through the unchanging order of natural law, is embraced in the doctrine of the Trinity; but the errors of Deism, which are that God is an absentee God, that He works only through second causes, that He is not in personal and loving contact with His people, and that He is therefore not concerned with their prayers and desires, is rejected·

Similarly, too, in regard to the heresies which have arisen within the Christian Church. The doctrine of the Trinity acknowledges the truth of Arianism, which is that Christ existed before the creation of the world and that He was possessed of supernatural power; but it rejects the errors of Arianism, which is that Christ was not co-eternal and co-equal with the Father, that He was in the final analysis only a creature and hence far short of Deity. With Sabellianism it acknowledges the full Deity and power of Christ and of the Holy Spirit, but denies its error, which is that it makes no proper distinctions between the Persons within the Godhead. With Nestorianism it acknowledges both the true Deity and the true humanity of Christ, but denies its error, which is that it separates the Divine and human natures in such a way as to render Him a dual personality.

Wherever the doctrine of the Trinity has been abandoned, with Christ as the connecting link between Deity and humanity, the tendency has been toward an abstract and immobile form of monotheism, toward the far-off God of Deism, or, recoiling from that, to lose God in the world of Pantheism. To identify God with nature is to attribute evil as well as good to Him; and this kind of religion had its logical outcome in the old worship of Baal, the supreme male divinity of the ancient Phoenicians, and of Ashtaroth, the goddess of love and fruitfulness, with all of their attendant and unmentionable abominations. The Christian doctrine of the Trinity supplies us with safeguards against both these errors, and at the same time provides us with the link between God and man, the link which philosophical speculation has striven so vainly to find. It is the true protection of a living Theism, which otherwise oscillates uncertainly between the two extremes of Deism and Pantheism, either of which is fatal to it.

This doctrine should, of course, be preached in every Christian Church. It is a mistake to say that people will no longer listen to doctrinal preaching. Let the minister believe his doctrines; let him present them with conviction and as living issues, and he will find sympathetic audiences. To-day we see thousands of people turning away from pulpit discussions of current events, social topics, political issues, and merely ethical questions, and trying to fill themselves with the husks of occult and puerile philosophies. In many ways we are spiritually poorer than we should be, because in our theological confusion and bewilderment we have failed to do justice to these great doctrinal principles. If rightly preached these doctrines are most interesting and profitable, and are in fact indispensable if the congregation is to be well grounded in the Faith. We are convinced that the chief need of the present age is great theology, and that only the emergence and dominance of great theology will produce an adequate basis for true Christian living.

It is certain that no merely speculative theory, and especially none so mysterious and so out of analogy with all other objects of human knowledge as is that of the Trinity, could ever have held such a prominent place and been so emphasized by all of the churches of Christendom as has this doctrine unless its controlling principle were vital. In the nature of the case Anti-trinitarianism inevitably leads to a radically different system of religion. Historically the Church has always refused to recognize as Christians those who rejected the doctrine of the Trinity. Also, historically, every great revival of Christianity down through the ages has been a revival of adhesion to fullest Trinitarianism. It is not too much to say, therefore, that the Trinity is the point on which all Christian ideas and interests focus, at once the beginning and the end of all true insight into Christianity.

Chapter IV.

THE PERSON OF CHRIST

1 Introduction

Probably the most earnestly discussed question in religious circles today is, "What Is Christianity?" But before we can reach a conclusion concerning that question we must settle another which is vitally related to it, namely, "Who Was, or Who Is Jesus Christ?"

There is practically unanimous agreement that a person bearing this name once walked the earth and that the movement which we know as Christianity sprang from Him. There is also practically unanimous agreement that for the last nineteen hundred years His influence has been the most potent and uplifting of all influences in shaping and moulding the life of our western world.

That Jesus was the finest specimen of humanity that the world has ever known, that His teachings were the purest and loftiest that the world has ever received, and that His actions were the most faultless that the world has ever seen, is admitted by practically every one. But from the time He walked the earth until this present hour there has been no end of controversy concerning His person and concerning the place that He occupies in the religion that He founded. More specifically the controversy has to do with the question whether Jesus was as the Scriptures represent Him to have been, the second person of the Trinity, God incarnate, who is to be worshipped and obeyed even as the Father, or whether He was only a man endowed with unusual spiritual insight, differing from other men not in kind but only in degree, and occupying a place in the Christian system not essentially different from that which Confucius occupies in Confusianism or Mohammed in Mohammedanism.

Historically the first great question that came up in the early Church had to do with the Person of Christ. The Church settled that question for herself once and for all by affirming that He is the divine Son of God, Deity incarnate. That decision was written into her authoritative creeds, and ever since that time Evangelical Christianity has been bold to assert that "The Church's one foundation is Jesus Christ her Lord." And this faith has been expressed not only in the creeds, but in the hymns and in the devotional writings of her representative spokesmen. Protestants and Catholics alike agree that Christ saves, although they differ in their opinions as to how He saves.

In comparatively recent times, however,—we may even say within the lifetime of our own generation—the faith of the Church has been seriously challenged not only from without but from within. The result is that today even among those who call themselves Christians there is no general agreement either as to who Christ is or as to what He does for our salvation. This in turn has led to endless confusion not only between denominations but also within individual churches. The doctrine of the Person of Christ is, therefore, not merely one of a number of equally important doctrines, but the most central and basic of the entire system, the very corner-stone of the temple of truth which is set forth in the Scriptures. And in accordance with this we would define Christianity as follows: *Christianity is that redemptive religion that offers salvation from the guilt and corruption of sin through the atoning death of Christ.* Consequently, we hold that to admit the Deity of Christ and to trust Him for salvation constitutes one a Christian, and that to reject His Deity marks one a non-Christian. The purpose of this book is to present the evidence which we believe is abundantly sufficient to prove that Christ was indeed Deity incarnate, the eternal Son of God, who came to this earth in order that He might provide a way of redemption for sinful men.

2 Christ's Own Testimony Concerning His Deity

The most important witness to the Deity of Christ is, of course, Christ Himself. The New Testament records make it abundantly clear that He possessed not only a sense of unbroken fellowship with God but a distinct consciousness that He Himself was God. From the age of twelve at least, when in reply to His mother's question He said, "How is it that ye sought me? knew ye not that I must be in my Father's house?", this sense appears, and it later becomes one of the dominant notes of His doctrine. He expressly claims equality with God the Father. "I and the Father are one," John 10:30. "He that hath seen me hath seen the Father," John 14:9. ". . . that all may honor the Son, even as they honor the Father. He that honoreth not the Son honoreth not the Father that sent Him," John 5:23. "He that believeth on me, believeth not on me, but on Him that sent me. And he that beholdeth me beholdeth Him that sent me," John 12:44, 45. He alone is the true Revealer of God to men. "All things have been delivered unto me of my Father: and no one knoweth the Son save the Father; neither doth any know the Father save the Son, and he to whomsoever the

Son willeth to reveal Him," Matt. 11:27. In the parable of the wicked husbandmen Jesus presents Himself as the Son and Heir of the vineyard, occupying a category higher than that of the prophets, who was rejected and slain, but who eventually is to be made "the head of the corner," Matt. 21:33-45. His activity is co-extensive with that of the Father: "For what things soever He doeth, these the Son also doeth in like manner," John 5:19,—a joint activity which from other sources we learn extends even to the resurrection and the judgment.

That Jesus' claim to Sonship and to oneness with the Father was understood by the Jews to imply Deity is quite clear. When on one occasion they took up stones to stone Him, He said, "Many good works have I showed you from the Father; for which of those works do ye stone me?", they replied, "For a good work we stone thee not, but for blasphemy; and because that thou, being a man, makest thyself God," John 10:32, 33. And when they accused Him before Pilate they said: "We have a law, and by that law He ought to die, because He made Himself the Son of God," John 19:7.

The last words of Jesus to His disciples as recorded in John, chapters 14 to 16, are the words of God to men. For a mere man to speak to other men as He speaks here would be blasphemy. He begins by exhorting His disciples to have the same faith in Him that they have in God: "Believe in God, believe also in me." He declares that He goes to heaven to prepare a place for them, and that He will come again and receive them. He declares that He is the way, the truth, and the life, and that no one comes unto the Father except through Him. To know Him is to know the Father, and to see Him, is to see the Father, for He and the Father are one. He goes to the Father, and promises that all of their prayers made in His name shall be answered. He promises to send them the Holy Spirit, another Divine Person, who is to take His place as their Comforter and Companion and Teacher, who is to be to them what He has been and to do for them what He has done, who is to render them infallible as teachers, and who is to give spiritual illumination to all believers. He declares that He is the true source of life to the Church, and that it is as necessary that every believer be united with Him as it is that the branch be united with the vine. They have not chosen Him but He has chosen them, with the result that such a tremendous gulf has been placed between them and "the world" that the world no longer recognizes them as of its kind and therefore hates them. Those who hate Him hate His Father also. All things whatsoever the Father has are His, and everything asked in His name will be granted. He came out from the Father into the world, and now He is to leave the world and go back to the Father.

In the intercessory prayer He prays that the Father may glorify the Son in order that the Son may glorify the Father. He claims authority to give eternal life to all those whom the Father has given Him, which life consists in knowing God and Himself. He prays that the Father may glorify Him with the Father's own glory, which glory He had with the Father before the world was.

During the trial before the Sanhedrin Jesus publicly and explicitly claimed deity and was condemned to death on the charge that He had spoken "blasphemy." In answer to the high priest's question, "Art thou the Christ, the Son of the Blessed?" (or, as Matthew says, "the Son of God"), Jesus replied, "I am: and ye shall see the Son of man sitting at the right hand of Power, and coming with the clouds of heaven." And then we are told that "the high priest rent his clothes. and saith, What further need have we of witnesses? Ye have heard the blasphemy: what think ye? And they all condemned Him to be worthy of death," Mark 14:61-64.

In giving the Great Commission to the disciples Jesus said: "All authority hath been given unto me in heaven and on earth. Go ye therefore, and make disciples of all the nations, baptizing them in the name of the Father and of the Son and of the Holy Spirit: teaching them to observe all things whatsoever I commanded you: and lo, I am with you always, even unto the end of the world," Matt. 28:18-20. There He placed His name at the center of the triune name of God. commanded that those who believe on Him should be baptized in that name, and promised to be with them always, even unto the end of the world. Concerning this Dr. Benjamin B. Warfield says: "Claiming for Himself all authority in heaven and on earth — which implies the possession of omnipotence — and promising to be with His followers 'always, even unto the end of the world' — which adds the implications of omnipresence and omniscience — He commands them to baptize their converts 'in the name of the Father and of the Son and of the Holy Spirit.' The precise form of the formula must be carefully observed. It does not read: 'In the names' (plural) — as if there were three beings enumerated, each with its distinguishing name. Nor yet: 'In the name of the Father, Son and Holy Spirit,' as if there were one person, going by a threefold name. It reads: 'In the name (singular) of the Father and of the (article repeated) Son, and of the (article repeated) Holy Spirit,' carefully distinguishing three persons, though uniting them all under one name. The name of God was to the Jews Jehovah, and to name the name of Jehovah upon them was to make them His. What Jesus did in this great injunction was to command His followers to name the name of God upon their converts, and to announce the name of God which is to be named on their converts in the threefold enumeration of 'the Father' and 'the Son' and 'the Holy Spirit.' As it is unquestionable that He here intended Himself by 'the Son,' He here places Himself by the side of the Father and the Spirit, as together with them constituting the one God. It is, of course, the Trinity which he is describing and that is as much as to say that He announces Himself as one of the persons of the Trinity." (*Biblical Doctrines*, p. 204.)

Certainly on the basis of His own teaching Jesus claimed Deity for Himself. No unprejudiced reader can reach any other conclusion. Such has been the impression of the great mass of those who have read the New Testament. This has led Dr. A. H. Strong to observe that "If He is not God, He is a deceiver or is self-deceived, and in either case, *Christ, if not God, is not good.*" And Dr. E. Y. Mullins has pointed out that if we deny His Deity then "we must conclude that, with all His moral beauty and excellence, Jesus was a pitiable failure as teacher if He did not succeed in guarding His message against corruptions which have led to His own exaltation as God, and to the existence through eighteen centuries of a system of idolatry of which He is the center."

3 Testimony of the Apostles

In full harmony with the claims and testimony of Jesus concerning His Deity are those of all of the others who speak in the New Testament. The angel Gabriel in announcing to Zacharias that he and Elizabeth were to have a son said that the mission of that son would be "to make ready for the Lord a people prepared for Him," Luke 1:17; and in announcing to Mary that she was to be the mother of a Son who without any human father was to be conceived through the power of the Holy Spirit he said: "He shall be great, and shall be called the Son of the Most High: and the Lord God shall give unto Him the throne of His father David: and He shall reign over the house of Jacob for ever; and of His kingdom there shall be no end," Luke 1:32, 33,— qualifications which can be met by no one who is less than Deity. His name was to be called "Jesus," "for it is He that shall save His people from their sins," Matt. 1:21,—again a work which can be performed by no one who is less than Deity. Matthew, citing one of the Messianic prophecies in the Old Testament, says: "Now all this is come to pass, that it might be fulfilled which was spoken by the Lord through the prophet, saying, Behold, the virgin shall be with child, and shall bring forth a son, And they shall call His name Immanuel; which is, being interpreted, God with us," 1:22, 23. The wise-men, finding the new-born babe after their long journey from the east and possessing a spiritual insight above that commonly given to men, "fell down and worshipped him," Matt. 2:11,—thereby rendering to Him the homage which it is idolatrous and sinful to render to any one other than Deity.

John the Baptist, stern preacher of righteousness that he was, acknowledged himself to be only the fore-runner of one who was coming later and declared that this one was so much greater than he that he was not even worthy to unloose the latchet of His shoes,—that is, not even worthy to be His servant. When Jesus did appear and was baptized John saw the heavens opened and the Spirit of God descending upon Him; and the Father's voice spoke from heaven, saying, "This is my beloved Son, in whom I am well pleased," Matt. 3:17. And the following day he pointed out Jesus as "the Lamb of God, that taketh away the sin of the world," as "He that baptizeth in the Holy Spirit," and as "the Son of God," John 1:29-34.

In the prologue of the Gospel of John we have a clear and unmistakable assertion of the Deity of Christ. "In the beginning was the Word, and the Word was with God, and the Word was God" (vs. 1). John applies to Christ a term which is not found anywhere else in the New Testament, and the predicates which he ascribes to Him can be ascribed to none other than full Deity. In our ordinary language a word reveals the idea which is behind it. What a word is to an idea, Christ is to God, that is, a Revealer. It is His Office to Make God known to His creatures. "No man hath seen God at any time; the only begotten Son, who is in the bosom of the Father, He hath declared Him" (vs. 18). His eternity is set forth by the statement that "in the beginning," when things began to come into existence, He already "was." The imperfect tense sets forth the notion of absolute supratemporal existence, so that, as Dr. Warfield says, "From all eternity the Word has been with God as a fellow: He who in the very beginning already 'was,' 'was' also in communion with God. Though He was thus in some sense a second along with God, He was nevertheless not a separate being from God: 'And the Word was God.' In some sense distinguishable from God, He was in an equally true sense identical with God. There is but one eternal God; this eternal God, the Word is; in whatever sense we may distinguish Him from the God whom He is 'with,' He is not another than this God, but Himself is this God." (*Biblical Doctrines*, p. 191.)

And in John's prologue not only is the Word taken entirely out of the category of creatures and declared to antedate all things; He

is declared to be the Creator of all things: "All things were made
through Him; and without Him was not anything made that hath been
made" (vs. 3). In verse 14 he says: "And the Word became flesh,
and dwelt among us (and we beheld His glory, glory as of the only
begotten from the Father), full of grace and truth." John would have
us realize that this Christ, who in still another connection he says has
"come in the flesh," I John 4:2, is not merely God's eternal fellow, but
that He is the eternal God Himself, and that even through the veil of
His humanity the disciples were able to behold something of His celestial glory. He uses the term "flesh" to indicate human nature in general,
with its implications of dependence and weakness. In his prologue then
John simply teaches that the eternal God entered upon a mode of existence in which the experiences that are common to human beings would
also be His; in short, that He became incarnate in Jesus Christ the man.

Peter doubtless spoke for most of the disciples when in his great
confession he said, "Thou art the Christ, the Son of the living God,"
Matt. 16:16. And as the revelation proceeded toward its climax even
the most dubious disciple came to the point where he fell down at
Jesus' feet with the acknowledgment, "My Lord and my God," John
20:28. Since those words went unrebuked by Jesus they were equivalent to an assertion on His own part of His claim to Deity.

The testimony of the apostles as they wrought miracles in His
name is further proof of His deity. "In the name of Jesus Christ of
Nazareth, walk," said Peter to the lame man at the door of the temple,
Acts 3:6. "If we this day are examined concerning a good deed done
to an impotent man," said he, "by what means this man is made whole;
be it known to you all, and to all the people of Israel, that in the name
of Jesus Christ of Nazareth, whom ye crucified, whom God raised from
the dead, even in Him doth this man stand here before you whole,"
Acts 4:9, 10. And Paul, casting out an evil spirit from a possessed
maid, said: "I charge thee in the name of Jesus Christ to come out
of her," Acts 16:18. As Stephen was being stoned to death as the
first Christian martyr, he gave his testimony: "Behold, I see the heavens
opened, and the Son of Man standing on the right hand of God," Acts
7:56.

Paul repeatedly and consistently teaches the Deity of Christ. Immediately after his conversion he went into the synagogues in Damascus and "proclaimed Jesus, that He is the Son of God," Acts 9:20.
Writing to the Colossians he set forth Christ as "the image of the
invisible God," 1:15, and declared that "In Him dwelleth all the fulness
of the Godhead bodily," 2:9,—in other words, that Christ is an incarnation of the Godhead in all its fulness, a form of statement that can-

not be harmonized with the view that He is anything less than God. To the Corinthians he wrote that "God was in Christ, reconciling the world unto Himself," II Cor. 5:19. Writing to the Romans he refers to the Jews as his kinsmen, "of whom," he says, "is Christ as concerning the flesh, who is over all, God blessed for ever," 9:5,—and a scholar and theologian of such unimpeachable authority as Dr. Warfield, translating from the Greek, insists that Paul here calls Christ by the supreme name of "God over all," so that the verse should read, "of whom is Christ as concerning the flesh, who is God over all, blessed for ever."

Exhorting the Philippian Christians to follow the example of Christ in humility and service Paul wrote: "Have this mind in you which was also in Christ Jesus: who, existing in the form of God" (that is, sharing fully in the Divine nature and possessing all of the attributes and qualities that make God what He is) "counted not the being on an equality with God a thing to be grasped" (did not selfishly choose to remain exclusively in that blessed condition while men continued to be victims of sin and misery), "but emptied Himself, taking the form of a servant, being made in the likeness of men; and being found in fashion as a man, He humbled Himself, becoming obedient even unto death, yea, the death of the cross" (that is, He took into union with His Divine nature a human nature, and that, of course, without losing or modifying His Divine nature, which is perfect and immutable, became incarnate, accepted the conditions of servanthood, and then, as God clothed in human nature, offered Himself as the Substitute for His people. In fulfilling His mission He thus submitted Himself to the prescribed penalty for sin, which is suffering and death). "Wherefore also," says Paul, "God highly exalted Him" (exalted the Divine-human Person, the God-man, since not the Divine nature as such but only the human nature is capable of receiving added glory and honor), "and gave unto Him the name which is above every name; that is the name of Jesus" (the name of the God-man, as God clothed in human nature, who is the object of worship) "every knee should bow, of things in heaven and things on earth and things under the earth, and that every tongue should confess that Jesus Christ is Lord, to the glory of God the Father" (the term "Lord" being used here not merely in the sense in which men are invested with authority or dignity, but in the sense of absolute sovereignty, the New Testament writers often applying to Jesus Old Testament texts in which the term "Lord" in the Hebrew is *Adonai* or *Jahweh,* translated Jehovah), Phil. 2:5-11

The writer of the Epistle to the Hebrews ascribes Deity to Christ when he says that God, having spoken in earlier times through the prophets and in other ways, in these later days has spoken unto us "in His Son, whom He appointed Heir of all things, through whom also He made the worlds; who being the effulgence of His glory and the very image of His substance, and upholding all things by the word of His power, when He had made purification of sins, sat down on the right hand of the Majesty on high," 1:1-3. And when in John's description of the Holy City, the new Jerusalem, we are told that "the city hath no need of the sun, neither of the moon, to shine upon it: for the glory of God did lighten it, and the lamp thereof is the Lamb" (Rev. 21:23), the last two clauses, according to the usual Hebrew parallelism, are synonymous and so teach the Deity of Christ.

The constant assumption of the writers throughout the New Testament as they record the teachings and miracles and promises of Christ is that He claimed to be and was Deity. After the testimony of Christ Himself the most competent witnesses to His Person and work are those who knew Him most intimately. "Ye also bear witness," said He, "because ye have been with me from the beginning," John 15:27. And their faithfulness to their Master is attested by the records of the early Church which tells us that practically all of them sealed their witness with their own life's blood.

Furthermore, the Roman centurion who witnessed the crucifixion adds his testimony: "Truly this man was the Son of God," Mark 15:39. And even the demons, fallen beings who had known Him in a former state of existence, at His command came out of possessed persons, saying, "What have we to do with thee, thou Son of God? art thou come hither to torment us before the time?" Matt. 8:29.

Christ's resurrection from the dead is also an inescapable proof of His Deity. Both His death and His resurrection were within His own power. Concerning His life He said, "No one taketh it away from me, but I lay it down of myself. I have power to lay it down, and I have power to take it again," John 10:18. Repeatedly He predicted His resurrection from the dead: "And the Son of Man shall be delivered unto the chief priests and the scribes; and they shall ... kill Him; and after three days He shall rise again," Mark 10:33, 34; 8:31; 9:31; Luke 18:33; 24:7; Matt. 20:19; 27:63. Paul points to the resurrection as a proof of Deity, saying that thereby He "was declared to be the Son of God with power, according to the spirit of holiness, by the resurrection from the dead," Rom. 1:4. It was this which convinced Thomas, the most dubious of the disciples, so that at the mere sight of Jesus he acknowledged Him as his Lord and His God (John 20:26-29).

4. Titles Ascribed to Jesus Christ

The name "Jesus," meaning "Saviour," was the name given to our Lord in accordance with the directions of the angel to Joseph and Mary: "Thou shalt call His name JESUS; for it is He that shall save His people from their sins," Matt. 1:21; Luke 1:31. It is the Grecianized form of the Hebrew name Joshua, which means "Jehovah is salvation." It became His personal name, and as such was designed to express the special office that He was to fulfill.

The term "Christ," meaning "anointed," was our Lord's official title, although often used as a proper name. It is from the Greek *Christos,* and corresponds to the Hebrew *Mashiah,* Messiah. The kings of Israel were anointed with oil as a part of their coronation, I Sam. 9:16; 10:1; II Sam. 19:10; and the king was sometimes called "Jehovah's anointed," I Sam. 24:6. The title "Christ" is therefore a reminder that He is a King in the highest sense. And the combined name, Jesus Christ, thus means that He is the anointed Saviour.

The New Testament records make it clear that Jesus accepted from men the loftiest titles, that He permitted men to render to Him and that He received as His just due all that God requires for Himself. He forbade others to be called Rabbi or Master (Matt. 23:8-10), but accepted for Himself the title Rabbi (John 4:31; 9:2), and expressly claimed the titles Teacher and Lord: "Ye call me, Teacher, and, Lord: and ye say well; for so I am," John 13:13. When preparing for the public entry into Jerusalem He sent two of the disciples to bring a colt, and instructed them to say to any one who might question them, "The Lord hath need of him," Mark 11:3.

Throughout the New Testament Christ is called "Lord," not merely in the sense in which men are invested with authority or dignity or ownership, but in the sense of Absolute and Supreme Sovereign, Preserver, Protector. He is Lord to the Christians in precisely the same sense that Jehovah was Lord to the people of the Old Testament. A few examples are: "For there is born to you this day in the city of David a Saviour, who is Christ the Lord," Luke 2:11; "The Son of Man is Lord of the Sabbath," Luke 6:5; "That every tongue should confess that Jesus Christ is Lord, to the glory of God the Father," Phil. 2:11; "The Lord of glory," I Cor. 2:8; "The Lord is at hand," Phil. 4:5; "Have mercy on me, O Lord," Matt. 15:22; "If thou shalt confess with thy mouth Jesus as Lord, and shalt believe in thy heart that God raised Him from the dead, thou shalt be saved," Rom. 10:9. "Preaching good tidings of peace by Jesus Christ (He is Lord of all)," Acts 10:36. "Holy, holy, holy, is the Lord God, the Almighty, who was and who is and who is to come," Rev. 4:8; "Worthy art thou, our Lord and our God, to receive the glory and the honor and the power: for thou didst create all things, and because of thy will they were, and were created," Rev. 4:11; "And He hath on His garment and on His thigh a name written, King of Kings, and Lord of Lords," Rev. 19:16. Christ is acknowledged to be the Lord of all, of those who are in heaven and of those who are on the earth. To Him all creatures are to bow and acknowledge His absolute dominion. He has a right in us and an authority over us which belongs only to One who is our Creator and Redeemer.

At the beginning of his letters Paul commonly places an introductory sentence in which the conjunct name, "God our Father and the Lord Jesus Christ," is used as the Christian pariphrasis for "God." (Cp. Rom. 1:7; I Cor. 1:3; II Cor. 1:2; Gal. 1:3; etc.). It is, in fact, a formula designating the Christian's God and setting forth the Father and the Son on a plane of absolute equality. The Father and the Son are thus indissolubly knit together as essentially one; yet they are not identified, for certain activities are ascribed to one which are not shared by the other, as when, for instance, in Gal. 1:1 we read of "Jesus Christ, and God the Father, who raised Him from the dead," and in Gal. 1:3 we read of "God the Father, and our Lord Jesus Christ, who gave Himself for our sins."

In the Apostolic Benediction, "The grace of the Lord Jesus Christ, and the love of God, and the communion of the Holy Spirit, be with you all," II Cor. 13:14, the name of the Lord Jesus Christ is linked on a plane of absolute equality with that of God the Father and the Holy Spirit as the source of all spiritual blessing.

In the New Testament various names which in tne Old Testament are applied only to Deity are applied to Christ. In recording the birth of Christ Matthew applies to Him the name Immanuel, saying, "Now all this is come to pass, that it might be fulfilled which was spoken by the Lord through the prophet, saying, Behold, the virgin shall be with child, and shall bring forth a son, And they shall call his name Immanuel; which is, being interpreted, God with us," 1:22, 23; and in Is. 7:14 we read: "Behold, a virgin shall conceive, and bear a son, and shall call his name Immanuel." In the New Testament Christ is constantly set forth as our King and Redeemer and as an eternal personage. Concerning his vision of the exalted and reigning Christ John says, "And when I saw Him, I fell at His feet as one dead. And He laid His right hand upon me, saying, Fear not; I am the first and the last, and the Living One; and I was dead, and behold, I am alive for evermore, and I have the keys of death and of hades," Rev. 1:17, 18; and again, "I am the Alpha and the Omega, the first and the last, the beginning and the end," Rev. 22:13; and in Is. 44:6 we read: "Thus saith Jehovah, the King of Israel, and his Redeemer, Jehovah of hosts: I am the first, and I am the last; and besides me there is no God." We have seen that in the New Testament Jesus Christ is repeatedly called Lord. In the Old Testament the predicted Messiah is sometimes called Lord: "Jehovah saith unto my Lord, Sit thou at my right hand, Until I make thine enemies thy footstool," Ps. 110:1 (compare with Matt. 22:44, where Jesus applies this verse to Himself); and in Mal. 3:1 we read: "The Lord, whom ye seek, will suddenly come to His temple."

Dr. Wm. C. Robinson, of Columbia Theological Seminary, has pointed out that "The Greek New Testament directly applies to Jesus the name 'God' some ten or more times (John 1:1, 18 [Aleph B. C. text]; 20:28; I John 5:20; Heb. 1:8; II Peter 1:1; Acts 20:28; Rom. 9:5; II Thess. 1:12; Titus 2:13; and perhaps Acts 18:26; I Tim. 3:16). And no less significant is the phenomenon, recognized by scholars of widely differing schools, that Jesus is identified by the New Testament writers as the Lord of the Old Testament when they apply to Him Old Testament texts in which the original is written of *Adonai* or *Jahweh* (Jehovah) (Is. 40:3; Mark 1:3; Joel 2:32; Acts 2:34; Rom. 10:13; Is. 45:23; Phil. 2:10; Jer. 9:24; I Cor. 1:31; 10:17; Ps. 68:18; Eph. 4:8: Is. 2:19; II Thess. 1:9; II Sam. 3:39; II Tim. 4:14; Rev. 22:13).)"

It is to be noted, therefore, that in the New Testament Christ is called: "Lord," Phil. 2:11; "Lord of Lords," I Tim. 6:15; "King of Israel," John 1:49; "The Saviour," II Peter 1:1; "Master," Matt. 23:10; Jude 4; "Son of God," John 1:34; 20:31; "Son of Man," Matt. 17:9; "Jesus," Matt. 1:21; "Christ," Matthew 16:16; "Saviour," John 4:42; Acts 5:31; "Messiah," John 1:41; 4:25. 26; "The Lamb of God," John 1:29; "The Word," John 1:1, "The Only Begotten Son," John 3:16; "Redeemer," Gal. 3:13; "The Lord of Glory," I Cor. 2:8; "The Image of God," II Cor. 4:4; "The Effulgence of His Glory," Heb. 1:3; "The Very Image of His Substance," Heb. 1:3; "Great High Priest," Heb. 4:14; "Mediator," Heb. 12:24; "The Author of our Salvation," Heb. 2:10; "The Author and Perfector of our faith," Eph. 5:23; "The Head of the Church," Eph. 5:23; "The Head of every man," I Cor. 11:3; "The Power of God, and the Wisdom of God," I Cor. 1:24; "The Bread of Life," John 6:35; "The Living Bread," John 6:51; "The True Vine," John 15:1; "The Door," John 10:7; "The Holy and Righteous One," Acts 3:14; "The Prince of Life," Acts 3:15; "God blessed for ever," Rom. 9:5; "The Alpha and the Omega," Rev. 21:6; "The Beginning and the End," Rev. 21:6; "The

First and the Last," Rev. 1:17; "The Living One," Rev. 1:18; "The Lord God," Rev. 1:8; "My Lord and My God," John 20:28; "The One who is and who was and who is to come," Rev. 1:8; "The Almighty," Rev. 1:8; "The Holy One of God," John 6:69; "The One through whom the world was made," John 1:3, 10; "The Heir of all things," Heb. 1:2. He thus accepted from men the loftiest titles, the most exalted honor, and the most absolute devotion. No one other than God could have allowed such titles to have gone unrebuked, or indeed have sought after or applied them to Himself.

Two of these titles, "Son of God," and "Son of Man," require more extended treatment and we shall take them up in the following sections.

5. The Son of God

One of the most exalted titles applied to Jesus is that of "The Son of God." It is a divine title or name which calls attention to the dignity of His Person, particularly to His Deity, and indicates that He is fully qualified to speak to men concerning the things of God. It was this side of His nature that impressed Nathaniel when, amazed at Jesus' familiarity with his past life, he exclaimed, "Rabbi, thou art the Son of God; thou art King of Israel," John 1:49. It was against this side of His nature that the Devil attempted to throw doubt when he issued the challenge, "If thou art the Son of God, command that these stones become bread," and, "If thou art the Son of God, cast thyself down" (from the pinnacle of the temple), Matt. 4:3, 6; and it was also against this side of His nature that the demons cried out when they said, "What have we to do with thee, thou Son of God? art thou come hither to torment us before the time?" Matt. 8:29. Lazarus' death and restoration to life was especially intended "for the glory of God, that the Son of God may be glorified thereby," John 11:4. Peter's great confession, "Thou art the Christ, the Son of the living God," Matt. 16:16, was prompted by his perception of Christ's essential Deity. And John declared specifically that his purpose in writing his Gospel was, "That ye may believe that Jesus is the Christ, the Son of God; and that believing ye may have life in His name," 20:31.

In connection with an earlier treatment of the doctrine of the Trinity we have pointed out that in theological language the terms "Father" and "Son" carry with them not our occidental ideas of, on the one hand, source of being and superiority, and on the other, subordination and dependence, but rather the Semitic and oriental ideas of *likeness* or *sameness of nature* and equality of being. It is, of course, the Semitic consciousness that underlies the phraseology of Scripture, and wherever the Scriptures call Christ the "Son of God" they assert

His true and proper Deity. It signifies a unique relationship that cannot be predicated of nor shared with any creature. As any merely human son is like his father in his essential nature, that is, possessed of humanity, so Christ, the Son of God, was like His Father in His essential nature, that is, possessed of Deity. The Father and the Son, together with the Holy Spirit, are co-eternal and co-equal in power and glory, and partake of the same nature or substance. They have always existed as distinct Persons. The Father is, and always has been, as much dependent on the Son as the Son is on the Father; for self-existence and independence are properties not of the Persons within the Godhead but of the Triune God. Consequently the terms "Father" and "Son" are not at all adequate to express the full relationship which exists between the first and second Persons of the Godhead. But they are the best we have. Moreover, they are the terms used in Scripture, and besides expressing the ideas of sameness of nature they are found to be reciprocal, expressing the ideas of love, affection, trust, honor, unity and harmony,—ideas of endearment and preciousness.

Christ is the Son of God by nature; we become the sons of God by grace. He is the Son of God in His own right; we become sons of God by adoption. He has existed thus from eternity; we become sons in time as we are regenerated to a new life and have His righteousness imparted to us. This, of course, does not mean that we ever come to partake of the nature of Deity. But it does mean that we have restored to us and perfected in us that moral and spiritual likeness of God with which we were created but which became lost through sin. God is the Father of the Lord Jesus Christ in a sense in which He is the Father of none other. Jesus did, indeed, speak to the disciples about "your Father who is in heaven," but in so doing He made it clear that the term was used only in a contingent sense. Their sonship with God came through Him and was dependent on their relations with Him: "The Father Himself loveth you, because ye have loved me, and have believed that I came forth from the Father," John 16:27; or as John so beautifully points out in another place, "As many as received Him, to them gave He the right to become children of God; even to them that believe on His name," 1:12.

The Scriptures do not teach a doctrine of the universal fatherhood of God and the universal brotherhood of men. That is one of the doctrines of present-day Modernism. The Scriptures teach, not a sonship based on the natural relationship which God bears to all men because of creation, but a sonship based on a spiritual re-creation, a sonship into which man comes through faith in Christ. In the broad sense it is, of course, true that God is the Father of all men since He has

created them; but in a narrower and far more important sense He is the
Father only of those who have been regenerated and who are therefore "in Christ" in such a sense that to some extent they partake of
His holiness, those who have been "born anew" (John 3:3). "If any
man is in Christ, he is a new creature," Paul wrote to the Corinthians,
II Cor. 5:17. And to the Romans he wrote: "As many as are led by
the Spirit of God, these are sons of God," 8:14. All true Christians
are "sons of God, through faith, in Christ Jesus," Gal. 3:26. "If ye
are Christ's, then are ye Abraham's seed," and therefore "heirs according to promise," Gal. 3:29. Outside of the sphere of redemption the
term "Father" can have only a very shallow meaning; for it is only
through Christ that we can really know God: "Neither doth any know
the Father, save the Son, and he to whomsoever the Son willeth to reveal
Him," Matt. 11:27. Those who are still in sin, fallen, unregenerate
worldlings, are said to be not sons of God but *sons of the Devil*, because
basically and in principle they are like the Devil and partake of his evil
nature. They are "by nature children of wrath," Eph. 2:3. To His
opponents Jesus said, "Ye are of your father the Devil, and the lusts of
your father it is your will to do," John 8:44; and again, "I speak the
things which I have seen with my Father: and ye also do the things
which ye have heard from your father. . . . If God were your Father,
ye would love me: for I came forth and am come from God," John
8:38, 42. Paul teaches this same truth. To Elymas the sorcerer he said:
"Oh full of all guile and all villiany, thou son of the Devil, thou enemy
of all righteousness, wilt thou not cease to pervert the right ways of the
Lord," Acts 13:10.

God is Father primarily because of the relationship which He sustains to Christ the Son; and only as we are spiritually united to Christ
do we become children of God. He has "foreordained us unto adoption as sons through Jesus Christ unto Himself," Eph. 1:5. Christ was
the Son of God in such a high sense that He Himself could say, "I
and the Father are one," John 10:30; "He that hath seen me hath
seen the Father," John 14:9; "He that honoreth not the Son honoreth
not the Father," 5:23; that Paul could say that He is "the image of
the invisible God," Col. 1:15; that "God was in Christ reconciling the
world unto Himself," II Cor. 5:19; that "In Him dwelleth all the fulness of the Godhead bodily," Col. 2:9; and that the writer of the Epistle
to the Hebrews could say that He is "the effulgence of His glory, and
the very image of His substance," 1:3. The recorded discourses of
Jesus make it perfectly clear that He was continually conscious of His
Deity, that He was the Son of God in a unique sense, gazing unbrokenly

into the depths of the Divine Being, knowing the Father fully even as He was known of the Father.

That the terms "Father" and "Son" as used by Jesus and as understood by His hearers carried with them the claim to equality and identity is made clear by the response of the Jews. When after healing a man on the Sabbath Jesus said to them, "My Father worketh even until now, and I work," we are told that "The Jews sought the more to kill Him, because He not only brake the Sabbath, but also called God His own Father, making Himself equal with God," John 5:17, 18. And a little later they said, "For a good work we stone thee not, but for blasphemy; and because that thou, being a man, makest thyself God," John 10:33. It was specifically for claiming to be "the Christ, the Son of God," that He was accused of blasphemy by the high priest and sentenced to death by the Sanhedrin (Matt. 26:63-66). "We have a law, and by that law He ought to die, because He made Himself the Son of God," said the Jews, John 19:7. And Jesus did not deny, but acknowledged, the accuracy of their charge. If they had been wrong a word from Him would have set them right, and it would have been nothing short of criminal for Him to have withheld it. But certainly He did not go to His death "for a metaphor," as some one has expressed it. It was not because of a slight misunderstanding of His claims that He allowed Himself to be murdered by His enemies, but because His claims were insisted upon by Him and accurately understood and resented by the Jews that He went to the cross.

From John Calvin comes the following useful observation concerning the title, "Son of God": "As He has received from His mother that which causes Him to be called the Son of David, so He has from His Father that which constitutes Him the Son of God, and this is something distinct and different from His humanity. The Scriptures distinguish Him by two names, calling Him sometimes 'The Son of God,' sometimes 'the Son of Man.' With respect to the latter, it cannot be disputed that He is styled the 'Son of Man,' in conformity to the common idiom of the Hebrew language, because He is one of the posterity of Adam. I contend, on the other hand, that He is denominated 'the Son of God' on account of His Deity and eternal existence; because it is equally reasonable that the appellation of 'Son of God' should be referred to the Divine nature, as that that of 'son of Man' should be referred to the human nature." (*The Institute,* Vol. I, p. 442).

It is thus abundantly clear that the name "Son of God" was designed to set forth Christ in His essential nature as Deity. He who was "born of the seed of David according to the flesh" is also "declared to be the Son of God with power," Rom. 1:3, 4; and He who "as concerning the flesh" came of the Jews is also declared to be "over all, God blessed for ever," Rom. 9:5. We are, therefore, to believe in the Son as we do in the Father, and to honor the one as we do the other.

6. The Son of Man

The title that Jesus most often used when speaking of Himself, and which therefore appears to have been His favorite title, was, "Son of Man." This much discussed title, whatever else it may mean, certainly was designed to call attention to the fact that He possessed real humanity. He is the representative man. We can point to Him and say, There is real manhood. In Him human nature is seen at its perfection, functioning as was intended when it left the hands of the Creator. He is the ideal after whom all others should pattern their lives. And since He thus possessed human nature in His own Person, He is vitally related to all other members of the human race and, by Divine appointment, is capable of acting as their representative before God.

In the eighth Psalm this title is used with reference to mankind in general: "What is man, that thou art mindful of him? And the son of man, that thou visitest him?" But as applied to Jesus in the New Testament it had more than human connotations. It went back to the heavenly figure in Daniel 7:13, 14, where, prophetic of the return of Christ to heaven after the completion of His work of redemption, "there came with the clouds of heaven one like unto a Son of Man, and He came even to the Ancient of Days, and they brought Him near before Him. And there was given Him dominion, and glory, and a kingdom, that all peoples, nations, and languages should serve Him: His dominion is an everlasting dominion, which shall not pass away, and His kingdom that which shall not be destroyed." To Jewish ears, therefore, it was a clear assertion of Messiahship. And that Jesus used it with full consciousness of its significance is very evident, for He Himself said: "Then shall appear the sign of the Son of Man in heaven: and then shall all the tribes of the earth mourn, and they shall see the Son of Man coming on the clouds of heaven with power and great glory. And He shall send forth His angels with a great sound of a trumpet, and they shall gather together His elect from the four winds, from one end of heaven to the other," Matt. 24:30, 31. And in the parallel passage in Luke He says, "Even so ye also, when ye see these things coming to pass, know ye that the *kingdom of God* is nigh," 21:31.

Some New Testament scholars have called the name "Son of Man" the "most celestial" of all of Jesus' titles. The Rev. Leonard Verduin, of the Christian Reformed Church, has thrown a great deal of light on its meaning in the following paragraphs. Says he:

"The name 'Son of Man' has its origin in the heavenlies. It harks back to that supersensitive region where the Council of Redemption met. The name finds its origin in that great conference and in the subject about which it met. At that Conference, as we know, the several persons of the Holy Trinity met to discuss redemption and to draw up a redemption program. Redemption strategy was determined upon. And since the proposed program of salvation for mortal men required the incarnation of Deity it had to be determined upon which of the three persons this task logically devolved. And for it the Son was indicated. Not the Father, nor the Spirit, but the Son was to be made after the fashion of men. He was to become very man, become such by assuming human nature, by becoming 'Son of Man' in a word. And that appelation became the exclusive property of the Son henceforth. This gives us the necessary background to any fair evaluation of the name 'Son of Man.' Needless to say, a generation of thinkers that is quite careless concerning the momentous doctrine of Christ's preexistence has by its very bias of unbelief insulated itself against a proper appreciation of the name 'Son of Man'."

"Now by common consent names are chosen to draw attention to that which is unique in the bearer. A boy with unusually red hair will likely be called 'Red' or 'Sandy.' If he is unusually tall he will soon be called 'Slim,' etc. Men are not named for that which is common but for that which is unique, uncommon. And in the mind of the eternal Son of God His own uniqueness lay not in His Deity—that He had in common with the Father and the Spirit. With them He shared His ubiquity, His eternity, His omniscience, etc. But the prospect of incarnation was His and His alone. Therein lay His uniqueness in the divine economy. Is it any wonder that in that heavenly society the name 'Son of Man' was invented and applied to this prospective visitor to earth and earth-men?" (Article in *The Calvin Forum*, Dec. 1940).

It should be observed further that since the term "Son of Man" was invented in connection with His proposed visit to earth Jesus quite often uses it when speaking of His coming, or going, or coming again. "The Son of Man came to seek and to save that which was lost," Luke 19:10. "The Son of Man goeth, even as it is written of Him," Matt. 26:24. "What then if ye should behold the Son of Man ascending where He was before?" John 6:62. "In an hour that ye think not the Son of Man cometh," Matt. 24:44. "When the Son of Man shall come in His glory, and all the angels with Him," Matt. 25:31. It is very appropriately been called a "transition" name, and it thus serves not only as a reminder of His union with mankind but also of His higher origin.

7. The Pre-Existence of Christ

In a rather remarkable series of statements Jesus conveys to our minds the idea that His existence did not merely begin when He was born in Bethlehem, but that He "came" or "descended" from heaven to earth, or that He was "sent" by the Father. Very evidently if He came or descended or was sent He must have existed before He came or descended or was sent. These verses afford not only a unique testimony to His divine mission, but also to His heavenly origin, and set Him forth not only as the greatest of the sons of men but as a pre-existent Person,—in some instances as an eternal Being. Unquestionably these sayings are spoken out of a consciousness of pre-existence, and cannot be fully satisfied by any other supplement than "from heaven," or "from the Father." And particularly is this true when the title, "Son of Man" (which, as we have just seen in the preceding section, itself implies pre-existence), is used in these verses. He thus sets Himself forth as of higher than human or earthly origin, and therefore as One uniquely qualified to speak to men concerning spiritual things.

Typical verses of this kind are as follows: "The Son of Man came to seek and to save that which was lost," Luke 19:10. "The Son of Man came not to be ministered unto, but to minister, and to give His life a ransom for many," Mark 10:45. "Think not that I came to destroy the law or the prophets: I came not to destroy, but to fulfil," Matt. 5:17. "Let us go elsewhere into the next towns, that I may preach there also; for to this end came I forth," Mark 1:38. "I was not sent but unto the lost sheep of the house of Israel," Matt. 15:24. "They that are whole have no need of a physician, but they that are sick: I came not to call the righteous, but sinners," Mark 2:17. "Think not that I came to send peace on the earth: I came not to send peace, but a sword. For I came to set a man at variance against his father, and the daughter against her mother, and the daughter-in-law against her mother-in-law: and a man's foes shall be they of his own household," Matt. 10:34-36 (meaning, of course, not that the ultimate and final purpose of His coming is to stir up strife, but that when the Gospel is preached in a sinful world the first reaction is one of strife with the opposing sinful environment, and that this opposition often disrupts even the most intimate family ties). "I came out from the Father, and am come into the world: again, I leave the world, and go unto the father," John 16:28. "I know whence I came, and whither I go; but ye know not whence I came, or whither I go. . . . I am not alone, but I and the Father that sent me," John 8:14, 16. "Ye are from beneath; I am from above: ye are of this world; I am not of this world," John 8:23. "He that cometh from above is above all: he that is of the earth is of the earth, and of the earth he speaketh: He that cometh from heaven is above all. What He hath seen and heard, of that He beareth witness. . . . He whom God hath sent speaketh the words of God," John 3:31-34. "No one hath ascended into heaven, but He that descended out of heaven, even the Son of Man, who is in heaven," John 3:13. "What then if ye should behold the Son of man ascending where He was before?" John 6:62.

Furthermore, Jesus teaches not only that He existed before coming into the world, but that He has existed from eternity. "And now, Father, glorify thou me with thine own self with the glory which I had with thee before the world was," John 17:5. "For thou (Father) lovedst me before the foundation of the world," John 17:24. "Before Abraham was born, I am," John 8:58,—a statement which infers that the ground of His existence is within Himself, and which also is reminiscent of the "I Am That I am," the name by which Jehovah announced Himself to Moses in the wilderness as the self-existent, eternal God. In fact, Jesus here applies to Himself the name which since the time of Moses had been known as the name of the eternal God. And in the book of Revelation the risen and glorified Christ says of Himself, "I am the Alpha and the Omega, the first and the last, the beginning and the end," 22:13.

Thus in explicit terms Jesus teaches not only His pre-existence but His eternal pre-existence. And with this agree the other witnesses who speak in the New Testament. "After me cometh a man who is become before me: for He was before me," said His forerunner, John the Baptist, John 1:30,—not that Jesus was born earlier than John the Baptist, but that He existed earlier, and therefore stands before him in rank. We have already had occasion to refer to the Prologue of John's Gospel, where concerning the pre-incarnate Word he declares that He possessed not only pre-existence but co-eternity and co-creatorship with the Father, that in time this Word "became flesh and dwelt among us, and we beheld His glory, glory as of the only begotten from the Father, full of grace and truth."

Setting it forth as one of the maxims of fundamental religious truth, Paul says, "Faithful is the saying, and worthy of all acceptation, that Christ·Jesus came into the world to save sinners," I Tim. 1:15. Writing to the Colossians he says, "In Him were all things created, in the heavens and upon the earth, things visible and things invisible, whether thrones or dominions or principalities or powers; all things have been created through Him, and unto Him; and He is before all things, and in Him all things consist," 1:16, 17. In I Tim. 3:16 preexistence is assumed when he refers to Christ as "He who was manifested in the flesh."

The writer of the Epistle to the Hebrews says, "Jesus Christ is the same yesterday and today, yea and for ever," 13:2,—the same through every change and chance of life, the same to this generation that He has been to any past generation. And because He is thus unalterably constant, He is set forth as the Christian's support and stay, the eternal refuge of His people.

Moreover, even the Old Testament predictions in regard to the Messiah who was to come set Him forth not merely as one who would be "born" like other men, but as One who existed before He came to earth, in fact, as One whose existence extends back into eternity. The prophet Micah wrote, "But thou, Bethlehem, Ephrathah, which art little to be among the thousands of Judah, out of thee shall one come forth unto me that is to be ruler in Israel; whose goings forth are from of old, from everlasting," 5:2. And Isaiah described the promised Messiah not only as the "Wonderful Counsellor" and "Prince of Peace," but as the "Mighty God" and as the "Everlasting Father," 9:6.

In all the history of the world Jesus emerges as the only "expected" person. No one was looking for such a person as Julius Caesar, or Napoleon, or Washington, or Lincoln to appear at the time and place that they did appear. No other person has had his course foretold or his work laid out for him centuries before he was born. But the coming of the Messiah had been predicted for centuries. In fact, the first promise of His coming was given to Adam and Eve soon after their fall into sin. As time went on various details concerning His Person and work were revealed through the prophets; and at the time Jesus was born there was a general expectation through the Jewish world that the Messiah was soon to appear, even the manner of His birth and the town in which it would occur having been clearly indicated.

Thus Jesus is consistently presented as one who existed before He came to earth. He is presented as One who "descended" from heaven to earth, as One who from all eternity has shared the Father's glory,—in fact, as One who "came out from the Father" (John 16:28) and who was in the most intimate way identified with God. His own words make it clear that He presented Himself as a visitant from a higher sphere, and that He thought of His work on earth as a mission on behalf of men,— in brief, that He came with the explicit purpose of saving the "lost."

It is quite evident that the doctrine of the pre-existence of Christ is a vital factor in any proper understanding of His Person. As Dr. Samuel G. Craig has pointed out, "In our study of Jesus Christ it is of the utmost importance that we interpret His life in the light of His pre-existence. It is important, in the first place, in order that we may keep constantly before us the fact that the Incarnation was not simply the birth of a great man but rather the entering into human conditions of the only-begotten Son of God, and hence that we may ever realize that in Jesus Christ we are face to face with the God-man. It is important, in the second place, in order that we may adequately appreciate the service He has rendered for us. It is simply impossible adequately to appreciate what Jesus has done for us unless we remember that the Son of Man *came* not to be ministered unto but to minister and give His life a ransom for many." (*Jesus As He Was and Is*, p. 58).

8. The Attributes of Deity Are Ascribed to Christ

Throughout the New Testament we find that the attributes of Deity are repeatedly ascribed to Christ, and that not merely in a secondary sense such as might be predicated of a creature but in such a sense as is applicable to God alone. The following attributes are ascribed to Him:

1. HOLINESS: "Thou art the Holy One of God," John 6:69. Peter affirms that He "did no sin, neither was guile found in His mouth," I Peter 2:22. Paul refers to Him as "Him who knew no sin." II Cor. 5:21. He was "holy, guileless, undefiled, separated from sinners," says the writer of the Epistle to the Hebrews, 7:26. "I do always the things that are pleasing to Him," said Jesus, John 8:29. "Which of you convicteth me of sin?" was His challenge to His enemies, John 8:46. Even the demons bore witness that He was "the Holy One of God," Luke 4:34.

2. ETERNITY: "In the beginning was the Word," John 1:1. "Before Abraham was born, I am," John 8:58. "The glory which I had with thee (the Father) before the world was," John 17:5. "Thou (Father) lovedst me before the foundation of the world," John 17:24. "He is before all things," Col. 1:17. In the Messianic prophecies He is called the "Everlasting Father," Is. 9:6, and is said to be One "whose goings forth are from of old, from everlasting," Micah 5:2. He is indeed the King of the Ages.

3. LIFE: "In Him was life," John 1:4. "I am the way, and the truth, and the life: no one cometh unto the Father, but by me," John

14:6. "I am the resurrection, and the life," John 11:25. "For as the Father hath life in Himself, even so gave He to the Son also to have life in Himself," John 5:26.

4. IMMUTABILITY: "Jesus Christ is the same yesterday and today, yea and for ever," Heb. 13:8. "They (the heavens) shall perish; but thou continuest. . . . They shall be changed: but thou art the same," Heb. 1:11, 12.

5. OMNIPOTENCE: "All authority has been given unto me in heaven and on earth," Matt. 28:18. "All things have been delivered unto me of my Father," Matt. 11:27. "He (God the Father) put all things in subjection under His feet, and gave Him to be head over all things to the Church," Eph. 1:22. "Upholding all things by the word of His power," Heb. 1:3. "The Lord God, who is and who was and who is to come, the Almighty," Rev. 1:8. In Messianic prophecy He is foretold as the "Mighty God," Is. 9:6. He possessed power to restore the dead to life (John 11:43, 44; Luke 7:14), and he declares that the final resurrection of all men will be accomplished through His power: "The hour cometh, in which all that are in the tombs shall hear His voice, and shall come forth: they that have done good, unto the resurrection of life; and they that have done evil, unto the resurrection of judgment," John 5:28, 29.

6. OMNISCIENCE: "Thou knowest all things," John 16:30. "Jesus knowing their thoughts," Matt. 9:4. "Knew all men . . . knew what was in man," John 2:24. "Jesus knew from the beginning who they were that believed not, and who it was that should betray Him," John 6:64. "Jesus therefore, knowing all the things that were coming upon Him, went forth," John 18:4. "Christ, in whom are all the treasures of wisdom and knowledge hidden," Col. 2:3. "No one knoweth the Son, save the Father; neither doth any know the Father, save the Son," Matt. 11:27,—a declaration in which Jesus Himself implies that the personality or being of the Son is so great that only God can fully comprehend it, and that the knowledge of the Son is so unlimited that He can know God to perfection; in other words, a declaration that His knowledge is infinite. Certainly the Gospels present Jesus as endowed with absolute and unlimited knowledge and foresight. Concerning this general theme Dr. J. Ritchie Smith has said: "How well He read the heart is illustrated in the case of Nathanael, of the woman of Samaria, of Judas, and of Peter. He foresaw the future, foretold His death, His resurrection, His return. The map of history was unrolled before Him, and He traced the unfoldings of the old economy, the mighty works to be wrought by His disciples, the overthrow of Satan, the triumph of the kingdom of God. Earth and heaven, time and eternity,

God and man lay open to His view." (*Studies in the Gospel of John,*
p. 134.)

7. OMNIPRESENCE: "The only begotten Son, who is in the bosom
of the Father," John 1:18. Here John declares that although Christ
became incarnate and lived on earth His communion with the Father
nevertheless continues in the most infinite and unmodified form. He
not merely "was" with God, but still "is" with Him, in the fullest sense
of the eternal relationship intimated in John 1:1. "No one hath
ascended into heaven, but He that descended out of heaven, even the
Son of Man, who is in heaven," John 3:13. Calvin has remarked concerning this verse that He was "incarnate, but not incarcerated;" and
then he adds: "The Son of God miraculously descended from heaven,
yet in such a manner that He never left heaven; He chose to be miraculously born of the virgin, to live on the earth, and to be suspended
from the cross; and yet He never ceased to fill the universe, in the
same manner as from the beginning." (*Institutes,* I, p. 435). Christ
Himself set forth His omnipresence when He said, "Where two or
three are gathered together in my name, there am I in the midst of
them," Matt. 18:20; and again, "Lo, I am with you always, even unto
the end of the world," Matt. 28:20. Assembled with His disciples on
the Mount of Olives after His resurrection, He assured them of His
continued presence and power and declared that His influence with
them would be, not that of a dead teacher, but of a living presence.
Being thus everywhere present, He is always accessible, able to guard
and comfort His people so that no affliction or suffering but such as
He sees to be for their own good can come upon them. And a remarkable fact which appears as we read the New Testament is that after
His resurrection His living presence was more real to His disciples
than His bodily presence ever had been before His death, their conviction concerning Him then became a conquering power whereas before
His death their estimate of Him was always wavering and doubtful.
Paul teaches the omnipresence of Christ when he refers to "the fulness
of Him that filleth all in all," Eph. 1:23.

8. CREATION: "All things were made through Him: and without
Him was not anything made that hath been made," John 1:3. "The
world was made through Him," John 1:10. "In Him were all things
created, in the heavens and upon the the earth, things visible and things
invisible, whether thrones or dominions or principalities or powers;
all things have been created through Him, and unto Him; and He is
before all things, and in Him all things consist," Col. 1:16, 17. "But
of the Son He saith, Thy throne, O God, is for ever and ever. . . .
Thou, Lord, in the beginning didst lay the foundation of the earth,

and the heavens are the works of thy hands," Heb. 1 :8, 10,—the writer here applies to Christ words which in the Old Testament are spoken concerning Jehovah, and thereby sets forth His Godhead in the most absolute sense. "One Lord, Jesus Christ, through whom are all things," I Cor. 8 :6. And the writer of the Epistle to the Hebrews informs us that even now He is "upholding all things by the word of His power," 1 :3.

Thus the Scripture writers set forth the relations which Christ sustains to the universe as a whole. While it is true that in Scripture the chief emphasis is thrown on the relations which He bears to us as Savior, Master, Teacher and Example, which is, of course, the most vital aspect of His work so far as we are concerned, we must not suppose that these relations comprehend His full significance. To limit Him to these is to rob Him of what are no doubt much greater and more important relations to the remainder of the universe. His significance for the entire universe is constantly assumed throughout Scripture, although not frequently mentioned. It is just because He is the Creator and Ruler of the entire universe that He can say, "All authority hath been given unto me in heaven and on earth," and that He is fitted to be the true Saviour and Master and Teacher of men. Concerning this point Dr. Craig has said: "We are told that it is He who created this universe with all that it contains of things visible and invisible. and hence that not only the physical universe with its myriads of suns and stars but that all forms of personal life, including the most potent of angelic beings, whether they be called thrones or dominions or principalities or powers, as well as men, are indebted to Him for their existence. He is imminent in the universe today, upholding it by His power and preserving it in unity so that it remains a cosmos and does not become a chaos. Finally we are told that as all things visible and invisible, had their source in Him so they move toward Him as their final goal. Not only were all things created 'through Him,' they were also created 'unto Him,' so that He is the last as well as the first, the end as well as the beginning." (*Jesus As He Was and Is,* p. 249).

9. AUTHORITY TO FORGIVE SINS: "And Jesus seeing their faith saith unto the sick of the palsy, Son, thy sins are forgiven,"—and when some of the scribes, pointedly conscious that this prerogative belongs to God alone, reasoned inwardly, saying, "Why doth this man thus speak? He blasphemeth: who can forgive sins but one, even God?" Jesus said unto them, "That ye may know that the Son of Man hath authority on earth to forgive sins (He saith to the sick of the palsy), I say unto thee, Arise, take up thy bed, and go unto thy house. And he arose, and straightway took up his bed, and went forth before them all," Mark

2:5-12. In instituting the Lord's Supper Jesus made it plain that the "remission of sins" was to be accomplished through His shed blood, Matt. 26:28. Not only does He calmly assume the authority to forgive sin in others, but asserts that in His own person and as their substitute He bears the penalty of sin for them. After His resurrection He declared to the disciples that "repentance and remission of sins should be preached in His name unto all the nations," Luke 24:47. John the Baptist bore witness to Him as "the Lamb of God, that taketh away the sin of the world," John 1:29. Peter declares that "every one that believeth on Him shall receive remission of sins," Acts 10:43. Paul refers to Him as "the Son of His love; in whom we have our redemption, the forgiveness of our sins," Col. 1:14. And John declares that "the blood of Jesus His Son cleanseth us from all sin," I John 1:7. He could forgive the sins of others because He Himself was to pay the price of that absolution.

To assume the authority to forgive sins is to assume one of the prerogatives of God. And to assume that authority unjustly is, of course, a very heinous offense. This, Paul tells us, is the offense of "the man of sin," "the son of perdition," who, he adds, "opposeth and exalteth himself against all that is called God or that is worshipped; so that he sitteth in the temple of God, setting himself forth as God," II Thess. 2:3, 4. But Christ claims this authority, and in doing so very definitely sets Himself forth as God. It is interesting to note just here that the Unitarians, who place a disproportionate emphasis on Christ's example to the detriment of His saviourhood, refuse to follow His example when He sets Himself over against His disciples and all others as the One who forgives sins.

10. THE AUTHOR OF SALVATION; THE OBJECT OF FAITH: "He that believeth on the Son hath eternal life; but he that obeyeth not the Son shall not see life, but the wrath of God abideth on him," John 3:36. "Believe on the Lord Jesus, and thou shalt be saved," Acts 16:31. "Believe in God, believe also in me," John 14:1. "For God so loved the world, that He gave His only begotten Son, that whosoever believeth on Him should not perish, but have eternal life. . . . He that believeth on Him is not judged: he that believeth not hath been judged already, because he hath not believed on the name of the only begotten Son of God," John 3:16, 18. "I am the resurrection, and the life: he that believeth on me, though he die, yet shall he live; and whosoever liveth and believeth on me shall never die," John 11:26. Faith in Christ is involved in, and in fact is declared to be identical with, faith in God: "And Jesus cried and said, He that believeth on me, believeth not on me, but on Him that sent me. And He that beholdeth me beholdeth Him

that sent me," John 12:44, 45. "They said therefore unto Him, What must we do that we may work the works of God? Jesus answered and said unto them, This is the work of God, that ye believe on Him whom He hath sent. . . . I am the bread of life: he that cometh unto me shall not hunger, and he that believeth on me shall never thirst. . . . This is the will of my Father, that every one that beholdeth the Son, and believeth on Him, should have eternal life; and I will raise him up at the last day," John 6:28-40. "I am the vine, ye are the branches: he that abideth in me, and I in him, the same beareth much fruit: for apart from me ye can do nothing. If a man abide not in me, he is cast forth as a branch, and is withered; and they gather them, and cast them into the fire, and they are burned," John 15:5, 6. "I am the door; by me if any man enter in, he shall be saved," John 10:9. "My sheep hear my voice, and I know them, and they follow me: and I give unto them eternal life," John 10:27, 28. "And this is life eternal, that they should know thee the only true God, and Him whom thou didst send, even Jesus Christ," John 17:3. "Come unto me, all ye that labor and are heavy laden, and I will give you rest," Matt. 11:28. "Be thou faithful unto death, and I will give thee the crown of life," Rev. 2:10. "And in none other is there salvation: for neither is there any other name under heaven, that is given among men, wherein we must be saved," Acts 4:12. "No one knoweth the Son, save the Father; neither doth any know the Father, save the Son, and he to whomsoever the Son willeth to reveal Him," Matt. 11:27. "Every one therefore who shall confess me before men, him will I also confess before my Father who is in heaven. But whosoever shall deny me before men, him will I also deny before my Father who is in heaven," Matt. 10:32. "Except ye believe that I am He, ye shall die in your sins," John 8:24. Even the name "Jesus" is not of human but of divine origin, and is the equivalent of the Hebrew "Joshua," meaning "Saviour." Even before He came into the world the purpose of His mission was thus designated: "And thou shalt call His name Jesus; for it is He that shall save His people from their sins," Matt. 1:21. And near the close of his Gospel the Apostle John states specifically his purpose in writing: "These (things) are written that ye may believe that Jesus is the Christ, the Son of God; and that believing ye may have life in His name," John 20:31.

These are indeed exceedingly great and precious promises. Certainly they make clear that faith in Christ is necessary for salvation, and that apart from Him there is no salvation. It is impossible for any one to make more stupendous claims than Jesus makes concerning His own Person and His influence over the lives of others. As Dr. Charles Hodge has said, "It is obvious that the infinite God Himself can neither promise nor give anything greater or higher than Christ gives to His people. To Him they are taught to look as the source of all blessing, the giver of every good and perfect gift. There is no more comprehensive prayer in the New Testament than that with which Paul closes his epistle to the Galatians: 'The grace of our Lord Jesus Christ be with your spirit.' His favor is our life, which it could not be if He were not our God." (*Systematic Theology*, I, p. 503).

11. PRAYER AND WORSHIP ARE ASCRIBED TO JESUS: It is universally acknowledged that God alone can hear and answer prayer, and that the worship of anything less than Deity is idolatry. Yet Jesus repeatedly sets Himself forth not only as the Revealer of God but as the object of worship. "Whatsoever ye shall ask in my name, that will I do," John 14:13. "If ye shall ask anything of the Father, He will give it you in my name. Hitherto ye have asked nothing in my name: ask, and ye shall receive, that your joy may be made full," John 16:23, 24. We read that on numerous occasions Jesus did receive worship while on earth. The Wise-men, having been divinely guided to the Christ-child, when they saw Him, "fell down and worshipped Him," Matt. 2:11. After Jesus had come to the disciples walking on the water, "they that were in the boat worshipped Him, saying, Of a truth thou art the Son of God," Matt. 14:33. Concerning the blind man whose sight was restored when he washed in the pool of Siloam it is said, "And he worshipped Him," John 9:38. On another occasion a certain Canaanitish woman "came and worshipped Him, saying, Lord, help me," Matt. 15:25. When confronted with the visible proof of Christ's resurrection, "Thomas answered and said unto Him, My Lord and my God," John 20:28,—a direct ascription of Deity to Christ, and since it went unrebuked it was the equivalent of an assertion of Deity on His part. After the resurrection the disciples went into Galilee, to the place where Jesus had appointed them, "And when they saw Him, they worshipped Him," Matt. 28:17. Luke says that at the time of the ascension, "He parted from them, and was carried up into heaven. And they worshipped Him," 24:51, 52. It is not His teachings nor the principles that He set forth, but He Himself that is the object of faith in religion. On numerous occasions Jesus accepted such worship as perfectly proper. Never did He reject it as improper or as misdirected. Promising that He will hear and answer prayer, that where two or three are gathered together in His name there He will be in the midst of them, and that He will be with His people always, even unto the end of the world, He laid direct claim to Deity and set Himself forth as the adequate supply of all of the spiritual needs of those who trust in Him.

With these words of Jesus agree, of course, all of the New Testament writers, the apostolic and the post-apostolic Church. Without exception they accord Him the honor and worship that is due to God alone. "That all may honor the Son, even as they honor the Father. He that honoreth not the Son honoreth not the Father that sent Him," said the Apostle John 5:23. Stephen died, "calling upon the Lord, and saying, Lord Jesus, receive my spirit," Acts 7:59. In answer to the most important question that man can ask, "What must I do to be saved?" Paul replied, "Believe on the Lord Jesus, and thou shalt be saved," Acts 16:31. "Confess with thy mouth Jesus as Lord," Rom. 10:9. "Whosoever shall call upon the name of the Lord shall be saved," Rom. 10:13. "That in the name of Jesus every knee should bow . . . and that every tongue should confess that Jesus Christ is Lord, to the glory of God the Father," Phil. 2:10, 11. "Let all the angels of God worship Him," says the writer of the Epistle to the Hebrews, 1:6. Peter refers to Him as "our Lord and Saviour Jesus Christ," II Peter 3:18. In the book of Revelation we read, "Worthy is the Lamb that hath been slain to receive the power, and riches, and wisdom, and might, and honor, and glory, and blessing. . . . Unto Him that sitteth on the throne, and unto the Lamb, be the blessing, and the honor, and the glory, and the dominion, for ever and ever," 5:12, 13.

At the beginning of each of Paul's letters we find a prayer in which he couples together on a plane of complete equality the names "God our Father" and "the Lord Jesus Christ" as the common source from which the gifts of grace and peace are sought. Yet to Paul there were not two objects of worship, nor two sources of blessing, but one. In I Cor. 8:4-6 he calls attention to the fact that we know that "there is no God but one." And the Apostolic Benediction—"The grace of the Lord Jesus Christ, and the love of God, and the communion of the Holy Spirit, be with you all," II Cor. 13:14, which is a prayer addressed to Christ for His grace, to the Father for His love, and to the Holy Spirit for His fellowship—is designed to exhibit at once the unity and the distinctness of the three Persons of the Trinity. On this formula, as in that of baptism, the Deity, and consequently the equality, of each of the Persons of the Godhead is taken for granted; and no other interpretation is rationally possible except that which the Church has held down through the ages, namely, that God exists in three Persons and that these three Persons are one in substance and equal in power and glory.

Consequently, when we compare these verses in which prayer and worship are ascribed to Christ with verses in which the unity of God and His exclusive right to the worship of men are set forth, such as,

"Look unto me, and be ye saved, all the ends of the earth; for I am God, and there is none else," Is. 45:22; "We know that . . . there is no God but one," 1 Cor. 8:4; and, "Thus saith the Lord, Cursed is the man that trusteth in man, and that maketh flesh his arm," Jer. 17:5, together with the repeated condemnation of idolatry, we are faced with this dilemma: Either the Christian doctrine of the Deity of Christ is true, or the Scriptures are self-contradictory; either the Scriptures recognize more Gods than one, or Christ, together with the Father and the Holy Spirit, is that one God.

Thus throughout the New Testament Christ is everywhere set forth as the proper object of prayer and worship. The relation which He sustains to His people is that which God alone can sustain to rational creatures. As Dr. Warfield has well said, "To the writers of the New Testament the recognition of Jesus as Lord was the mark of a Christian; and all their religious emotions turned on Him. . . . To the heathen observers of the early Christians, their most distinguishing characteristic, which differentiated them from all others, was that they sang praises to Christ as God." (*Christology and Criticism,* p. 372). And Dr. Hodge says: "Christ is the God of the Apostles and early Christians, in the sense that He is the object of all their religious affections. They regarded Him as the person to whom they specially belonged; to whom they were responsible for their moral conduct; to whom they had to account for their sins; for the use of their time and talents; who was ever present with them, dwelling in them, controlling their inward, as well as their outward life; whose love was the animating principle of their being; in whom they rejoiced as their present joy and as their everlasting portion. This recognition of their relation to Christ as their God, is constant and pervading, so that the evidence of it cannot be gathered up and stated in a polemic and didactic form. But every reader of the New Testament to whom Christ is a mere creature, however exalted, must feel himself to be out of communion with the Apostles and apostolic Christians, who avowed themselves and were universally recognized by others as being the worshippers of Christ. They knew that they were to stand before His judgment seat; that every act, thought, and word of theirs, and of every man who shall ever live, was to lie open to His omniscient eye; and that on His decision the destiny of every human soul was to depend. . . . True religion in their view consists not in the love or reverence of God, merely as the infinite Spirit, the Creator and Preserver of all things, but in the knowledge and love of Christ." (*Systematic Theology,* I, 498).

12. JUDGMENT OF ALL MEN: The idea of final judgment occupies a prominent place in the teaching of Jesus. But not only did He empha-

size the thought of judgment. He taught that He Himself is to be the Judge, and that as such He will pass on the merits and demerits of all men, assigning to each individual his eternal destiny. "For neither doth the Father judge any man," said Jesus, "but He hath given all judgment unto the Son . . . for the hour cometh, in which all that are in the tombs shall hear His voice, and shall come forth; they that have done good, unto the resurrection of life; and they that have done evil, unto the resurrection of judgment," John 5:22-29. In the great eschatological discourse in the twenty-fifth chapter of Matthew He pictures Himself as the final Judge of all the nations and as the "King": "But when the Son of Man shall come in His glory, and all the angels with Him, then shall He sit on the throne of His glory: and before Him shall be gathered all the nations: and He shall separate them one from another, as the shepherd separateth the sheep from the goats; and He shall set the sheep on His right hand, but the goats on the left. Then shall the King say unto them on His right hand, Come ye blessed of my Father, inherit the kingdom prepared for you from the foundation of the world. . . . Then shall He say also unto them on the left hand, Depart from me, ye cursed, into the eternal fire which is prepared for the Devil and his angels. . . . And these shall go away into eternal punishment: but the righteous into eternal life," vss. 31-46. Even in the early part of His ministry, as recorded in the Sermon on the Mount, Jesus pictures Himself as the Lord and Judge who determines human destiny: "Not every one that sayeth unto me, Lord, Lord, shall enter into the kingdom of heaven; but he that doeth the will of my Father who is in heaven. Many will say unto me in that day, Lord, Lord, did we not prophesy in thy name, and by thy name cast out demons, and by thy name do many mighty works? And then will I profess unto them, I never knew you: depart from me, ye that work iniquity," Matt. 7:21-23. Peter testifies that "this is He who is ordained of God to be the Judge of the living and the dead," Acts 10:42. And Paul says, "We must all be made manifest before the judgment-seat of Christ; that each one may receive the things done in the body, according to what he hath done, whether it be good or bad," II Cor. 5:10. Furthermore, it is generally acknowledged that the New Testament not only expresses the beliefs of those who wrote it, but that it also directly and indirectly bears witness to the beliefs of the early Christian community as a whole; and there is scarcely any better witness to the profound impression that Jesus made on the early Christian community than this, that they accepted His claims and trusted in Him even when He claimed to be the Judge of the world.

Thus we find that throughout the whole range of His activity Jesus does not hesitate to lay His hands on the highest prerogatives of Deity. He claims for Himself, and others readily ascribe to Him, all of the essential attributes of Deity: holiness, eternity, life, immutability, omnipotence, omniscience, omnipresence, creation, authority to forgive sins, the power to save the souls of men, the right to receive prayer and worship, and the authority to pass final judgment on all men. He promises to be to men all that God can be, and to do for them all that God can do, and so to be God in a more ultimate sense than He is man. To the Unitarians and Modernists who deny the Deity of Christ but who claim to accept Him as a moral teacher it should be perfectly evident that His authority as an ethical teacher stands or falls with His claims to possess the attributes of Deity and to be the object of worship. For if as a mere man He asked and received worship from other men and so led them into idolatry, how can He be considered an authority in teaching men the way to please God? How can we eulogize Him as proclaimer of the Beatitudes and the Golden Rule and at the same time condemn Him for usurping the prerogatives which belong to God alone? It is utterly impossible to accept Christ as a great teacher and yet deny His Deity. We can feel nothing but indignation toward those so-called leaders in the Church who, while rendering lip service to Christ, reject His Deity and criticize irreverently the inspired records of His Person and work. The alternative is clear: Either Jesus is God, or He is not good. Either He is supernatural or sub-normal. Either He was the Messiah as He claimed to be, or He was the greatest imposter that ever walked this earth. Either He possessed and still possesses power to save men, or He has succeeded in perpetuating a fraud which through the ages has victimized innumerably more people than has any other false system.

It is superabundantly clear that a merely human Jesus such as is imagined by the Unitarians and Modernists—a mere man who mistakenly thought of himself as the Messiah possessed of supernatural power, rising from the dead, and sitting as judge over all peoples and nations—could never have made the impression on his followers that the historical Jesus made, and could never have become the source of the stream of religious influence which we call Christianity. The assumption that a deluded fanatic or a deliberate imposter could have given the world what is incomparably the loftiest moral and spiritual system that it ever received is simply ridiculous. "Who is the liar but he that denieth that Jesus is the Christ? This is the antichrist, even he that denieth the Father and the Son. Whosoever denieth the Son the same hath not the Father; he that confesseth the Son hath the

Father also," I John 2:22, 23. No one who is familiar with Scripture evidence and who knows the influence that Christianity has had throughout the world during the past twenty centuries can reasonably deny that Christ was what He claimed to be, truly Divine and truly the Saviour of the world.

9. Jesus' Life the Fulfillment of a Divine Plan

As we study the portrait of Jesus as it is presented in the four Gospels there is impressed upon us the teaching that He came to earth on a specific mission, and that His whole life was lived and His work of redemption was accomplished in accordance with a divinely predetermined plan. At least from the outset of the public ministry that plan lay before His mind in clear outline. He had no time to lose, yet He was never in a hurry. He was never the victim but always the master of circumstance. Unswerved by the opposition of men, He went unflinchingly forward with the work that had been ordained for Him in the counsels of eternity. His whole life was governed by a divine "must" or "necessity." "I must preach the good tidings of the kingdom of God to the other cities also: for therefore was I sent," Luke 4:43, said He early in His ministry. Mark tells us that "He began to teach them, that the Son of Man must suffer many things, and be rejected by the elders, and the chief priests, and the scribes, and be killed, and after three days rise again," 8:31. And on the resurrection morning the angel reminded the women that during His public ministry Jesus had foretold these very things. In discussing His preexistence we have already cited verses which teach that He "came" or "was sent" to perform a specific mission. Particularly were the events concerned with His going out of the world a matter of Divine necessity. His final journey to Jerusalem, His rejection by the chief priests and elders, Judas' betrayal, His arrest, sufferings, death by crucifixion, and His resurrection on the third day, were not merely predicted but were presented as necessary in the fulfillment of His mission. And after His resurrection He said to the disciples: "These are my words which I spake unto you, while I was yet with you, that all things must needs be fulfilled, which are written in the law of Moses, and the prophets, and the psalms, concerning me. Then opened He their minds, that they might understand the Scriptures; and he said unto them, Thus it is written, that the Christ should suffer, and rise again from the dead the third day; and that repentance and remission of sins should be preached in His name unto all the nations, beginning from Jerusalem." Luke 24:44-47.

For a Divine Person to undertake such a mission involved humiliation at every point. Not only was there humiliation in the poverty, weariness and hunger which He endured, in the persistent opposition which was carried on by His opponents, in the public rejection of Him by the rulers in Church and State, and in His final suffering, death and burial. In the first place it involved deep humiliation for a Divine Person to submit Himself to human birth, to exist as a helpless babe, and to experience for a period of thirty-three years the whole series of limitations and weaknesses to which human nature is subject. Yet His mission is represented as being in every step and stage of it voluntary and as having been carried through to complete fulfillment. Every suggestion of escape from it, whether by the use of His supernatural powers for personal gratification, or of evading or lessening His suffering, was treated by Him as a temptation from the Devil. He came into the world with the express purpose of making an atonement for sin through His own suffering and death; and the events which led up to that climax were determined in their precise order and time not for Him but by Him.

"Determining all things, determined by none," says Dr. Warfield, "the life He actually lived, leading up to the death He actually died, is in the view of the Evangelists precisely the life which from the beginning He intended to live, ending in precisely the death in which, from the beginning, He intended this life to issue, undeflected by so much as a hair's breadth from the straight path He had from the start marked out for Himself in the fullest prevision and provision of all the so-called chances and changes which might befall Him. Not only were there no surprises in life for Jesus and no compulsions; there were not even 'influences,' as we speak of 'influences' in a merely human career. The mark of this life, as the Evangelists depict it, is its calm and quiet superiority to all circumstances and conditions, and to all the varied forces which sway other lives; its prime characteristics were voluntariness and independence. Neither His mother, nor His brethren, nor His disciples, nor the people He came to serve, nor His enemies bent on His destruction, nor Satan himself with his temptations, could move Him one step from His chosen path. When men seemed to prevail over Him they were but working His will; the great 'No one taketh my life away from me! I have power to lay it down, and I have power to take it again' (John 10:18), is but the enunciation for the supreme act of the principle that governs all His movements. His own chosen pathway ever lay fully displayed before His feet; on it His feet fell quietly, and they found the way always unblocked. What He did, He came to do; and He carried out His programme with unwavering purpose and indefectible certitude." (*Biblical Doctrines,* p. 74).

Certainly the Gospel writers present the suffering and death of Christ not as an accident or calamity, but as an achievement, an accomplishment. At the time of the Transfiguration Moses and Elijah appeared to Jesus and "spake of His decease which He was about to accomplish at Jerusalem," Luke 9:31. "I have a baptism to be baptized with; and how am I straitened till it be accomplished," Luke 12:50, said He with reference to the ordeal which lay ahead. When the time came for Him to suffer God measured to Him the contents of the cup, and determined what He should endure. He, not His enemies, set the date of His death. Strange and incredible though His crucifixion and death seemed to the disciples, it was all according to plan, designed to become the ground of forgiveness for men, the doorway into a new and abiding kingdom of righteousness and life.

In the book of Acts this same emphasis on the sovereignty and over-ruling providence of God as it relates to the events of Jesus' life is set forth clearly and strongly. The crucifixion, which is beyond doubt the most sinful event in all the history of the world, is even declared to have been fore-ordained. "For of a truth in this city against thy holy servant Jesus, whom thou didst anoint, both Herod and Pontius Pilate, with the Gentiles and the people of Israel, were gathered together, to do whatsoever thy hand and thy counsel fore-ordained to come to pass," Acts 4:27, 28. And further: "Him being delivered up by the determinate counsel and foreknowledge of God, ye by the hands of lawless men did crucify and slay," Acts 2:23; "The things which God foreshadowed by the mouth of all the prophets, that His Christ should suffer, He thus fulfilled," Acts 3:18; "For they that dwelt in Jerusalem, and their rulers, because they knew Him not, nor the voice of the prophets which are read every Sabbath, fulfilled them in condemning Him. And though they found no cause of death in Him, yet asked they of Pilate that He should be slain. And when they had fulfilled all things that were written of Him, they took Him down from the tree, and laid Him in a tomb," Acts 13:27-29.

But while these things were foreordained and predicted, they were carried out by agents who acted by their own free choice and who were therefore fully responsible for what they did. Those who abused Jesus were ignorant of the fact that they were laying on Him precisely the burden of suffering that God had ordained that His Christ should bear. Hence through all this we see the sovereignty of God marvelously displayed in that the actions of Christ's enemies, sinful though they were because done with evil motives, were overruled for the redemption of the world.

There is, of course, no basis whatsoever for the Modernistic view that Jesus first aimed at a temporal kingdom only to abandon the idea when the people failed to respond. The facts are that, first, at the very beginning of His ministry, He repudiated temporal power in the temptations immediately after His baptism; and, secondly, in His earliest preaching, particularly in the Sermon on the Mount, the requirements for membership in His kingdom were spiritual, namely faith and repentance.

Furthermore, in this connection it is important to notice the air of authority with which Jesus spoke. There had been many prophets in Israel who prefaced their words with "Thus saith the Lord," and then proceeded to speak God's word to the people sternly and uncompromisingly. But Jesus went much farther. He did not refer to an authority outside of Himself but, placing Himself in the relation of God to His people, spoke in His own name and as the final authority. In the Sermon on the Mount He spoke as the sovereign Law-Giver, and proceeded to elaborate more fully or to modify the word of God as given in the Old Testament. Repeatedly His commands are equated with the law of God: "Ye have heard that it was said . . . But I say unto you . . ." Those who are persecuted for His sake are equated with the prophets who suffered for the cause of God, Matt. 5:11, 12. He assumed the role of the final judge in admitting people into, or in excluding them from, the kingdom of heaven: "Not every one that saith unto me, Lord, Lord shall enter into the kingdom of heaven; but he that doeth the will of my Father who is in heaven. Many will say unto me in that day, Lord, Lord, did we not prophesy in thy name, and by thy name cast out demons, and by thy name do many mighty works? And then will I profess unto them, I never knew you: depart from me, ye that work iniquity," Matt. 7:21-23. We are told that at the conclusion of the Sermon on the Mount "the multitudes were astonished at His teaching: for He taught them as one having authority, and not as their scribes," Matt. 7:28, 29. He assumed authority over the sacred ordinances of Israel, not only over the law but also over the temple and the Sabbath; "One greater than the temple is here ... The Son of Man is Lord of the Sabbath," Matt. 12:6, 8. To the disciples He said, "Heaven and earth shall pass away, but my words shall not pass away," Matt. 24:35. The men of Nineveh and the queen of the south are to rise up in the judgment and condemn that generation because He, the greater than Jonah who preached to the Ninevites and than Solomon whose glories attracted the queen of Sheba, was present among them and had given them greater opportunities than had been given to any former generation. For us who are accustomed to think of the law, the temple and the Sabbath in the light of New Testament teaching and to look to Jesus as our divine Master, it is hard to realize how revolutionary all of this must have sounded to the orthodox Jew.

While we are told that "the Son of Man came not to be ministered unto, but to minister, and to give His life a ransom for many," Matt. 20:28, we are to note that His manner of behaviour throughout the period of his early life was distinctly not that of a servant. He claimed and received obedience and reverence, and His followers recognized Him as their Master and Lord. We have already seen that He applied to Himself and accepted from others the highest titles. Even in this saying the title "Son of Man" and the assertion that He "came" on a particular mission sets Him apart as a transcendent Being. It was not the *manner* of His earthly life, but the mere *fact* that He, the Heavenly One, had become incarnate and subjected Himself to the limitations of earth that needed explanation. And in this verse He gives that explanation, which was that He might render a particular service for His people in redeeming them from the power of sin.

There can be no doubt but that in His teaching Jesus presented Himself not as one needing salvation but as the Saviour of men, not as a member of the Church but as the head of the Church, not as the example but as the object of faith, not merely as a suppliant praying to God but as the one to whom prayer is to be made, not merely as a teacher of men but as their sovereign Lord. If Jesus was only a man, not essentially different from the rest of us, then, of course, there would be no reason why we should accept His statements as binding on our conscience. In that case we would be warranted in classing Him along with Socrates, Plato, Confucius, etc., as one of the world's wisest and most influential teachers. But if He was the Person He claimed to be, Deity incarnate, He has the fullest right to speak to us in this authoritative tone and we do but show ordinary common sense when we heed His voice as the voice of God.

10. The Miracles of Jesus

ANOTHER special proof of the Deity of Christ is that afforded by His miracles. A miracle may be defined as an event in the external world, wrought by the immediate power of God, and designed to accredit a message or a messenger. It is, in short, an appearence of the supernatural within the realm of the natural. The miracles wrought by Jesus differed from those wrought by the prophets or the apostles in that they were wrought by His own inherent power rather than by power delegated to Him. When the prophets or the apostles wrought miracles they expressly disclaimed that it was by any power within themselves. When the waters of the Red Sea were divided Moses ascribed the work to God (Ex. 14:13), as also did Joshua (Joshua 3:5), Elijah (I Kings 18:36), and the other prophets when similar marvelous works were performed; and in the New Testament when Peter and John had healed the lame man at the door of the temple Peter very quickly met the curiosity of the crowd with these words: "Why marvel ye at this man? or why fasten ye your eyes on us, as though by our own power or godliness we had made him to walk?" Acts 3:12, and when at Lystra Paul healed a lame man and the multitudes were ready to offer sacrifice to him and Barnabas they sprang forward and confessed themselves to be "men of like passions" with them and gave God the glory (Acts 14:15). But when Jesus healed the sick, or cast out demons, or raised the dead, or calmed the raging sea, it was by the exercise of His own limitless power. "The works that I do in my Father's name, these bear witness of me," said He to the Jews in Jerusalem, John 10:25. "If I do not the works of my Father, believe me not. But if I do them, though ye believe not me, believe the works; that ye may know and understand that the Father is in me, and I in the Father," John 10:37, 38. "If I had not done among them the works which none other did, they had not had sin; but now have they both seen and hated both me and my Father," John 15:24. When the disciples of John the Baptist came to ask if He were the Messiah He did not give them a yes or no answer but, letting the evidence speak for itself, said: "Go tell John the things which ye hear and see: the blind receive their sight, and the lame walk, the lepers are cleansed, and the deaf hear, and the dead are raised up, and the poor have good tidings preached to them," Matt. 11: 4, 5. Since the laws of nature have been ordained of God they can be changed or suspended only by Him. And in every instance where Jesus exercised that power He manifested His glory and thus gave visible proof of His Deity to those who had eyes to see.

The number of miracles worked by Jesus was undoubtedly large; for while only about thirty-five or forty are recorded—these being given as examples which showed His power in healing diseases which were incurable so far as human help was concerned, in raising the dead, in demonstrating His power over the forces of nature, etc.,—there are occasional blanket statements to the effect that "Jesus went about in all Galilee, teaching in their synagogues, and preaching the Gospel of the kingdom, and healing all manner of disease, and all manner of sickness among the people," Matt. 4:23; "And when the sun was setting, all they that had any sick with divers diseases brought them unto Him; and He laid His hands on every one of them, and healed them," Luke 4:40. See also Matt. 4:24; 15:30; etc. Hence for a time disease and death were reduced to a minimum throughout the land,—a blessing which in itself, because of the almost complete lack of medicines and surgical skill in that day, must have meant a radical change in the life of the nation.

But more important, of course, than the miracles wrought by Jesus was His teaching, which in its insight and its foresight was as supernatural as were His miracles and manifested His Deity as clearly as did they. Moreover, it was with authority, very much unlike that of the scribes and Pharisees. The net result of both His teaching and His miracles was that His fame spread through all parts of the country, even to such an extent that He could not openly enter into the cities because of the multitudes which thronged about Him. And that, in turn, rendered all the more heinous and inexcusable the opposition of the scribes and Pharisees.

That the miracles of Jesus were designed to prove His Deity and to inspire faith on the part of the people, and that they did have exactly that effect on unprejudiced minds, is clearly stated in the Gospel records. "This beginning of His signs did Jesus in Cana of Galilee, and manifested His glory; and His disciples believed on Him," John 2:11. Mark records that "the common people heard Him gladly," 12:37. Luke says that after healing a leper early in His ministry "great multitudes came together to hear," 5:15, and Mark adds that "they came to Him from every quarter," 1:45. The man whose eyes were opened after he washed in the pool of Siloam rebuked the unbelief of the Pharisees with these words: "Why, herein is the marvel, that ye know not whence He is, and yet He opened mine eyes. . . . Since the world began it was never heard that any one opened the eyes of a man born blind. If this man were not from God, He could do nothing," John 9:30-33. When Lazarus was raised from the dead "many of the Jews, who came to Mary and beheld that which He did, believed on Him," John 11:45. Thomas, the most skeptical of all the disciples, when confronted with the resurrection body of Jesus, was fully convinced and cried out, "My Lord and my God," John 20:28. Certainly nothing less than this conclusion, as also the conclusion to which Peter came, "Thou art the Christ, the Son of the living God," Matt. 16:16, can explain the miracles of the New Testament. Jesus Himself marvelled that any people could see these mighty works which so wonderfully displayed the limitless power and wisdom and love of God and still not believe (Mark 6:1-6), and in burning language He foretold the judgments which were to be visited on the cities that rejected these signs (Matt. 10:1-15; Luke 10:1-15).

The miracles of Jesus are, of course, an integral part of the New Testament record. They cannot be rejected without destroying the credibility of the entire record. The problem raised is not merely that of the bare possibility of supernatural works, but that of the supernatural Person of Jesus and His redemptive work, plus miracles. We very readily admit that if we were to hear of even one such event having been performed by a mere man anywhere in the world today we would not believe it. The absolutely wrong way to study the miracles is to look at them as detached and isolated happenings having no connection with any plan of redemption. If Christ was what He declared Himself to be, Deity incarnate, living a perfectly normal yet sinless life in this world and giving Himself up to suffer and die in man's stead and for his sin, then the working of miracles as a means of accrediting His Person and message would appear to have been a most natural and normal accomplishment for such a life. In fact, we can hardly conceive of God working out such a plan of redemption without just such displays of supernatural power as are recorded in the Gospels. The miracles are, as it were, sparks emitted by the fires within. Nowhere was this more convincingly displayed than in the Transfiguration, at which time the limitations of earth were partially removed and the glory of the Divine Christ shone out through the veil of flesh. We can no more separate the miraculous and the non-miraculous elements in the Bible than we can separate the body and soul in man. A Bible without a supernatural Christ and supernatural works would be like a temple without God. Hence, the question, Did the miracles really happen? is subordinate to the questions, Who was Jesus? and, What was the nature of His work? If we get those questions settled correctly we shall have no difficulty in believing the miracles.

11. Importance of Belief in the Deity of Christ

The Deity of Christ is thus taught in Scripture so explicitly and repeatedly that the question is settled for all those who accept the Bible as the word of God. There can be no question but that Jesus Himself as He is portrayed in the New Testament records presented Himself as God incarnate. Nor is there any doubt but that the writers of the New Testament personally held this same high estimate of Him and worshipped Him as God, or that the Church in all ages in all its great branches, whether Roman Catholic, Greek Catholic, Lutheran, Reformed, Presbyterian, Episcopal, Methodist, Baptist, or Congregational, as its faith has been expressed through its creeds and hymns and devotional writings, has likewise conceived of Him. And throughout the ages the great mass of those who have read the New Testament have come to the same conclusion.

In view of this great mass of evidence we are completely unable to understand how any fair-minded person can rise up and say, as do the Unitarians and Modernists, that Christ was not Deity, or that He did not claim Deity. In fact, we must go farther and say that such opposition appears to be based on nothing other than blind opposition and a determination not to accept that evidence no matter how clear and strong it may be. Any denial of the Deity of Christ, together with the implication that He was merely a great teacher or prophet, gives one a viewpoint other than that from which the Scriptures are written and makes it impossible for him to comprehend the system of truth that is revealed in Scripture. Such denial throws one out of harmony with the great Source of wisdom and truth, which is God, and causes him to attempt to explain intellectually that which can only be discerned spiritually.

The pre-eminent importance of the doctrine of the Deity of Christ in the Christian system is shown by the fact that this is the test by which we are to distinguish between true and false prophets, between spirits which are of God and spirits which are not of God. The Apostle John, after giving the warning, "Beloved, believe not every spirit, but prove the spirits, whether they are of God; because many false prophets are gone out into the world," adds these words: "Hereby know ye the Spirit of God: every spirit that confesseth that Jesus Christ is come in the flesh is of God: every spirit that confesseth not Jesus is not of God: and this is the spirit of the antichist, whereof we have heard that it cometh, and now it is in the world already," I John 4:1-3. Here we are plainly told that every one who acknowledges that Christ has come in the flesh is of God, and that every one who denies the Deity of Christ is antichrist. Regardless of how eloquent the speaker may be, how pleasing or magnetic his personality, how widespread his influence, or even how sincere his motives, the prophet or preacher or teacher who denies the Diety of Christ is branded in Scripture as a false prophet or preacher or teacher. And to the same effect Paul says: "No man speaking in the Spirit of God saith, Jesus is anathema; and no man can say, Jesus is Lord, but in the Holy Spirit," I Cor 12:3. Here Paul declares that only by the spiritual insight which the Holy Spirit gives as He regenerates a soul can that soul form a true judgment of the Deity of Christ. No one recognizes Christ as

Lord and as his Lord unless he has been born again. The man who looks at Jesus only with his own unenlightened eyes sees in Him only a man, perhaps a great man with many lofty principles and ideals, yet a man who has claimed too much for Himself and who has committed blasphemy by calling himself the Son of God. But when the Holy Spirit comes into his life, renewing and enlightening him spiritually, he then sees himself a guilty, condemned sinner who merits nothing but God's wrath and punishment. But he is also given to see, by the eye of faith, that Jesus is the Son of God, that He lived on this earth, that He was crucified for the sins of His people, that He arose from the grave, and that He now reigns from heaven. Never does a mortal man see the Lord Jesus thus, and never does he accept Him as his Lord, unless it is so given him by the Holy Spirit. Thus Paul says that no person can acknowledge Jesus as Lord unless he has been enlightened by the Holy Spirit. And, incidentally, in these words he also tells us that the person who does thus acknowledge Jesus as Lord has been regenerated and is therefore assured of salvation.

In concluding our discussion of this great basic doctrine of the Deity of Christ we can do no better than to quote the words of Dr. Charles Hodge. He says: "Whoever believes that Jesus is the Son of God, i. e., whoever believes that Jesus of Nazareth is God manifested in the flesh, and loves and obeys Him as such, is declared to be born of God. Any one who denies that truth, is declared to be antichrist, denying both the Father and the Son, for the denial of the one is the denial of the other. The same truth is expressed by another Apostle, who says, 'If our gospel is hid it is hid to them that are lost, in whom the god of this world hath blinded the minds of them which believe not, lest they should see the glory of God as it shines in the face of Jesus Christ.' They are lost, according to this Apostle, who do not see, as well as believe, Jesus to be God dwelling in the flesh. Hence such effects are ascribed to the knowledge of Christ, and to faith in Him; such hopes are entertained of the glory and blessedness of being with Him, as would be impossible or irrational if Christ were not the true God. He is our life. He that hath the Son hath life. He that believes on Him shall live forever. It is not we that live, but Christ that liveth in us. Our life is hid with Christ in God. We are complete in Him, wanting nothing. Though we have not seen Him, yet believing in Him, we rejoice in Him with joy unspeakable. It is because Christ is God, because He is possessed of all divine perfections, and because He loved us and gave Himself for us, and hath redeemed us and made us kings and priests unto God that the Spirit of God says, 'If any man love not the Lord Jesus Christ, let him be anathema.' The denial of the divinity of the Son of God, the refusal to receive, love, trust, worship, and serve Him as such, is the ground of the hopeless condemnation of all who hear and reject the Gospel. And to the justice of this condemnation all rational creatures, holy and unholy, justified and condemned, will say, Amen. The divinity of Christ is too plain a fact, and too momentous a truth, to be innocently rejected. Those are saved who truly believe it, and those are already lost who have not eyes to see it. He that believeth not is condemned already, because he hath not believed on the name of the only begotten Son of God. He that believeth on the Son hath everlasting life; and he that believeth not the Son shall not see life, but the wrath of God abideth on him. It is the doctrine of the New Testament, therefore, that the spiritual apprehension and the sincere recognition of the Godhead of the Redeemer constitutes the life of the soul. It is in its own nature eternal life; and the absence or want of this faith and knowledge is spiritual and eternal death. Christ is our life; and therefore he that hath not the Son hath not life."*

12. The Humanity of Christ

In answer to the question, "Who is the Redeemer of God's elect?" the Westminster Shorter Catechism says: "The only Redeemer of God's elect is the Lord Jesus Christ, who, being the eternal Son of God, became man, and so was, and continueth to be God, and man, in two distinct natures, and one person, for ever." And in answer to the question, "How did Christ, being the Son of God, become man?" the Catechism says: "Christ, the Son of God, became man, by taking to Himself a true body and a reasonable (i. e., reasoning) soul, being conceived by the power of the Holy Ghost, in the womb of the Virgin Mary, and born of her, yet without sin."

While as we have seen in the preceding chapters Christ was Deity in the highest sense, possessed of all the attributes and titles of God and free from any taint of sin or error, we are not to forget that He was also perfect humanity, bone of our bone and flesh of our flesh, and that during His earthly career He lived on this earth as a man among men, subject to all of the trials and temptations and sufferings which are common to men. He is as truly one with us on the side of His humanity as He is one with God on the side of His Deity. As a babe He came to consciousness; as a child and youth He "advanced in wisdom and stature, and in favor with God and men;" and as a man He fulfilled perfectly the divine ideal of what God made man and meant man to be.

---

*Systematic Theology, I, 498.

All of the rest of us are only sketches or suggestions of manhood, having had our speech and action and sometimes even our bodies grotesquely marred by the destructive influences of sin. He alone had a strictly normal development, having been born into the world without the fatal entail of original sin, and having grown from childhood to manhood governed always by purity and righteousness. From the mouth of His mother He first learned the sacred things of God, and at her knee He often knelt to pray. He grew up in the obscure town of Nazareth. Doubtless the wonders of His infancy were kept a secret by Joseph and Mary, although after His crucifixion Mary may have related these to the intimate group of the disciples and thus they may have found their way into Matthew's and Luke's Gospel. In all probability as He grew up His companions and the family saw nothing in Him to lead them to believe that He was a supernatural Being, but were only impressed with His remarkable mental force and moral purity. It seems probable that Joseph died before Jesus entered upon His public ministry, and that since He was the firstborn the responsibility of supporting His mother and the rest of the family fell upon His shoulders. As a carpenter He knew what every-day toil was. How much we should have missed if the Last Adam had appeared on earth as did the first Adam, mature! Instead He has passed through all the stages of human experience, from childhood to manhood. He knows human life fully, by personal experience.

The reality of Jesus' human nature and the genuineness of the human life is everywhere assumed and endlessly illustrated throughout the Scriptures. The first promise of a Redeemer, recorded in Genesis 3:15, to the effect that the seed of the woman should bruise the head of the serpent, indicated quite clearly that God purposed to use a human agent. The promise was made to Abraham that the everlasting covenant would be established with his seed (Gen. 17:19; 22:18), which promise Paul says was fulfilled not in the Jewish people as such but in Christ (Gal. 3:16, 29). David was promised that His seed should sit upon His throne for ever (II Sam. 7:12-16; II Chr. 6:16). "Of the fruit of thy body will I set upon thy throne," Ps. 132:11. Isaiah foretold the advent of the Messiah (9:6, 7), even saying that He should be born of a virgin (7:14). And Micah said that He should be born in Bethlehem (5:2).

In dozens of places the New Testament ascribes to Jesus the reactions and experiences which are common to human nature. The following will serve as a fairly representative list. (1) Birth: "Now when Jesus was born in Bethelehem," Matt. 2:1; "There is born to you this day in the city of David a Saviour," Luke 2:11. (2) Growth: "And the child grew, and waxed strong, filled with wisdom," Luke 2:40; "And Jesus advanced in wisdom and stature, and in favor with God and men," Luke 2:52. (3) Fatigue: "Jesus therefore, being wearied with His journey, sat thus by the well," John 4:6. (4) Sleep: "The boat was covered with the waves: but He was asleep," Matt. 8:24; "And they awake Him," Mark 4:38. (5) Hunger: "And when He had fasted forty days and forty nights, He afterward hungered," Matt. 4:2; "Now in the morning as He returned to the city, He hungered," Matt. 21:18. (6) Thirst: "Jesus . . . saith, I thirst,," John 19:28. (7) Indignation: "But when Jesus saw it, He was moved with indignation," Mark 10:14; "And when He had looked round about on them with anger, being grieved at the hardening of their heart," Mark 3:5. (8) Compassion: "But when He saw the multitudes, He was moved with compassion for them," Matt. 9:36; "And being moved with compassion (toward the leper), He stretched forth His hand, and touched him," Mark 1:41. (9) Love: "Jesus looking upon him loved him," Mark 10:21; "One of His disciples, whom Jesus loved," John 13:23. (10) Joy: "These things have I spoken unto you, that my joy may be in you, and that your joy may be made full," John 15:11. (11) Sorrow and anxiety: "And He . . . began to be sorrowful and sore troubled," Matt. 26:37; "Jesus wept," John 11:35; "Now is my soul troubled," John 12:27. (12) Temptation: "Then was Jesus led up of the Spirit into the wilderness to be tempted of the Devil," Matt. 4:1; "For we have not a high priest that cannot be touched with the feeling of our infirmities; but one that hath been in all points tempted like as we are, yet without sin," Heb. 4:15; "For in that He Himself hath suffered being tempted, He is able to succor them that are tempted," Heb. 2:18. (13) Prayer: "He went up into the mountain apart to pray," Matt. 14:23; "Who in the days of His flesh, having offered up prayers and supplications with strong crying and tears," Heb. 5:7; "And being in an agony He prayed more earnestly; and His sweat became as it were great drops of blood falling down upon the ground," Luke 22:44. (14) Suffering: "He was wounded for our transgressions, He was bruised for our iniquities; the chastisement of our peace was upon Him; and with His stripes we are healed," Is. 53:5; "Thus it is written, that the Christ should suffer," Luke 24:46; "Though He was a Son, yet learned obedience by the things which He suffered," Heb. 5:8; "for it became Him . . . to make the Author of their salvation perfect through suffering," Heb. 2:10. (15) Death: "And Jesus cried with a loud voice, and yielded up His spirit," Matt. 27:50; "Christ died for our sins according to the Scriptures," I Cor. 15:3.

Thus we are given to understand that Jesus was a truly human person, that He exercised the normal powers and was subject to normal reactions of human nature. The completeness of our Lord's human nature is made plain by the writer of the Epistle to the Hebrews when he says that "in all things" He was "made like unto His brethren" (2:17). He expressly called Himself "man"; "Ye seek to kill me, a man that hath told you the truth," John 8:40; and He is called "man" by others; "Pilate saith unto them, Behold, the man!" John 19:5; "Jesus of Nazareth, a man approved of God unto you," Acts 2:22; "One Mediator also between God and men, Himself man, Christ Jesus," I Tim. 2:5. The genealogies given in Matt. 1:1-17 and Luke 3:23-38 make plain His human descent, and prove Him to have been the royal and legal heir of David. And the title, "Son of Man," regardless of how much more it may mean, certainly means that He was truly human. Down through the ages the Christian Church has always believed that her Christ was not only Divine but also human.

The limitations of Jesus in the realm of knowledge present an interesting study. We have already noted that He "advanced in wisdom" as well as in stature and in favor with God and men. But as man He did not and never can become omniscient, for the simple reason that human souls by their very nature are finite. He "marvelled" at the faith of the centurion, Luke 7:9. In one of the discourses given during His last week on earth He specifically told the disciples that He did not know the time of the end of the world: "But of that day and hour knoweth no one, not even the angels of heaven, neither the Son, but the Father only," Matt. 24:36 (see also Mark 13:32). In other Sripture we are given to understand that in the plan of God it is not intended that men should know when the end of the world is coming. Hence there was no need or occasion for that revelation to be made to men. And since Jesus Himself was true man His own human soul was subject to the same limitation. The Holy Spirit revealed to the human soul of Jesus many things concerning the future; but this was not among them. As Dr. J. Ritchie Smith has observed, however, "It was only the time of His coming that was hidden from Him. The precedents, concommitants, and consequences He foresaw and foretold. This single acknowledgment of ignorance serves to confirm our faith in Him by assuring us that He taught only what He knew. His ignorance pertained to His human nature, and He recognized the limits of His knowledge because they were self-imposed. He is the only man that ever lived who could describe the boundaries of His knowledge with absolute precision. There was with Him no region of speculation or conjecture intermediate between certain knowledge and conscious ignorance, as in the case of all men besides. He did not suppose or infer. He knew or He did not know, and the line of division was to Him precise and clear. Whenever He speaks, He speaks with authority." (Studies in the Gospel of John, p. 136).

In a number of other instances Jesus asked and received information from human sources, but used supernatural power as He dealt further with the situations. Although when touched by the woman with the issue of blood He asked, "Who touched my garments," He immediately manifested His power to heal her of the affliction (Mark 5:25-34). While the news of Lazarus' sickness was brought to him by human messengers, He knew without any further message that Lazarus was dead, and that this death was not to be permanent but that it was "for the glory of God, that the Son of God may be glorified thereby." He asked, "Where have ye laid him?" and wept with the bereaved sisters; yet He put forth supernatural power and raised him from the dead, John 11:1-44. In Mark 11:12, 13, we read: "And on the morrow, when they were come out from Bethany, He hungered. And seeing a fig tree afar off having leaves, He came, if haply He might find anything thereon; and when He came to it, He found nothing but leaves;" yet at the same time He had power to wither it away from the roots (vss. 14, 20).

Concerning this general subject Dr. Warfield says: "Jesus Himself has told us that He was ignorant of the time of the day of Judgment (Mark 13:32); He repeatedly is represented as seeking information through questions, which undoubtedly were not asked only to give the appearance of a dependence upon information from without that was not real with Him: He is made to express surprise; and to make trial of new circumstances; and the like. There are no human traits lacking to the picture that is drawn of Him; He was open to temptation; He was conscious of dependence on God; He was a man of prayer; He knew a 'will' within Him that might conceivably be opposed to the will of God; He exercised faith; He learned obedience by the things that He suffered. It was not merely the mind of a man that was in Him, but the heart of a man — a man without error and sin — is, and must be conceived to have grown, as it is proper for a man to grow, not only during His youth, but continually through life, not alone in knowledge, but in wisdom, and not alone in wisdom, but 'in reverence and charity' — in moral strength and in beauty of holiness alike." He then goes on to state that Jesus continued to increase in wisdom and in all of the traits of His humanity, not only during His entire earthly life but that He continues to do so even since the time of His ascension: "For Christ, just because He is the *risen* Christ, is man and true man — all

that man is, with all that is involved in being man—through all the
ages and unto the eternity of the eternities.

"We may not fear, therefore, that we may emphasize too strongly
the true, the complete humanity of Christ. All that man as man is,
that Christ is to eternity. The Reformed Theology which it is our
happiness to inherit, has never hesitated to face the fact and rejoice
in it, with all its implications. With regard to knowledge, for example,
it has not shrunk from recognizing that Christ, as man, had a finite
knowledge and must continue to have a finite knowledge for ever.
Human nature is ever finite, it declares, and is no more capable of
infinite *charismata* than of the infinite *idiomata* or attributes of the
divine nature; so that it is certain that the knowledge of Christ's
human nature is not and can never be the infinite wisdom of God
itself. . . . It is again nothing but gain, to realize in all its fulness
that our Lord was man even as we are men, made 'in all things like
unto His brethren' (Heb. 2:17) . . .

"Alongside of these clear declarations and rich indications of His
true and complete humanity, there runs an equally pervasive attribution
to Him of all that belongs to Deity. If, for example, He is represented
as not knowing this or that matter of fact (Mark 13:32), He is equally
represented as knowing all things (John 21:17; John 16:30). If He is
represented as acquiring information from without, asking questions
and expressing surprise, He is equally represented as knowing without
human information all that occurs or has occurred — the secret prayer
of Nathaniel (John 1:47), the whole life of the Samaritan woman
(John 4:29), the very thoughts of His enemies (Matt. 9:4), all that
is in man (John 2:25). Nor are these two classes of facts kept separate; they are rather interlaced in the most amazing manner. If it is by
human informants that He is told of Lazarus' sickness (John 11:3, 6),
it is of no human information that He knows him to be dead (John
11:11, 14); if He asks 'Where have ye laid him?' and weeps with the
sorrowing sister, He knows from the beginning (John 11:11) what
His might should accomplish for the assuagement of this grief. Everywhere, in a word, we see a double life revealed before us in the drama-
tization of the actions of Jesus among men; not, indeed, in the sense
that He is represented as acting inconsistently, or is inconsistently
represented as acting now in one order and now in another; but rather
in the sense that a duplex life is attributed to Him as His constant
possession. If all that man is is attributed to Him, no less is all that
God is attributed to Him, and the one attribution is no more pervasive
than the other." (Article in *The Bible Student,* Jan., 1900).

Something of the importance of a correct doctrine of the humanity of Christ can be seen when we look at the errors into which the Roman Catholics have been led. They have emphasized His majesty and Deity to the almost total exclusion of His human qualities, with the result that they have come to think of both the Father and the Son as far removed from them. Almost invariably their pictures and images have represented the human Christ either as a helpless babe in a manger, or a dead Christ on a cross. Yet through all this they have continued to feel the need of a Divine-Human Mediator, One who as man can act as their true representative when He stands before the throne of God, and One who as Deity is able to intercede effectively with God. But since the Roman Catholic theology did not present this kind of a Mediator they have been forced to invent something else, and in their groping they have turned to the idolatrous worship of the Virgin Mary. They have hailed her as the "Mother of God" and have enthroned her as the "Queen of Heaven," thus for all practical purposes exalting her to a position of equality with God. We say this, not because we wish to give Mary any less honor than that which is her just due as the most blessed of women, but because we consider the Roman Catholic practice very misleading and wholly without Scripture warrant. Those who know the Jesus who is set forth in the New Testament find Him to be not only a man but the most sympathetic and the most approachable of men. Witness the readiness of the mothers to bring their children to Him, the ease with which the woman of Samaria entered into conversation with Him at the well, His deep sympathy for Mary and Martha at the death of their brother Lazarus. The poor, rough, uncultured fishermen of Galilee became His intimate and trusted friends. And we who live nearly two thousand years after these events find ourselves bound to Him with strong personal ties of love and friendship. To us, as to the early Christians, He says, "Ye are my friends." Although He is our Creator and Lord, if we trust and obey Him it is not presumptuous for us to call Him our Friend; and in fact we have not fully entered upon our inheritance in Him unless we do know Him not only as our Creator and Lord but also as our Friend. To the disciples He said, "No longer do I call you servants; for the servant knoweth not what his lord doeth: but I have called you friends; for all things that I have heard from my Father I have made known unto you," John 15:15. And from age to age He stands saying, "Come unto me, all ye that labor and are heavy laden, and I will give you rest," Matt. 11:28. Every true Christian, conscious of what Jesus has done for him, should feel that in a true sense he, like the disciple John, can designate himself as "the disciple whom Jesus loved." What a serious error it is, then, for any one to suppose that this our most intimate and loving Friend can be approached only through the intercession of some one else. Such practice pushes the Saviour far away and robs the Christian of one of his most precious possessions.

13. The Humiliation of Christ

The Apostle Paul tells us that Christ in order that He might accomplish His work of redemption "humbled" Himself (Phil. 2:8). The meaning of this is perhaps expressed more clearly and briefly in the Shorter Catechism than anywhere else when in answer to the question, "Wherein did Christ's humiliation consist?" the answer is given: "Christ's humiliation consisted in His being born, and that in low condition, made under the law, undergoing the miseries of this life, the wrath of God, and the cursed death of the cross; in being buried, and continuing under the power of death for a time."

According to this statement the first stage in the humiliation of Christ was His birth. For the Prince of Glory, who partakes of the same nature as the Father, to have condescended to take into personal and permanent union with Himself a nature which is infinitely lower than His own, even had He entered the world as a king clothed in purple and crowned with gold, would have been an immeasurable condescension. But for Him to be born a helpless infant entirely dependent on His mother, to be so poor as not to have a place where to lay His head, to have His life immediately sought after by a cruel king and His parents made fugitives from the wrath of this king, was in itself an act of condescension in our behalf utterly beyond anything that our minds can grasp. As He grew up He accommodated Himself to the limitations of human existence. Though He was the Giver of the Law, He submitted to circumcision, took His place under the Law as if He were an ordinary Israelite, and assumed its obligation in man's place and stead. As the Lutheran theologian, Dr. Joseph Stump, has observed: "His home was in the humble and despised village of Nazareth, amid rough and uncouth neighbors, in a narrow and contracted environment, and in the deepest obscurity. . . . Though Lord of all, He was subject to Joseph and Mary like an ordinary child of men, labored at the carpenter's bench, and subjected Himself to the hardships and limitations of the poor and lowly. . . . His public ministry brought Him into contact with all sorts of men, the best of whom were weak and sinful, and the worst of whom were quite depraved. Though divine and holy, He associated with them day by day as if He were simply one of them. He mingled with all kinds and classes of people, and dined with despised publicans and with self-righteous Pharisees. He was often hungry and thirsty, had no place to lay His head, like the lowest of them, and endured bitter hostility and persecution at the hands of the ruling classes of the Jews." *The Christian Faith*, p. 168. (Muhlenberg Press).

While the humiliation and suffering of Jesus continued in greater or lesser degree throughout the whole period of His earthly life, it increased in intensity as His career neared its close. The opposition and hatred of His enemies became more intense. The indifference and callousness of the people, as well as the dreadful doom which He foresaw coming upon the whole Jewish nation — the nation to which He belonged and which He loved—weighed heavily upon Him. But the climax was reached as He endured the shameful suffering and death by crucifixion, which is the most horrible and agonizing form of death that has ever been invented by man. Nor were the physical sufferings all that He had to endure on the cross. As the sin-offering for His people He was treated as if He were sinful in His own person. The Father's presence, of which He had been so conscious throughout his entire life, was now withdrawn, as was also the light of the sun. His sensitive soul was left to suffer alone and in violent conflict with the forces of evil which sought desperately on this last occasion to cause His downfall and defeat His redemptive work. The anguished cry, "My God, my God, why hast thou forsaken me?" is an indication of the extremity of His suffering. In the nature of the case we can understand but faintly what He endured as He hung there. But this we do know, that He who did no sin, and on whom death therefore had no claim, voluntarily took our place and suffered the penalty which was due to us and so made atonement for our sin. We shall not shift to the Jews of that day, nor to the Romans, the responsibility for His crucifixion, but penitently confess that in its broader aspects it was our sin as well as theirs that brought that suffering upon Him — specifically that it was for the redeemed individually, regardless of what age they may live in, that He carried that burden.

The humiliation of Christ was completed in His burial, in which His sacred body was put away in the grave as if He shared the common end of men who die and are buried, whose bodies decay and cease to be. But His body was not given over to decay. Instead, three days later it was raised in a glorious resurrection.

14. The Exaltation of Christ

In answer to the question, "Whence consisteth Christ's exaltation?" the Shorter Catechism says: "Christ's exaltation consisteth in His rising again from the dead on the third day, in ascending up into heaven, in sitting at the right hand of God the Father, and in coming to judge the world at the last day."

In the first place it must be apparent to all that the exaltation of Christ, as well as His humiliation, relates not to His Divine nature, which is and always has been infinitely blessed and glorious, but only to His human nature. His divine nature is immutable, and therefore not capable of either increase or diminution. His humiliation was temporary. It began with His birth and was completed with His burial, and it can never be repeated. His exaltation is permanent. It began with His resurrection and ascension. It continues now as He sits at the right hand of God the Father and directs the affairs of His advancing kingdom. It will be more fully revealed when at the end of the world He comes in the glory of His Father and with the holy angels to judge the nations and to assign to each individual his eternal destiny.

The resurrection of Christ was not only the first step in His glorification. It was also one of the most important truths of the Gospel. For by this act Christ conquered death and came forth alive out of the tomb. It was the proof that His work of redemption had been fully successful, that He had made a complete conquest of death. It showed that His work had fully satisfied the demands of the law (the law which God established at the original creation, that the soul that committed sin should die), and that death therefore had no further hold on Him nor on any of those for whom He died. It proved further that He was what He claimed to be, the Son of God, equal with the Father, God manifested in the flesh. And since He suffered and died not for any sin of His own but as the federal head and representative of His people, His resurrection is the guarantee that at the appointed time His people who are vitally related to Him shall also be raised in a glorious resurrection. It means that the Gospel is true, that Satan has been finally and completely defeated, and that the triumph of life over death, of truth over error, of good over evil, and of happiness over misery, is forever assured. Paul set forth the real importance of the resurrection when he said: "If Christ hath not been raised, then is our preaching vain, your faith also is vain. . . . If Christ hath not been raised, your faith is vain; ye are yet in your sins. Then they also that are fallen asleep in Christ have perished. If we have only hoped in Christ in this life, we are of all men most pitiable. But now hath Christ been raised from the dead, the first-fruits of them that are asleep. For since by man came death, by man came also the resurrection from the dead. For as in Adam all die, so also in Christ shall all be made alive. But each in his own order: Christ the first fruits; then they that are Christ's at His coming," I Cor. 15:14-23.

The first and most impressive result of the resurrection, and, in fact, we may say the strongest proof of the resurrection, was found in the complete transformation which took place in the minds and hearts of the disciples. Whereas after the crucifixion they were utterly disheartened and were on the point of losing faith in Christ as the Messiah, they then became firmly convinced that He had risen from the dead and that He was the Son of God, the promised Messiah, the Saviour of the world. From that time on nothing could shake them from that conviction. They went forth and preached everywhere, and showed themselves ready to suffer and die if need be for the Gospel. We know that some of them did lose their lives in the service of their Lord. Tradition tells us that most of them thus died.

The second step in the exaltation of Christ was His ascension. Mark records very briefly that after He had spoken with the disciples, "He was received up into heaven, and sat down at the right hand of God," 16:19, which is, of course, the position of honor and influence, of power and majesty. Luke says that "He led them (the disciples) out until they were over against Bethany; and He lifted up His hands, and blessed them. And it came to pass, while He blessed them, He departed from them, and was carried up into heaven," 24:50, 51. But the fullest account of the Ascension is given in the book of Acts. After recording the last words of Christ to the disciples it adds: "And when He had said these things, as they were looking, He was taken up; and a cloud received Him out of their sight. And while they were looking steadfastly into heaven as He went, behold two men stood by them in white apparel; who also said, Ye men of Galilee, why stand ye looking into heaven? This Jesus who was received up from you into heaven, shall so come in like manner as ye beheld Him going into heaven," 1:9-11.

Concerning these verses Dr. Hodge says: "It appears, (1) That the ascension of Christ was of His whole person. It was the Thean-thropos, the Son of God, clothed in our nature, having a true body and a reasonable soul, who ascended. (2) That the ascension was visible The disciples witnessed the whole transaction. They saw the person of Christ gradually rise from the earth and 'go up' until a cloud hid Him from their view. (3) It was a local transfer of His person from one place to another; from earth to heaven. Heaven is therefore a place. In what part of the universe it is located is not revealed. But according to the doctrine of Scripture it is a definite portion of space where God specially manifests His presence, and where He is surrounded by His angels (who not being infinite, cannot be ubiquitous), and by the spirits of the just made perfect." *Systematic Theology,* II, p. 630.

Heaven is Christ's home, His throne, His temple. The ascension was the counterpart of His descent to earth. In an earlier section we discussed His pre-existence, and have seen that He "came" or "was sent" on a specific mission of redemption. Having brought that work to a wholly successful conclusion He returned to His heavenly home. This world with its present load of sin is not suited for the Redeemer's abode in His state of exaltation, and will not become so until it has undergone its great process of regeneration so as to become a new heaven and a new earth.

Furthermore, since Christ has provided an objective atonement and so satisfied all of the legal requirements for His people, it was necessary that that work should be effectively applied by the Holy Spirit to those for whom it was intended. It is the Holy Spirit who regenerates the souls of men and prepares them fully for the heavenly abode. In order to accomplish this He enlightens them spiritually, induces faith and repentance, and brings them through the whole process of sanctification. Apart from His regenerating power men would have remained in their sins for ever and Christ's work would have been in vain. But before the Holy Spirit could begin His work it was necessary that Christ return to the Father. "It is expedient for you that I go away; for if I go not away, the Comforter will not come unto you; but if I go, I will send Him unto you," John 16:7. To quote Dr. Hodge again, "The great blessing which the prophets predicted as characteristic of the Messianic period, was the effusion of the Holy Spirit. To secure that blessing for the Church His ascension was necessary. He was exalted to give repentance and the remission of sins; to gather His people from all nations and during all ages until the work was accomplished. His throne in the heavens was the proper place whence the work of saving men, through the merits of His death, was to be carried on." (*Systematic Theology,* II, p. 635).

It may be well to point out further in this connection that God's dealing with men in this world embraces three distinct dispensations in which the particular work of one of the persons of the Trinity is predominant. In the eternal plan of God there was what we may call a division of labor among the different persons of the Trinity and a definite order of events to be followed. That of the Father came first. It had to do primarily with creation and with the government or providential control of all things. It extended through the entire Old Testament period and up until the birth of Jesus in Bethlehem. That of the

Son had to do particularly with redemption. It began with His birth in Bethlehem and continued until the day of Pentecost. During that time He provided an objective atonement and fulfilled all of the legal requirements for His people so that they might be brought from their estate of sin and misery into a state of salvation. That of the Holy Spirit had to do primarily with salvation or the application to the hearts of men of this atonement which was provided for them by Christ. This dispensation began with the day of Pentecost and extends until the end of the world. This, of course, does not mean that during the dispensation of any one member of the Trinity the other two were inactive, but only that in matters pertaining to salvation the different members of the Trinity perform different functions.

In connection with Christ's resurrection and ascension it may be well to point out that it is in the person of the risen and glorified Christ that we shall see God. It would seem to be impossible for us ever to see God the Father or God the Holy Spirit as distinct persons of the Trinity, for each is pure spirit and infinite as regards space. But we shall see God the Son in His resurrection body. Moreover, we should also remember that Christ Himself said: "I and the Father are one," John 10:30; "I am in the Father, and the Father in me," John 14:11; and, "He that hath seen me hath seen the Father," John 14:9.

The third step in the exaltation of Christ is His sitting at the right hand of God. From there He directs the affairs of His advancing kingdom and maintains its perfect schedule. In order that His mediatorial reign should be wholly successful it was necessary that He should be given absolute dominion. "All authority hath been given unto me in heaven and on earth," Matt. 28:18, said He as He commissioned the disciples for their task of world-wide evangelism. "He must reign till He hath put all His enemies under His feet," said Paul; and then he added, "The last enemy that shall be abolished is death," I Cor. 15:25, 26—which means, of course, the complete subjugation of the forces of sin, since sin and sin alone is the cause of death. His disciples are commanded to go and "make disciples of all the nations," Matt. 28:19, claiming their people for the true God through baptism "in the name of the Father and of the Son and of the Holy Spirit." And the message to be proclaimed in this universal evangelism is, of course, the full-orbed Gospel, — "teaching them to observe all things whatsoever I commanded you," Matt. 28:20. We shall have more to say about the mediatorial reign of Christ when we come to discuss the subject, "Christ as King."

The fourth and last step in the exaltation of Christ will be His coming again with power and great glory to be the final Judge of the entire world. He is then to appear in His resurrection body, surrounded by all the angels, and is to sit on the throne of His glory (Matt. 25 :31) ; every eye is to see Him (Rev. 1 :7), this same Jesus who while on earth was rejected by His own people and arraigned as a criminal at the bar of Pilate, who was unjustly condemned and crucified with malefactors. From His lips all men are to receive their final rewards or punishments. Then, with His mediatorial reign completed and crowned with complete success, He is to deliver up the kingdom to the Father and resume His original relation to the other Persons of the Trinity, sharing fully in the glory which He had with the Father before the world was, and, together with the Father and the Holy Spirit, He is to reign forever as King over the redeemed ; "And when all things have been subjected unto Him, then shall the Son also Himself be subjected to Him that did subject all things unto Him, that God may be all in all," I Cor. 15 :28.

This, then, is what we mean by the exaltation of Christ. And again we would remind our readers that it is not the divine nature but the human nature of Jesus that is exalted, that it was the man Jesus Christ who received a resurrection body, who ascended to heaven, who shares in the mediatorial reign, and who will be seen by all peoples when He comes again at the last day.

15. The Relation of the Two Natures in Christ

In the Westminster Confession of Faith we find this very clear and complete statement concerning the person of Christ: "The Son of God, the second person of the Trinity, being very and eternal God, of one substance, and equal with the Father, did, when the fulness of time was come take upon Himself man's nature, with all the essential properties and common infirmities thereof, yet without sin : being conceived by the power of the Holy Ghost, in the womb of the Virgin Mary, of her substance. So that the two whole, perfect, and distinct natures, the Godhead and the manhood, were inseparably joined together in one person, without conversion, composition, or confusion. Which person is very God and very man, yet one Christ, the only Mediator between God and man." (Chapter VIII, Section 2).

Many of the critics have gone astray in their study of the person of Christ for no other reason than that they have based their conclusions on the assumption that He must be either Divine or human. That He might be both Divine and human seems never to have entered their minds. They are therefore confronted at the very outset with an irreconcilable dilemma, for the whole historical tradition testifies to a Divine-human Jesus, a Jesus who is intensely supernataural and yet who is possessed of a perfectly normal human nature. The tendency of these critics is to tear apart the natural and the supernatural elements in the Gospels, then to assign the natural elements to a supposedly "earlier" or "historical" narrative while discounting the supernatural elements as "accretions" or "myths." Such criticism, however, is utterly illegitimate. It is based not on historical or textual criticism, which presents not a shred of evidence for a merely human Christ, but entirely on *a priori* reasoning. Specifically, it is based on the philosophical assumption that the supernatural is impossible.

The evidence that we have concerning the historical Jesus comes primarily from the New Testament and secondarily from the beliefs and practices of the early Christians. This evidence admittedly sets forth a Divine-human Jesus. It is abundant and is consistently maintained in the various sources. It bears on its face the marks of honesty and sincerity. To reject it in the interests of a merely human Jesus who may perchance fit in more harmoniously with the critic's personal notion of what is real or possible, when that notion has not the slightest scrap of historical evidence to support it, is certainly highhanded and inexcusable. Whether the supernatural is possible or not, either in the person of Jesus or in the world at large, is not a question of historical or textual criticism, — which criticism should deal impartially and exclusively with the text of the New Testament that has been handed down to us and which, incidentally, fully supports belief in the supernatural. It is rather a question of philosophical world-view, and cannot be disposed of by an arbitrary rejection of unwanted elements in the Gospel narratives. In this chapter it is our purpose to show that it is entirely reasonable to believe that the two natures which the Gospel narratives ascribe to Jesus did function in His person with perfect harmony, and that only such a two-natured person would be capable of providing salvation for mankind.

In the incarnation our Lord added to His divine nature, not another person (which would have given Him a double personality), but impersonal, generic human nature, so that He was and continues to be God and man, in two distinct natures and one person for ever. There is, to be sure, mystery here which we cannot explain. Probably the nearest analogy we have to it is that which is found in man's own being. Man is composed of two radically different substances, — an immaterial soul or spirit which is subject to mental and spiritual influences, and a material body which is subject to all of the physical and chemical and electrical forces which operate in the world about him. These two natures are not fused or mixed so as to produce a third which is different from either of the others, but exist side by side in perfect harmony with all of their distinct attributes. Each continues to obey the laws of its realm as definitely as if detached from the other. And as in man the soul is the dominant and controlling factor, so in Christ the divine nature is dominant and controlling. In man the attributes or peculiarities of either nature are the attributes or peculiarities of the person. What can be affirmed of either of his natures can be affirmed of the person. If his spirit is moral or immoral, happy or sorrowful, wise or foolish, or if his body weighs one hundred and fifty pounds, is tall or short, has blue eyes, suffers pain or is sick, we do not bother to point out to which nature it is that these things apply but simply say that he as a person has these qualities or experiences these things. It will be acknowledged that each of these qualities or conditions applies exclusively to one nature and not to the other. The soul cannot be wounded or burnt or made lame or deaf; nor can the body think, or be happy or sorrowful, or have a good conscience or suffer remorse. Yet what the man is or experiences in either nature he is or experiences as a person.

Hence in view of the fact that Christ has two natures, and depending on which nature we have in mind, it is proper to say that He is infinite or that He is finite, that He existed from eternity or that He was born in Bethlehem, that He was omniscient or that He was limited in knowledge. In His composite personality He was, on the one side, "of the seed of David according to the flesh," and on the other He was "declared to be (that is, proved to be) the Son of God with power, according to the Spirit of holiness, by the resurrection from the dead," Rom. 1:3, 4. Consequently the Scriptures present Him as the son of David, yet David's Lord. He is born an infant, yet is the Ancient of Days. He is the son of Mary, yet at the same time God over all, blessed forever. He is weary with His journey, yet He upholds all things by the word of His power. He can do nothing without the Father, yet without Him was not anything made that hath been made. He is bone of our bone and flesh of our flesh, yet might readily have clung exclusively to His equality with God. He takes the form of a servant, yet His proper and natural form was the form of God. He increases in stature, yet is the same yesterday, today and for ever. He increases in wisdom, yet knows the Father perfectly. He is born under the law and keeps the law, yet in His own name He gives a new and more perfect law and proclaims Himself the Lord of the Sabbath and greater than the temple. His soul is troubled, yet He is the Prince of Peace. He goes to His death at the command of the Roman governor, yet He is the King of kings and Lord of lords. He is received up into heaven out of the sight of His disciples, yet continues to be with them even to the end of the world. Hence the Gospel writers sometimes present Him as Divine, sometimes as human, — not that we are to take the one and leave the other, but that we are to accept Him as a Divine-human person, incarnate Deity, whose whole earthly life was but an episode in the existence of a heavenly Being.

We have said that the two natures in Christ are so united that the attributes or peculiarities of either nature can be predicated of the person. And since we mean exactly the same person whether we call Him Jesus or Christ, God or man, the Son of God or the Son of Man, it is perfectly correct to say that Jesus was thirsty or that God was thirsty, that Jesus suffered or that God suffered, that Jesus took man's place on the cross and died for him or that God took man's place on the cross and died for him, provided, of course, that we keep in mind the particular nature through which the action is accomplished. In Scripture the attributes and powers of either nature are ascribed to the one Christ, and conversely the works and characteristics of the one Christ are ascribed to either of the natures in a way which can be explained only on the principle that these two natures were organically and indissolubly united in a single person. The Scriptures tell us, for instance, that sinful men "crucified the Lord of glory," I Cor. 2:8. Paul refers to "the Church of the Lord which He purchased with His own blood," Acts 20:28, and declares that "there is one God, one Mediator also between God and men, Himself man, Jesus Christ," I Tim 2:5. John writes of "that which was from the beginning, that which we have heard, that which we have seen with our eyes, that which we beheld, and our hands handled, concerning the Word of life," I John 1:1, and in another place declares that "they shall look on Him whom they pierced," John 19:37. When Jesus asked, "What then if ye should behold the Son of Man ascending where He was before?" John 6:62, a term which had special reference to His human nature was used to designate the person when the thing referred to was true only of His divine nature.

The expression, "Mary, mother of God," used so repeatedly in the Roman Catholic Church, is usually offensive to Protestant ears. Yet there is a sense in which it is true, provided that we keep in mind that Mary was the mother not of His divine nature but only of His human nature. But since it is so likely to be misunderstood by uninformed listeners and lends itself so readily to the propagation of error its use would be better discontinued.

It was necessary that the Redeemer of mankind should be both human and Divine. It was necessary that He be human if He was really to take man's place and suffer and die, for Deity as such was not capable of that. And it was necessary that He should be Divine if His suffering and death were to have infinite value. Briefly, His humanity made His suffering possible, while His Deity gave it infinite value. Had He been only man He would have needed to have worked out salvation for Himself, and even though He had been sinless He could not have paid a ransom sufficient for the deliverance of others. But since He possessed two natures united in perfect harmony and was no less truly Divine than truly human, the atonement which He made was infinitely meritorious and therefore sufficient to save as many members of this fallen race as put their faith in Him. Furthermore, since the race fell through the action of one man who acted in his representative and official capacity, it was possible for salvation to be provided in the same way. As Calvin has so well expressed it, in order that man might be reconciled to God it was necessary "that man, who had ruined himself by his own disobedience, should remedy his condition by obedience, should satisfy the justice of God, and suffer the punishment of his sin. Our Lord then made His appearance as a real man; He put on the character of Adam, and assumed his name, to act as his substitute in his obedience to the Father, to lay down our flesh as the price of satisfaction to the justice of God; and to suffer the punishment which we deserved, in the same nature in which the offense had been committed. As it would have been impossible, therefore, for one who was only God to suffer death, or for one who was a mere man to overcome it, He associated the human nature with the Divine, that He might submit the weakness of the former to death, as an atonement for sins; and that with the power of the latter He might contend with death, and obtain a victory on our behalf. Those who despoil Christ, therefore, either of His Divinity or His humanity either diminish His majesty and glory, or obscure His goodness." (*Institutes*, I, 421).

We have said that it was not with another man that the Second Person of the Trinity united Himself, but with impersonal generic human nature. This human nature had no personality apart from the Divine nature, but came to consciousness and found its personality only in union with the Divine, in much the same way that our physical bodies if separated from our spirits are devoid of all reason and sensation and are as nothing, but when united with our spirits they share our true personal life because we, whose bodies they are, are persons. In this union the Divine nature was basic and controlling, so that this was not the case of a man being exalted to Deity, but of God voluntarily humbling Himself and descending to the plane of man in such a manner that He shared equally with us the experiences which are common to men. In the same manner that our spirits take precedence over and control our bodies, the Divine nature in Christ took precedence over and controlled the human; yet each nature continued to have its own distinctive attributes or properties and to fulfill its own functions.

Incidentally, the fact that Christ took into union with Himself not another person but impersonal generic human nature throws considerable light on the problem of His immaculate conception by the Virgin Mary. It has often been asked how Christ could be born a member of the human race and yet be free from original sin. But the fact of the matter is that sin and guilt are attached not to human nature as such, but to individual persons,—specifically to all who are sons of Adam by ordinary generation. Furthermore, had Jesus been born not of a virgin but of a human father and mother there would have been some reason for believing that it was a complete human being which He took into union with Himself. In the realm of the human it requires both a father and a mother to produce a new being possessing body and soul. But since Jesus had only a human mother He could have taken into union with His Divine nature not a human person but only impersonal human nature, in which nature, however, He was able to experience all of the limitations and sufferings which are common to men. Hence the entail of original sin which rests upon all other members of the human race had no hold on Him. This consideration also shows how unnecessary and even ridiculous is the Roman Catholic doctrine of the immaculate conception of the Virgin Mary as an explanation of the sinlessness of Christ's nature.

In treating of the two natures of Christ we must ever keep in mind the unity of His person. Though as truly God as is God the Father and as truly man as we are, in the New Testament records He invariably speaks of Himself and is spoken of as but a single personality. Never are the pronouns "I," "thou," or "He," used to distinguish between the Divine and human nature as is done to distinguish between the different persons of the Trinity, and never does Christ use the plural number in referring to Himself. The distinction seems to lie in the fact that the different members of the Godhead have distinct (that is, individual) subsistence with powers of consciousness and will, but that the human nature of Christ does not and is therefore of itself not a distinct personality. Throughout the New Testament Jesus is presented as a Divine person living and moving in the flesh. It is but one and the same person of whom birth, growth, life, death, eternity, omniscience, omnipotence, and all the other attributes, whether human or Divine, are predicated. For any one to pick out certain statements in that tradition which emphasize the humanity of Jesus and on the basis of those to represent Him as merely human, is as erroneous as to pick out certain other statements which emphasize His Divinity and to represent Him as purely Divine. And for any one to confound the two natures so that they are merged into a third which is neither Divine nor human (as was the heresy of the Eutychians — condemned by the Council of Chalcedon, 451 A. D.), or to separate the two natures so as to give Christ a double personality (which was the heresy of the Nestorians — condemned by the Council of Ephesus, 431 A.D.), is equally erroneous. Each of these errors has tended to crop up time and again, and can be disposed of only through a correct understanding of His person.

This doctrine of the two natures united in one person is found to be the key which unlocks all of the treasures of Biblical instruction concerning the person of Christ and enables the reader to arrange the Scripture declarations into a fully intelligent and consistent system. It is inconceivable that the key which unlocks such a complicated lock can fail to be the true key. As Dr. Warfield has said concerning this doctrine: "The doctrine of the Two Natures supplies, in a word, the only possible solution of the enigmas of the life-manifestation of the historical Jesus. It presents itself to us, not as the creator, but as the solvent of difficulties—in this, performing the same service to thought which is performed by all the Christian doctrines. If we look upon it merely as a hypothesis, it commands our attention by the multiplicity of phenomena which it reduces to order and unifies, and on this lower ground, too, commends itself to our acceptance. But it does not come to us merely as a hypothesis. It is the assertion concerning their Lord of all the primary witnesses of the Christian faith. It is, indeed, the self-testimony of our Lord Himself, disclosing to us the mystery of His being. It is, to put it briefly, the simple statement of the fact of Jesus, as that fact is revealed to us in His whole manifestation. We may reject it if we will, but in rejecting it we reject the only real Jesus in favor of another Jesus — who is not another, but is the creature of pure fantasy. The alternatives which we are really face to face with are, Either the two-natured Christ of history, or — a strong delusion." (*Christology and Criticism*, p. 309).

And in another connection the same writer says concerning the New Testament portrait of Jesus that it is "the portrait not of a merely human life, though it includes the delineation of a complete and completely human life. It is the portrayal of a human episode in the divine life. It is, therefore, not merely connected with supernatural occurrences, nor merely colored by supernatural features, not merely set in a supernatural atmosphere: the supernatural is its very substance, the elimination of which would be the evaporation of the whole. The Jesus of the New Testament is not fundamentally man, however divinely gifted: He is God tabernacling for a while among men. with heaven lying about Him not merely in His infancy, but throughout all the days of His flesh.

"The intense supernaturalism of this portraiture is, of course, an offense to our anti-supernaturalistic age. It is only what was to be expected, therefore, that throughout the last century and a half a long series of scholars, imbued with the anti-supernaturalistic instinct of the time, have assumed the task of desupernaturalizing it. Great difficulty has been experienced, however, in the attempt to construct a historical sieve which will strain out miracles and yet let Jesus through; for Jesus is Himself the greatest miracle of them all. Accordingly at the end of the day there is a growing disposition, as if in despair of accomplishing this feat, to construct a sieve so as to strain out Jesus too; to take refuge in the council of desperation which affirms that there never was such a person as Jesus, that Christianity had no founder, and that not merely the portrait of Jesus but Jesus Himself, is a pure projection of later ideals into the past. The main stream of assault still addresses itself, however, to the attempt to eliminate not Jesus Himself, but the Jesus of the Evangelists, and to substitute for Him a desupernaturalized Jesus." (*Christology and Criticism*, p. 163).

Throughout the whole study of the relationship which exists between the two natures we are, of course, face to face with impenetrable mystery. It is one of those mysteries which the Scriptures reveal but which they make no effort to explain. Christ is an absolutely unique person; and although in every age much study has been expended upon His personality it remains a profound mystery, in some respects as baffling as the Trinity itself. All we can know are the simple facts which are revealed to us in Scripture, and beyond these it is not necessary to go. As a matter of fact we do not understand the mysterious union of the spiritual and physical in our own natures; nor do we understand the attributes of God. But the essential facts are clear and are understandable by the average Christian. These are that the Second Person of the Trinity added to His own nature a perfectly normal human nature, that His life on earth was passed as far as was fitting within the limits of this humanity, that His life remained at all times the life of God manifest in the flesh, that His action in the flesh never escaped beyond the boundary of that which was suitable for incarnate Deity, and that all of this was done in order that in man's nature and as man's Substitute He might assume man's obligation before the law, suffer the penalty which was due to him for sin, and so accomplish his redemption.

16. The Incarnation

In answer to the question, "How did Christ, being the Son of God, become man?" the Shorter Catechism replies: "Christ, the Son of God, became man, by taking to Himself a true body and a reasonable (that is, reasoning) soul, being conceived by the power of the Holy Ghost, in the womb of the Virgin Mary, and born of her, yet without sin."

Man, in contrast with all of the animals of the field, was created in the image of God, with a spiritual and rational nature, and was given an immortal soul. Paul says that God is "not far from each one of us," and that "in Him we live, and move, and have our being," Acts 17:27, 28. The divine and the human, though distinct from each other, are not foreign to each other or mutually exclusive. Man is, as it were, a spark out of the great fire, or, to change the figure, he is an empty vessel to be filled from the infinite Fountain, and fulfills his appointed purpose only when in union with the divine. Since he was created in the image of God and was appointed a ruler in the earth he is in effect a miniature God. This, too, is in harmony with Scripture, for in Ps. 82:6 we read: "I said, Ye are gods, And all of you sons of the Most High;" and Christ Himself said, "Is it not written in your law, I said, Ye are gods?" John 10:34. Hence a union between the Divine and the human, while not inherently necessary, and while in all probability it would never have been made apart from God's work of redemption, was very definitely within the realm of possibility, and, given God's desire to rescue man from sin, is seen to have been a most natural and effective method of procedure. "God may assume the form of man," says Dr. J. Ritchie Smith, "because man was made in the likeness of God. The Eternal Word may become the Son of Man because man is by nature the son of God. He could not take upon Him a nature wholly foreign to His own, nor become that which is altogether unlike Himself."

The incarnation was not an end in itself, but a means toward that end. Since man by his fall into sin had cut himself off from God and made himself utterly incapable of working out his own salvation, Christ in His infinite mercy assumed that task for him. It was for that purpose that He became incarnate, so that, as God dwelling in a human body, God clothed in human flesh, He might assume man's place before the law and satisfy Divine justice. Only a truly human person could suffer and die, and only a truly Divine person could give that suffering infinite value. The ultimate end of Our Lord's incarnation is therefore declared to be that He might die. "Since then the children are sharers in flesh and blood, He also Himself in like manner partook of the same; that through death He . . . might deliver all them who through fear of death were all their lifetime subject to bondage . . . Wherefore it behooved Him in all things to be made like unto His brethren, that He might become a merciful and faithful high priest in things pertaining to God, to make propitiation for the sins of the people," Heb. 2:14-17.

The doctrine of the Deity of Christ is, of course, not dependent on the doctrine of the Incarnation. As Dr. J. Gresham Machen has pointed out, "The doctrine of the Deity of Christ is part of the Biblical teaching about God. This person whom we know as Jesus Christ would have been God even if no universe had been created and even if there had been no fallen man to save. He was God from everlasting. His Deity is quite independent of any relation of His to a created world. The doctrine of the incarnation, on the other hand, is part of the doctrine of salvation. He *was* from everlasting, but He *became* man — at a definite moment in the world's history, and in order that fallen man might be saved. That He became man was not at all necessary to the unfolding of His own being. He was infinite, eternal and unchangeable God when He became man and after He became man. But He would have been infinite, eternal and unchangeable God, even if He had never become man. His becoming man was a free act of His love. Ultimately its purpose, as the purpose of all things, was the glory of God; and that purpose does not conflict at all with the fact that it was a free act of mercy to undeserving sinners. He became man in order that He might die on the cross to redeem sinners from the guilt and power of sin." (Article in *The Presbyterian Guardian*).

Paul's doctrine of the Incarnation is perhaps expressed most fully in Phil. 2:5-11, where he refers to Christ as "existing in the form of God," and as "taking the form of a servant, being made in the likeness of men, and being found in fashion as a man." Numerous other allusions are found throughout his epistles. In II Cor. 8:9, for instance, we are reminded of the graciousness of "Our Lord Jesus Christ, who, though He was rich, yet for our sakes became poor, that we through His poverty might become rich." In Gal. 4:4 we are told that "When the fulness of the time came, God sent forth His Son, born of a woman, born under the law, that He might redeem them that were under the law, that we might receive the adoption of sons."

Concerning the statement in Gal. 4:4 Dr. Warfield makes the following comment: "The whole transaction is referred to the Father in fulfillment of His eternal plan of redemption, and it is described specifically as an incarnation: the Son of God is born of a woman — He who is in His own nature the Son of God, abiding with God, is sent forth from God in such a manner as to be born a human being, subject to law. The primary implications are that this was not the beginning of His being; but that before this He was neither a man nor subject to law. But there is no suggestion that on becoming man and subject to law, He ceased to be the Son of God or lost anything intimated by that high designation." And then concerning this general subject he continues: "Paul teaches us that by His coming forth from God to be born of a woman, Our Lord, assuming a human nature to Himself, has, while remaining the Supreme God, become also true and perfect man. Accordingly, in a context in which the resources of language are strained to the utmost to make the exaltation of Our Lord's being clear — in which He is described as the image of the invisible God, whose being antedates all that is created, in whom, through whom and to whom all things have been created, and in whom they all subsist — we are told not only that (naturally) in Him all the fulness dwells (Col. 1:19), but, with concrete explication, that 'all the fulness of the Godhead dwells in Him bodily' (Col. 2:9); that is to say, the very Deity of God, that which makes God God, in all its completeness, has its permanent home in Our Lord, and that in a 'bodily fashion,' that is, it is in Him clothed with a body. He who looks upon Jesus Christ sees, no doubt, a body and a man; but as he sees the man clothed with the body, so he sees God Himself, in all the fulness of His Deity, clothed with humanity. Jesus Christ is therefore God 'manifested in the flesh' (I Tim. 3:16), and His appearance on earth is an 'epiphany' (II Tim. 1:10), which is the technical term for manifestations on earth of a God. Though truly man, He is nevertheless also our 'great God' (Titus 2:13)." (*Biblical Doctrines*, 6. 183).

The incarnation not only made it possible for God to provide redemption for man. It made possible a much fuller revelation of God to men, which in turn meant that His truth and ideals would become the ruling principles in the inner life of an ever-increasing number of men down through the ages. During the Old Testament dispensation God spoke to the people through the prophets, revealing to them something of His own nature, of man's sinful and lost condition, and of the plan of salvation. But the glory of the present dispensation is that in Christ God *came personally,* and through His own person and work has given man an incomparably more advanced revelation concerning both His own nature and the plan of salvation. The great God who made this world actually came down to the world that He had made, and walked and talked with the people whom He had created. "When men looked upon Jesus," said Dr. Machen, "they actually saw with their eyes one who was truly God. That is the marvel of the incarnation. To behold with one's bodily eyes one who was truly God — what greater wonder can there possibly be than this?"

We may say further that Christ is the final and perfect revelation of God to men, and that He will continue to be such not only on this earth but also in heaven. For while we dare not speak with assurance concerning mysteries so high, yet it seems inconceivable that God in His essential nature as an infinite Spirit can ever be seen by men either in this world or in the next. He it is "whom no man hath seen, nor can see," I Tim. 6:16. But in Christ the Infinite Spirit manifests Himself in finite, human form, that the creature may apprehend Him. We have said that it would seem that even in heaven our vision of God will be that of Christ in His glorified body, which will be finite and limited to one particular place, — not that His body will always remain in the same place, but that it, like our own resurrection bodies, will be in only one place at a time. It is well to remember that the book of Revelation repeatedly pictures Christ on the throne in heaven, and that it is before His throne that the redeemed sing their praises and give thanks for the marvelous deliverance that has been provided for them. We shall then see God in Christ; but apparently we shall not see God the Father nor God the Holy Spirit as such, but only know of their presence through their love for us and their influence over us. Assuming this to be true, the Lord Jesus Christ stands out all the more clearly as the final and perfect revelation of God to men.

It should be observed that as Christ entered into this vital, personal relationship with human nature He conferred upon it an inestimable blessing in that our nature was taken, as it were, into the very bosom of Deity. It was thereby lifted far above that of the angels. With no other creatures in the entire universe does He sustain such a close and intimate relation. As the writer of the Epistle to the Hebrews says, "Since then the children are sharers in flesh and blood, He also Himself in like manner partook of the same. . . . For verily not to angels doth He give help, but He giveth help to the seed of Abraham," 2:14-16. Furthermore, the human nature which Jesus assumed in the incarnation is His forever. He brought it with Him when He rose from the grave and with it He returned to the Father. In heaven He appeared to John like unto a Son of Man, in human form, Rev. 1:13; and the dying Stephen saw the Son of Man standing on the right hand of God, the position of honor and power, Acts 7:56. Through the resurrection and the further exaltation of Christ human nature has in truth attained to the very throne of the universe.

The sojourn of Christ on earth was therefore not a mere theophany or temporary appearance of God in human form, but a real and permanent incarnation. Various Old Testament persons had seen theophanies: Abraham (Gen. 18:1-33); Jacob (Gen. 32:24-30); Moses (Ex. 24:9-11; 34:5, 6); Joshua (Josh. 5:13-15); the father and mother of Sampson (Ju. 13:2-22); Isaiah (Is. 6:1-5); Daniel's three friends (Dan. 3:24, 25); etc. But the incarnation of Christ was quite different. In the incarnation God was born a babe in Bethlehem. For a period of thirty-three years that union continued in a form which manifested the human much more clearly than the Divine, although on numerous occasions the Divine made itself manifest through supernatural works. Particularly on the mount of transfiguration the veil was partially removed and the Divine showed out in its true glory. But with the resurrection and ascension human nature, by virtue of its union with Deity, was glorified far beyond anything of which it was capable in this world.

Concerning the probability or improbability that there would be an incarnation, and the amount of evidence that would be required to convince the average person that an incarnation had taken place, Dr. Craig makes the following worthwhile comment: "We all know that the amount of evidence required to produce faith in an event varies with the nature of the event itself. If, for instance, one or two persons of ordinary veracity should tell you that they had seen a man knocked down by an automobile you would no doubt believe them, since there is nothing very improbable about such an event. If, however, twelve of the most intelligent and upright men of this community should tell you that they had seen a man with the feet of a dog and the wings of a bird, it is not probable that you would believe them. In the one case you would believe on very slight evidence; in the other you would refuse to believe in the face of exceedingly strong evidence. It is not surprising, therefore, that men should admit that the evidence in favor of the Incarnation is strong and yet that they should refuse to admit that such an event ever took place."

And then he continues: "Now, is there such an antecedent presumption against the Incarnation as these would have us believe? I do not think so. In fact, I maintain that when this event is looked at in the light of its purpose we are warranted in saying rather that the presumption is in favor of its occurrence. At this point everything hinges, so it seems to me, upon the moral and spiritual condition of this world. If we think that this world is, on the whole, in a normal condition, morally and spiritually; that men do not stand in any real need of a Saviour from the guilt and power of sin, we will think it more or less inconceivable that God's Son should have assumed flesh and dwelt among us — because we will be unable to perceive that there was any real need for such an act on His part. But if, on the other hand, we believe that this world is in an abnormal condition, morally and spiritually; that it has gone wrong, seriously wrong, so wrong that it is a lost and condemned world; then for those who believe in the existence of a God who is interested in the welfare of His creatures, the presumption is in favor of the notion that He will intervene, that He will put forth His hand to save and to redeem."

"I hold, therefore, that the credibility of the Incarnation is bound up with the question of the moral and spiritual condition of mankind. I am not alone in this. Men in general hold with me in this, as is evident from the fact that we find a close connection between men's views of the moral and spiritual condition of the race and their attitude toward the Incarnation. Generally speaking, where we find men thinking that there isn't much the matter with this world, or at least that it is in as good condition as we can fairly expect at this stage of its development, we find men who refuse to believe in Christ as God manifest in the flesh; but where we find men who recognize that this is a lost world, a world that left to itself would fester in its corruption from eternity to eternity, there we find men who perceive the need of an Incarnation and so men who are ready to assign due weight to the evidence that goes to show that God did indeed so love this world that He gave His only-begotten Son that whosoever believeth in Him might not perish but have eternal life." (*Jesus As He Was and Is*, p. 62).

The importance of the doctrine of the Incarnation in the Christian system can hardly be over-estimated, for the integrity of Christianity as the redemptive religion divinely set forth stands or falls with this doctrine. Nowhere is this more clearly stated than in the First Epistle of John which, written late in the life of the Apostle and at a time when many had begun to apostatize and deny the faith, was designed primarily to establish the faith of believers in the midst of widespread errors. Chief of these errors was the denial, in one form or other, of the incarnation of the Son of God. John not only insists strenuously on the acknowledgment that Jesus Christ has come in the flesh, but makes this the fundamental doctrine of the Gospel. "Every spirit that confesseth that Jesus Christ is come in the flesh," says he, "is of God; and every spirit that confesseth not Jesus is not of God: and this is the spirit of the antichrist, whereof ye have heard that it cometh; and now it is in the world already," I John 4:2, 3. "Whosoever believeth that Jesus is the Christ is begotten of God. . . . And who is he that overcometh the world, but he that believeth that Jesus is the Son of God? . . . He that hath the Son hath life; he that hath not the Son of God hath not the life. . . . We know that the Son of God is come, and hath given us an understanding, that we know Him that is true, and we are in Him that is true, even in His Son Jesus Christ. This is the true God, and eternal life." I John 5:1-20. Judged by this infallible touchstone Modernism, Unitarianism, Christian Science, and all other systems which deny the Deity of Christ or His incarnation stand condemned as false religions.

17. The Sinlessness of Jesus

In any study of the person of Christ it is important to keep in mind that He was altogether free from sin. The Apostle Peter, who had occasion to know Him well, describes Him as "the Holy One of God," John 6:69, and affirms that He "did no sin, neither was guile found in His mouth," I Peter 2:22. The Apostle John declares that "In Him is no sin," I John 3:5. The writer of the Epistle to the Hebrews says that He was "holy, guileless, undefiled, separated from sinners," 7:26, that He was "in all points tempted like as we are, yet without sin," 4:15, and that He "through the eternal Spirit offered Himself without blemish unto God," 9:14. Paul's witness is that He "knew no sin," II Cor. 5:21. The angel Gabriel, in announcing to Mary that she was to become the mother of Jesus, said, "The holy thing which is begotten shall be called the Son of God," Luke 1:35.

Various other sources also testify to the sinlessness of Jesus. The traitor Judas, smitten with remorse, declared, "I have sinned in that I betrayed innocent blood," Matt. 27:4. Pilate's wife warned her husband, "Have thou nothing to do with that righteous man," Matt. 27:19. Pilate weakly proclaimed the innocence of Jesus when he washed his hands before the multitude, saying, "I am innocent of the blood of this righteous man," Matt. 27:24. One of the thieves who was crucified with Him said, "We receive the due reward of our deeds; but this man hath done nothing amiss," Luke 23:41. And the Roman centurion who witnessed the death of Jesus said, "Truly this was the Son of God," Matt. 27:54.

But most important of all in establishing His sinlessness is the testimony of Jesus Himself. "I do always the things that are pleasing to Him," John 8:29. "The prince of the world cometh: and he hath nothing in me," John 14:30. To His enemies, the very ones who were most anxious to point out some flaw in His character, He threw out the challenge, "Which of you convicteth me of sin?" John 8:46, — and the challenge went unanswered. As He stood within the shadow of the cross and reviewed His life He could find no failure of duty, no stain upon His life: "I have kept my Father's commandments," John 15:10; and again, "I have glorified thee on the earth, having accomplished the work which thou hast given me to do," John 14:7 Nowhere in the records do we find that Jesus ever betrayed the slightest consciousness of sin. He prayed often, but never for pardon. He prayed, "Father, forgive them," Luke 23:34, and taught His disciples to pray, "Forgive us our debts," Matt. 6:12; but never does He pray, "Father, forgive me." He went often to the temple, but never offered sacrifice (the essential principle behind sacrifice being, as we are taught in the Old Testament, to acknowledge one's sin and propitiate offended Deity). Death was for Him not the wages of sin, but a voluntary sacrifice for the sake of others. Free both from hereditary depravity and from actual sin, He carried morality to the highest point attained or even attainable by humanity. In His own person He presented the rare spectacle of a life uniformly noble and consistent with His own lofty principles, so that in the Christian religion His own conduct has become the ideal which all of His followers seek to imitate. No other teacher has ever approximated the standards of Jesus, and both friend and foe are almost unanimous in acknowledging His moral grandeur. It was, of course, necessary that the One who was to redeem the world should Himself be free from sin: for no one who was a sinner and who therefore had forfeited his own life could atone for others.

Jesus' claim to sinlessness, and the serenity of His moral and spiritual life, are all the more impressive when we remember that, (1) He was a Jew, trained in the Old Testament with its strong emphasis on the holiness of God and the sinfulness of all men, — compare, for instance, the words of the pious Jew as expressed by Peter when the centurion Cornelius attempted to worship him: "Stand up; I myself also am a man," Acts 10:26; or the words of Paul when the multitude at Lystra would have worshipped him and Barnabas: "We also are men of like passions with you," Acts 14:15. (2) He was keenly conscious of the prevalence and power of sin, and quick to detect it in others . (3) He more than any other teacher pointed out the spiritual meaning of the law as it related to the inner life, motives and character of men. (4) Self-righteousness was to Him the most abhorrent and the most strongly condemned of sins. And, (5) the holiest among the saints of earth have been most conscious of their unworthiness and most sensitive of their sin. Certainly throughout His teaching and the general mode of His life, including the working of many miraculous cures and works of mercy, Jesus acts precisely as we would expect incarnate Deity to act.

As a matter of fact, it was impossible for Christ to commit sin. For in His essential nature He was God, and God cannot sin. This does not mean that He could not be tempted; for as the writer of the Epistle to the Hebrews says, "We have not a High Priest that cannot be touched with the feeling of infirmities; but one that hath been in all points tempted like as we are, yet without sin," 4:15. In order for us to understand how Christ could have been tempted while at the same time there was no possibility that He would fall it is necessary that we keep in mind the real nature of temptation. This has been well expressed by the Lutheran theologian, Dr. Joseph Stump, who says: "Temptation is literally a testing, to see whether the tested one will choose God's service or not. This does not necessarily imply the possibility of a failure to stand the test. Gold may be tested as well as dross. And gold can never fail to stand the test. Theoretically, that is, as long as we do not know that the metal in question is gold, there may be the possibility in our minds that it will fail when put to the proof. But actually there is no such possibility. The gold, just because it is gold, will stand the test and cannot possibly fail to do so. If we were in ignorance of the true nature of Christ's person, we should suppose that He might have failed in the hour of temptation. But knowing, as we do, that He is the veritable Son of God, we know that He could not have sinned. Being pure gold, He could not fail to stand the test. He might be tempted by Satan in many ways; but it was not possible that He should fall, because He was the Son of God." (*The Christian Faith,* p. 148).

Since Christ was free from every taint of either inherited or personal sin, there was nothing in Him to which sin could appeal, nothing to which it could commend itself as attractive. This was the meaning of the words, "The prince of the world cometh; and he hath nothing in me," John 14:30. The Devil could find not the slightest evil tendency or desire in the personality of Jesus to which he could make an appeal, no basis on which He could be persuaded to accomplish His ends by other than lawful means. Since His Divine nature was the dominant and controlling principle in His personality, His human will, which was always in full harmony with His Divine will, was kept steadily inclined toward the right. Consequently, sin, regardless of the form in which it was presented, was always repulsive to Him. Sin often does seem attractive to us and we become its victims, because we still have remnants of the old sinful nature clinging to us, although happily we do find some persons who have made such progress in the Christian way that sin is practically always repulsive to them. And if in this life we find that some of those who have been redeemed reach a state in which they almost invariably turn from sin with contempt, it is not strange that the holy nature of Jesus, which was entirely free from all mental and moral aberrations and from all inherited and personal sin, should unerringly have rejected all temptations to do evil. Christ's inability to commit sin was, strictly speaking, not a limitation, but a perfection; for certainly there is no surer proof of imperfection than that when confronted with a choice between good and evil the person is capable of choosing evil. Consequently, one of the rewards that we look forward to in heaven is that of being confirmed in holiness so that we too shall be unable to commit sin.

18. The Virgin Birth

In the opening chapters of Matthew's and of Luke's Gospel we are given an account of the virgin birth of Jesus. This miracle has been the occasion for considerable debate both within and without the Church, and has often served as a kind of touchstone to indicate whether or not a person is an evangelical. As a general rule one who accepts the virgin birth as true will also accept the other miraculous elements in Scripture, while one who rejects it will also reject a considerable portion of the other miracles. It is therefore of more than average importance, not only because of its bearing on the doctrine of the person of Christ, but also because of its representative character.

We are frequently told nowadays that the presumption is altogether against the notion that miracles should have happened, since they involve a break in the order of nature. If we take into consideration only the physical world the presumption against miracles is, no doubt, almost overwhelming; for it is very evident that we live in an ordered world in which events are casually connected and in which there is no place for chance or caprice. So far as ordinary events are concerned the reign of natural law is invariable. The redemption of mankind, however, is not an ordinary, but a most extraordinary event. In fact, since it is something which determines our eternal condition for happiness or misery we cannot conceive of an event more extraordinary. If we take into consideration moral and spiritual values and grant that the human race is in a very abnormal condition morally and spiritually —that it has, in fact, gone so seriously wrong that if left to itself its condition would be hopeless—the whole matter assumes a different aspect. The presumption then becomes strongly in favor of the view that a loving and merciful God would intervene for the salvation of His people; and such intervention, in the very nature of the case, would involve the miraculous. Miracles then are seen, not as isolated wonders or prodigies for the occurrence of which no good reason can be given, but organically related events in a great system of redemption, at the very center of which stands Christ Himself. Hence the miracles recorded in both the Old and the New Testament, and particularly the miracles of the incarnation and the Resurrection, have to do not with things trivial but with things supremely important. Granted that Christ is the supernatural person that we believe Him to be, it was most appropriate that His entrance into the world and His exit from the world should have been accompanied and accredited by manifestations of the supernatural. Hence the question whether or not miracles have occurred turns on the question whether or not God has provided redemption for His people; and to scoff at the miraculous is to scoff at the reality of redemption.

By way of background for a discussion of the virgin birth it may be well to remind ourselves of the general circumstances which attended that event. These have been set forth beautifully and logically in the following paragraph by Dr. George T. Purves: "Joseph was a carpenter by trade, a man of humble station though of high descent, and a devout Israelite. To Mary the angel announced that she was to become the mother of Messiah (Luke 1:28-38) by the power of the Holy Spirit working in her, and that the child, who was to be called Jesus, should have the throne of His father David. . . . Joseph, seeing her condition, was disposed quietly to put her away without public accusation, but even this gentle treatment was forestalled. An angel revealed to Him in a dream the cause of Mary's condition; told him that he was to have Messiah for his child; and that, as Isaiah had foretold, the latter was to be born of a virgin. With faith, equal to Mary's, Joseph believed the message and made Mary his legal wife. It was thus secured that Mary's child was born of a virgin, and at the same time that He had a legal human father and His mother protected by the love and respectability of a husband. . . . The narrative of Christ's birth beautifully harmonizes with what we now know of His dignity and His mission upon earth. The Messiah was to be the perfect flower of Israel's spiritual life; and so Jesus was born in the bosom of this pious family circle where the pure religion of the Old Testament was believed and cherished. The Messiah was to appear in lowliness; and so Jesus came from the home of the Nazarene carpenter. The Messiah was to be the son of David, and so Joseph, His legal father, and probably

Mary, His actual mother, were descendants from David. The Messiah was to be the incarnation of God, a Divine Person uniting to Himself a human nature, and so Jesus was born of a woman but miraculously conceived by the power of the Holy Spirit." (*Davis Bible Dictionary*, p. 382).

As a matter of fact, it is just in proportion as men lose their sense of the Divine personality of Christ that they come to doubt the reality or the necessity of the virgin birth. If we believe that He existed as God before He came to earth, that His birth was heralded by the appearance of a star and by the announcement of the angels to the shepherds, and that miracles constantly attended His public ministry and were especially conspicuous at the time of His death, resurrection and ascension, then the virgin birth will seem but the natural and normal thing in the advent of such a person. A natural birth would have been a most unnatural thing for such a person as Jesus. Grant the Deity of Christ, and all trouble concerning miracles vanishes away. It then becomes easy to accept all that the Gospels record concerning Him. It is then seen as entirely appropriate that the miraculous life should have been bounded on the one side by the virgin birth and on the other by the resurrection and the ascension. It would, indeed, have been strange and incredible if Deity had entered the human race any other way. There is, in fact, nothing about His person which is not unusual. He Himself is the great miracle, and we expect Him to move in the atmosphere of the supernatural where both His person and His message can be accredited by indisputable proofs. The miracles then become the reasonable thing, not the unreasonable; the credible, not the incredible. In proportion as the Christianity of the New Testament remains vivid and vital to men they instinctively feel that the virgin birth alone is consistent with the person and work of Christ, that He should acknowledge no other father than the Father who is in heaven, from whom alone He came forth to save the world. In fact, had His birth been otherwise we should have felt instinctively that something was amiss. Had He had an ordinary birth with a human father a strong discordant note would have been struck which would have thrown all of the other elements out of tune, and an invitation would thereby have been given for the world to have conceived of the supernatural Saviour as but a natural man. "Born into our race He might be and was; but born of our race, never—whether really or only apparently," says Dr. Warfield.

The close connection between the Deity of Christ and the accounts concerning the virgin birth as given in the Gospels of Matthew and Luke is clearly expressed in the following paragraphs by Dr. Craig.

Says he: "Are we to regard these accounts as sober statements of truth, or are we to place them on a par with the mythological tales of a somewhat similar nature that meet us in other connections? Assuredly our reply cannot be made without reference to the question whether the life and career of Jesus stamp Him as a divine being. If I believe that there was nothing in His life and career inconsistent with my regarding Him as a mere man, *i.e.,* one who was wholly the product of the forces ordinarily energizing in this world, I might not esteem the story of the virgin birth credible. In that case I might feel certain not only that He had a human mother but that He had a human father like the rest of us, and look upon the accounts of Matthew and Luke as containing myths and legends rather than history. But as I cannot consider the life and character and influence of Jesus without having forced upon me the conclusion that He was more than a man, that He was indeed God manifest in the flesh, these accounts of a supernatural birth seem altogether credible to me. In other words, if I were to cease to regard Jesus Christ as a divine being I might easily cease to believe in the virgin birth. . . . But surely there is nothing incredible in the notion that a supernatural being should have come into the world in a supernatural manner."

"I hold, therefore, that the question of the virgin birth is inextricably bound up with the question of Christ's divinity. If, then, one should say to me, I do not believe in the virgin birth, I would straightway ask him, Do you believe in the divinity of Jesus? If he answered No, and could not be moved from that position, I would cherish little hope of being able to persuade him that a virgin was the mother of Jesus. But if he answered Yes, then I would cherish such a hope because I should feel that a mere acquaintance with the facts of the case would be sufficient to convince him of this truth. That I am warranted in this is evidenced by the fact that practically all of those who reject the divinity of Jesus reject at the same time the virgin birth, while practically all of those who accept the divinity of Jesus accept at the same time the virgin birth. . . . . The question of the virgin birth is but part of the larger question of Christ's divinity, or, to speak strickly, of His Deity. Do we on Christmas Day merely commemorate the birth of a great man? Then the accounts of Matthew and Luke may well seem incredible. Do we on that day commemorate the coming into this world of the only begotten Son of God? Then there is nothing incredible in the Gospel accounts, because everything is in perfect harmony with what might be expected at the coming of such a being into this world." (*Jesus As He Was And Is,* p. 50).

We have already pointed out that when Christ became incarnate He took into union with Himself not another human person but impersonal human nature, and that for two different reasons: first, to have taken another person into union with Himself would have given Him a double personality; and secondly, union with another person would have involved Him in original sin; for all of Adam's sons have his sin imputed to them. We have also pointed out that guilt and depravity are attached not to human nature as such, but to individual persons, specifically to all those for whom Adam stood in the covenant of works. Since Christ already possessed personality in His divine nature, He needed only to add to Himself impersonal human nature in order that He might enter into all of the experiences which are common to men. And the Scriptures, from which we derive all our knowledge concerning our covenant relationship both with Adam and with Christ, tell us that Christ was born of the Virgin Mary, God alone being His Father. Hence while He inherited human nature from His mother, He did not inherit a personality and was therefore not chargeable with Adam's sin. Hence the vital importance of the doctrine of the virgin birth, indicating not only the supernatural character of the person so born, but also His absolute separateness from the sin of Adam.

Concerning this subject Dr. Wm. C. Robinson has said: "As our Lord's divine nature had no mother, so His human nature has no father. The Son of man is no man's son. The virgin birth has guided the Church in her efforts to understand and state the union of God and man, and this break in the ordinary generations descending from Adam has presented One unstained by original sin to be the sinner's substitute. The virgin birth is integral to the virgin life and the vicarious death, to the full truthfulness of the Gospels, and to the Church's faith in the incarnation of the pre-existing Lord." (Article in the *Moody Monthly*).

And Dr. Warfield says: "It is only in its relation to the New Testament doctrine of redemption that the necessity of the virgin birth of Jesus comes to its full manifestation. For in this Christianity the redemption that is provided is distinctly redemption from sin; and that He might redeem men from sin it certainly was imperative that the Redeemer Himself should not be involved in sin. . . . Assuredly no one, himself under the curse of sin, could atone for the sin of others; no one owing the law its extreme penalty for himself could pay this penalty for others. And certainly in the Christianity of the New Testament every natural member of the race of Adam rests under the curse of Adam's sin, and is held under the penalty that hangs over it.

If the Son of God came into the world therefore—as that Christianity asserts to be a 'faithful saying'—specifically in order to save sinners, it was imperatively necessary that He should become incarnate after a fashion which would leave Him standing, so far as His own responsibility is concerned, outside that fatal entail of sin in which the whole natural race of Adam is involved. And that is as much as to say that the redemptive work of the Son of God depends upon His supernatural birth." (*Christology and Criticism*, p. 455).

The fact of the matter is that the great Evangelical truths are strongly bound together as with a golden cord. Christ's entrance into this life, like His exit from it, was different from that of other men. And history shows that when the Church becomes lax as to the manner of His entrance, it soon becomes indifferent as to the manner of His departure.

The doctrine of the Virgin Birth thus emerges as an essential doctrine of the Christian system, not in the sense that it is impossible for one to be saved unless he has a clear knowledge and firm conviction of it, but in the sense that no statement of the Christian system which ignores or denies it can be considered consistent or complete.

19. Christ the Messiah of Old Testament Prophecy

We have observed that revelation concerning all of the great doctrines of the Bible has been progressive, that what was only vaguely intimated at first is set forth clearly and fully as time goes on. This we find to be particularly true in regard to the person and work of the Messiah. In the very nature of the case men could have no adequate comprehension of His person and work until He actually came and lived among them; and yet since the whole system of redemption was so vitally and necessarily tied up with Him it was only reasonable to suspect that some intimations of His person and work would have been given in the Old Testament. In the providence of God this wonderful personality of the Messiah was not flashed before our eyes like the sun rising at midnight to dazzle and blind us, but was revealed gradually by the succession of the prophets until our understanding was prepared to receive the whole truth. It is our purpose in this chapter to trace the course of that development and to show that the Old Testament revelations concerning the person and work of the Messiah led up to and had their complete fulfillment in Christ.

The first promise concerning the coming of a Messiah who was to redeem His people is found in the third chapter of Genesis. Immediately after the fall of our first parents a curse was pronounced upon Satan who had been the immediate cause of their fall, and in that curse is contained a veiled promise of redemption: "I will put enmity between thee and the woman, and between thy seed and her seed: He shall bruise thy head, and thou shalt bruise His heel," Gen. 3:15. But while this promise was deeply veiled it was a definite ray of light in the dark night of sin which had settled down over Adam and Eve, and as such it was sufficient to keep them from despair. "The meaning of this promise and prediction," says Dr. Hodge, "is to be determined by subsequent revelations. When interpreted in the light of the Scriptures themselves, it is manifest that the seed of the woman means the Redeemer, and that bruising the serpent's head means His final triumph over the powers of darkness. In this protevangelium, as it has ever been called, we have the dawning revelation of the humanity and divinity of the great deliverer. As seed of the woman His humanity is distinctly asserted, and the nature of the triumph which He was to effect, in the subjugation of Satan, proves that He was to be a divine person. In the great conflict between the kingdom of light and the kingdom of darkness, between Christ and Belial, between God and Satan, He that triumphs over Satan is, and can be nothing less than divine. In the earliest books of Scripture, even in Genesis, we have therefore clear intimations of the two great truths; first, that there is a plurality of persons in the Godhead; and secondly, that one of those persons is specially concerned in the salvation of men,—in their guidance, government, instruction, and ultimate deliverance from all the evils of their apostasy." (*Systematic Theology*, I, 484).

We may add further concerning this promise found in Genesis 3:15 that within it is inferred both the completeness of Christ's victory and also something of the great cost at which that victory would be secured, in that to bruise or crush the head is to inflict a fatal wound, while the bruised heel, though very painful, is not fatal.

It is quite possible that Adam and Eve, like the people of every later generation, looked for or at least hoped for the fulfillment of that promise within their lifetime. When their first son Cain was born Eve said, "I have gotten a man with the help of Jehovah," Gen. 4:1; and when Cain turned out bad and a later son in which they had great hope was born Eve called his name Seth. "For, said she, God hath appointed me another seed instead of Abel," Gen. 4:25. Generations later when Noah was born this same hope seems to have been in evidence, for we read that his father gave him this name (which means "rest"), saying, "This same shall comfort us in our work and in the toil of our hands, which cometh because of the ground which Jehovah hath cursed," Gen. 5:29. Likewise it is quite possible that some of the promises made to David concerning the greatness of his Son who was to sit on his throne, which promises had a preliminary and partial fulfillment in Solomon, led some to believe that the appearance of the Redeemer was near.

In Gen. 22:18 is recorded the promise given to Abraham: "In thy seed shall all the nations of the earth be blessed." To quote Dr. Hodge again, "He who was promised to Adam as the seed of the woman, it was next declared should be of the seed of Abraham. That this does not refer to his descendants collectively, but to Christ individually, we know from the direct assertion of the Apostle (Gal. 3:16), and from the direct fulfillment of the promise. It is not through the children of Abraham as a nation, but through Christ, that all the nations of the earth are blessed. And the blessing referred to, the promise to Abraham, which, as the Apostle says, has come upon us, is the promise of redemption. Abraham therefore saw the day of Christ and was glad, and, as our Lord said, Before Abraham was I am. This proves that the person predicted as the son of the woman and as the seed of Abraham, through whom redemption was to be effected, was to be both God and man. He could not be the seed of Abraham unless man, and he could not be the Saviour of men unless God." *Systematic Theology*, I, 485).

In Gen. 49:10 the dying Jacob, speaking by inspiration and foretelling what would happen to the different tribes in the latter days, says concerning Judah:

> *"The sceptre shall not depart from Judah,*
> *Nor the ruler's staff from between his feet,*
> *Until Shiloh come;*
> *And unto Him shall the obedience of the peoples be,"*

— and while the meaning here is not altogether clear, it is generally understood to mean that Judah was to continue as a nation with at least a nominal king until the coming of the Messiah (which as a matter of historical record is what did happen, the Jews being finally dispersed shortly after that) ; from which time the Lords' people were to know their Messiah personally, to acknowledge Him as their true and rightful King, and so to give their allegiance to Him.

The prophet Balaam, when besought by Balak, king of Moab, to pronounce a curse on the Israelites pronounced instead a blessing, which, while having its preliminary fulfillment in David, evidently can have its complete fulfillment only in Christ:

> *"There shall come forth a star out of Jacob,*
> *And a sceptre shall rise out of Israel,*
> *And shall smite through the corners of Moab*
> *And break down all the sons of tumult."*   Nu. 24:17

In Deut. 18:18, 19 we find a remarkable prophecy given through Moses: "I will raise them up a prophet from among their brethren, like unto thee; and I will put my words in His mouth, and He shall speak unto them all that I shall command Him. And it shall come to pass, that whosoever will not hearken unto my words which He shall speak in my name, I will require it of him."

In II Samuel 7:12-16 we find a great promise made to King David: "When thy days are fulfilled, and thou shalt sleep with thy fathers, I will set up thy seed after thee, that shall proceed out of thy bowels, and I will establish his kingdom . . . I will be his father, and he shall be my son. . . . my loving kindness shall not depart from him. . . . And thy house and thy kingdom shall be made sure for ever before thee: thy throne shall be established for ever." In Ps. 89:3, 4, 36 the same promise is repeated:

> "I have made a covenant with my chosen,
> I have sworn unto David my servant:
> Thy seed will I establish for ever,
> And build up thy throne to all generations . . .
> His seed shall endure for ever,
> And his throne as the sun before me."

This promise received a preliminary fulfillment in David's son Solomon, but in the very nature of the case could not be completely fulfilled in him. Its real fulfillment, as we learn from the New Testament, was reserved for the Messiah, of whom it is said that He was "the son of David," Matt. 1:1; that "He shall be great, and shall be called the Son of the Most High: and the Lord God shall give unto Him the throne of His father David; and He shall reign over the house of Jacob for ever; and of His kingdom there shall be no end," Luke 1:32, 33. In Heb. 1:5 the writer specifically applies to Christ the words of the promise spoken to David in II Sam. 7:14:

> "I will be to Him a Father,
> And He shall be to me a Son;"

as also in Heb. 1:8 he applies to Christ the words of the Messianic 45th Psalm (vs. 6):

> "Thy throne, O God, is for ever and ever;
> And the sceptre of uprightness is the sceptre of thy kingdom."

In the Messianic psalms the coming King is set forth as One who is Deity. In the 110th we read,

"Jehovah saith unto my Lord, Sit thou at my right hand,
Until I make thine enemies thy footstool."

—words of one Jehovah spoken to another (and understandable only in the light of the doctrine of the Trinity), in which David, speaking by inspiration of the Holy Spirit, acknowledges that his greater Son shall be his Lord, words which Christ declared found their fulfillment in Himself (Matt. 22:41-44). In the 96th Psalm the coming of Jehovah to establish a reign of righteousness in all the earth is exultantly announced:

"Let the heavens be glad, and let the earth rejoice;
Let the sea roar, and the fulness thereof;
Let the field exult, and all that is therein;
Then shall all the trees of the wood sing for joy
Before Jehovah; for He cometh,
For He cometh to judge the earth:
He will judge the world with righteousness,
And the peoples with His truth," vss. 11-13.

"I will tell of the decree;
Jehovah said unto me, Thou art my Son;
This day have I begotten thee.
Ask of me, and I will give thee the nations for thine inherit-
ance,
And the uttermost parts of the earth for thy possession,"

Ps. 2:7, 8,—quoted by the writer of the Epistle to the Hebrews (1:5) as having been spoken of Christ.

"Thy throne, O God, is for ever and ever:
A sceptre of equity is the sceptre of thy kingdom,"

Ps. 45:6,—declared in Heb. 1:8 to have been fulfilled in Christ.

The book of Isaiah contains a wealth of material descriptive of the Messiah. In chapter 6 Isaiah records the glorious vision in which he saw Jehovah sitting upon a throne high and lifted up and surrounded by the hosts of adoring angels who worship Him; and in the New Testament the Apostle John, after quoting the words which were spoken to Isaiah at the time of this vision and comparing the unbelief of the people in Christ to that which prevailed in Isaiah's day, declared that the person who was seen by Isaiah was none other than Christ: "These things said Isaiah, because he saw His glory; and he spake of Him," John 12:41. The divinely appointed sign by which the Messiah was to be recognized was that He should be born of a virgin: "Therefore the Lord Himself will give you a sign: behold, a virgin shall conceive, and bear a son, and shall call His name Immanuel," Is. 7:14—than which a name more expressive of His Deity could not have been given; and Matthew, after declaring that this prophecy had its fulfillment in the virgin birth of Christ, adds that the name Immanuel, "being interpreted," means "God with us," i.e., God in our nature (1:23).

In Is. 9:2 the prophet says concerning the inhabitants of Zebulun and Naphtali: "The people that walked in darkness have seen a great light: they that dwelt in the land of the shadow of death, upon them hath the light shined;" and Matthew declares that these words were fulfilled when Christ came and dwelt in the city of Capernaum (4:13-16).

In Is. 9:6, 7 we have a very remarkable and impressive description of the Messiah: "For unto us a child is born, unto us a Son is given; and the government shall be upon His shoulder: and His name shall be called Wonderful Counsellor, Mighty God, Everlasting Father, Prince of Peace. Of the increase of His government and of peace there shall be no end, upon the throne of David, and upon His Kingdom, to establish it, and to uphold it with justice and with righteousness from henceforth even for ever." Here both His humanity and His Deity are clearly foretold, and it is declared that His kingdom, which is to be founded on justice and righteousness, shall be everlasting and universal. Here the term "Mighty God" is applied directly to the Messiah; and the fact that this same term is used again in chapter 10:21 where it means Jehovah shows clearly that the Messiah is declared to be God in the very same sense in which Jehovah is God. To apply those great titles to a merely human representative of Jehovah would involve the Old Testament revelation in self-contradiction; and by no manner of treatment, however ingenious, could that self-contradiction be resolved, without doing violence to all linguistic propriety. It is resolved, however, by the New Testament miracle of the Incarnation of the Son of God, so that the Messiah is at one and the same time Divine and human, the God-man. That this prophecy relates to the Messiah was not disputed even by the Jews until the violence and bitterness of the anti-Christian controversy drove them from the ground which their own progenitors had steadfastly maintained.

In Is. 11:1-10 we have another description in figurative language of the reign of the Messiah as the King of the Golden Age, in which righteousness and peace are to be triumphant over all the earth and forces which have been perpetually at enmity with each other are to be reconciled in Him: "There shall come forth a shoot out of the stock of Jesse, and a branch out of his roots shall bear fruit. And the Spirit of

Jehovah shall rest upon Him, and the spirit of wisdom and understanding, the spirit of counsel and might, the spirit of knowledge and of the fear of Jehovah. And His delight shall be in the fear of Jehovah; and He shall not judge after the sight of His eyes, neither decide after the hearing of His ears; but with righteousness shall he judge the poor, and decide with equity for the meek of the earth: and He shall smite the earth with the rod of His mouth; and with the breath of His lips shall He slay the wicked. And righteousness shall be the girdle of His waist, and faithfulness the girdle of His loins.

"And the wolf shall dwell with the lamb, and the leopard shall lie down with the kid; and the calf and the young lion and the fatling together; and a little child shall lead them. And the cow and the bear shall feed; their young ones shall lie down together; and the lion shall eat straw like the ox. And the sucking child shall play on the hole of the asp, and the weaned child shall put his hand on the adder's den. They shall not hurt nor destroy in all my holy mountain; for the earth shall be full of the knowledge of Jehovah, as the waters cover the sea.

"And it shall come to pass in that day, that the root of Jesse, that standeth for an ensign of the peoples, unto Him shall the nations seek; and His resting-place shall be glorious."

Note the striking parallel between Isaiah's description of the Messiah's complete conquest over the forces of evil when he says, "He shall smite the earth with the rod of His mouth; and with the breath of his lips shall He slay the wicked: (11:4), and the description of Christ's complete conquest of the world by the preached word of the Gospel as given by John in the book of Revelation: "And out of His mouth proceedeth a sharp sword, that with it He should smite the nations: and He shall rule them with a rod of iron" (19:15). Surely no one can deny that Isaiah and John were describing the same person.

In Is. 35:5-10 the very signs and miracles which were to mark the advent of the Messiah were foretold: "Then the eyes of the blind shall be opened, and the ears of the deaf shall be unstopped. Then shall the lame man leap as a hart, and the tongue of the dumb shall sing. . . ." And when the disciples of John the Baptist came to Jesus and asked if He were the Messiah or if they should look for another, it was to these very miracles that He pointed as proof that He was the Messiah: "Go and tell John the things which ye hear and see: the blind receive their sight, and the lame walk, the lepers are cleansed, and the deaf hear, and the dead are raised up, and the poor have good tidings preached to them," Matt. 11:4, 5.

In Is. 42:1-7 the prophet again speaks of the coming age of justice and righteousness, with special mention of blessing to the Gentiles which is a distinctive characteristic of the Gospel age. To the same effect he says in 49:6: "I will give thee for a light to the Gentiles, that thou mayest be my salvation unto the end of the earth." And in the New Testament Luke tells us that when the infant Jesus was presented in the temple the aged and saintly Simeon was given to see that this was the long expected Messiah, and that he praised God with these words:

> *"Now lettest thou thy servant depart, Lord,*
> *According to thy word in peace;*
> *For mine eyes have seen thy salvation,*
> *Which thou hast prepared before the face of all peoples;*
> *A light for revelation to the Gentiles,*
> *And the glory of thy people Israel"* (2:29-32).

Paul calls special attention to this promise that the blessings of the Gospel are to be extended unto the uttermost parts of the Gentile world, Acts 13:47, as does also the Apostle James, Acts 15:17.

The most familiar and the most complete of all the Messianic prophecies is, of course, that found in the 53rd chapter of Isaiah (with which also belongs Is. 52:13-15). Here the nature of His work as suffering, together with its purely vicarious or substitutionary character, is clearly set forth as the only ground on which the sins of His people are forgiven:

"Who hath believed our message? and to whom hath the arm of Jehovah been revealed? For He grew up before Him as a tender plant, and as a root out of a dry ground: He hath no form nor comeliness; and when we see Him, there is no beauty that we should desire Him. He was despised, and rejected of men; a man of sorrows, and acquainted with grief: and as one from whom men hide their face he was despised; and we esteemed Him not.

"Surely He hath borne our griefs, and carried our sorrows; yet we did esteem Him stricken, smitten of God, and afflicted. But He was wounded for our transgressions, He was bruised for our iniquities; the chastisement of our peace was upon Him; and with His stripes we are healed. All we like sheep have gone astray; ye have turned every one to his own way; and Jehovah hath lain on Him the iniquity of us all.

"He was oppressed, yet when He was afflicted He opened not His mouth; as a lamb that is led to the slaughter, and as a sheep that before its shearers is dumb, so He opened not His mouth. By oppression and judgment He was taken away; and as for His generation, who among them considered that He was cut off out of the land of the living for the transgression of my people to whom the stroke was due? And they made His grave with the wicked, and with a rich man in His death; although He had done no violence, neither was any deceit in His mouth.

"Yet it pleased Jehovah to bruise Him; He hath put Him to grief: when thou shalt make His soul an offering for sin, He shall see His seed, He shall prolong His days, and the pleasure of Jehovah shall prosper in His hand. He shall see of the travail of His soul, and shall be satisfied; by the knowledge of Himself shall my righteous servant justify many; and He shall bear their iniquities. Therefore will I divide Him a portion with the great, and He shall divide the spoil with the strong; because He poured out His soul unto death, and was numbered with the transgressors: yet He bare the sin of many, and made intercession for the transgressors."

Isaiah 65:17-25 and 66:22, 23 portray the glorious kingdom which eventually is to result from the Messiah's work, as the Gospel is preached to ever larger numbers of men and the world is effectively turned to righteousness. The Lord's people are to be redeemed not only from the Babylonian captivity, but from all evil; and not merely the Jews but the Gentiles as well are to share in these blessings,—when "the residue of men," and "all the Gentiles," are to "seek after the Lord." Amos 9:11, 12; Acts 15:17. For Jehovah is no mere tribal deity, but "the God of the whole earth." Up to the present time we have had only a foretaste of this great Golden Age, and that in very limited communities. But we see the forces of righteousness advancing, and the forces of evil in retreat; and we look forward to the time when the Gospel shall have won its complete victory and when (as a result of man's increased diligence and his advanced knowledge in the realms of agriculture, biology, chemistry, engineering, etc.) even nature shall reflect gloriously the change that has occurred in the hearts of men,— "when the wilderness and the dry land shall be glad; and the desert shall rejoice and blossom as the rose," Is. 35:1.

In Jer. 23:5, 6 we have another Messianic prophecy: "Behold, the days come, saith Jehovah, that I will raise unto David a righteous Branch, and He shall reign as King and deal wisely, and shall execute justice and righteousness in the land. In His days Judah shall be saved, and Israel shall dwell safely; and this is His name whereby He shall be called: Jehovah our righteousness." In these verses we are told that the restoration of God's people is to be accomplished by One who is. (1) a descendant of David; (2) who is to be a king; (3) whose kingdom is to be founded, not on political or military power, but on wisdom, justice and righteousness; (4) who is called the "Branch," a term which in the book of Isaiah is applied to the Messiah; (5) His reign shall bring peace and harmony,—Judah and Israel, i.e., the Lord's people, are to be united; and (6) He is expressly called "Jehovah our righteousness" (the New Testament makes it clear that we are saved not by any righteousness of our own but by the righteousness of Christ imputed to us and received by faith alone). Consequently the name identifies Him as Christ, the Messiah. And the parallel passage of Jer. 33:14-18 declares that the kingship and the priesthood are to be permanently established through the work of this righteous Branch.

In Dan. 2:44 the kingdom of the Messiah (which was to be preceded by four great world kingdoms, the last of which was the Roman) was foretold as everlasting and as designed to supercede and absorb all other kingdoms: "And in the days of those kings shall the God of heaven set up a kingdom which shall never be destroyed, nor shall the sovereignty thereof be left to another people; but it shall break in pieces and consume all these kingdoms, and it shall stand for ever." Nearly two thousand years have elapsed since the Christian kingdom was set up by the advent of Christ in Palestine. It is still far from its consummation, but it is making progress and its triumph is certain. Already its influence is felt in almost every part of the world. To us who live in the twentieth century, as to the Christians who have lived in each preceding century, it is given to witness a small part of this mighty struggle, this battle of Armageddon, as the forces of good and evil are locked in a titanic battle for the mastery of the world,—while indeed "the kingdom of the world" is slowly but surely becoming "the kingdom of our Lord, and of His Christ," Rev. 11:15.

In the vision recorded in Dan. 7:13, 14 we witness a veritable coronation act which, in the light of the New Testament, we recognize as the reward conferred upon Christ for His work of redemption: "I saw in the night-visions, and, behold, there came with the clouds of heaven one like unto a Son of Man, and He came even to the Ancient of Days, and they brought Him near before Him. And there was given Him dominion, and glory, and a kingdom, that all the peoples, nations, and languages should serve Him: His dominion is an everlasting dominion which shall not pass away, and His kingdom that which shall not be destroyed." Here the transcendental element of the Messianic figure, the "Son of Man," is so strongly stressed that the human traits are almost obscured. Here He is represented as coming with the clouds, which symbolize divine majesty,—a description which is never applied to any other than the Lord of nature, for He alone can ride on the clouds of heaven. It was from this description that Jesus derived His favorite title, "Son of Man," in the use of which He presented Himself as a heavenly Being come to earth on a mission of mercy to lost men. At the trial of Jesus before the Sanhedrin it was His use of this title together with its appropriate setting from Dan. 7:13, 14, which so infuriated the high priest that he rent his garments and declared that Jesus had spoken blasphemy (Matt. 26:64).

In Micah 5:2-5 is found the well-known prediction that the Messiah was to be born in Bethlehem: "But thou, Bethlehem Ephrathah, which art little to be among the thousands of Judah, out of thee shall one come forth unto me that is to be ruler in Israel; whose goings forth are from of old, from everlasting. . . . And He shall stand, and shall feed His flock in the strength of Jehovah, in the majesty of the name of Jehovah His God: and they shall abide; for now shall He be great unto the ends of the earth. And this man shall be our peace." Concerning these verses Dr. Hodge says: "The prophet Micah predicted that one was to be born in Bethlehem, who was to be, (1) The Ruler of Israel, i.e., of all the people of God. (2) Although to be born in time and made of a woman, His 'goings forth are from of old, from everlasting.' (3) He shall rule in the exercise of the strength and majesty of God, i.e., manifest in His government the possession of divine attributes and glory. (4) His dominion shall be universal; and (5) Its effects peace, i.e., perfect harmony, order, blessedness." (Systematic Theology, I, 493). And that these verses were understood by the Jews to predict the advent of the Messiah is proved from Matt. 2:4-6, where, in response to Herod's inquiry as to where the Christ should be born, the priests and scribes readily replied by quoting Micah 5:2

In Zechariah the Messiah is described as the "King," who is "just, and having salvation; lowly, and riding upon an ass, even upon a colt the foal of an ass," 9:9 (with which compare Matthew's account of Jesus' public entry into Jerusalem, 21:1-11); whose dominion is to be universal: "His dominion shall be from sea to sea, and from the River to the ends of the earth," 9:10; who is to be sold for thirty pieces of silver, 11:12, 13 (with which compare Matthew's account of Judas' treachery 26:14-16). Because the Jews rejected the Messiah they have brought upon themselves untold suffering and reproach and have been given up to long dispersion. This too was foretold by Zechariah: "I will scatter them with a whirlwind among all the nations which they have not known," 7:14,—and this is precisely what they have experienced during these nineteen centuries that have elapsed since that time. But happily Zechariah tells us something more. At long last God is to pour out upon the people of Israel "the spirit of grace and of supplication," and many are to turn to the Messiah and repent: "And they shall mourn for Him, as one mourneth for his only son, and shall be in bitterness for Him, as one that is in bitterness for his first-born," 12:10. This was fulfilled in part at least on the day of

Pentecost, when Peter preached with such power and conviction that "they were all amazed, and were perplexed, saying one to another, What meaneth this?" — and "about three thousand souls." all Jews. were converted in one day, Acts 2:12, 41. Furthermore, says Zechariah, Messiah's kingdom is to triumph and become universal: "Jehovah shall be king over all the earth," 14:9.

And Malachi, the last of the Old Testament prophets, declares that "The Lord, whom ye seek, will suddenly come to His temple; and the Messenger of the covenant, whom ye desire, behold, He cometh, saith Jehovah of hosts," 3:1; and again, "Unto you that fear my name shall the Sun of Righteousness arise with healing in its wings," 4:2. Like the other prophets, he too foretells a reign of righteousness and peace, emphasizing that the Gentiles as well as the Jews are to share its blessings "For from the rising of the sun even unto the going down of the same my name shall be great among the Gentiles; and in every place incense shall be offered unto my name, and a pure offering: for my name shall be great among the Gentiles, saith Jehovah of hosts," 1:11 (also 3:2-5, 11, 12; 4:3). And at the very close of his book and of the Old Testament, as if it were a sign post pointing across the silent centuries to the New Testament, we find the prophecy that Elijah the prophet is to return and prepare the way for the Messiah (4:5, 6),—which prophecy, Matthew tells us, was fulfilled in John the Baptist, who came in the spirit and power of Elijah and prepared the way for Jesus (11:10; 17:10-13).

Thus we find that from the very first the Old Testament clearly and repeatedly predicts the advent of a divine person clothed in our nature, who was to be the Redeemer of His people. As the revelation is unfolded by the procession of the prophets He is set forth as truly man, the seed of the woman, the seed of Abraham, of the tribe of Judah. a prophet like unto Moses, of the house of David, a man of sorrows and acquainted with grief, to be born of a virgin, in the village of Bethlehem; He is to be lowly in manner, He is to be heralded by one reminiscent of the prophet Elijah, and He is suddenly to come to His Temple. Yet it was no less clearly revealed that He was to be a divine person, the Mighty God, One who would exercise divine prerogatives and receive divine worship from men and angels, One who would accredit Himself before the people by working miracles of healing on the blind, the lame, the deaf and the dumb, a triumphant King whose dominion is to be extended until it embraces the entire world. Sometimes the Divine, sometimes the human side of His nature is held up more prominently by the prophets. And, as the New Testament makes clear, these prophecies were literally fulfilled in Christ. The specific purpose for which they were given was to make it possible for the people to recognize the Messiah at once by comparing these descriptions with His person and work. But alas, that the very people to whom the Scriptures were entrusted were so blind that they not only failed to recognize Him, but rejected Him completely with the most shameful and abusive treatment!

Thus the outstanding element in the eschatological system of the Old Testament was the expectation that in some majestic way God would again come to His people and walk and talk with them as He had done in the Garden of Eden. From the very beginning the Jewish religion was a religion of hope, and also from the very beginning it was prepared sometime to become the world-religion. Far from the Messianic idea being merely the expectation of an outstanding earthly king and having been developed late in the history of Israel as some of the critics would have us believe, the devout-minded in Israel had ever before them the hope that their salvation would be made sure through the appearance of Jehovah in person. Throughout the Old Testament period they looked for salvation to the same Christ that we look to, and never were they encouraged to look to any other.

The New Testament takes up the narrative concerning the Messiah at just the point where the Old Testament had left off. Everywhere the Christ of the New Testament is presented as the One who fulfills the Messianic prophecies of the Old. Matthew begins his Gospel by tracing the genealogy of Jesus through David and Abraham. He records the virgin birth of Jesus as the fulfillment of the prophecy in Is. 7:14, His birth in Bethlehem as the fulfillment of Micah 5:2, and the ministry of John the Baptist as the fulfillment of Is. 40:3. Mark begins his Gospel by declaring that Jesus Christ is the Son of God, and that the ministry of John the Baptist fulfills the prophecies in Is. 40:3 and Mal. 3:1. Luke, in recording the words of the angel Gabriel, says concerning Jesus that "He shall be great, and shall be called the Son of the Most High: and the Lord God shall give unto Him the throne of His father David: and He shall reign over the house of Jacob for ever; and of His kingdom there shall be no end," 1:32, 33. He also records the testimony of the aged and saintly Simeon who, when Jesus was presented in the temple, recognized Him as the Messiah through whom God would provide salvation, and as "A light for revelation to the Gentiles, And the glory of thy people Israel," 2:32. John begins his Gospel with a Prologue in which he sets forth the Deity of the incarnate "Word," and relates Jesus intimately to the Old Testament doctrine of redemption with the designation, "The Lamb of God, that taketh away the sin of the world," 1:29.

There is, of course, no doubt but that Jesus Himself claimed to be the Messiah. Early in His ministry, in response to the words of the woman of Samaria, "I know that Messiah cometh," He said: "I that speak unto thee am He," John 4:26. He accepted as accurate and as His just due the words of Peter, "Thou art the Christ, the Son of the living God," Matt. 16:16, and declared that this truth had been revealed to him not by men but by His Father who is in heaven. He accepted also the testimony of Martha: "I have believed that thou art the Christ, the Son of God, even He that cometh into the world," John 11:27. To the Pharisees He said, "Except ye believe that I am He, ye shall die in your sins," John 8:24,—than which a more stupendous claim could hardly be made. In His controversy with the Pharisees He pointed out that their ideas of the Messiah fell far below the teaching of their own Scriptures; for while they thought of Him only as David's son, the Scriptures presented Him also as David's Lord (Matt. 22:41-45). When the disciples of John the Baptist came to ask if He were the Messiah, or if they should look for another, He replied, "Go and tell John the things which ye hear and see: the blind receive their sight, and the lame walk, the lepers are cleansed, and the deaf hear, and the dead are raised up, and the poor have good tidings preached to them," Matt. 11:4, 5. These and similar miracles were the very signs that Isaiah had said would accompany the work of the Messiah (35:5, 6). In response to the request of the Jews that if He were the Christ He tell them plainly, Jesus said, "I told you, and ye believe not: the works that I do in my Father's name, these bear witness of me," John 10:25. These miracles should have been sufficient evidence to have convinced any one. Such evidence was sufficient for the woman at the well in Samaria who, free from prejudice and acting only on her simple faith and common sense and with characteristic reticence, said to the people of the town, "Come, see a man, who told me all things that ever I did: can this be the Christ?" John 4:29. They were sufficient to convince the disciples (John 2:11; Luke 5:8), as well as many of the common people (John 6:14; 10:42; 11:45; 12:11), Jesus' public entry into Jerusalem at the beginning of passion week was especially designed to manifest publicly His claims to Messiahship (Luke 19:29-40). And during the trial before the Sanhedrin He claimed under oath and in a most public and explicit manner that He was the Messiah. In response to the charge of the high priest, "I adjure thee by the living God, that thou tell us whether thou art the Christ, the Son of God," Jesus answered, "Thou hast said: nevertheless I say unto you, Henceforth ye shall see the Son of Man sitting at the right hand of Power, and coming on the clouds of heaven," Matt. 26:64.

As Jesus met with the disciples after the resurrection He completed the revelation that He had been making concerning Himself, pointing out to them how the Old Testament had predicted His sufferings and the glory that was to follow. In Luke 24:25-27 we are told that Jesus, as He walked with the disciples on the road to Emmaus, rebuked them for not perceiving the clear teaching of the Old Testament concerning His sufferings: "O foolish men, and slow of heart to believe in all that the prophets have spoken! Behooved it not the Christ to suffer these things, and to enter into His glory? And beginning from Moses and from all the prophets, He interpreted to them in all the Scriptures the things concerning Himself." No doubt He brought out the meaning of many other texts which we have not yet understood. Earlier He had said to the Jews, "If ye believed Moses, ye would believe me; for he wrote of me," John 5:46. Even before His incarnation and suffering lighted up so many dark passages of the ancient Scriptures it should have been apparent that the Messiah was to be not merely a son of David according to the flesh but also Deity, and not merely a King but also One who was to bear a burden of suffering. And since the sacrificial system with its emphasis on the pascal lamb pervaded the entire religious life of the Jewish people and prefigured the atonement which was to be worked out by the Messiah, this in itself should have given a strong lead as to what the mission of the Messiah would be when He came. Hence it is clear that the Old Testament did set forth the person and work of the Messiah who was to come. Had the Jewish people been spiritually awake they would have had no difficulty at all in recognizing the Messiah.

We should also point out that the testimony of the disciples to the Messiahship of Jesus is equally strong. The Gospels are, of course, distinctly not biographies of Jesus in the sense in which we usually think of biographies. Rather they are theses written to prove that He was the promised Messiah. John in particular states the purpose of his book when he says: "Many other signs therefore did Jesus in the presence of the disciples, which are not written in this book; but these are written, that ye may believe that Jesus is the Christ, the Son of God; and that believing ye may have life in His name," 20:30, 31. Each of the Gospels is composed primarily of recorded incidents or teachings which are designed to prove the Deity or Messiahship of Christ, and the details concerning His life are brought in only incidentally. This method, however, most effectively reveals the background and brings the attributes of the supernatural Being into view in the most natural way; and the practical purpose of the writers, that of being spiritually helpful to their readers, is most effectively served. Peter, speaking for the disciples, the group that knew His life most intimately, said, "Thou art the Christ, the Son of the living God," Matt. 16:16; and again he said, "To Him bear all the prophets witness," Acts 10:43. And Phillip's interpretation of the prophecies of Isaiah led the Ethiopian eunuch to the conclusion that Jesus was the Messiah so that he desired to be baptized in His name, Acts 8:26-40. Moreover in this connection it should be kept in mind that the facts concerning the person and actions of Christ were well known to the early Christians to whom the Gospels and the Epistles were written, and that consequently nowhere is the doctrine of the person of Christ formally expounded. The writers very naturally did not feel the need of giving instructions concerning that which was already common property among the Christians, but in most cases only alluded incidentally to the elements in the doctrine of the person of Christ as they set Him forth as an example of conduct for others. Even in Phil. 2:5-9 where Paul, the most didactic of the New Testament writers, intimates more fully than anywhere else his conception of the person of Christ, his primary object is to set Him forth as an example of unselfishness. Although He existed as Deity before His incarnation, says Paul, He did not look selfishly upon His condition of equality with God, but emptied Himself, took the form of a servant and became obedient even to the death of the cross in order that others might share in His true riches and fulness.

The early Christian Church strongly pressed the claim that Christ was the Messiah who was foretold in the Old Testament. Peter pointed out that David, "foreseeing this spake of the resurrection of Christ, that neither was He left unto hades, nor did His flesh see corruption. This Jesus did God raise up," Acts 2:31, 32 (compare Ps. 16:8-11 and Acts 2:24-32). The point here made is that the resurrection is a proof that Jesus was the Messiah. Stephen gave his witness unflinchingly before the rulers of Israel, declaring that they had betrayed and killed "the Righteous One" whose coming had been foretold by the prophets, Acts 7:52. Paul affirms that "they that dwell in Jerusalem, and their rulers, because they knew Him not, nor the voices of the prophets which are read every Sabbath, fulfilled them by condemning Him," Acts 13:27. The belief that Jesus was the Christ was, of course, the very corner stone of belief in the early Christian Church, the distinguishing mark which set it apart from continuing Judaism.

It is very evident that the Old Testament portrait of the Messiah was largely misunderstood by the Jewish people. The turbulent political life through which they were passing naturally had its effect on their religious life. For nearly six hundred years they had suffered under the tyranny of foreign invaders. Thus molded by oppression and poverty they had come to think of the Messianic kingdom in terms of political empire and material prosperity. So far as the official classes were concerned the purely religious hopes of the Old Testament had been almost forgotten, and even among the common people the idea of a spiritual kingdom had been largely displaced by that of an earthly kingdom. They longed for a restoration of the kingdom as it had been under David and Solomon, with added power and wealth. There were, however, some few righteous and devout souls, such as Joseph and Mary, Zecharias and Elizabeth, Simeon, the shepherds and the wise-men who saw the true spiritual import of the Messianic prophecies. But when Jesus explained to Nicodemus that entrance into the kingdom of God meant such a change of character and conduct that a man might truly be said to have been born anew, Nicodemus, although a trained religious thinker of the Jews, could not understand; and the disciples even after three years of intimate association with Jesus still found it hard to subordinate the political and military and economic aspects of the kingdom to the spiritual. Witness their question as He talked to them just before His ascension: "Lord, dost thou at this time restore the kingdom to Israel?" It is true, of course, that the Old Testament prophesies do foretell a great golden age of political freedom and material prosperity in connection with the Messianic kingdom; but this phase of the kingdom was subordinated to the spiritual, and in fact is largely future even in our own day.

We have also noted that one prominent element in the Messianic prophecies was the promise that the Gentiles were to share in the future blessings. While in Old Testament times God's revelation was given almost exclusively to the Jews (not that they might selfishly hoard it for themselves, but that they might be blessed by it and in turn pass it on to the Gentiles, in which task, however, they proved extremely derelict), and while even in the New Testament we are reminded that "Salvation is from the Jews," John 4:22 (in that our only Saviour, Jesus Christ, "as concerning the flesh," Rom. 9:5, was a Jew and the Bible is of Jewish origin), the old distinctions have been abolished and Jews and Gentiles now stand as equals before God. Within the Christian realm the distinction between Jew and Gentile, like the distinction between bond and free or male and female, means nothing. Paul tells us that all true Christians are "sons of God, through faith, in Christ Jesus. For as many of you as were baptized into Christ did put on Christ. There can be neither Jew nor Greek, there can be neither bond nor free, there can be no male and female; for ye are all one man in Christ Jesus," Gal. 3:26-28. In writing to the Gentile church in Ephesus Paul reminded them of their former condition, saying, "Ye, the Gentiles in the flesh ... were at that time separate from Christ, alienated from the commonwealth of Israel, and strangers from the covenants of the promise, having no hope and without God in the world." And then he added: "But now in Christ Jesus ye that once were afar off are made nigh in the blood of Christ. For He is our peace, who made both one, and brake down the middle wall of partition ... And He came and preached peace to you that were afar off, and to them that were nigh: for through Him we both have our access in one Spirit unto the Father. So then ye are no more strangers and sojourners, but ye are fellow-citizens with the saints, and of the household of God, being built upon the foundation of the apostles and prophets, Jesus Christ Himself being the chief cornerstone." Eph. 2:11-20.

Furthermore, in matters pertaining to salvation the spiritual relationship is stronger than the physical. This principle was set forth by Christ Himself: "Whosoever shall do the will of my Father who is in heaven, he is my brother, and sister, and mother," Matt. 12:50. Paul sets forth Abraham as the typical example of the true believer, and declares that the believing Gentile is in a truer sense a son of Abraham than is an unbelieving Jew. "Know therefore that they that are of faith, the same are sons of Abraham," Gal. 3:7. And again, "If ye are Christ's then are ye Abraham's seed, heirs according to promise," Gal. 3:29. The fact of the matter is that Jews have no other righteousness than that which comes through faith in Christ, no standing whatever with God except as they acknowledge Christ as their Saviour; and Gentile believers possess fully this same righteousness by faith alone.

During the past two thousand years the Christian Church has been largely a Gentile Church, and the attitude of the Jews has been mainly that of opposition—due in part to a blind prejudice which has not allowed them to examine fairly and openly the evidence for Christianity, and also in part, it must be admitted, to the indifference or even persecution which professing Christians, both Protestants and Catholics, have directed against them. It should be pointed out, however, that such persecution is utterly contrary to all Christian principles and repulsive to all true Christians, that all true Christians have a deep sympathy for the Jews as God's ancient people and as the race from which our Saviour came, and that such persecution as has taken place has been instigated by misguided or unchristian people who were betraying the very principles which they professed to hold.

It is a mistaken view which expects a future period in which God will single out the Jews and bless them above the Gentiles. Their primary mission as the channel through which the oracles of God were given, and as the race which was to provide the Saviour of the world, has been fulfilled, and they now stand on exactly the same footing as do the Gentiles, needing equally the righteousness of Christ for salvation and being utterly without hope apart from that righteousness. There are, however, numerous promises in Scripture that they, along with the Gentiles, are to be converted to Christianity. We have already noted the prophecy that they shall look upon Him whom they pierced, and that they are to mourn for Him as one mourns for his first-born. In the eleventh chapter of Romans Paul likens the Jews to the natural branches of the olive tree which were broken off and the Gentiles to wild branches which have been grafted in. He points out that "by their fall salvation is come unto the Gentiles, to provoke them to jealousy," and adds: "Now if their fall is the riches of the world, and their loss the riches of the Gentiles; how much more their fulness?" In contrast with that of the Gentiles, the spiritual energy and zeal with which they are capable of responding to their own religion is likened to "life from the dead." Paul says pointedly that "God is able to graft them in again," and that "a hardening in part hath befallen Israel, until the fulness of the Gentiles be come in; and so all Israel shall be saved: even as it is written, There shall come out of Zion the Deliverer; He shall turn away ungodliness from Jacob," Rom. 11:23, 25, 26. How tragic it is that all these years the Jewish people should have rejected Him who in the highest sense is "the glory of His people Israel." But events sometimes take unexpected courses and, strange as it may seem, the second World War has produced a marked change in the attitude of the Jews toward Christ. Whereas for ages they have been governed by a blind hatred and opposition to Him, the very mention of His name being forbidden in the Ghetto and in the synagogue, the attitude of the Christian Church as it has attempted to sheild them from persecution and to minister to them in the dictator-dominated countries has caused them to see Christianity in a new light. While no considerable numbers have yet acknowledged Christ as Messiah, many outstanding teachers and leaders have tried to outdo themselves in acknowledging Him as an incomparable teacher and leader. This in itself is, of course, not enough, but it is a long step in the right direction.

In concluding this phase of our study, then, we would point out that the Christ of the New Testament is the perfect fulfillment of the Old Testament Messianic prophecies. In His Divine-human person, the manner of His birth, His teaching, His miracles, the death He died, the redemption He accomplished, and the nature of the kingdom that He has established, the distinguishing marks of the Messiah are fully satisfied.

20. The Personal Appearance of Jesus

One rather surprising thing which emerges in connection with a study of the person of Christ is that no authentic records which we possess make any attempt to describe His physical features. Artists have painted their pictures and sculptors have made their statues, but the likenesses are imaginary. So far as His general appearance was concerned He undoubtedly appeared to be only a man, a perfectly normal man. There is, of course, not the slightest evidence which would lead us to believe that a halo of light surrounded His head, either in infancy or in later years. Isaiah's prophecy that "He hath no form nor comeliness; and when we see Him, there is no beauty that we should desire Him" (53:2), seems to indicate that He was to be a perfectly normal man, that He was to possess no outward qualities which would set Him off from other men as such. But He was a very outstanding man. The phrase, "Son of Man," seems to indicate that He answered to the idea of perfect humanity as it was intended in the original creation. We are told that the people who heard Him in the days of His flesh remarked, "Never man so spake," John 7:46; that they "wondered at the words of grace which proceeded out of His mouth," Luke 4:22; and that His teaching, as contrasted with that of the scribes, was with "authority," Matt. 7:29. His were words of wisdom and power always, and we believe there never was another human voice so full of music and resonance and grace as was the voice of the Lord Jesus. It must have been a rare privilege to have heard Him speak to men, and an even more rare privilege to have heard Him when He spoke to God in prayer. It was after the disciples had heard Him pray that they felt in their hearts a great desire to be able to pray as He did, and they said, "Lord, teach us to pray, even as John also taught his disciples," Luke 11:1.

And where else in all humanity do we find such a marvelous union and balance of opposite traits as in the personality of Jesus? As Dr. E. Y. Mullins has said: " Where does humanity shine with such a radiance as in Him? Who among the sons of men were ever so 'meek and lowly in heart?' Did ever weary humanity feel a touch so tender? Did patience ever conquer so splendid a Kingdom? Did modesty and gentleness ever find so complete an incarnation? Or self-denial ever master a life so completely? Over against these lowly virtues note the heroic ones. 'All power has been given unto me,' He said. 'Woe unto you scribes and Pharisees, hypocrites,' was His own hot blast of judgment. Speaking of Himself He said if this stone fall on a man it will grind him to powder. He alone was Lord and Master, the disciples were brethren. What mortal is it that hurls out this challenge, 'Which of you convicteth me of sin?' He it was who was filled with an ambition to rule the race and predicted His coming on the clouds of heaven surrounded by angels. The union of opposites in perfect balance appears in Jesus. Other men are fragments. He is the complete man. He is weary and asleep on the boat as any tired apostle might have been; but He stands up and with a voice of power stills a tempest. He weeps with the other broken-hearted ones at a grave; but with a divine voice calls forth the dead Lazarus. He yields to His captors as any culprit might have done; but works a miracle to restore a severed ear and rebuke the rash disciple who smote it off." (*Why Is Christianity True?* p. 21.)

There are those who have been led to see in Jesus only a sort of mild effeminate character who, while markedly free from evil, was decidedly lacking in strength and ruggedness of character. Unfortunately most of the artists have presented Him as a delicate man with a thin face and small hands. But the New Testament presents Him quite differently. The Jesus there presented was a carpenter who earned His living with His own hands; and a carpenter's hands have more of strength than delicacy, more muscle than fineness of shape. We do not know how He looked, except that He was a Jew and an oriental. But surely He was vigorous and masculine and strong, a man's man in every respect. He won the devotion of a select group of men friends. At Nazareth He walked boldly through the midst of a hostile mob that had gathered to hurl Him over a cliff; and in the garden of Gethsemane when voluntarily surrendering Himself He stepped from the shadows with such majestic personality that those who had come to arrest Him recoiled backward and fell to the ground. Bravely He went to a dreadful death and bore the world's sin in His own body on the cross. Certainly the Gospels give us to understand that He was strong, and that the whole bearing of His personality was impressive and commanding.

In this same connection the present writer on another occasion has said: "Too long the picture of Jesus as a weak, inoffensive, harmless soul has been allowed to go unchallenged. The New Testament certainly does not present Him as such a person. These characteristics have been inferred partly, no doubt, by the fact that in dealing with the erring and with those who were afflicted or in sorrow He was gentle and sympathetic; partly because of His admonition to 'resist not him that is evil' (Matt. 5:39, where the context makes it clear that He forbids the taking of revenge, not that He advocated non-resistance in general); and partly because of the fact that during His public ministry women were drawn with peculiar loyalty to His service and in many instances have been more active than men in the Church since that time. In regard to this latter consideration it is well to keep in mind that in the ordinary relationships between men and women it is the masculine qualities of strength, initiative and leadership, not the feminine qualities, which women most admire in men. The disciples and all others who saw and heard Jesus were strongly impressed with His courage, His fearlessness, His tireless energy, and His air of supreme self-confidence and leadership. Repeatedly the Gospel writers use the words 'power' and 'authority' in connection with Him. From the beginning of His public ministry until He was nailed to the cross He was in courageous opposition to the scribes and Pharisees, showing how they perverted the Scriptures, denouncing them as liars and hypocrites, and exposing their fraudulent practices. Single-handed and alone He stood against those organized groups which were holding His people in mental and spiritual bondage. He called His disciples not to a life of ease and comfort and safety, but to one of hardship and sacrifice and danger. He sent them out on a mission which would take them to the ends of the earth, and warned them that they would suffer many persecutions and in some instances death. Certainly no weakling could have inspired men for such service as that."

While at first it may strike us as strange that none of the New Testament writers has given any description of Jesus, not even so much as one of His physical features having been mentioned, that was undoubtedly a wise provision in the divine plan. It was designed in part, at least, to prevent idolatry. In all ages men have shown themselves very prone to make and worship idols. Witness not only the almost universal practice of idol worship among heathen, but also the strong tendency toward it among the Jews in Old Testament times, and even today in the professedly Christian Roman Catholic Church where countless images of Christ, the Virgin and the saints are given reverent adoration. We can hardly imagine to what extent this abuse would have been carried, especially among the more ignorant of the people, if they had possessed a real likeness of Christ. As in the earlier dispensation the grave of Moses was kept secret (Deut. 34:6) and thereby safely out of the reach of idolatry and special veneration, so here a wise directing providence has concealed the true likeness of Christ. "God is a Spirit," says John, "and they that worship Him must worship in spirit and truth," John 4:24.

It is of interest, however, to note that we have very definite information concerning one item of Jesus' dress. The pious Jew had God's command to wear a blue fringe on the border of his outer garment.

The Hebrew and Greek words used to describe this fringe are variously translated by different scholars: fringe, hem, border, lace. But at any rate it was something blue on the edge of the garment. Blue is a heavenly color, the color of the sky, a reminder of God. It was one of the principal colors of the tabernacle; and one of the high priest's outer garments was of blue. The command concerning the blue fringe was given by Moses and is found in Nu. 15:37-40. After an object lesson of sin and punishment, the people then and throughout their generations were commanded to wear a blue fringe on their garments as a reminder of God and His commandments. Of the Scribes and Pharisees in Jesus' day it was said that they "made broad their phylacteries, and enlarged the borders of their garments," Matt. 23:5. It is the blue fringe that is referred to in Matt. 9:20, where we are told that the woman with an issue of blood "came behind Him, and touched the border of His garment"; and again in Matt. 14:36, where we are told that the men of Gennesaret brought to Him all that was sick, and that "they besought Him that they might only touch the border of His garment: and as many as touched were made whole." Jesus was a true Jew and preached to Jews. He came not to destroy but to fulfill the law. He was born under the Old Testament dispensation and scrupulously observed the ceremonial law throughout His entire earthly life. It was in fact His death on the cross which closed the Old Testament dispensation and ushered in the New. He was the real Lamb of God, and His sacrifice was the reality to which the Old Testament sacrifices looked forward and of which they were but the symbols and shadows. Undoubtedly He wore the blue fringe.

There is an old tradition—on what authority it rests we do not know—which says that Jesus was never seen to laugh a single time, but that He was seen to weep. Whether that was true or not at least the spirit of it is good. That He did weep we are told in Scripture,—John 11:35. That He was never seen to laugh may at first seem strange to some. But for One who saw and fully understood fallen human nature, who knew that apart from divine grace every member of the race was hopelessly lost and on the way to eternal destruction, and who was conscious that the whole burden of redemption rested exclusively on His shoulders, life could be no laughing matter. We can laugh and enjoy life because our burden has been borne by another. Indeed, the world now has much of happiness and joy in it. But let us remember that that happiness and joy was purchased for us by One who suffered in our stead and who paid in His own person and in full the awful price that sin entails. Jesus could not be off guard for one moment, nor enter into the light-hearted pleasures in which we indulge so freely. Rather His attitude toward life would seem to be reflected more accurately by such statements as that of Luke 9:51 where we read that "He steadfastly set His face to go to Jerusalem" (when He knew that crucifixion awaited Him), and that of Luke 12:50: "I have a baptism to be baptized with; and how am I straightened till it be accomplished!" This means primarily that His attitude toward life was one of extreme earnestness, but not that He was in any sense gloomy or morose. Witness His presence with His disciples at the wedding in Cana, where He turned the water into wine in order that the wedding festivities might proceed normally. The multitudes, we are told, heard Him gladly and sometimes were attracted to Him in such great numbers that it was humanly impossible for Him to minister to all of them. His birth was heralded by the angels as bringing "good tidings of great joy which shall be to all the people," Luke 2:10. Repeatedly He spoke of spiritual and heavenly joys, which in reality are the only permanent and abiding joys: Matt. 25:21; Luke 6:23; 15:7, 10; John 3:29; 15:11; 16:20, 22, 24; etc. From childhood to old age people in Christian lands have many joys which are unknown to those who live in non-Christian lands. Furthermore we may add that Christianity, far from being a kill-joy religion as so many would have us believe, is in reality the only true basis for happiness. The word "Gospel" literally means *good news,* the good news of what Christ has done for us. In fact, Christians are the only persons in this sinful world who have a genuine cause to be happy. For, despite whatever trials and hardships they may have (which trials, Paul says, "are not worthy to be compared with the glory which shall be revealed to us-ward," Rom. 8:18), their eternal happiness is assured and each passing day only brings them that much closer to that rich inheritance. But non-Christians, despite whatever worldly pleasures they may have, are, so long as they remain astray from God, only living in a fool's paradise, and each new day only brings them that much nearer their final destruction. Incidentally Matthew gives us an interesting item concerning the home life of Jesus, to the effect that He had four brothers and at least three sisters. He records that when Jesus returned to His home town of Nazareth the people were astonished at His teaching and said, "Is not this the carpenter's son? is not his mother called Mary? and his brethren, James, and Joseph, and Simon, and Judas? And his sisters are they not all with us?" Matt. 13:55, 56. Undoubtedly those were the natural brothers and sisters of Jesus, or, strictly speaking, half-brothers and half-sisters, since Jesus was the supernaturally born Son of Mary only, while the others were the natural children who were later born to Joseph and Mary. There is no Scriptural ground whatever for holding, as does the Roman

Catholic Church, that these were merely cousins or other distant relatives, for in the original Greek the words here translated brothers and
sisters are the same as those used for natural brothers and sisters in
other parts of the New Testament. The Roman Catholic interpretation
is of course influenced by their doctrine of the perpetual virginity of
Mary, and also no doubt by their doctrine of the celibacy of the clergy
and the unmarried state of the nuns.

21 The Offices of Christ

The mediatorial work of Christ is most conveniently treated under
three heads or offices. This does not mean that it can be divided into
three separate and independent parts, for it cannot. But it does mean
that in this form it can be presented more logically and systematically.
These three offices, together with the nature of the work accomplished
under each, are clearly stated in the Shorter Catechism. In answer to
the question, "What offices doth Christ execute as our Redeemer?"
(Question 23), the answer is given: "Christ, as our Redeemer, executeth the offices of a prophet, of a priest, and of a king, both in His
estate of humiliation and exaltation."

1. CHRIST AS PROPHET

In answer to the question, "How doth Christ execute the office
of a prophet?" the Catechism answers: "Christ executeth the office
of a prophet, in revealing to us, by His Word and Spirit, the will of
God for our salvation." A prophet, as the term is used in Scripture,
is one who speaks for another, specifically, one who is qualified and
authorized to speak for God to men. Christ was, of course, the greatest
of the prophets, the prophet *par excellence*. The Old Testament
prophets, although real prophets who spoke God's word to the people,
were in this regard but types of Christ who spoke not merely for God
but as God. The revelation which they made was elementary and
incomplete; that which He made was complete and final. They prefaced
their messages with, "Thus saith the Lord," never presuming to speak
in their own authority but only in that of God; but He said, "I say
unto you." Concerning the pre-eminent place of Christ among the
prophets the Apostle John says, "no man hath seen God at any time;
the only begotten Son, who is in the bosom of the Father, He hath
declared Him," 1:18; and the writer of the Epistle to the Hebrews
begins his writing with these words: "God, having of old time spoken
unto the fathers in the prophets by divers portions and in divers manners, hath at the end of these days spoken unto us in His Son, whom
He appointed heir of all things, through whom also He made the

world, who being the effulgence of His glory, and the very image of His substance, and upholding all things by the word of His power, when He had made purification for sins, sat down on the right hand of the Majesty on high," 1:1-3.

In both the Old and the New Testament Christ is called a prophet. "Jehovah thy God will raise up unto thee a prophet from the midst of thee, of thy brethren, like unto me," said Moses, Deut. 18:15; and in Acts 3:22 this prophecy is declared to have been fulfilled in Christ. Christ called Himself a prophet when He said, "A prophet is not without honor, save in his own country, and in his own house," Matt. 13:57; and again, "Nevertheless I must go on my way today and tomorrow and the day following: for it cannot be that a prophet perish out of Jerusalem," Luke 13:33. He was also recognized by the people as a prophet: "When therefore the people saw the sign which He did, they said, This is of a truth the prophet that cometh into the world," John 6:14.

Christ was, of course, not merely a prophet in the narrow sense of foretelling future events, but (and this is much more important) in the broad sense of being pre-eminently the Interpreter and Revealer of divine truth. It was through Him that God's message of redemption in its fulness was communicated to man. The Old Testament prophets did sometimes predict future events, but such predictions were comparatively rare and were only incidental to their main work, which was that of calling men to repentance by earnest preaching of the law, and to faith through their proclamation of the coming redemption.

Because Christ drew from the fountainhead of all wisdom, He taught as one having authority, and not as the scribes. In all of His teaching there was never a note of indecision or doubt, never a tendency to reason things out or speculate, but always an air of authority and finality. He alone had original knowledge of God, and He alone knew the real condition of men's spiritual nature and the remedy for that condition.

In His office as prophet, then, Christ reveals to us the will of God for our salvation. Or, in other words, He proclaims to us the Gospel. That proclamation was indeed begun by Him in Old Testament times as He sent the Holy Spirit upon the prophets who testified beforehand of His coming and gave an elementary revelation of the way of salvation. But when we think of Christ as prophet we think primarily of the revelation that He gave after becoming man. All of His teaching during His earthly ministry is here included. But His work as prophet did not end with His earthly career. Before leaving the disciples He gave them the promise that the Holy Spirit would be sent to continue this work: "But when the Comforter is come, whom I will send unto you from the Father, even the Spirit of truth, who proceedeth from the Father, He shall bear witness of me: and ye also bear witness, because ye have been with me from the beginning," John 15:26, 27; "The Comforter, even the Holy Spirit, whom the Father will send in my name, He shall teach you all things, and bring to your remembrance all that I said unto you," John 14:26; "When He, the Spirit of truth, is come, He shall guide you into all the truth," John 16:13.

Christ also continued to speak through His apostles. In preparing them to meet the persecution and opposition which inevitably would come upon them as they carried the Gospel out through the world He said, "Settle it therefore in your hearts, not to meditate beforehand how to answer: for I will give you a mouth and wisdom, which all your adversaries shall not be able to withstand or to gainsay," Luke 21:14, 15. "We are ambassadors therefore on behalf of Christ," said Paul, "as though God were entreating by us: we beseech you on behalf of Christ, be ye reconciled to God," II Cor. 5:20. Thus the prophetic work of Christ continued as the Holy Spirit enlightened the Apostles and rendered them infallible in their capacity as teachers and as authors of the New Testament books, although that infallibility did not extend to their personal conduct nor to their personal ideas on other subjects. And while infallibility did not extend beyond the Apostles and some few of their immediate associates, ministers of the Gospel down through the ages are, in a secondary but nevertheless true sense, prophets prophesying in Christ's stead. They are His ambassadors. The Gospel ministry is therefore at once the most exalted and the most responsible office in the world. The prophetic work of Christ is also continued down through the ages as the Holy Spirit enlightens the minds of His people and leads them to understand spiritual truth which otherwise would be incomprehensible to them.

Furthermore, since Christ reveals the Father, and since the Father is infinite, His prophetic work will be endless. "These things have I spoken unto you in dark sayings: the hour cometh, when I shall no more speak unto you in dark sayings, but shall tell you plainly of the Father," John 16:25, said Jesus to His disciples shortly before He left them; and again, "I have yet many things to say unto you, but ye cannot bear them now," John 16:12. Indeed, as Dr. Strong very fittingly says: "In heaven Christ will be the visible God. We shall never see the Father separate from Christ. No man or angel has at any time seen God, 'whom no man hath seen, nor can see.' 'The only begotten Son ... He hath declared Him,' and He will forever declare Him." (John 1:18; I Tim. 6:16)." (Systematic Theology, p. 713).

2. CHRIST AS PRIEST

In answer to the question, "How doth Christ execute the office of a priest?" the Shorter Catechism says: "Christ executeth the office of a priest, in His once offering up of Himself as a sacrifice to satisfy divine justice, and reconcile us to God, and in making continual intercession for us."

We have seen that a prophet is one who is qualified and authorized to speak for God to men. A priest, by way of contrast, is one who is qualified and authorized to treat in behalf of, or to represent men before the throne of God. Man in his fallen condition is a guilty sinner, in open and definant rebellion against God. He therefore has neither the right nor even the desire to come into God's presence. A priest is one who, acting on man's behalf, undertakes to restore harmonious relations between God and man. In order to accomplish this he publicly acknowledges man's sin, offers gifts and sacrifices to God in order to expiate that sin and make God propitious, and then, having gained access to God, intercedes in man's behalf.

Since man in his fallen condition is blinded by sin, he does not realize the utter hopelessness of his condition. His tendency is to put God out of his thoughts, to think that he is the master of his fate and the captain of his soul, and that he is able to turn from evil to good whenever he chooses. But his reasoning is based on utterly false premises. Hence if he is to be saved it is necessary that God take the initiative and rescue him. And this, the Scriptures tell us, is precisely what God has done. Entirely at His own cost, and through pure grace alone, He has provided a system of redemption. "Christ died for the ungodly," says Paul, Rom. 5:6; and then he continues: "God commendeth His own love toward us, in that, while we were yet sinners, Christ died for us. Much more then, being now justified by His blood, shall we be saved from the wrath of God through Him. For if, while we were enemies, we were reconciled to God through the death of His Son, much more, being reconciled, shall we be saved by His life," Rom. 5:8-10.

The New Testament makes it plain that Christ is our Priest, our great High Priest. This function He performed in that He offered sacrifice and interceded effectively with God in our behalf. The supreme purpose of His coming, the writer of the Epistle to the Hebrews tells us, was "to put away sin by the sacrifice of Himself," 9:26. Specifically, He offered Himself through His suffering and death on the cross as a sacrifice to God to satisfy divine justice and reconcile us to God, and that in such a manner that He was at one and the same time the sacrifice and the priest who offered it. The Epistle to the Hebrews is in fact concerned almost exclusively with showing that He is our great High Priest and that it is through His sacrifice that our salvation has been made possible. "Having then a great High Priest, who hath passed through the heavens, Jesus the Son of God, let us hold fast our confession," Heb. 4:14. "For such a High Priest became us, holy, guileless, undefiled, separated from sinners, and made higher than the heavens; who needeth not daily, like those high priests, to offer up sacrifices, first for his own sins, and then for the sins of the people: for this He did once for all, when He offered up Himself," Heb. 7:26, 27. "Thou art a priest for ever, after the order of Melchizedek," Heb. 5:6. The Old Testament priests, offering the blood of goats and bulls which had no saving power in itself, were required to offer their sacrifices repeatedly. "But Christ," we are told, "having come a high priest of the good things to come, through the greater and more perfect tabernacle, not made with hands, that is to say, not of this creation, nor yet through the blood of goats and calves, but through His own blood, entered in once for all into the holy place, having obtained eternal redemption. . . . For Christ entered not into a holy place made with hands, like in pattern to the true; but into heaven itself, now to appear before the face of God for us: nor yet that He should offer Himself often, as the high priest entereth into the holy place year by year with blood not his own; else must He often have suffered since the foundation of the world: but how once at the end of the ages hath He been manifested to put away sin by the sacrifice of Himself," Heb. 9:11, 12, 24-27. "Behold, the man whose name is the Branch . . . He shall be a priest upon His throne," said Zechariah (6:12, 13) as he predicted the advent of the Messiah and set Him forth as a royal priest. And Matthew tells us that "The Son of Man came not to be ministered unto, but to minister, and to give His life a ransom for many" (20:28). When viewed against the background of Jewish ritual and Old Testament sacrifice, it is perfectly clear that the death of Christ was designed to make possible the forgiveness of sin. The trail of blood that first appears outside the Garden of Eden leads unerringly to the cross on Calvary.

Furthermore, the priesthood of Christ did not cease with the completion of His work on earth, but continues for ever. His work of sacrifice was, of course, finished with His offering of Himself. But His work of intercession, which was begun on earth and which reached its climax in the high priestly prayer recorded in the seventeenth chapter of John, is continued in the presence of God as He fulfills this the second office of the priest. But He now prays not with strong

crying and tears as in the days of His flesh (Heb. 5:7), but with the
sovereignty and prevailing power of One who by His own work has
achieved eternal redemption for His people. This intercession is
repeatedly mentioned. In the Levitical system it was necessary that
there be a succession of priests, "priests many in number, because that
by death they are hindered from continuing: but He, because He
abideth for ever, hath His priesthood unchangeable. Wherefore also
He is able to save to the uttermost them that draw near unto God
through Him, seeing He ever liveth to make intercession for them,"
Heb. 7:23-25. "If any man sin, we have an Advocate with the Father,
Jesus Christ the righteous," said the Apostle John, I John 2:1. "It is
Jesus Christ that died, yea rather, that was raised from the dead, who
is at the right hand of God, who also maketh intercession for us," said
Paul, Rom. 8:34. "He bare the sin of many, and made intercession for
the transgressors," said Isaiah (53:12) in anticipation of the advent of
the Messiah.

We have said that the Old Testament priests, like the Old Testament prophets, were but types and shadows of the Great One who was
to come later. But while they were only types and shadows they had
not, like the priests in the heathen religions, usurped their offices but
were truly appointed by God. Their priesthood was effective in bringing
salvation to men because it was a promise of, and pointed forward to,
the one true Priest who on Calvary was to offer the only sacrifice that
can take away the sins of men. And since the merely human priesthood
was but a shadow of that which was to come it was but temporary.
Just as we put out our artificial lights when the sun rises, and as the
blossom falls away when the fruit appears, so the entire ceremonial and
sacrificial system of the Old Testament has fulfilled its function and
ceased to be when Christ's work was completed. This being the nature
of the Christian priesthood, it is clearly evident that all those today
who, in the Roman Catholic or any other church, pretend to function
as priests mediating between God and man are simply usurpers of
divine authority.

3. CHRIST AS KING

The third office that Christ executes as our Redeemer is that of
king. The Shorter Catechism, in answer to the question, "How doth
Christ execute the office of a king?" says: "Christ executeth the
office of a king, in subduing us to Himself, in ruling and defending us,
and in restraining and conquering all His and our enemies."

The kingly office of Christ relates primarily to the risen and glorified
Christ who, seated at the right hand of the Father and possessing all

authority in heaven and on earth, directs the advancing affairs of His kingdom and secures the salvation of His people. Exercising His authority through the agency of the Holy Spirit, through whom He is ever present with His people, He effectively applies to His people the redemption which He has worked out for them and effectively restrains the forces of evil which would thwart their redemption. As the Second Person of the Trinity Christ possessed divine power and glory from eternity, and so was King of the entire universe. But during the time of His career on earth He voluntarily subjected Himself to the limitations and privations of human nature, and His divine power and glory were veiled except for occasional miracles which bore testimony to the nature of His mission and work. But with the completion of His work of redemption He, as the God-Man, ascended to heaven in His glorified nature and now directs every step in the advancement of His kingdom.

That Christ is a king is taught clearly and repeatedly in Scripture. In the first place His name, "Christ," means "anointed." In Old Testament times the anointing of the king signified his appointment to the kingly office. To Samuel God said, "Fill thy horn with oil, and go: I will send thee to Jesse, the Bethlehemite; for I have provided me a king among his sons. . . . Then Samuel took the horn of oil, and anointed him in the midst of his brethren: and the Spirit of Jehovah came mightily upon David from that day forward," I Sam. 16:1, 13. After announcing to Mary that she should have a Son whose name was to be called Jesus, the angel Gabriel added "He shall be great, and shall be called the Son of the Most High: and the Lord God shall give unto Him the throne of His father David: and He shall reign over the house of Jacob for ever and ever; and of His kingdom there shall be no end," Luke 1:32, 33. At the very beginning of His public ministry Nathanael, impressed with His supernatural insight, acknowledged His true kingship: "Rabbi, thou art the Son of God, thou art King of Israel," John 1:49. Christ Himself claimed to be a king, and announced the establishment of His kingdom, which is variously called the kingdom of heaven, the kingdom of God, the kingdom of Christ. Mark tells us that early in His ministry, "Jesus came into Galilee, preaching the Gospel of God, and saying, The time is fulfilled, and the kingdom of God is at hand: repent ye, and believe in the Gospel," 1:14, 15. In the Sermon on the Mount He made it plain that not mere lip service but only true allegiance from the heart would secure admittance into His kingdom: "Not every one that saith unto me, Lord, Lord, shall enter into the kingdom of heaven; but he that doeth the will of my Father who is in heaven," Matt. 7:21. In the eschatological discourse

of Matt. 25:31-46 Christ pictured Himself as seated upon the throne
of universal judgment, before whom is to be gathered all the nations,
whose voice pronounces sentence and assigns to the good and the evil
their eternal rewards and punishments. In conformity with the accepted
custom of the Roman Empire that the newly designated king, coming
to the capital city for the first time in his official capacity, should be
mounted on a proud spirited horse and publicly welcomed by a multitude of his people who shouted his praise and strewed flowers in his
path, Jesus so entered Jerusalem on Palm Sunday, except that instead
of the proud spirited horse he used the lowly ass, symbol of service and
humility,—thus literally fulfilling the words of the prophet Zechariah:
"Rejoice greatly, O daughter of Zion; shout, O daughter of Jerusalem:
behold, thy King cometh unto thee; He is just, and having salvation;
lowly, and riding upon an ass, even upon a colt the foal of an ass,"
Zech. 9:9; Matt. 21:5. On this same occasion He was welcomed by
the crowd with the words, "Blessed is the King that cometh in the
name of the Lord," Luke 19:38,—which welcome He accepted as
entirely appropriate. During His trial before Pilate His enemies made
the charge: "We found this man . . . saying that He Himself is Christ
a king," Luke 23:2. In reply to Pilate's question Jesus said: "My
kingdom is not of this world: if my kingdom were of this world, then
would my servants fight, that I should not be delivered to the Jews;
but now is my kingdom not from hence," John 18:36; and when asked
directly, "Are thou a king then?" He answered affirmatively: "Thou
sayest that I am a king. To this end have I been born, and to this
end am I come into the world, that I should bear witness unto the
truth," John 18:37.

Paul's testimony to the kingship of Christ is, of course, clear and
abundant. In the Epistle to the Ephesians he declares that "God raised
Him from the dead, and made Him to sit at His right hand in the
heavenly places, far above all rule, and authority, and power, and
dominion, and every name that is named, not only in this world, but
also in that which is to come: and He put all things in subjection
under His feet, and gave Him to be head over all things to the Church,"
1:20-23. To sit at the right hand of the Father is to occupy the position
of honor and power. In these words Paul tells us that Christ, in His
theanthropic nature, now presides at the tribunal of heaven, that all
creatures, celestial and terrestrial, admire His majesty, obey His will,
and are subject to His power. In the Epistle to the Philippians he
declares that "God highly exalted Him, and gave unto Him the name
which is above every name; that in the name of Jesus every knee should
bow, of things in heaven and things on earth and things under the

earth, and that every tongue should confess that Jesus Christ is Lord, to the glory of God the Father," 2:9-11. In First Corinthians he says that "He must reign, till He hath put all His enemies under His feet," 15:25. And in First Timothy he declares that Christ is "the blessed and only Potentate, the King of kings, and Lord of lords," 6:15.

In Heb. 2:8, 9 we read: "For in that He subjected all things unto Him, He left nothing that is not subject to Him. But we behold . . . Jesus . . . crowned with glory and honor." And in Heb. 1:8 the 45th Psalm is quoted as having its fulfillment in Christ: "Thy throne, O God, is for ever and ever; and the sceptre of uprightness is the sceptre of thy kingdom."

The book of Revelation is one sustained hymn of praise to Christ as King, setting forth the glory of His person and the triumph of His kingdom. He is declared to be "the Ruler of the kings of the earth," 1:5. He has "made us to be a kingdom, to be priests unto His God and Father; to Him be the glory and the dominion for ever and ever," 1:6. In chapter 5 He is pictured as sitting on the throne and receiving homage and worship from all the hosts of heaven and earth. All opposition is to be utterly crushed: "and out of His mouth proceedeth a sharp sword, that with it He should smite the nations: and He shall rule them with a rod of iron. . . . And He hath on His garment and on His thigh a name written, KING OF KINGS, AND LORD OF LORDS," 19:15, 16,—not that He will use violence or military force, but rather that His conquest of the nations is to be accomplished by the preaching of the Gospel, as is indicated by the fact that the sword proceeds "out of His mouth;" and, continuing with the same figure of speech, while it will be an immeasurable pleasure and privilege for His people to be ruled by Him, His rule will be as complete and effective as if enforced with a rod of iron.

The Old Testament too sets forth His kingship. The predicted Messiah is set forth as the King of the Golden Age in which the wolf and the lamb lay down together, Is. 11:1-10. In the Messianic vision recorded in Daniel 7:13, 14 we read: "There came with the clouds of heaven one like unto a Son of Man, and He came even to the Ancient of Days, and they brought Him near before Him. And there was given Him dominion, and glory, and a kingdom, that all the peoples, nations, and languages should serve Him: His dominion is an everlasting dominion, which shall not pass away, and His kingdom that which shall not be destroyed." The Messianic psalms strongly emphasize the kingly nature of the coming One, some making special mention of His conquest of the wicked: "I have set my King upon my holy hill in Zion," 2:6; "Thy throne, O God, is for ever and ever," 45:6 (quoted in Heb. 1:8 as having its fulfillment in Christ) ; "Ask of me, and I will give thee the nations for thine inheritance, and the uttermost parts of the earth for thy possession. Thou shalt break them with a rod of iron; Thou shalt dash them in pieces like a potter's vessel," Ps. 2:8, 9; "Jehovah saith unto my Lord, Sit thou at my right hand, until I make thine enemies thy footstool," Ps. 110:1 (quoted five times in the New Testament as having its fulfillment in Christ).

The inward spiritual nature of His kingdom as well as its present existence was set forth by Christ Himself when, being asked by the Pharisees concerning the time of its appearance, He said, "The kingdom of God cometh not with observation"—that is, not with outward and spectacular signs or events—"neither shall they say, Lo, here! or There! for lo, the kingdom of God is within you," Luke 17:21, 22. The kingdoms of this world are established with mighty armies, great conquests, violence and cruelty. But how different was the advent of Jesus, without earthly eminence, without arms, without wealth. Individuals are brought into His kingdom one by one as the Holy Spirit regenerates their hearts and implants a new principle of spiritual life. The Christian, although in the world, is no longer of it. Actuated by new motives and new desires and acknowledging Christ as His only Lord and Master, he looks forward to a new heavens and a new earth wherein dwelleth righteousness. Paul fittingly says that "our citizenship is in heaven," Phil. 3:20.

The writer of the Epistle to the Hebrews, after having called the roll of the outstanding faithful, says that these "confessed that they were strangers and pilgrims on the earth," 11:13, and later adds that "we have not here an abiding city, but we seek after the city which is to come," 13:14,—"the city which hath the foundations, whose builder and maker is God," 11:10. The visible representation of the kingdom on earth is, of course, the Church, in so far as the Church is composed of true believers.

In order to make clear the nature of Christ's kingdom in its broadest outlines it probably can be best presented under three heads: *The Kingdom of Power; The Kingdom of Grace;* and, *The Kingdom of Glory.*

(1). *Christ's Kingdom of Power* relates to the universe at large as, by virtue of His Divine nature and His work of creatorship, He upholds (that is, preserves in existence) all things visible and invisible, governs (throughout the realm of nature as well as in the affairs of men), and passes final judgment on the entire race of men. That He was the active agent, although not the exclusive agent, in the creation of all things is repeatedly taught in Scripture: "All things were made through Him; and without Him was not anything made that hath been made . . .

the world was made through Him," John 1 :3, 10; "Through whom also He made the worlds," Heb. 1 :2; "All things have been created through Him, and unto Him; and He is before all things, and in Him all things consist," Col. 1 :16, 17. He rules or governs all things, for the glory of God and the effective execution of the divine plan: "All authority hath been given unto me in heaven and on earth," Matt. 28 :1ᴿ; "Wherefore also God highly exalted Him, and gave unto Him the name which is above every name; that in the name of Jesus every knee should bow, of things in heaven and things on earth and things under the earth, and that every tongue should confess that Jesus Christ is Lord, to the glory of God the Father," Phil. 2 :9-11; "The exceeding greatness of His power . . . which He (that is, God the Father) wrought in Christ, when He raised Him from the dead, and made Him to sit at His right hand in the heavenly places, far above all rule, and authority, and power, and dominion, and every name that is named, not only in this world, but also in that which is to come: and He put all things in subjection under His feet, and gave Him to be head over all things to the Church, Eph. 1 :19-22; "For in that He subjected all things unto Him. He left nothing that is not subject to Him. But now we see not yet all things subject to Him. But we behold . . . Jesus . . . crowned with glory and honor," Heb. 2 :8, 9. And that He is to be the final Judge of all men is set forth with equal clearness: "But when the Son of Man shall come in His glory, and all the angels with Him, then shall He sit on the throne of His glory: and before Him shall be gathered all the nations. . . . Then shall the King say unto them on His right hand, Come, ye blessed of my Father, inherit the kingdom prepared for you from the foundation of the world. . . . Then shall He say also unto them on the left hand, Depart from me, ye cursed, into the eternal fire which is prepared for the Devil and his angels," Matt. 25 :31-41. His conquest of the nations, which is to be accomplished through the preaching of the Gospel, and His effective government of them in righteousness is foretold in figurative language in the book of Revelation: ". . . Upon His head are many diadems. . . . And the armies which are in heaven followed Him upon white horses, clothed in fine linen, pure and white. And out of His mouth proceedeth a sharp sword, that with it He should smite the nations: and He shall rule them with a rod of iron. . . . And He hath on His garment and on His thigh a name written, KING OF KINGS, AND LORD OF LORDS," 19 :12-16. Thus His kingdom of power embraces the material world, the course of history, and all angels and men.

(2) *The Kingdom of Grace.* Christ's Kingdom of Grace is that spiritual kingdom in which He rules in the hearts and lives of believers. It is a kingdom which is here and now: "The kingdom of God is within

you," Luke 17:21. It was originally founded by Him, being made possible by His atoning work on the cross. It receives its laws from Him. In all ages He administers its affairs and defends it against all enemies. Its membership on earth is identical with that of the true Church, which is composed of all those who from the heart believe in Christ as Saviour and Lord. It is a kingdom which is in the world but not of it: "They are not of the world, even as I am not of the world," John 17:16; "If ye were of the world, the world would love its own; but because ye are not of the world, but I chose you out of the world, therefore the world hateth you," John 15:19; "My kingdom is not of this world: if my kingdom were of this world, then would my servants fight, that I should not be delivered to the Jews: but now is my kingdom not from hence," John 18:36. Its distinguishing characteristics are not earthly or carnal: "For the kingdom of God is not eating and drinking, but righteousness and peace and joy in the Holy Spirit." Rom. 14:17. It is made effective, not by any external display of power or magnificence, but by a divine work of the Holy Spirit as He regenerates the hearts and gives spiritual insight to the minds of men: "The kingdom of God cometh not with observation," Luke 17:20; "Except one be born anew, he cannot see the kingdom of God," John 3:3; "Not by works done in righteousness, which we did ourselves, but according to His mercy He saved us, through the washing of regeneration and renewing of the Holy Spirit," Titus 3:5. But while the coming of the kingdom is not heralded by external signs, its effect within the individual is immediately felt in that he becomes conscious of a new relationship to God and of new governing principles which make for holiness, sobriety and uprightness; and in due time the effects thus wrought in individuals are reflected in the improved social, economic and political conditions of the whole community or nation.

Christ's kingdom of grace embraces all types of men, recognizing no distinctions of nationality, color, class, rank, person or sex. "There can be neither Jew nor Greek, there can be neither bond nor free, there can be no male and female; for ye are all one man in Christ Jesus," says Paul, Gal. 3:28. That it was not intended for the Jews alone but for all nations and races was set forth clearly in the Old Testament Messianic passages and was repeatedly emphasized in the New Testament: "Ask of me, and I will give thee the nations for thine inheritance, And the uttermost parts of the earth for thy possession," Ps. 2:8; "I will also give thee for a light to the Gentiles, that thou mayest be my salvation unto the end of the earth," Is. 49:6; "From the rising of the sun even unto the going down of the same my name shall be great among the Gentiles," Mal. 1:11; "I will give thee for a covenant of the people, for a light of the Gentiles," Is. 42:6; "And it shall come to pass afterward that I will pour out my Spirit upon all flesh," Joel 2:28. When the infant Jesus was presented in the temple the aged but spiritually minded Simeon recognized Him as "A light for revelation to the Gentiles, And the glory of thy people Israel," Luke 2:32. "Of a truth I perceive that God is no respecter of persons: but in every nation he that feareth Him, and worketh righteousness, is acceptable to Him," said Peter when he realized the full meaning of the vision he had seen while on the housetop, Acts 10:34, 35. "Is God the God of Jews only? is He not the God of Gentiles also? Yea, of Gentiles also," said Paul, Rom. 3:29. And the last command of Christ to His disciples was, "Go ye therefore, and make disciples of all the nations," Matt. 28:19.

We wish particularly to stress the fact that Christ is in the truest sense of the word our King today, that, having established His Church as the fellowship of believers, He now is seated on the throne of the universe from whence He directs the affairs of His advancing kingdom, that He animates His people with new spiritual life and defends them against all the forces of evil, and that He is thus to continue until all His enemies have been placed under His feet. It is our duty never to despair of the Church, nor of the world, which eventually is to be conquered by the Church. Since the Kingdom of Grace is not terrestrial or carnal, but spiritual, we must not be surprised if during our course through a world in which there still remains so much that is evil we often suffer persecutions, sickness, poverty, cold, hunger, and other disagreeable circumstances. For all of these things have their appointed place in God's providential control of the world, and as they come upon believers they are designed not as punishments but as disciplines or chastisements for their improvement. We have the assurance of our King that He will never forsake us—"Lo, I am with you always, even unto the end of the world"—and that He will supply, not our every desire, but our "every need . . . according to His riches in glory," Phil. 4:19. Being truly united with Christ and depending on the power of His Spirit, we shall not doubt but that we shall be finally victorious over the Devil and every kind of evil that he can bring against us. We look upon science, education, invention, art, music, commerce, statesmanship, sociology, etc., each in its own field so far as it is based on truth, as a revelation of the wisdom and glory of Christ, who is the Light of the world and the Ruler of the nations. Each of these represents an accomplishment in man's conquest of the forces of nature, which was the task assigned to him when immediately after his creation he was commanded to "subdue" the earth; and each of these is a prophecy of the complete establishment of Christ's kingdom. Let us ever remember that Christ is our King here and now, that He is ruling and overruling through the whole course of human history, making the wrath of men to praise Him and able even to bring good out of that which men intend for evil.

And since Christ is thus our King it is our duty in every sphere of life's activity to render to Him that homage and obedience which is His due. In the following paragraph Dr. Craig sets forth this obligation very clearly. "It is important," says he, "that we note the all-inclusiveness of Christ's rule. Not only does He demand obedience from all men; He demands obedience from them in all things. . . . There is no sphere of life conceivable where Jesus does not maintain His demand that He be honored and obeyed. As King, therefore, Christ ought to be supreme in our private lives. Within this sphere we ought to strive to bring every thought and activity into captivity to Him. As King, Christ's will ought, also, to be supreme in our social and business lives. Within these spheres we should be guided by the golden rule; we should place the emphasis upon our duties rather than upon our rights. Still further, as King, Christ's will ought to be supreme in our political lives. To deny this is tantamount to saying that politics ought to be Christless. This is not to say that the Church, as an institution, ought to mix in politics, but it is to say that, if we are Christians, our Christianity will manifest itself in the sphere of politics as well as in the other spheres of life. Let us not imagine, then, that Christ's kingship has to do with only a part of life; it has to do with the whole life. Wherever we may be, whatever we may do, in the world of action or of thought, we are under the dominion of, and as such responsible to, Jesus Christ." (*Jesus As He Was and Is,* p. 84).

Furthermore, whether in human or divine affairs, the relationship between king and subjects is a reciprocal relation. Not only do the subjects have obligations towards their king, but the king also has obligations toward his subjects. In this connection Dr. Craig has said: " For our comfort and encouragement let us remind ourselves that —assuming that we are endeavoring to yield Him that obedience that is His due—Christ has placed Himself under obligations to us. As subjects of the King we do, indeed, owe Him homage and obedience. At the same time, however, He, as our King, grants us support and protection. What holds good of our relations to the State holds good, in a true sense, of our relations to King Jesus. As long as we obey the laws of the State, the State will protect and defend us. If others seek to take away our life, our liberty or our possessions we are not dependent upon our own resources: all the resources of the State are pledged for the support and defense of even the weakest and most insignificant of its citizens. And so as long as we serve Jesus as King, all His power and strength is pledged to our support and defense. No matter how weak and helpless we may be in ourselves; no matter how strong and reliant they may be who are against us, we need not fear, for greater is He that is for us than they that be against us. No doubt, if left to ourselves, we would soon be overcome of evil; but as it is King Jesus watches over us and defends us, and thus we are enabled to prevail not because of our own strength but because of the strength of Him in whom we have put our trust. Let us then be of good cheer. Though all the hosts of earth and hell should conspire together to accomplish the undoing of the weakest of Christ's true subjects they would not succeed. Unto Him that watches over us and defends us has been committed all power and authority in heaven and on earth." (*Craig*, p. 85).

Today Christ's kingship is, of course, widely ignored. In this connection we find another valuable comment in the writings of Dr. Craig. Says he: "Everywhere there are those who say by their action if not by their words that they do not recognize His right to rule over them. It is necessary, therefore, to distinguish between His *de facto* and His *de jure* rule, i.e., between the obedience that is actually yielded Him and the obedience that is His by law and right. According to law and right Jesus is entitled to universal obedience. As a matter of fact only a relatively few render Him the homage and obedience that is His due. We may be sure, however, that things will not always remain as they are in this respect. Jesus being what He is we may be confident that He will make good His claims and that the time is coming when all men, willingly or unwillingly, will acknowledge His lordship. Let no one suppose that Jesus' right to rule rests on the consent of men, that He exercises rightful authority only over those who acknowledge His lordship. It is not for you or for me, it is not for any man to say, whether he will live in Christ's kingdom. This is true, in some degree at least, of the kingdoms of this world. If we do not like the way in which authority is exercised in that one in which we happen to be, we may move to one more to our liking. Nothing like this is possible, however, in connection with the kingdom of Christ. His kingdom is not confined to any special territory. Go where we may, we are still within His jurisdiction and answerable to His authority. We might as well suppose that we can go where the law of gravitation does not operate as suppose we can go where Christ does not hold sway. Hence just as it is the part of wisdom to adjust ourselves to the law of gravitation so that it will operate for our advantage and not to our disadvantage it is the part of wisdom to adjust ourselves to the Lord Jesus in such a way that His rule will bring us weal not woe, gain not loss, life not death." (*Craig*, p. 82).

That Christ does exist as King is recognized by Roman Catholics as well as by Protestants—a fact which could hardly be denied since it is set forth so clearly in Scripture—although they differ quite radically in regard to the manner in which He exercises His authority. Roman Catholics hold that He has appointed the Pope as His vice-regent on earth, and that His kingly authority is thus exercised through the instrumentality of a human being. We hold, however, with the whole Protestant world that not only is there no Scripture authority to support such a claim but that such a claim is contrary to the plain teaching of Scripture, and that the authority by which the Pope presumes to speak and act in the name of Christ is simply usurped authority. We hold that every believer is directly responsible to King Jesus Himself, and that it is our God-given right to go directly to Him in prayer without the intervention of any earthly pope or hierarchy. Our conviction in this regard is only strengthened when we examine more closely into the private lives and conduct of many of the popes and priests who have presumed to exercise this authority. A church which has incorporated so much error into its teaching and which has engaged in such shameless oppressions and persecutions as has the Roman Catholic Church is plainly not the authorized agency of Christ on earth.

In this treatment we have given undue space to the Kingdom of Grace, since that is the phase of Christ's kingdom in which we now are and since it is also the phase concerning which we have the most information. There is, however, a third phase, and we must now turn our attention to that.

(3). *The Kingdom of Glory.* Christ's Kingdom of Glory is that state in which He rules over the redeemed in heaven and over the holy angels. It began with His ascension, and it reaches its consummation and completion at the end of the world and the final judgment. Entrance into the Kingdom of Glory is through the Kingdom of Grace; and it grows and develops as the members of the Church Militant, one by one, are translated into the Church Triumphant. In anticipation of his estate in this kingdom Paul wrote to the Philippians, "For me to live is Christ, and to die is gain," 1:21; and in the same connection he declared that he had "the desire to depart and to be with Christ," which, said he, "is very far better," Phil. 1:23. John pronounces blessed those who are privileged to share in the glories of this kingdom: "Blessed are the dead who die in the Lord," Rev. 14:13. In the highly figurative passage of Rev. 20:4-6 John gives us an insight into the joys experienced by those who are privileged to share in this kingdom as, released from all earthly cares and limitations, they "lived, and reigned with Christ a thousand years,"—which period of time, we believe, is to be understood not as an exact one thousand years but a comparatively long period, specifically, as relates to each individual, the period between his death here and the consummation of the kingdom at the end of the world. For some of the redeemed, perhaps for most of them, this period will continue much longer than a literal one thousand years. All of those who have suffered and died for Christ, that is, all of those who in one way or another have given their lives in Christian service, are described as having been "beheaded for the testimony of Jesus, and for the word of God," Rev. 20:4. If this be taken literally to include only those martyrs who actually have been beheaded, to the exclusion of all those who have been burned at the stake or who have suffered torture or privation in other ways, the number partaking of the joys of this reign would be relatively insignificant. As a matter of fact many of those who have been put to death by being beheaded have suffered much less than those who have died by other means, or who after a life of Christian service have died natural deaths. Consequently we understand this to mean that all those who have suffered for Christ have a part in His mediatorial reign. Furthermore, as these persons are awaiting the resurrection they are in a disembodied state and are described not as men and women but as "souls," and their estate there is figuratively described as "the first resurrection." It is an inestimable privilege to share in this intermediate reign, and those who are thus privileged are described as "blessed and holy." "Over these," John tells us, "the second death"—by which he evidently means the state of torture into which the wicked are to be cast—"hath no power; but they shall be priests of God and of Christ, and shall reign with Him a thousand years," Rev. 20:6. Furthermore, when seen in this light death should hold no horrors for the Christian, but should be looked upon primarily as a transition from this world to Christ's Kingdom of Glory, or as the gateway through which he enters a far better and more glorious life than can ever be attained here.

The mediatorial reign of Christ closes with His second coming and the final judgment. The work of redemption then will have been completed, divine grace will have been fully manifested, and the fate of all men, good or bad, fixed forever. Then Christ, having gained the complete victory and having reigned till He has put all His enemies under His feet, shall deliver up the kingdom to God the Father, ". . . that God may be all in all," I Cor. 15:23-28. This does not mean that from that time on Christ will cease to have any part in the kingdom, but that, the work of redemption having been completed and the elect gathered in, it will cease to be pre-eminently His kingdom, that He will return to the original relationship which He had with the Father and the Holy Spirit, and that the triune God will reign eternally over the perfected kingdom.

In conclusion, then, Christ is at one and the same time our Prophet, our Priest, and our King. This is the terminology under which His work is set forth in Scripture. It is to John Calvin that we are indebted for developing more clearly than anyone else has done this threefold nature of the work of redemption. But while we use this terminology we are not to assume that these are separate offices as are those of President, Chief Justice and Senator in the affairs of State, or that these functions are performed successively and in isolation. Rather they are concurrent and mutually imply one another as do lungs, heart and brain in the human body—functionally distinct, yet interdependent and together constituting the one life. With varying degrees of emphasis Christ is always a royal Priest, a priestly King, a priestly Prophet, and a prophetical Priest. His work as Prophet, through which he reveals God to us, is rightly understood only when we know Him as the One who through His priestly work has redeemed us and who is our heavenly King. His work as Priest—His offering up Himself as a sacrifice to satisfy divine justice and reconcile us to God—is made known to us through His work as prophet as He reveals to us the true meaning of His suffering and death. And His work as King can be rightly understood only when through His work as Prophet He reveals Himself as the One who has purchased us with His own blood, whose possession therefore we are.

In the typical economy of Israel's long history there were three distinct offices, that of the prophet, of the priest, and of the king. In the historical order the prophetic order was established first. Abraham was a prophet (Gen. 20:7); Jacob performed this function (Gen. 49:1); and Moses was officially called to be a prophet before he led the Children of Israel out of Egypt. The priests were appointed soon after Israel became a nation. The kings, however, did not begin to reign until some four hundred years later, Israel in the meantime existing as a theocracy in which God as their King governed through the prophets. As the Old Testament prophets were types of the great Prophet, and the Old Testament priests were types of the great Priest, so were the Old Testament kings types of the great King. The three functions which ran in separate though parallel lines during Old Testament times were thus merged and brought to perfection in Christ. But even in Him the emphasis on the three offices still fell in the historical order, so that during His public ministry He acted primarily as Prophet; in His suffering and death on the cross and in His intercession for us before the throne of God, he acted primarily as Priest; and in His Kingdom of Grace and His Kingdom of Glory He has revealed Himself primarily as King.

Furthermore, as a result of Christ's work of redemption, all believers, under the New Covenant, are made prophets, priests and kings. We are constituted prophets in that we are commanded to proclaim the Gospel and to show forth the excellencies of Him who called us out of darkness into His marvelous light (Matt. 28:18-20). Peter sets forth the priesthood when he says, "Ye are an elect race, a royal priesthood, a holy nation, a people for God's own possession," I Peter 2:9, and likewise John when he says, "He made us to be a kingdom, to be priests unto His God and Father," Rev. 1:6. And the kingly estate of the Lord's people is set forth when Peter declares that believers are a "royal" priesthood, and when John declares that those in the intermediate state "shall reign with Him a thousand years," Rev. 20:6, and that those in heaven "shall reign for ever and ever," Rev. 22:5. Thus the three offices which for centuries ran parallel in Israel and then were united in the Lord Jesus Christ reappear in all those who believe in Him. Each believer ideally and potentially has all three offices. Some are pre-eminently prophets in that they proclaim the Gospel. Others are pre-eminently priests, not that they offer any more sacrifices for sin, for Christ alone offered that sacrifice, but in that they minister under their great High Priest and offer up for themselves and others spiritual sacrifices, which sacrifices include (1) themselves as living sacrifices in service to God, (2) their possessions, (3) prayer, (4) praise, and (5) thanksgiving. And while the kingly office is largely reserved for the future, some even in this life through the instrumentality of their office in Church or State exercise authority over their fellow men.

22. Erroneous Views Concerning the Person of Christ

In order that we may keep more clearly in mind the true doctrine concerning the person of Christ it may be helpful to make a brief survey of the erroneous views that have emerged during the course of Church history. As we have stated at the very beginning of this study, the first question that must be settled by any one professing to be a Christian is, "What think ye of the Christ?" (Matt. 22:42) ; and as that question is answered the truth or falsity of that person's Christianity becomes evident. As a matter of historical record the full statement concerning the person of Christ was arrived at only after protracted and violent controversies, during the course of which every possible interpretation of the biblical data was examined, its elements of truth sifted out and preserved while the elements of error which deformed it were exposed and discarded.

1. EBIONISM

The earliest heretical view concerning the person of Christ was that known as "Ebionism." In the interests of a supposedly pure monotheism the Ebonites denied the Deity of Christ and held that He was merely a man on whom the Spirit of God rested in its fulness. God and man were regarded as always external to each other. It denied the possibility of a union of the divine and the human nature and so ruled out the doctrine of the Incarnation. Some Ebionites acknowledged His supernatural birth, while others rejected it and held that His baptism marked the time at which He was especially endowed with the Holy Spirit. All agreed that after His death He was exalted to kingship. But this means that they acknowledged Him only as a great prophet or teacher during His earthly career and so definitely a part of the creaturely existence,—all of which in turn means that the worship paid Him by the Church was simply idolatry. They held that the old Jewish law was still obligatory upon the Lord's people. Hence their system appears to have been simply Judaism within the pale of the Christian Church.

2. DOCETISM

Chronologically, the next important error to develop concerning the person of Christ was Docetism. This term was derived from the Greek word *dokeo,* meaning to "seem," or to "appear." While the Ebionites believed that Christ had only a human nature, the Doceti held precisely the opposite error, asserting that He had only a divine nature and that His appearance in this world was only an illusion, or, more correctly, a theophany. According to this view He did not have a real human body and therefore could not have had a real human life. This meant further that He suffered no real pain and died no real death.

This peculiar belief was based on the philosophical assumption that matter is inherently evil. Since Christ was acknowledged to be altogether pure they could not admit that He was in any way connected with a physical body. Docetism was therefore simply pagan philosophy within the Church. It appeared quite early, about the year A. D. 70, and continued for approximately a century. The Patripassion and Sabellian heresies which appeared later may well be considered sects of the Docetic heresy since they too denied any real humanity in Christ.

The Scripture refutation of Docetism is found in John's declaration that "The Word became flesh, and dwelt among us (and we beheld His glory, glory as of the only begotten from the Father), full of grace and truth," 1:14; and also in the unequivocal statement of Heb. 2:14: "Since then the children are sharers in flesh and blood, He also Himself in like manner partook of the same." Incidentally we may add that the early appearance of Docetism with its strong emphasis on the Deity of Christ is eloquent testimony showing that the impression made upon those who saw and heard Him in the flesh was that He was a supernatural Being.

3. ARIANISM

A third error that arose in the early Church, more serious than either of the preceding ones, was Arianism. This view denied the true Deity of Christ and held rather that He occupied a position somewhere between that of God and man, that He was the first created being and the creator of all other creatures. He was thus regarded not as possessing absolute Deity, but only as the highest of created beings. Because of the claims which He made, the authority which He assumed, the miracles He worked, and the glory He displayed particularly in His resurrection, the great majority of the early Christians recognized Him as truly God. The Arians, however, misinterpreted certain Scripture statements relating to His state of humiliation and assumed that temporary subordination to the Father meant original and permanent inequality. Origen, the most outstanding of the early church fathers, in connection with his doctrine of the eternal generation of the Son, had taught inherent subordination. Arius carried this idea much farther and declared that the generation of the Son had taken place in time, thus definitely making Him a creature.

This controversy was brought to a head in the early part of the fourth century by the teaching of Arius, a presbyter in the Church at Alexandria, Egypt. Because of the widespread difference of opinion concerning the person of Christ an Ecumenical Council was called by the first Christian Emperor, Constantine, for the purpose of formulating a general doctrine which should be accepted by the whole Church. The council met in the year 325, at Nicaea, in Asia Minor, and was attended by bishops and presbyters from practically all parts of the empire. The real controversy centered around the question as to whether Christ was to be considered as truly God, or as only the first and greatest creature. The Arians maintained that Christ was not eternal, that He was created by the Father out of nothing and was therefore the first and highest of all creatures, that He in turn created the world, and that because of the power delegated to Him He is to be looked upon as God and is to be worshipped. He was, therefore, to be called God only by courtesy, in much the same way that we give a Lieutenant Governor the title of Governor. His pre-eminence was due to the fact that He alone was created immediately by God and that supernatural power was given to Him, while all other creatures were created by Him. Most of the Arians also held that the Holy Spirit was the first and greatest of the creatures called into existence by His power. All of this meant, of course, a God who had a beginning, and who might therefore have an end; for a creature, no matter how highly exalted, must ever remain finite. Hence the Arians, in demanding worship of Christ, were in fact asserting the central principle of heathenism and idolatry, the worship of a creature.

The Arians asserted that Christ was not of the same substance (homo-ousia) with the Father, but of similar substance (homoi-ousia). We may be tempted today to wonder how the whole Christian world could have been convulsed over the rejection of a single letter of the alphabet; but in reality the absence or the presence of the iota signified the difference between a Saviour who is truly God and one who is only a creature,—between a Christianity which is able to save the souls of men and one which can not. In the Council of Nicaea the Church faced what we believe to have been the greatest crisis in the entire history of doctrine. It was, however, in effect, although in a slightly different form, the same question that it faces in the twentieth century dispute between the Evangelical Faith and Modernism.

The noble champion of the orthodox cause was Athanasius, who later became Bishop of Alexandria. Under His influence the Council declared for the full and eternal Deity of Christ, who was declared to be "God of God, Light of Light, Very God of Very God, being of one substance with the Father." Opposition continued strong for some time after the Council had made this pronouncement, but under the zealous and skillful leadership of Athanasius the doctrine gradually won official acceptance by the entire Church. It was seen that a created Christ was not the Christ of the New Testament, nor could He be the Christ who, by His death and resurrection, became the Author of eternal salvation.

4. Apollinarianism

The next error that the Church had to face concerning the person of Christ was that of Apollinarianism. This system denied the completeness of His human nature. It acknowledged His true Deity, and also that He possessed a real body and a soul which would continue after death; but it denied that He had a truly human mind, i.e., a reasoning mind that reached conclusions through mental processes as do ours. It asserted in effect that He was simply God masquerading in human flesh, and that ignorance, weakness, obedience, worship, suffering, etc., were to be predicated of the Logos, that is, of the Deity or Divine nature as such. If, by way of comparison, we can imagine a man's mind implanted in the body of a lion and the lion thereafter governed not by lion or animal psychology but by a human mind we shall have something analogous to what the Apollinarian system set forth concerning the incarnation of Christ. Apollinarius was a tricotomist, and his system was based on the assumption that there were three elements in man's nature: a material body, an immortal soul, and a reasoning mind. We believe, however, that man is composed of only two elements, body and soul, and that the mind with which man reasons in this life is the same as the soul or spirit which lives on after death. Hence it is evident that, reduced to dicotomist terms, Apollinarianism granted Christ a human body but not a complete human soul. But if Christ was to have a real incarnation it was necessary that He add to His divine nature not merely a human body but also a human mind or soul; for humanity consists not merely in the possession of a body but of a body and soul. Apollinarianism was plainly an inconsistent explanation of the person of Christ, and it was condemned by the Council of Constantinople in the year 381.

5. NESTORIANISM

Another error that had a widespread influence in the early Church, ranking next to Arianism in importance and even resulting in a considerable portion of the Church splitting off from the main body, was that of Nestorianism. The error of Nestorius was that he carried the dual nature of Christ too far. This gave Christ a double personality, two natures and two persons instead of two natures and one person. Christ was thus regarded as a man in very close union with God, and Nestorius' favorite analogy to explain the person of Christ was that of the union of the believer with Christ. This, however, gave us not an incarnate God, but only a deified man,—one who came from below, not from above. Far from giving us a real incarnation, this system gave us only an alliance between God and a man. Somewhat after the fashion of the Siamese twins, Chang and Eng, God and man were joined together.

We have insisted repeatedly, of course, that Christ is an unique person, that in Him true Deity and true humanity are joined to form one person, and that He is as truly God as is God the Father and as truly man as we are. But we have also pointed out that there is nothing in Scripture to indicate that He was conscious of a double personality. It was not a man but manhood, that is, impersonal generic human nature, that He took into union with Himself. Since He had two natures He also had two wills, the human, however, being always in perfect harmony with and subordinate to the divine. This latter aspect of His personality was best illustrated in His prayer, "Not my will but thine be done." We are thus able to distinguish, but not to divide, the two natures in Christ. The chief error of the Nestorian system was that in separating the divine and the human natures in Christ it deprived His human sufferings of the value and efficacy that they must have if they are to be sufficient for the redemption of mankind. As we have pointed out earlier, only when His divine and human nature are organically and indissolubly united in one person can the acts of either nature have the value of both. Hence we are always to insist upon His true Deity, His true humanity, and the unity of His person.

6. EUTYCHIANISM

Perhaps the most peculiar of all of the Christological heresies was that of Eutychianism. This teaching denied the distinction between the divine and the human nature and held that the two were fused to form a third which was neither divine nor human. Christ was thus supposed to be neither God nor man, but possessed of a nature somewhere between the two. But since the divine nature was the greater it followed that for all practical purposes the human was really absorbed into the divine, but with the effect that the divine was also somewhat changed. Eutyches held that two natures implied two persons. Hence he acknowledged in Christ but one life, one intelligence, and one will. Since Eutychianism denied the human element in Christ it denied the real union of God and man and therefore the possibility of an atonement through the human nature. This blending or fusing of the two natures was, of course, the precise opposite of the Nestorian heresy which had so divided the natures as to give a double personality. Eutychianism was too unstable to gain a large following and it was condemned by the Council of Chalcedon in the year 451.

In conclusion, then, we would point out that the orthodox doctrine of the person of Christ has been the common heritage of the Church since the Council of Chalcedon, 451 A. D. It is not a doctrine that was easily arrived at, but one that was worked out only after long and patient study of the Scriptures and after lively debate in the church councils. Numerous other solutions were tried and found wanting. But in this the Church found rest and has continued to rest until our own day. In it alone, it is safe to say, do the Scripture representations of Christ as God and also as man find harmonious adjustment. "To the onlooker from this distance of time," says Dr. Warfield, "the main line of the progress of the debate takes on an odd appearance of a steady zigzag advance. Arising out of the embers of the Arian controversy, there is first vigorously asserted, over against the reduction of our Lord to the dimensions of a creature, the pure Deity of His spiritual nature (Apollinarianism) ; by this there is at once provoked, in the interests of the integrity of our Lord's humanity, the equally vigorous assertion of the completeness of His human nature as the bearer of His Deity (Nestorianism) ; this in turn provokes, in the interest of the oneness of His person, an equally vigorous assertion of the conjunction of these two natures in a single individuum (Eutychianism) : from all of which there gradually emerges at last, by a series of corrections, the balanced statement of Chalcedon, recognizing at once in its 'without confusion, without conversion, eternally and inseparably' the union in the person of Christ of a complete Deity and a complete humanity, constituting a single person without prejudice to the continued integrity of either nature. The pendulum of thought had swung back and forth in ever-decreasing arcs, until at last it found rest along the line of action of the fundamental force. Out of the continuous controversy of a century there issued a balanced statement in which all the elements of the biblical representation were taken up and combined. Work so done is done for all time ; and it is capable of ever-repeated demonstration that in the developed doctrine of the Two Natures and in it alone, all the biblical data are brought together in a harmonious statement, in which each receives full recognition, and out of which each may derive its sympathetic exposition. This key unlocks the treasures of the biblical instruction on the person of Christ as none other can, and enables the reader as he currently scans the sacred pages to take up their declarations as they meet him, one after the other, into an intelligently consistent conception of his Lord." (*Christology and Criticism*, p. 264).

The foregoing survey of the erroneous views concerning the person of Christ would seem to show that history has exhausted the possibilities of heresy and that future denials of the doctrine must be, in essence, only variations of views which have already been advanced and refuted. For, as Dr. A. H. Strong says, "All controversies with regard to the person of Christ must, of necessity, hinge on one of the three points : first, the reality of the two natures ; secondly, the integrity of the two natures ; thirdly, the union of the two natures in one person. Of these points, Ebionism and Docetism deny the reality of the two natures ;

Arianism and Apollinarianism deny their integrity; while Nestorianism and Eutychianism deny their proper union. In opposition to all these errors, the orthodox doctrine held its ground and maintains it to this day." (*Systematic Theology*, p. 672). And there is much truth in the comment of Dr. A. P. Peabody made in another connection to the effect that "The canon of infidelity was closed almost as soon as that of the Scriptures,"—modern unbelievers having done little more than repeat the long exploded heresies of former centuries. From its earliest origin the Church has believed in both the Deity and the humanity of Christ. Only in the outlawed and comparatively insignificant Ebionite and Docetic sects do we find a belief in a one-natured Christ. Not until the rise of Socinianism in the sixteenth century do we find an important defection from the Church doctrine; and that was in substance a recrudescence of the ancient Ebionite heresy which denied the Deity of Christ. Present day Unitarianism and Modernism, which are essentially denials of the supernatural in religion, trace their origin back to that same movement.

23. Conclusion

Thus is portrayed in Scripture the wonderful character of Jesus Christ. It is of the utmost importance that we have right views concerning His person and work. Otherwise we shall never be able to render Him that honor and respect and devotion that He properly deserves, nor shall we be able to understand the system of truth that He has set forth. The question that Christ Himself put to the Pharisees, "What think ye of the Christ? whose Son is He?" is still the critical question, and no one is entitled to the name of Christian who cannot answer that question aright.

What we think of Christ is of supreme importance because our destiny is determined by our attitude toward Him. Within the circle of His redemptive grace is life; all without is death. Those who sincerely accept Him as their Lord and Master are saved and are destined to enjoy an eternity of blessedness. Those who reject Him are lost, and if they persist in that attitude are destined to an eternity of misery and suffering. Scripture and experience unite in affirming that there is no saving knowledge of God apart from Christ, and that all who enter heaven do so only through the atonement that He has provided.

Nothing is more clear than that Christ cannot be explained by any humanistic system. He does not fit into any theory of natural evolution, for in that case the perfect flower of humanity should have appeared at the end of human history and not in the middle of it. Unquestionably His advent was thousands of years too soon to fit that theory. He differs from all other men not only in degree but also in kind. He is, of course, the central figure in the New Testament, and also in the Old when it is read in the light of the New. No explanation other than that He was Deity incarnate is sufficient to account for the majesty of His person and the uplifting influences that have followed wherever His Gospel has been made known.

The advent of Christ has proved to be the central event in all history. Time before His birth is recorded as B. C. (before Christ), and time since as A. D. (*Anno Domini,* in the year of Our Lord). Every time we write a letter, sign a contract, or print a newspaper we state that we are doing so so many years, months and days after the birth of Christ in Bethlehem. And that a mistake of some four years was later discovered to have been made by those who arranged the calendar does not alter the central fact that His advent was the dividing point in history.

A mere glance at the course of history is sufficient to show that at a particular time in the affairs of men a new influence began to be felt and that, despite the slowness with which men have responded, in the midst of all the other kingdoms of the world there has been implanted this ethical and spiritual kingdom which gradually is pervading society and sweetening all its varied forms of life. The contrast between the Christian era and the preceding era has been well expressed by Dr. C. E. Macartney in the following words: "Do not be misled or deceived by Satanic outbursts of animalism and tyranny and human ferocity, which curse and shadow our world today. In spite of all that, as compared with 'that hard pagan world' into which the Gospel first came, the world today is a world that has been 'turned upside down.' Is the world's labor done today by slaves? Is one-half the population of the world slaves? Are prisoners when taken in battle put to the sword? Are little children exposed and left to die by their parents on the hill-sides, and in the forests? Is woman a plaything and chattel of mankind? To ask these questions is to answer them. The power that wrought this great change was the Gospel of Christ. Call up one by one the systems of darkness and tyranny and superstition which have cursed the earth, and which have long since disappeared. Call them out of their graves and ask them, 'Who smote you? What made you pass?' And one by one they answer, 'Christ smote us and we died.'"

We sometimes hear Christ mentioned along with Socrates, Plato, Buddha, Confucius, Mohammed, etc., as if He were only one of a class of outstanding leaders or reformers. But even the veriest amateur in spiritual things should know better than to pull Him down to the level of those men. Socrates, perhaps the greatest of the Greeks, was guilty of sinful excesses, even living in open sin with a harlot, and on his death-bed with cold indifference kept his family waiting outside the room while he discussed speculative philosophy with some of his associates. As for Plato, read his *Republic* and discover how low and degrading were his views in regard to the family, slavery, the treatment that men should accord women, etc. Or consider Buddha, withdrawing from mankind instead of sharing their hardships, spending his life in the objective contemplation of the world's ills, and giving rise to a system of morals which are so low that to this day in all Buddhistic countries human values have remained very cheap. Or Confucius, collecting and summarizing the wisdom of the past but essentially atheistic in his outlook and completely lacking of any true appreciation of spiritual values. Or Mohammed, with his well-known polygamous practices, his fiendish cruelty in war, his disdain for all people who were not of his following, and his atrocious system of morals which still lays as a blight on all Moslem lands. No, Christ cannot be put in the same class with the world's supposedly great men. He demands a special category, and cannot be explained on any other grounds than that He was the pure, radiant Son of God. The elements of truth that are found in each of the pagan systems are only borrowed or reflected rays from the Sun of Righteousness. In those systems certain elements of truth are curiously intertwined and confused with fatal error, while in the Christian system these same elements, together with a flood of other truth, are presented in their true relationship and are preserved from all error. When we compare Christian ethics with the best of the codes that have been developed by the Greek, Roman, Chinese, or any other non-Christian philosophers or teachers we see immediately how great is the contrast. In the breadth of their scope, in the motives urged for their practice, and in the fundamental qualities of the precepts themselves the contrast is so striking that no serious critics even pretend that there is any real comparison.

Through all the weary centuries man apart from God has never been able to find peace. But in Christ he does find peace and is acutely aware that he has passed out of death into life. The tragic fact, however, is that under the influence of Modernism, materialistic evolution. and so-called higher criticism many of our present day churches have lost much of their witnessing power. The words of Dr. A. H. Strong, written a generation ago, seem even more applicable today. "Many of our teachers and preachers," said he, "have swung off into a practical denial of Christ's deity and of His atonement. We seem upon the verge of a second Unitarian defection that will break up churches and compel secessions, in a worse manner than did that of Channing and Ware a century ago. American Christianity recovered from that disaster only by vigorously asserting the authority of Christ and the inspiration of the Scriptures. We need a new vision of the Saviour like Paul saw on the way to Damascus and John saw on the isle of Patmos, to convince us that Jesus is lifted above space and time, and that His existence antedated creation, that He conducted the march of Hebrew history, that He was born of a virgin, suffered on the cross, rose from the dead, and now lives forevermore, the Lord of the universe, the only God with whom we have to do, our Saviour here and our Judge hereafter. Without a revival of this faith our churches will become secularized, mission enterprise will die out, and the candlestick will be removed out of its place as it was with the seven churches of Asia, and as it has been with the apostate churches of New England."

What a marvelous person is this Christ of the Ages! Every true Christian should be a witness for his Lord and Master, and his witness in order to be effective should be corroborated by a consistently upright manner of life. It is both our duty and privilege to tell others of this wonderful Saviour and of the redemption that has been purchased for them by Him. For His Gospel is the answer to all of the worlds' ills; and above and beyond that it is the power of God unto salvation to every one that believeth, our ground of comfort and our hope of glory. Would that this vision might be clearly presented to every human being on the whole face of the earth, and that mankind in general might come to realize the poverty that is theirs without Christ and the joy that might be theirs with Christ.

CHAPTER V

THE ATONEMENT

1. The Atonement

The two great objectives to be accomplished by Jesus Christ in His mission to this world were, first, the removal of the curse under which mankind labored as a result of the disobedience and fall, and second, the restoration of men to the image and fellowship of God. Both of these were essential to salvation. The work of Christ in reconciling God and men we call the Atonement; and this doctrine, we believe, lies at the very heart of the Christian system.

In the nature of the case we are altogether dependent on Scripture for our knowledge concerning this doctrine and can know only what God has seen fit to reveal concerning it. Human philosophy and speculation can contribute practically nothing toward its solution, and should be held in abeyance. Our present purpose is to give a systematized account of what the Scriptures teach concerning it, and to show that this fits in perfectly with the longings and aspirations of an enlightened spiritual nature.

In one of Paul's most condensed statements of Christian truth we read: "For I delivered unto you first of all that which also I received: that Christ died for our sins according to the Scriptures; and that He was buried; and that He hath been raised on the third day according to the Scriptures," I Cor. 15:3. In this statement first place is given to the death of Christ. "Christ died for our sins" was the fundamental fact of the early Christian message, the corner-stone of its faith. But as soon as this simple fact is stated a number of vital questions are bound to arise. In order that we may have an intelligent understanding of this vital truth it is necessary that we know precisely what it was that Christ accomplished on the cross and how He did it. We cannot rest content with teaching that leaves the central doctrine of our faith shrouded in mystery and uncertainty. This does not mean that all mystery can be removed. But the Scriptures do supply the interpretation of the death of Christ that the inquiring mind legitimately asks for, and the salient factors concerning it should be known by all Christian people. Believing that the Bible is God's word to man, and that the statements of Scripture regarding the death of Christ

270

were meant to be understood by ordinary Christian men and women, we shall not be deterred from this study by those who deprecate any "theory of the atonement." Rather we hold it to be our task and privilege under the promised guidance of the Holy Spirit to "search the Scriptures" until we reach that understanding which satisfies the mind and heart and conscience, and leads to certainty and finality.

We cannot expect to give a full explanation of the Atonement any more than we can give a full explanation of the nature of electricity, or of the force of gravity, or of our own mental and physical processes. But the main outlines of the plan of salvation are clearly revealed in the Scriptures, and it is both our privilege and our duty to acquaint ourselves with as much of that plan as God has seen fit to reveal. We are told, for instance, in broad terms that we are members of a fallen race, that God has given His only-begotten Son for our redemption, and that salvation is through Him and not through any works which we ourselves are able to do. Certainly anyone who accepts these facts and acts upon them will be saved. Yet, accepting these facts and acting upon them would appear to represent only a minimum of faith, and God has made it possible for us greatly to enrich and expand our knowledge of the way of salvation if we will but give careful attention to His word.

By way of background for this subject we are to remember that after God had created man He established certain moral laws by which man was to be governed, and solemnly announced that disobedience to these laws would bring an awful punishment. As a pure test of obedience man was given permission to eat of every tree of the garden except of the tree of the knowledge of good and evil. In regard to that tree he was told: "In the day that thou eatest thereof thou shalt surely die." But man deliberately and defiantly disobeyed that command. Through that disobedience he not only corrupted his moral nature, but made necessary the infliction of the prescribed penalty. In view of God's previously expressed good will toward man, the large degree of liberty granted to him, and his full knowledge of the consequences, this disobedience was especially heinous; because through it man in effect transferred his allegiance from God to the Devil.

Moreover, by his fall Adam corrupted not only himself but all of his posterity, since by divine appointment in this test he acted as their federal head and representative. Had man been left to suffer the penalty alone, he would have experienced not only physical death, but spiritual death as well, which means eternal separation from God and therefore endless progress in sin and suffering. Like the Devil and the demons, who also are fallen creatures and who have been abandoned to their fate, man was morally polluted and guilty and had neither the desire nor the ability to reform himself. Furthermore, it is very evident that no member of this fallen race was capable of paying the debt owed by any other, since each one was preoccupied with his own sin. Even if it had been possible to have found a truly righteous man who was also willing to bear the penalty for others, he could at most have delivered but one other person since he himself was only a man. Nowhere outside the Trinity was there a person either capable or willing to take the place of another, no one capable of suffering and dying, the one for the many. Nor had man the slightest grounds on which to base a request that he be excused from the penalty of the law. Hence his condition was truly desperate.

But fortunately for man there was One both able and willing to perform that service. It was for this purpose that the Lord Jesus Christ, the second Person of the Trinity, became incarnate and performed for man a double service, discharging, on the one hand, the penalty through His own suffering and death, and on the other, restoring to man holiness and life through His perfect obedience to the moral law. Thus was redeemed a multitude which no man can number. How appropriate, then, the words of Peter, "Ye were redeemed, not with corruptible things, with silver or gold, from your vain manner of life handed down from your fathers; but with precious blood, as of a lamb without blemish and without spot, even the blood of Christ," I Peter 1:18, 19. And how appropriate the words of the heavenly songs, "Worthy art thou to take the book, and to open the seals thereof: for thou wast slain, and didst purchase unto God with thy blood men of every tribe, and tongue, and people, and nation, and madest them to be unto our God a kingdom and priests; and they reign upon the earth," Rev. 5:9, 10; "Blessing, and glory, and wisdom, and thanksgiving, and honor, and power, and might, be unto our God for ever and ever," Rev. 7:12; "Great and marvellous are thy works, O Lord God, the Almighty; righteous and true are thy ways, thou King of the ages. Who shall not fear, O Lord, and glorify thy name? for thou only art holy; for all the nations shall come and worship before thee; for thy righteous acts have been made manifest," Rev. 15:3, 4.

The Infinite Value of Christ's Sacrifice

The chief mystery in regard to the Atonement appears to lie in the fact that God chooses to accept the unmerited sufferings of Christ as a just equivalent for the suffering due to sinners. The question then arises, How can the suffering of an innocent person be set to the account of a guilty person in such a way that the guilty person is freed

from the obligation to suffer? Or, to state the question more specifically, How can the suffering which was endured by Christ be set to the
credit of His people, and how can that suffering suffice to save the
millions of mankind, or even all of the people of the world if they
would but trust Him? Or again, as it is sometimes asked although
somewhat erroneously, How can God, the first person, take the sin of a
guilty man, the second person, and lay it on Christ, an innocent third
person?

That this last form of the question does not state the case correctly
is quite evident; and here we get at the heart of the matter. For when
God, the first person, takes the sin of a guilty man, a second person,
and lays it on Christ, He lays it not on a third person but on Himself.
There is no third person in this transaction, because Christ is God,
Deity incarnate. This last consideration many people fail to keep in
mind, and their failure to do so is oftentimes the reason for their
rejection of the whole Christian system, which then is, of course, made
to appear fantastic, unreal, unjust. If God had taken the sin of one
man and laid it on another mere man, that would indeed have been a
flagrant violation of justice as the Unitarians and Modernists charge.

In view of the fact that Christ is God, and therefore a Person of
infinite value and dignity, we have no hesitation in saying that the
crucifixion of Christ was not only the world's worst crime, but that
it was *a worse crime than that which would have been committed if the
entire human race had been crucified.* Isaiah tells us that in comparison
with man God is so great that even "the nations are as a drop in a
bucket, and are accounted as the small dust of the balance," 40:15.
Christ's Deity and creatorship is set forth by John when he says, "In
the beginning was the Word, and the Word was with God, and the
Word was God . . . All things were made through Him; and without
Him was not anything made that hath been made . . . He was in the
world, and the world was made through Him, and the world knew Him
not," 1:1, 3, 10. Paul declares that "God was in Christ reconciling
the world unto Himself," II Cor. 5:19; and in another place adds, "In
Him were all things created, in the heavens and upon the earth, things
visible and things invisible, whether thrones or dominions or principalities or powers; all things have been created through Him, and unto
Him; and He is before all things, and in Him all things consist," Col.
1:16, 17. Even the first chapter of Genesis, which gives an account of
the original creation, declares this same truth; for when read in the
light of the New Testament we see that it was counsel within the
Trinity when it was said, "Let us make man in our image." Paul states
this same general truth in even more graphic words when he declares

that the rulers of this world "crucified the Lord of glory," I Cor. 2:8, and when he refers to "the Church of the Lord" (the King James Version reads, "the Church of God") "which He purchased with His own blood," Acts 20:28. For sinful man thus to crucify his God was an infinitely heinous crime. Whatever may be said about the Atonement, it certainly cannot be said that the debt paid by Christ was of lesser value than that which would have been paid if all of those for whom He died had been left to suffer their own penalty.

In order to illustrate a little more clearly the infinite value of Christ's atonement we should like to use a very simple illustration. Doubtless all of us, for instance, have killed thousands of insects such as ants, beetles, grasshoppers. Perhaps we have even killed millions of them if we have plowed a field or set a large brush fire. Or perhaps we have killed a considerable number of birds or animals, either for food or because they had become pests. Yet we suffer no accusing conscience. But if we kill just one man we do have an accusing conscience which condemns us bitterly; for in that case we have committed *murder*. Even if we could imagine a whole world full of insects or animals and if we could kill them all at one stroke, we would have no accusing conscience. The reason for this difference is that man was created in the image of God, and is therefore of infinitely greater value than the insects or animals. Now in a manner similar to this, Christ, who was God incarnate, was not only of greater value than a man but was of greater value than the sum total of all men; and therefore the value of His suffering and death was amply sufficient to redeem as many of the human race as God sees fit to call to Himself. Christ did not, of course, suffer eternally as men would have done, nor was His pain as great as the sum total of that which would have fallen on man; but because He was a Person of infinite value and dignity His suffering was what God considered a just equivalent for that which was due to all of those who were to be redeemed.

And as we who have been redeemed read that awful account of the crucifixion let us remember that we had a part in it, that it was for our sin and as our Substitute that He suffered and died, regardless of whether or not we personally clamored for His death or drove the nails.

In order for us to understand how it was possible for Christ to have accomplished this work of redemption it is necessary for us to keep in mind the fact that He possessed two natures, one Divine and the other human, and that it was in His human nature that He suffered on the cross. But in our own persons — which are composed of two natures in vital union, the spiritual and the physical — whatever can be affirmed of either of our natures can be affirmed of us as persons. If a certain man is good, or if he is a keen thinker, or happy, or sorrowful, we say that he as a person is good, intellectual, happy, or sorrowful. If his body weighs one hundred and fifty pounds, or if he suffers a broken leg, or is sick, we say that that person weighs that amount or suffers those things. Our spiritual nature is the more important, more dominant and controlling; yet what happens to either of our natures happens to us as persons. In a similar manner, Christ's Divine nature was the more important, more dominant and controlling; but since the two natures were vitally united what He experienced in either He experienced as a Person. Hence His suffering on the cross was God's suffering, and His death was in a real sense God's death for His people. This means that the death of Christ, through which the Atonement was accomplished, was a stupendous event; the most important event in the history of the universe, the central event in all history.

That an atonement of some kind was necessary if human beings were to be pardoned is very evident. The justice of God demands that sin shall be punished as definitely as it demands that righteousness shall be rewarded. God would not be just if He failed to do either. Consequently, the law which was set forth in the beginning, that the punishment for sin should be death—involving, of course, not only destruction of the body, but eternal separation of the spirit from God—could not simply be brushed aside or nullified. The honor and holiness of God were at stake, and when man sinned the penalty had to be paid. The idea of vicarious suffering underlay the entire sacrificial system of the Jews, impressing upon them the fact that a righteous God could make no compromise with sin, and that sin must be and eventually would be punished with its merited recompense, death.

In the Incarnation human nature is taken, as it were, into the very bosom of Deity, and is thus accorded an honor far above that given to angels. Although Christ's work of Atonement is completed, He still retains His resurrection body and will retain it forever; and thus will be exhibited one of the strongest possible evidences of God's unity with man and His measureless love for man.

No Injustice Done When Our Penalty Was Laid on Christ

Unitarians and Modernists sometimes object to this doctrine on the grounds that it is unjust to punish one person for the sins of another, and assert that the idea of vicarious suffering is abhorrent. We reply that there can be no injustice or impropriety connected with it when the person who suffers is the same one who, having made the law that such and such an offense should be followed by such and such a penalty and himself actuated by love and mercy, steps in and receives the penalty in his own person while at the same time he makes provision for the reformation of the offender. In financial matters we readily see that there is no injustice when a creditor remits a debt, provided that he assumes the loss himself. Now what God has done in the sphere of redemption is strictly parallel to this. He has assumed the loss Himself and has set us free. In this case God, who is the offended party, took the initiative and (1) permitted a substitution, (2) provided a substitute, and (3) substituted Himself. If after man fell, God, as the sovereign Ruler of the universe and with the purpose of manifesting His attributes of love and mercy before men and angles throughout eternal ages, voluntarily chose to pay man's debt, surely there are no grounds for objecting that such action was not right. And this, Paul tells us, is precisely what God has done: "God, being rich in mercy, for His great love wherewith He loved us, even when we were dead through our trespasses, made us alive together with Christ (by grace have ye been saved), and raised us up with Him, and made us to sit with Him in the heavenly places, in Christ Jesus: that in the ages to come He might show the exceeding riches of His grace in kindness toward us in Christ Jesus: for by grace have ye been saved through faith; and that not of yourselves, it is the gift of God," Eph. 2:4-9. The work of redemption, including its purpose, method and result, could hardly be stated in clearer language than this.

But it is small wonder that the Unitarians and Modernists object to the Christian doctrine of the Atonement. Since they see in Jesus only a man the Atonement can be, from their point of view, nothing but a colossal travesty, an insult to man's intelligence and to God. Unless Christ was both Divine and human, the whole Christian system is reduced to foolishness. Had Christ been only a man He no more could have saved others than could Stephen, or Huss, or Lincoln, or any other martyr. God cannot take the sins of a criminal and lay them on a good man, but He can take them and lay them on Himself; and that is what the doctrine of the Atonement teaches us that He has done.

2. The Significance of Christ's Death

If we compare the manner in which the service of the world's greatest men have been rendered, and that in which Christ's work of redemption was rendered, we are immediately impressed with an outstanding contrast. While the service of men is rendered during their lifetime, and while Christ too, for that matter, lived a life of unparalleled service, the climax of His work came at its very close, and our salvation is ascribed pre-eminently to His suffering and death. Practically all of the material recorded in the Gospels has to do with the events which occurred during the last three years of His life, and approximately one-third of the material has to do with the events of the last week, commonly known as Passion Week. The prominence thus given to the closing scenes indicates very clearly that the distinctive work of Our Lord was accomplished not by His life but by His death. Neither His example nor His teaching reveals the love and mercy and justice of God so convincingly as does His death; and consequently the cross has become *par excellence* the Christian symbol.

During the latter part of the public ministry Jesus spoke repeatedly and insistently of the death which He was to suffer at Jerusalem. "From that time," says Matthew, marking the beginning of a period. "began Jesus to show unto His disciples, that He must go unto Jerusalem, and suffer many things of the elders and chief priests and scribes, and be killed," 16:21. "He took unto Him the twelve," says Luke, "and said unto them, Behold, we go up to Jerusalem, and all the things that are written through the prophets shall be accomplished unto the Son of man. For He shall be delivered up unto the Gentiles, and shall be mocked, and shamefully treated, and spit upon: and they shall scourge and kill Him," 18:31-33. When Moses and Elijah appeared in glory at the time of the Transfiguration they talked with Jesus concerning "His decease which He was about to accomplish at Jerusalem," Luke 9:31. We are told that when the time drew near that He should be received up "He steadfastly set His face to go to Jerusalem," Luke 9:51, knowing full well what awaited Him there. With such majestic determination did He press forward toward the cross that the disciples were "amazed" and "afraid," Mark 10:32. "I have a baptism to be baptized with; and how am I straightened till it be accomplished," He said to the disciples, Luke 12:50. Loving His people with an infinite love, and having come to earth specifically for their redemption, He longed to suffer and to accomplish His appointed work. In these and numerous other statements He shows His preoccupation with His death, and that in such a manner as to make clear that in His mind it constituted the most significant part of His work.

That the specific purpose of Christ's death was to secure forgiveness for others is taught directly in Scripture. "This is my blood of the covenant, which is poured out for many unto remission of sins," said He as He instituted the Lord's Supper which through all succeeding generations was to be observed as a memorial of His death, Matt. 26:28. "The Son of man came not to be ministered unto, but to minister, and to give His life a ransom for many," Mark 10:45. "I lay down my life for the sheep," John 10:15. "Therefore doth the Father love me, because I lay down my life, that I may take it again. No one taketh it away from me, but I lay it down of myself," John 10:17, 18.

It is not enough to recognize Christ as a teacher while rejecting Him as the atoning Saviour. In the conversation with Nicodemus He promptly brushed aside the complimentary words, "we know that thou art a teacher come from God," and declared that until one is born anew he cannot even so much as see the kingdom of God. And similarly the pity of the "Daughters of Jerusalem," although doubtless sincere, was rejected apparently because it did not recognize the fact that His suffering was not for Himself but for others,—"Weep not for me, but weep for yourselves," Luke 23:28. And the rending of the veil of the temple, which symbolized that the way into the presence of God had been opened for all men, occurred not at His baptism, nor at the Sermon on the Mount, but at His death.

The same teaching concerning the death of Christ is found throughout the New Testament. The Apostle Paul, for instance, pointedly conscious that he had received the cleansing which comes through faith in Christ, places His atoning death at the very heart of his theological system. "Christ redeemed us from the curse of the law, having become a curse for us," Gal. 3:13. "Him who knew no sin He [that is, God] made to be sin on our behalf [that is, laid on Him the punishment due for sin]; that we might become the righteousness of God in Him," II Cor. 5:21. "Christ died for our sins according to the Scriptures," I Cor. 15:3. He is the One whom "God set forth to be a propitiation, through faith, in His blood," Rom. 3:25. "I determined not to know anything among you, save Jesus Christ and Him crucified," I Cor. 2:2.

Peter declares that "Christ also suffered for sins once, the righteous for the unrighteous, that He might bring us to God," I Peter 3:18; and again that He "bare our sins in His body upon the tree," I Peter 2:24. John says, "The blood of Jesus His Son cleanseth us from all sin," I John 1:7; and "He is the propitiation for our sins," I John 2:2. "Apart from shedding of blood there is no remission," wrote the author of the Epistle to the Hebrews, 9:22; and again, "Now once at the end of the ages hath He been manifested to put away sin by the sacrifice of Himself," 9:26. And in John's Revelation the triumphant Christ is pictured as "arrayed in a garment sprinkled with blood," 19:13.

Even in the Old Testament this doctrine was clearly anticipated. In the Messianic 53rd chapter of Isaiah we read: "He was wounded for our transgressions, He was bruised for our iniquities; the chastisement of our peace was upon Him; and with His stripes we are healed. All we

like sheep have gone astray; we have turned every one to his own way:
and Jehovah hath laid on Him the iniquity of us all . . . He was cut off
out of the land of the living for the transgression of my people to
whom the stroke was due . . . When thou shalt make His soul an offering for sin . . . He shall justify many; and He shall bear their iniquities
. . . He bare the sin of many, and made intercession for the transgressors," vss. 5-12.

In appointing the lamb as the principal animal for the morning and
evening sacrifice in ancient Israel, God chose the animal which is at one
and the same time the most harmless and gentle and the most attractive
and pleasing of all the domestic animals, and thus emphasized both the
innocence and the inherent value of the victim whose life was taken.
The people were thus taught that their sins were forgiven and their
lives spared only because another who was innocent and virtuous took
their place and died in their stead. The term "Lamb of God,"
when applied to Christ, calls to mind the Old Testament sacrifices and
invariably refers to His sacrificial death. John the Baptist, for instance,
pointed out Jesus as "the Lamb of God, that taketh away the sin of
the world," John 1:29. Peter says that we were redeemed, "not with
corruptible things, with silver or gold . . . but with precious blood, as
of a lamb without blemish and without spot, even the blood of Christ,"
I Peter 1:18, 19. In the Book of Revelation the redeemed are portrayed
as those who have "washed their robes, and made them white in the
blood of the Lamb," 7:14. And since Christ in His relationship with
His people manifests so preeminently the attributes of gentleness and
tenderness, and since He rules them in and through love, we are further
given to understand that all opposition to Him is unprovoked and
malignant.

SIGNIFICANCE OF THE TERM "BLOOD"

The term "blood" as used in theological language is, of course, to be
understood as a figure of speech. It is used as a synonym for Christ's
atoning death, and it designates the price which He paid for the redemption of His people. There are, as might be expected, many in our day
who take offense at the term "blood," and wish to earn their salvation
by their own good works. But the New Testament, as if anticipating
this very offense, not only repeatedly asserts that salvation is not by
works, but makes direct reference to the "blood" of Christ some thirty-
five or forty times; and in the Old Testament there are innumerable
references to the blood of the animals which were used in the ceremonies and rituals which prefigured the death of Christ. Salvation in
all ages has been through Christ alone; and the Old Testament saints

who worshipped God in His appointed way of sacrifice and poured-out blood looked to the same Saviour as do we who live in the Christian era. "The life of the flesh is in the blood," said the Lord to Moses, "and I have given it to you upon the altar to make atonement for your souls: for it is the blood that maketh atonement by reason of the life," Lev. 17:11. When the blood is poured out, the person or animal dies. Under the ceremonial law the blood with which atonement was made was secured in such a way that the life of the victim was always forfeited. In the twelfth chapter of Exodus we are given an account of the Passover, with its sprinkling of blood and the deliverance of all the firstborn of Israel from death. On the day of annual Atonement the high priest was to sprinkle the blood of the bullock and of the goat over the mercy seat and upon the horns of the altar, Lev. 16:1-34. The various Old Testament blood rituals were but prophetic types or prefigurements of the great sacrifice which later was to be made by Christ when He offered Himself for the sins of His people.

The teaching of the New Testament concerning the blood is very explicit. We have seen that Jesus' own words in instituting the Lord's Supper were, "This is my blood of the covenant, which is poured out for many unto remission of sins," Matt. 26:28. Paul repeatedly asserts this truth: "Now being justified by His blood, we shall be saved from the wrath of God through Him," Rom. 5:9. "Jesus Christ . . . in whom we have our redemption through His blood, the forgiveness of our trespasses, according to the riches of His grace," Eph. 1:3, 7. "But now in Christ Jesus ye that once were afar off are made nigh in the blood of Christ," Eph. 2:13. Christ has "made peace through the blood of His cross," Col. 1:20. The writer of the Epistle to the Hebrews, contrasting the work of Christ with that of the high priest in ancient Israel, says that "Christ having come a high priest . . . not through the blood of goats and calves, but through His own blood, entered in once for all into the holy place, having obtained eternal redemption. For if the blood of goats and bulls, and the ashes of a heifer sprinkling them that have been defiled, sanctify unto the cleanness of the flesh: how much more shall the blood of Christ, who through the eternal Spirit offered Himself without blemish unto God, cleanse your conscience from dead works to serve the living God?" Heb. 9:11-14. John writes, "The blood of Jesus His Son cleanseth us from all sin," I John 1:7. And in the songs of praise to the Redeemer, recorded in the book of Revelation, we hear the words, "Worthy art thou to take the book, and to open the seals thereof: for thou wast slain, and didst purchase unto God with thy blood men of every tribe, and tongue, and people, and nation. . . . Worthy is the Lamb that hath been slain to receive the power, and riches, and wisdom, and might, and honor, and glory, and blessing," Rev. 5 :9, 12.

So let no one take offense at the term "blood." Since salvation was purchased for us by the vicarious suffering and death of Christ, and since that suffering and death is symbolized by the blood, it is but natural that both the Old and the New Testament should mention the blood repeatedly. Many persons have tried to gain salvation by other methods, by church membership, pledge signing, good resolutions, meritorious works, etc., only to find that such methods invariably end in failure. So clearly and constantly and emphatically do the New Testament writers assert that the efficacy of Christ's work is to be ascribed to His death, His blood, His cross, that we are justified in asserting that the Scripturalness or un-Scripturalness of the various present day theories of the atonement can be fairly tested by the place which they give to His death.

To the unsaved nothing seems more unreasonable and meaningless than the assertion that salvation is to be obtained through the blood of Christ. The Scriptures, of course, recognize this condition of the unregenerate heart, and declare that, "The word of the cross is to them that perish foolishness," and then add by way of contrast, "but unto us who are saved it is the power of God," I Cor. 1 :18. Those who have experienced the cleansing and forgiveness which comes through this faith know that the crucified and risen Lord is able to save to the uttermost those who draw near unto God through Him, and that there is no salvation in any other.

And unless Christ did thus give His life a sacrifice for others we are at a loss to know why He died. We have seen that the penalty which God originally prescribed for sin was the loss of life,—and like any other penalty it can be justly inflicted only where the law has been violated. But Christ suffered the penalty of death even though He had no sin of His own. Consequently He must have died for the sins of others. Unless He did thus die, His voluntary surrender to death, and that at the early age of thirty-three, must be looked upon as utter foolishness, as, in fact, criminal suicide.

Not Merely a Martyr's Death

There are many who deny that the death of Christ had any value as an atonement. The most common alternative view is that He died merely as a martyr. But apart from the fact that a mere martyr's death would leave most of the distinctive Christian doctrines without any adequate foundation, the narratives themselves make it quite clear that something profoundly different was involved. Compare His feeling, in view of death, with that of Paul: "having the desire to depart," Phil. 1:23; "The time of my departure is come. I have fought the good fight, I have finished the course, I have kept the faith: henceforth there is laid up for me the crown of righteousness, which the Lord, the righteous judge, shall give to me at that day; and not to me only, but also to all them that love His appearing," II Tim. 4:6-8. Jesus, on the other hand, was filled with anguish. "Now is my soul troubled; and what shall I say? Father, save me from this hour," John 12:27. We are told that "His sweat became as it were great drops of blood falling down upon the ground," Luke 22:44. And as He hung on the cross we hear the despairing cry, "My God, my God, why hast thou forsaken me?" Matt. 27:46. As Dr. A. H. Strong has said, "If Christ was simply a martyr, then He was not a perfect example; for many a martyr has shown greater courage in prospect of death, and in the final agony has been able to say that the fire which consumed him was 'a bed of roses.' Gethsemane, with its mental anguish, is apparently recorded in order to indicate that Christ's sufferings even on the cross were not mainly physical sufferings."

As Jesus hung on the cross He was, in His human nature, the true sin-offering for His people, and as such, it was necessary that He suffer alone. God can have no association whatever with sin, since in His sight it is infinitely heinous. And, as in the Old Testament ritual for the sin-offering, this was symbolized by the burning of the flesh of the bullock outside of the camp (even the offering itself being treated as offensive and polluted since in the mind of the offerer it stood representative of and was in some way associated with his sin), so Jesus, as He bore in His own body the full weight of the penalty of sin, was temporarily cut off from the Father's presence and paid the entire cost of redemption without help from any other. The darkened heavens, and the cry, "My God, my God, Why hast thou forsaken me?" indicate as much. He was acutely conscious not only of the pain from the nails, but also of a break in that intimate and loving fellowship which He had always enjoyed with the Father. Since Jesus in His human nature was subject to the limitations which are common to men, it was as possible for Him to experience the sense of separation from the Father as it was for Him to be ignorant of the time of the end of the world, or to suffer pain or hunger. But during the crucifixion, as He bore a burden of sin such as had never been borne and could never be borne by any mere man, He went through an experience far more awful and terrifying than is possible for any mere martyr. In contrast with His sufferings, the Christian martyrs were deeply conscious of God's presence as they yielded up their lives. If Christ's death was only a martyr's death it might well fill us with terror and despair, for it would show that the holiest man who ever lived was utterly forsaken by God in the hour of His greatest need.

Death is primarily the separation of the soul from God; and physical death, or the separation of the soul from the body, is only a by-product and a relatively unimportant consequence of that greater catastrophe. Jesus did not suffer the pangs which are experienced by lost souls in hell, but in paying the penalty for His people, He did suffer death in its most essential nature, which is separation from God. And while His sufferings were not identical, either in intensity or in length of time endured, with those which His people would have suffered had they been left to their own sin, in view of the infinite worth and dignity of the Sufferer they were nevertheless a full equivalent for those sufferings.

Let us keep in mind that it was not Christ's divine nature, but only His human nature, which was subject to suffering and death, as it was only His human nature which was subject to temptation, hunger, thirst, sleep, etc. While we do not fully understand the relationship which exists between His two natures, we have a faint analogy in our own persons in which a spiritual and a physical nature are united; and on the basis of our own experience we know that what He experienced in either nature He experienced as a person, that is, as the God-man. This latter fact is of the utmost importance since it explains why His work of redemption was possessed of infinite value, sufficient to save all those who put their trust in Him. And again, while we do not fully understand the relationship which exists between the two natures, and while the analogy does not hold at all points, we may picture His divine nature during the crucifixion as not only fully sympathetic with His human nature, but as looking down upon His human nature calmly and serenely as the moon in its majesty looks down upon the troubled sea.

It seems quite evident that the work of redemption, which together with its wider effects may also be designated as the spiritual re-creation of the souls of men, was a greater work than the original creation of the universe. When the starry heavens were brought into existence and spread throughout the vast bounds of space, that work, while requiring great power and wisdom, was accomplished at God's spoken command. Such creation was comparatively easy, and is referred to as but "the work of His finger," Ps. 8:3. "He spake, and it was done; He commanded, and it stood fast," Ps. 33:9. But when the work of redemption was to be accomplished, God, in the person of Christ, took upon Himself human nature with its attendant weaknesses, was born a helpless babe in low condition, underwent the hardships of this life, was scoffed at and rejected by the religious and political rulers of the nation, suffered the cruel pain and cursed death of the cross, was buried, and continued under the power of death for a time. While the work of creation was accomplished through a mere exercise of power and wisdom, the work of redemption was accomplished only at an infinite cost of suffering on the part of God Himself. As man's soul is of incomparably greater value than his body, so the redemption of the souls of men was an incomparably greater work than the original creation of the universe. Christ's work of redemption is now seen to have been the central event of all history.

We do not mean to imply that man's salvation was completed by the work of Christ on the cross. His words, "I have accomplished the work which thou hast given me to do," John 17:4, and "It is finished," John 19:30, relate to the objective atonement which He provided for the sins of men. But the great purpose of His coming, that of making men subjectively just and holy, was not yet fulfilled. As the work of providence follows the work of creation, so the subjective cleansing of the sinner is a continuing process as the redemption which was purchased by Christ is applied by the Holy Spirit to those for whom it was intended. Here enter the works of regeneration, justification, adoption, sanctification, and glorification. But this opens up a whole new field of theology, that of the person and work of the Holy Spirit, which we have not space to discuss in this present work.

Thus the death of Christ emerges as the central truth in the Christian doctrine of redemption. It is the link which holds together all of the other distinctive doctrines. The mark of His blood is upon them all and signifies their ownership, as the scarlet thread running through every cord and rope of the British navy signifies that it is the property of the crown. It hardly seems possible that, with this central truth written so plainly and so repeatedly across the pages of Scripture, any honest or serious minded persons could arise, as do the Unitarians and Modernists, and declare that the essence of Christianity consists in our following the example of Christ in lives of social service, or that the chief purpose of the Church is to build a new social order in this world. It is very evident, of course, that in our daily lives we are to follow the example of Christ as closely as possible. And in due course of time a new social order, based on justice and improved living conditions, will gradually arise as Christian principles are applied first to the lives of individuals and through them to the life of the community. In many limited social groups we already see the effects of this uplifting process. But Christ's expiatory death is no more an object for our imitation than is the creation of the world. For in His death He took man's place and rendered to divine justice a satisfaction which man himself was utterly unable to render. That Christianity is not primarily a social movement, but a redemptive religion, setting forth a way of escape from sin, is as plain as it is possible for words to make it.

3. The Satisfaction View of the Atonement

Before we can have any adequate understanding or appreciation of the work that Christ has done for us it is necessary that we know something of the nature and effect of sin in the human soul. In substance the Bible tells us that sin is open and defiant rebellion against the law of God. There are, of course, many forms in which it may manifest itself, such as murder, robbery, adultery, lying, profanity, idolatry, pride, envy, covetousness, disrespect for parents, etc. But regardless of the different forms which it may assume it is essentially and definitely one thing: It is crime committed against God. Perhaps the best known formal definition of sin is that of the Westminster Confession which says, "Sin is any want of conformity unto, or transgression of, the law of God." The law of God is moral in the highest sense, and has been given for the good of mankind. It is a revelation of, or a transcript of, God's own character, and is therefore perfect and immutable.

The person who commits sin transfers his allegiance from God to the Devil, although but few seem to realize that they are actually serving the Devil. But the Scripture says, "He that doeth sin is of the Devil," I John 3:8. Paul was divinely appointed to preach to the Gentiles, "to open their eyes, that they may turn from darkness to light and from the power of Satan unto God," Acts 26:18. We have the word of Jesus that "Every one that committeth sin is the bond-servant of sin" John 8:34; and to the Pharisees who maliciously opposed Him He said, "Ye are of your father the Devil, and the lusts of your father it is your will to do," John 8:44.

The nature of sin being what it is, it is not surprising that the penalty that God has established against it is severe. That penalty is *death*. "In the day that thou eatest thereof thou shalt surely die," Gen. 2:17, was the clearly announced penalty spoken to Adam at the very beginning of the race. It was repeated by the prophets, e.g., "The soul that sinneth, it shall die." Ezek. 18:4; and in the New Testament, "The wages of sin is death," Rom. 6:23.

We have already pointed out that death in this sense included a great deal more than physical death, which is the separation of the soul from the body, that it was primarily spiritual death, or the eternal separation of the soul from God. In this broader sense death means an abandoned spiritual condition such as that of the Devil and the demons. It involves the immediate loss of the divine favor, the sense of guilt, the corruption of the moral nature (resulting of course in the commission of other and more flagrant transgressions), and the pains of hell. The reward promised for obedience, as is clearly implied in the Genesis account and in later Scripture, was *life,* the exact opposite of the penalty threatened, not merely physical life as we know it, but eternal life such as is enjoyed by the holy angels. And since Adam by divine appointment stood representative for all of those who were to come after him by natural descent and acted precisely as they would have acted under similar circumstances, the reward for his obedience or the penalty for his disobedience was designed to fall not only on him but equally on them. Thus situated, Adam made his choice,—and fell. The results were disastrous, for by that fall he brought himself and his descendants into a state of depravity, guilt, and condemnation, a state in which the intellect is blinded to spiritual truth, the affections corrupted, and the will enslaved. From that condition there was no possible way of escape—except by divine grace.

That the penalty for sin did relate primarily to man's spiritual nature is seen in the fact that Adam did not die a physical death for 930 years after he had disobeyed, although he died spiritually and felt himself estranged from God the very instant he sinned. It is also shown by the fact that Adam's unregenerate posterity since that time have invariably and persistently gone the way of evil, displaying the same aversion to righteousness and the same affection for sin.

Unchangeable Nature of the Law Against Sin

The moral law which God gave to man in the beginning was no arbitrary or whimsical pronouncement, but an expression of His being. It showed man what the nature of God was, and was designed to bring man's nature into closer conformity with His nature. It was very explicit, both in its command and in its threatened penalty. Now sin is the absolute contradiction of that nature, and cannot therefore be lightly set aside. In all of His dealings God reveals Himself as a holy, just, and truthful God. As a holy God He hates sin and burns against it with a consuming zeal. As a just God he scrupulously rewards righteousness and punishes sin, for strict justice is as insistent in its demand that sin shall be punished as it is in its demand that righteousness shall be rewarded. God cannot give the reward of obedience for disobedience. The same God who is a God of mercy and who in virtue of His mercy desires to save human souls, is also a God of justice and in virtue of His justice must punish sinners. And as a truthful God He must put into effect the penalty which He has said would be enforced against transgressors. For Him to fail to punish sin would be for Him to remove the penalty against it, to consent to it or to become partaker in it, and therefore to violate His own nature and to destroy the moral order of the universe. Consequently when sin is committed it simply cannot be ignored or cancelled out with mere pardon. The penalty must be paid. God's honor and justice are at stake. However much God in His love might have desired to have saved man, it was not possible for Him to do so until satisfaction was made to the divine law. Hence the truth of the Scripture statement: "Apart from shedding of blood [i.e., the payment of the prescribed death penalty] there is no remission" (of sin), Heb. 9:22.

Hence even if man possessed the power to repent and turn to God, forgiveness could not be granted on the basis of mere repentance. For repentance does not expiate crime, even under civil government. The fact that the murderer, or robber, or adulterer, or liar is sorry does not excuse him from obligation. He must restore what he has taken. He must make right what he has made wrong. Otherwise the injury remains. We instinctively feel that wrong-doing must be balanced by a corresponding penalty. This feeling is especially noticeable after a particularly atrocious crime has been committed. We say that the crime calls for vengeance, and that a moral order which would allow it to go unpunished would not be right. The truly penitent man never feels that his repentance constitutes a ground of acceptance, either with God or with his fellow men. The more sincerely he repents the more truly he recognizes his need of reparation and expiation.

Fortunately for us, God meets the demands of His own holiness and justice and of man's conscience by Himself providing an atonement, a satisfaction. He does not forgive sin merely because He cares so little about it, nor because He is so exclusively the God of love that all other considerations fall into insignificance beside it; but in His own person and by the sacrifice of Himself He pays the penalty which frees man from obligation and provides that righteousness which alone admits him into heaven. For as Dr. Wm. C. Robinson has recently said, "The cross is not a compromise, but a substitution; not a cancellation, but a satisfaction; not a wiping off, but a wiping out in blood and agony and death." Thus mercy does not cheat justice. Holiness is rewarded, sin is punished, and the moral order of the universe is maintained in its perfection.

Years ago in England and in our own country there were debtor's prisons in which those who could not pay their debts were incarcerated. The law was inexorable. The man who had borrowed money and squandered or mismanaged it had to go to prison. He could not make things right merely by saying that he was sorry. Some one had to stand the loss, either the borrower or the person from whom it had been borrowed. But if a wealthy friend of the borrower came forward and paid the debt he was set free. In fact, in such a case his freedom became mandatory, for the law was satisfied. And so it is with the Christian doctrine of the atonement. Christ has done for His people exactly what a man does for his friend,—He has paid the debt for them. That is the meaning of the cross. God Himself assumed man's nature, and in that nature took man's place before His own law, suffered its penalty, and saved man through pure grace.

It must be perfectly evident to every one that if God allowed sin to go unpunished, or if He dealt with it in a free and loose manner, it would mean that justice had been cast to the winds and that He was governed by weak sentimentality. In the original creation God made man in His own image and implanted in him a deep sense of moral responsibility. He would be unfaithful to Himself if after having implanted that great principle He did not rule in accordance with it. For He is not only a loving Father, but also a righteous Judge. He cannot permit His righteous laws to be violated with impunity. If the sinner is to be forgiven, then for his own sake as well as for the sake of truth and righteousness, that forgiveness must not come in such a way as to diminish or benumb his sense of guilt. While God's love and tenderness are manifested in His forgiveness of sin, that forgiveness must not be accomplished in a manner which fails to show sin to be what it really is, something hateful and painful to God, diametrically opposed to His holy nature and subversive of His rule throughout the universe. Otherwise man will be misled into an easy-going, good-natured carelessness, and will have no adequate understanding or appreciation of the favor that has been granted to him.

For the righteousness of God is not, as so many people seem inclined to believe, mere disinterested benevolence which can pass lightly over sin. It is rather a distinct and separate attribute of the divine nature which demands that sin shall receive its adequate punishment. We regret that so much of our modern theological literature shows an almost complete lack of any adequate sense of the heinousness and guilt of sin. It is only when men hold superficial views of sin and think that it can be cast off by simple repentance that they deny the need of an expiatory atonement. But in proportion as an aroused conscience tells us that we are sinners we realize how deep is our guilt and cry out for that Saviour who alone is "able to save to the uttermost them that draw near unto God through Him."

HOLINESS IS PRIOR TO AND CONDITIONS LOVE

The most fundamental attribute of God's nature is, not love, but holiness. His holiness may be defined as His self-perpetuating righteousness or purity, in virtue of which He eternally wills and maintains His own moral excellence. He has constituted the universe, and humanity as a part of it, so that it shall express His holiness,—positively by connecting happiness with righteousness, and negatively by connecting unhappiness or suffering with sin. Love, in itself, is irrational and capricious except as it is governed by holiness. And the fact that holiness is logically prior to and conditions love makes it impossible for sin to be pardoned without an atonement. There must be an adequate infliction of misery to offset that sin. Many of the Greek gods were notoriously immoral. But our God is a God of holiness, a God of perfect morality; and He can tolerate no sin. If the forgiveness of sin depended only on the sovereign will of God, there would, of course, be no need for an atonement. In Mohammedanism, for instance, where the sovereignty of God is so emphasized that all other attributes are dwarfed beside it, no need is felt for satisfying divine justice. Mohammedanism holds that God can pardon whom He will, and on whatever grounds He pleases. The immeasurable superiority of Christian theology is evidenced by its clear and emphatic demand that the justice and holiness of God must be maintained and that the affront which has been offered to it by human sin shall not go unpunished. The tendency in some modern systems of theology is to merge holiness and love and to assume that God can forgive sin without an atonement. But such an easy-going optimism either does not know what the holiness of God involves, or fails utterly to understand the heinous nature of sin.

That God is love is, of course, one of the clear revelations of Scripture. And to us who would be forever lost if it were not for His love, that is the crowning revelation of Christianity. But love is not all that God is, and can therefore never adequately express all that God is. It is equally true that God is just and that He must punish sin. The writer of the Epistle to the Hebrews says that His attitude toward the workers of iniquity is that of "a consuming fire" (12:29). The popular literature of our day abounds with many ill-considered assertions of the indiscriminate love of God, as though He were too broadly good to hold man to any real account for sin. But we can never know the depth of the meaning of God's love until it is thrown up against the background of those other lofty conceptions which arise from and are based on a true view of His holiness, righteousness and justice. In brief, we may say that whereas the Modernist reasons, God is love and therefore there is no need for an atonement, the truth is, God is love and therefore He provides an atonement.

This brings us to the question, What is true love? We may say that one person truly loves another when he has a greater desire to please that person than he has to please himself. And the correlated truth is: One person truly loves another when he would rather suffer himself than see that one suffer. In the final analysis there are just two moral principles which may govern one's action: the first is that which has one's own interests as its final motive or supreme object, and is therefore the *selfish* principle; the second is that which has the interests of others as its final motive and is therefore the self-giving, *sacrificial* principle. This second is the principle which God manifests in His relations with His people. Consequently the greatest message that any one can hear is that *"God is love,"* (I John 4:16); for that means that God's holy nature seeks to express itself actively toward him, and that he will therefore be fitted for the divine presence.

On Calvary more than anywhere else the great loving heart of God has been revealed to man. There was love, unspeakable love, "When God the mighty Maker died for man the creature's sin." This redeeming love originated in the Trinity and was first exhibited in God's attitude toward man, not in man's attitude toward God; for man showed only opposition and hatred for everything that was good. "Herein is love, not that we loved God, but that He loved us, and sent His Son to be the propitiation for our sins," I John 4:10. "God commendeth His own love towards us, in that, while we were yet sinners, Christ died for us," Rom. 5:8. The atonement is not the cause, but the effect, of God's love for His people. Because He loved them He redeemed them. In the cross there was revealed to us the love of the Father who proposed the covenant of grace, the love of the Son who in His own body freely accomplished that redemption, and the love of the Holy Spirit who makes that love effective in our hearts. This general thought has been beautifully expressed in a recent book by Dr. Wm. C. Robinson. Says he: "In the very being of God Himself there are eternal love relationships. 'God is love.' And hence out of that self-moving and self-motivated love ever· existing between the Persons of the adorable

Trinity love came forth into this world of sin. Out of God's great eternal love, out of the heart of the Trinity came the love of Calvary. Before the foundation of the world He did in love predestinate us unto the adoption of sons through Jesus Christ unto Himself (Eph. 1:4, 5). The eternal Son brought the love of heaven into this world of hate, and lifted it so high on that hill called a skull that every nation shall behold its light, every age be mellowed by its glow,"—*The Word of the Cross,* p. 118.

The great classical passage with reference to the Atonement is Rom. 3:25, 26. There Christ is declared to be the One "Whom God set forth to be a propitiation, through faith, in His blood, to show His righteousness because of the passing over of the sins done aforetime, in the forebearance of God; for the showing, I say, of His righteousness at this present season: that He might Himself be just, and the justifier of him that hath faith in Jesus." Here we are told, (1) that God set forth Christ as an effective propitiatory offering; (2) that man is saved by the exercise of faith in the substitutionary suffering and death of Christ; (3) that while up to this time God, in His mercy and in anticipation of the certain coming of a Redeemer, had saved men without exacting an adequate punishment for their sins. He determines that at this time He will provide that adequate and public exhibition of the punishment of sin; and (4) that the purpose of this sacrifice is that God Himself may be just while forgiving and saving the sinner. Because God had in pre-Christian times saved sinners while allowing their sins to go unpunished His own righteousness had been lost sight of and obscured, and it was necessary that an adequate exhibition of the punishment of sin be made before men and angels. The sacrifices of animals in Old Testament times were not real atonements, but only signs and tokens pointing to the real atonement which was to come later. As the Baptist theologian, Dr. A. H. Strong, has boldly expressed it, "Before Christ's sacrifice, God's administration was a scandal,—it needed vindication. The Atonement is God's answer to the charge of freeing the guilty."

Hence the first and primary effect of the atonement is upon God Himself in that through it He is enabled to remain righteous even when pardoning the sinner,—"that He might Himself be just, and the justifier of him that hath faith in Jesus." Because God Himself, in the person of Christ, has borne the penalty for sin, He is now able to show Himself as perfectly just and holy while at the same time He grants forgiveness and eternal life to those who put their faith in Christ.

CHRIST ALONE ABLE TO REDEEM MEN

We have said that man's condition after the fall was one of absolute helplessness, that he was morally alienated from God, and that his whole attitude toward God, so far as he thought of God at all, was one of opposition and enmity. In Scripture language he was "dead" in trespasses and sins (Eph. 2:1, 5). In that fallen state, however, he was still able to do works which considered only in themselves or in reference to his fellow men were good,—he was still able to love his family, to deal honestly with his neighbors, to feed the hungry and comfort the sorrowing, etc. But in doing these things he acted only from selfish or humanitarian motives. In no instances were they done with the purpose of honoring or glorifying God. He might give a million dollars to build a hospital, but he could not give so much as a cup of cold water to a disciple *in the name of Christ*. However good his works might appear in themselves, none of them were done with right motives toward God. All of them, therefore, had a vitiating principle, a fatal defect, and could in no wise merit salvation. Man's vital need, then, was not good advice, nor an impressive example of right conduct, but to be "made alive" spiritually (Eph. 2:1, 5), to be "born anew" (John 3:3), to experience "regeneration" and "renewing" by the Holy Spirit (Titus 3:5).

Since men were in that ruined and helpless condition there was only one possible way by which they might be saved. That was for another person of infinite value and dignity to take upon himself their nature, that is, human nature, and, with the consent of God, suffer the penalty which was due to them. His higher personality would give unlimited value to his suffering, which would then be a just equivalent for that which was due to them. And at this point comes in the importance of the Christian doctrine of the Trinity. For God is not only unity, but tri-personality, so that there are within the Godhead three Persons, each possessing full Deity, the same in substance and equal in power and glory. Hence because of this fact alone it was possible that there might be One who would offer Himself as Mediator between God and man, One possessing a personality of infinite value and dignity who therefore as man's Agent could work out an atonement of infinite value. Christ, the second Person of the Trinity, did offer Himself as such a Mediator between God and man. In order to accomplish that work He became incarnate, uniting Deity and humanity in His person as intimately and harmoniously as our souls and bodies are united in ours. Only Christ, then, in His Divine-human person, that is, as the God-man, was qualified to accept that penalty and discharge that obligation. No other person in all the universe was capable of assuming that role. The sacrifice of no creature could have availed anything. Nor could either the Father or the Holy Spirit as such have performed that work. Only the two-natured Christ was capable of providing redemption. And only in His organic and official union with His people can we find that vital relation which makes His vicarious suffering either possible or just. The entire Bible from Genesis to Revelation is God's account of the work that He has done for man. In strict literalness it might have been called, "The History of Redemption," for the main features dealt with are the original creation of man, his fall, his condition after the fall, God's merciful staying of the full execution of the penalty, the long course of preparation for the coming of the Redeemer, the nature of the work performed by the Redeemer when He did come, His ascension to heaven and His future coming when He shall assign all men their eternal rewards.

Consequently, we find that in the accomplishment of that work Christ did not die a natural death. The kind of death that He died was particularly designed to show that satisfaction was being made to divine justice, that somehow He was dying because the penalty of sin is death. Had He been unexpectedly assassinated, or died as a result of accident, or disease, or old age, there would have been no appearance of a satisfaction having been made to satisfy the demands of divine justice. But when He is placed as a criminal before a tribunal, accused, overpowered by the testimony of witnesses, officially condemned to death, and crucified and His life taken from Him in the very prime of His manhood, we are given to understand that on this righteous Person was inflicted the punishment due to criminals, to malefactors,— in short, the punishment due to us as sinners. He died not merely a corporal death, but a particular kind of death in which He experienced the severity of the divine vengeance against sin. By paralleling even in detail the Old Testament ritual for the sin-offering it was made plain that He was our sin-bearer. What He did and suffered He did and suffered, not for any sin of His own, but for that of His people, in their name and on their account. Hence Paul could say, and we can say with him, "I have been crucified with Christ; and it is no longer I that live, but Christ liveth in me." Gal. 2:20.

Since man's sin was directed against God, who is an infinitely holy and just Being, and since fallen man if left to himself would have continued to sin throughout endless ages as do the Devil and the fallen angels, it is very evident that nothing less than an atonement of infinite value could have rescued him from that condition. This does not mean that Christ suffered as much during the space of one lifetime as His people would have suffered in an eternity of punishment. But it does mean that since the divine and human natures were united in the person of Christ, His suffering possessed a value equal to or rather greater than that which all of His people deserved, and that it was therefore amply sufficient for the redemption of all who put their trust in Him. His suffering was not the same as theirs either in kind or in duration; for He could suffer no remorse because He had no personal sin, and His was terminated within a few hours whereas theirs, due to their endless persistence in sin, would have continued through all eternity. A finite being could never have exhausted that penalty, but an infinite Being can exhaust it in a comparatively short time. But while not identical with the sufferings that sinners would have borne, His sufferings were of such kind and degree and duration as divine wisdom, interpreting divine justice, decreed was a full legal equivalent of that penalty when suffered vicariously by a divine person. Only when Calvary is regarded as revealing eternal principles of the divine nature can we see how the sufferings of those few hours can suffice to save millions of mankind. Certainly the fundamental conception of Christ's redeeming work as it is set forth in the Scriptures is that through His vicarious suffering and death He made full satisfaction to the justice of God and by His vicarious obedience He has merited eternal life so that all those who by faith accept Him as their Lord and Savior receive, firstly, deliverance from the guilt of sin, so that they are no longer under obligation to suffer for it; secondly, emancipation from the power of sin, so that they are cleansed from it and enabled to live a holy life; and, thirdly, a life of eternal blessedness in heaven.

To those who are accustomed to look upon man as sufficient for all things, the death of Christ and redemption through blood atonement is, of course, nonsense. When it was first announced it was "unto Jews a stumblingblock, and unto Gentiles foolishness," but unto them that believed it was "the power of God, and the wisdom of God," I Cor 1:23. Some call it repulsive. It is indeed repulsive and humiliating to the self-confident natural man. When Unitarians and Modernists represent it as a cruel demand on God's part and as an expiation from without in which one man's sin is laid on another while they themselves profess to believe in a God of love, they consciously or unconsciously caricature the Christian doctrine. For the plain and repeated teaching of Scripture is that it was not an outsider but God Himself in the person of Christ who met the demands of His own justice in order that He might be free to save man. For "God was in Christ reconciling the world unto Himself," II Cor. 5:19. Nor is this doctrine difficult to understand. A little child can understand its essential features, and can receive it to the salvation of his soul. And certainly it is not a system of human invention, for all men naturally feel that they should earn salvation by their own good works. A system of salvation by grace is so radically at variance with what man sees in the natural world where every thing and person is evaluated in terms of works and merits that he has great difficulty in bringing Himself to believe that it can be true. There is real point in the words of the great English preacher, C. H. Spurgeon: "The doctrine of substitution must be true; it could not have been invented by human wit." In one way or another all of the pagan religions and all of the philosophical systems teach that man must earn his own salvation. Christianity alone sets forth a system of salvation by grace. Time and again the Scriptures repeat the assertion that salvation is by grace, as if anticipating the difficulty which men would have in coming to the conclusion that they could not earn it by their own good works.

The Difference Between Commercial and Penal Debt

It has sometimes been charged that the satisfaction view represents the sacrifice of Christ as a purely commercial transaction. There is, however, a wide difference. In a commercial or pecuniary debt the point is not *who pays,* but *what is paid,* and the payment of the thing owed *ipso facto* frees the debtor from any further obligation whatsoever. If a third person offers to pay the debt, the creditor has no other choice than to accept the payment. He then has no further claim on the person of the debtor. He cannot be said to have extended any grace or indulgence toward the debtor; for he has received the precise *thing* which was due him. But penal debt is far different. In this case the obligation rests upon the *person* as well as upon the thing due. Not only must the prescribed penalty be suffered, but it must be suffered by the person who has committed the crime. A vicarious suffering of the penalty is permissible only at the discretion of the sovereign or judge. If it is permitted, it is a matter of grace to the criminal; and the rights which are acquired by the vicarious suffering all accrue to the sponsor or substitute who has borne the suffering. The claims of the law upon the sinner are not automatically dissolved by such a transaction. Instead, the benefits are passed on to him only at such times and on such conditions as have previously been agreed upon between the sovereign and the sponsor. Hence it is that the benefits of Christ's suffering were not immediately set to the account of His people at the time He suffered, but accrue to them as individuals down through the ages, in greater or lesser degree, and in many varied conditions, in accordance with the terms of the secret covenant which was made between the Father, the Son and the Holy Spirit. Hence, too, it is that God is absolutely sovereign in bestowing these benefits, and that salvation is of pure grace. God can give or withhold these benefits in each individual case as He pleases. The vicarious suffering of Christ thus emerges as an infinite benefit to those who are saved, and as no injury or disadvantage whatever to any who may be left to bear the penal consequences of their own sin.

In the following illustration Dr. Robert L. Dabney, the noted theologian of the Southern Presbyterian Church, has brought out quite clearly the distinction between (1) commercial debt; (2) the satisfaction view; and (3) a compromise system in which something less than the equivalent of the original obligation is paid: "A mechanic is justly indebted to a land-owner in the sum of one hundred pounds; and has no money wherewith to pay. Now, should a rich brother offer the landlord the full hundred pounds, in coin of the realm, this would be a legal tender; it would, *ipso facto,* cancel the debt, even though the creditor captiously rejected it. Christ's satisfaction is not *ipso facto* in this commercial sense. There is a second supposition: that the kind brother is not rich, but is himself an able mechanic; and seeing that the landlord is engaged in building, he proposes that he will work as a builder for him two hundred days, at ten shillings *per diem* (which is a fair price), to cancel his poor brother's debt. This proposal, on the one hand, is not a 'legal tender,' and does not compel the creditor. He may say that he has already enough mechanics, who are paid in advance; so that he cannot take the proposal. But, if he judges it convenient to accept it, although he does not get the coin, he gets an actual equivalent for his claim, and a fair one. This is *satisfactio.* The debtor may thus get a valid release on the terms freely covenanted between the surety and the creditor" (—the same principle applying here as in the Reformed or Calvinistic system, which holds that Christ made a full satisfaction for the sins of His people). "But there is a third plan: The kind brother has some 'script' of the capital stock of some company, which, 'by its face' amounts nominally to one hundred pounds, but all know that it is worth but little. Yet he goes to the creditor, saying: 'My brother and I have a pride about bearing the name of full payment of our debt. We propose that you take this 'script' as one hundred pounds (which is its nominal amount), and give us a discharge, which shall state that you have payment in full.' Now, if the creditor assents, this is payment *per acceptilationem"* (the same principle applying here as in the Arminian system, which holds that since the sinner could not pay his debt God, as a result of Christ's suffering on the cross, no longer demands perfect obedience, but now offers salvation on lower terms, on the basis of such "faith and evangelical obedience" as the crippled sinner is able to offer). "Does Christ's satisfaction amount to no more than this? We answer emphatically, it does amount to more. This disparaging conception is refuted by many Scriptures, such as Is. 42:21; 50:6. It is dishonorable to God, representing Him as conniving at a 'legal fiction,' and surrendering all standards of truth and justice to confusion. On this scheme, it is impossible to see how any real necessity for satisfaction could exist. The Reformed assert then, that Christ made penal satisfaction, by suffering the very penalty demanded by the law of sinners." *Theology*, p. 504.

Contrast Between the Gospels and the Epistles

In recent years some critics have attempted to discredit the doctrine of the atonement by setting the teaching of Jesus over against that of Paul. It is true, of course, that Jesus did not say a great deal about the atonement. A careful examination of His teaching, however, will show that its reality was constantly assumed, and that on some occasions He expressed it clearly. This lack of emphasis concerning it in the Gospels as compared with its repeated statement in the Epistles has led some to say that true Christianity is based on the former and that the latter must be rejected.

But the reason for this difference of approach is very evident when we remember that the primary purpose of Jesus in His earthly mission was not to preach the Gospel but to work out an atonement so that there might be a Gospel to preach,—to be the sacrifice rather than to speak of it. The cross had to be endured before it could be explained; and when we consider the slowness, or even the inability, of the apostles to grasp the meaning of the atonement until after the day of Pentecost this becomes all the more evident. Jesus Himself proclaimed the incompleteness of His own words, declaring that He had yet many things to say unto the apostles although they were not then able to bear them, and promising that the Holy Spirit who was soon to be given would guide them into all truth (John 16:12, 13). Furthermore, this reticence on the part of Jesus is just what we might have expected since the doer of a great deed usually has the least to say about it. It was not for the Redeemer, but for the redeemed, to magnify the cost of salvation.

Also in this connection we are to remember that in reality the Gospels are supplementary to the Epistles, not the Epistles to the Gospels as so many people are accustomed to assume,—the Epistles being more concerned with setting forth the great fact of redemption while the

Gospels are mainly concerned with filling out our knowledge of the person of Christ and showing at what an infinite cost redemption was procured. The fact that the material in the Gospels deals almost exclusively with the events which occurred during the last three years of Jesus' life and that the closing scenes are given special prominence—approximately one-third of all the material being devoted to the events of the last week—is evidence that not His life, but His death, was the great work of our Lord. Furthermore, one of the two ordinances which He established, the Lord's Supper, was designed to keep His death prominently in the minds of His people. The fact is that the Gospels and the Epistles unite in affirming that the death of Christ lays the basis for our salvation.

The world at large has long been inclined to blame the Jews for the death of Christ, and the Jews in turn have been inclined either to deny it outright or to shift the blame to the Romans. But a truer analysis of the whole affair was recently given by a Jewish speaker addressing an American Jewish audience. After asking, "Did the Jews kill Christ?" he gave the answer in these words: "In a larger sense the death of Jesus was not an accident; the greed of the mercenary priests and the vacillation of Pontius Pilate the Roman, were merely incidental to it. The New Testament teaches that the death of Christ was a divine act, that His death was sacrificial; and the intelligent follower of Jesus, be he Jew or Gentile, does not shift the blame to the shoulders of Jews, but assumes equal responsibility for the tragedy that took place on Golgotha's hill. There is a Christian litany which runs:

> *"Who was the guilty? Who brought this upon Thee?*
> *Alas my treason, Jesus, hath undone Thee.*
> *'Twas I, Lord Jesus, I it was denied Thee:*
> *I crucified Thee."*

"The cleavage of the centuries can be bridged. The misunderstandings and the hates which have kept Jew and Gentile apart can be removed by a common acknowledgment that in the person of the High Priest our people were led into a fatal act, and through Pontius Pilate and the Roman soldiery the whole Gentile world became sharers in the immolation of Christ. We are both guilty, Jew and Gentile, and have need to smite our breast and cry for the forgiveness of God."

A true understanding of the nature of the atonement makes it crystal clear that the responsibility for the death of Christ does rest on Jew and Gentile alike, and that it rests primarily upon all of us who were to be redeemed through the ages, and, heinous and cruel though it was, only secondarily and incidentally on the men of that generation who actually laid the burden of suffering upon Him.

4. The Active and Passive Obedience of Christ

We have said that the two great objectives to be accomplished by Christ in His mission to this world were, first, the removal of the curse under which His people labored as a result of the fall, and, second, their restoration to the image and fellowship of God. It is perfectly evident that both of these elements were essential to salvation. In the preceding section we pointed out that because of the federal relationship which, through appointment of God, Adam bore to his posterity, all mankind since that time have been born into the state into which he fell, and that the purpose of Christ was to rescue His people from that condition and to bring them into a state of holiness and blessedness. In order that He might accomplish that purpose He entered into a vital relationship with them by taking their nature upon Himself through incarnation. Then, acting as their federal head and representative in precisely the same manner that Adam had acted when he plunged the race into sin, He assumed their place before the divine law, fulfilling, on the one hand, its every precept, and on the other, receiving in His own person the penalty due for their transgressions. He thus lived the particular kind of life and suffered the particular kind of death that we read of in the Gospels. These two phases of His work are known as His "Active" and His "Passive" obedience.

Throughout the history of the Church most theological discussions have stressed Christ's passive obedience (although not often calling it by that name), but have had very little to say about His active obedience. The result is that many professing Christians who readily acknowledge that Christ suffered and died for them seem altogether unaware of the fact that the holy, sinless life which He lived was also a vicarious work in their behalf, wrought out by Him in His representative capacity and securing for them title to eternal life.

A moment's reflection should convince us that the suffering and death of Christ, although fully effective in paying the debt which His people owed to divine justice, was in a sense only a negative service. Being of the nature of a penalty it could relieve His people from the liability under which they labored, but it could not provide them with a positive reward. Its effect was to bring them back up to the zero point, back to the position in which Adam stood before the fall. It provided for their rescue from sin and its consequences, but it did not provide for their establishment in heaven. Life in heaven is the reward for the perfect keeping of the moral law through a probationary period. Had the work of Christ stopped with the mere payment of the debt which was owed by His people, then they, like Adam, would still have been under obligation to have earned their own salvation through a covenant of works and, also like Adam, subject again to eternal death if they disobeyed. But the covenant of works had had its day and had failed. Very evidently if salvation is to be attempted a second time it will be on a different plan. For what would be the sense of rescuing a man from a torrent which had proved too strong for him merely to put him back into the same situation? Having rescued His people once God would not permit them to be lost a second time and in precisely the same way. This time not man but God will be the Actor; not works but grace (which is the free and undeserved love or favor of God exercised toward the undeserving, toward sinners) will be the basis; and not failure but complete success will crown the effort. Hence Christ, in His human nature and as a perfectly normal man among men, rendered perfect obedience to the moral law by living a sinless life during the thirty-three years of His earthly career, and thus fulfilled the second and vitally important part of His work of redemption.

THE SINLESS LIFE OF CHRIST

That Christ did live this life of perfect love and unselfish service to God and man is clearly set forth in Scripture. He "did no sin, neither was guile found in His mouth," I Peter 2:22. He was "holy, guileless, undefiled, separated from sinners," says the writer of the Epistle to the Hebrews. 7:26. "I do always the things that are pleasing to Him," said Jesus, John 8:29. "Which of you convicteth me of sin?" was His challenge to His enemies, John 8:46. Even the demons bore witness that He was "the Holy One of God," Luke 4:34. As He was being crucified He prayed, "Father, forgive them." But never did He pray, Father, forgive me. It is not uncommon for the greatest of saints, when they come to the hour of death, to pour out their souls in fresh confessions; desiring to obtain renewed consciousness of sins forgiven. But there is no trace of sin-consciousness to be found anywhere in the life of Jesus. He made no confession of sin, nor did He at any time offer a sacrifice for Himself in the temple. At the time of His death there was no shadow of a cloud between Him and the Father except as He assumed the consequences of sin on behalf of others.

By that life of spotless perfection, then, Jesus acquired for His people a positive righteousness which is imputed to them and which secures for them life in heaven. All that Christ has done and suffered is regarded as having been done and suffered by them. In Him they have fulfilled the law of perfect obedience, as also in Him they have borne the penalty for their sins. By His passive obedience they have been rescued from hell; and by His active obedience they are given entrance into heaven.

SALVATION BY GRACE

Paul's teaching that we are saved, not by a self-acquired, but by an imputed righteousness is very clear and definite. He strongly rebuked those of His own race who, "being ignorant of God's righteousness, and seeking to establish their own, did not subject themselves to the righteousness of God," Rom. 10:3; and he declared that he willingly suffered the loss of all things in order that he might "gain Christ, and be found in Him, not having a righteousness of mine own, even that which is of the law, but that which is through faith in Christ," Phil. 3:9. "Him who knew no sin He made to be sin on our behalf; that we might become the righteousness of God in Him," II Cor. 5:21,— that is, our guilt and punishment was transferred to Christ, in order that His righteousness and purity might be transferred to us. To the Ephesians he wrote, "We are His workmanship, created in Christ Jesus for good works, which God afore prepared that we should walk in them," 2:10. Notice that he does not say that this change in character came about because we did good works, but that he ascribes the workmanship to God and says that its purpose was that we might bear fruit in good works and that these were not original on our part but that they were afore prepared or planned out that we should do them. In his declarations that, "If there had been a law given which could make alive, verily righteousness would have been of the law," Gal. 3:21, and "If righteousness is through the law, then Christ died for nought," Gal. 2:21, he disposes completely of the notion that man can earn his own salvation by good works. If we had been able to have worked out our own salvation there would have been no need for Christ to have become incarnate and to have submitted to such humiliation and suffering. And, of course, in that case He most certainly would not have done so. How profoundly grateful we should be that not only our suffering for sin, but also our probation for heaven, has been assumed for us by Christ, that each of these is now a thing of the past, and that we are safe forever in God's care!

The salvation which the Scriptures offer to mankind is therefore a salvation provided entirely by God Himself. It is not adulterated in any way by human works. And because it is of this nature the

Scripture writers never tire of asserting that it is by grace and not by works. Even the faith through which salvation is received is induced by the Holy Spirit and is a gift: "By grace have ye been saved through faith; and that not of yourselves, it is the gift of God; not of works, that no man should glory," Eph. 2:8, 9. We are "justified freely by His grace," Rom. 3:24. Man's own righteousness, in the words of Isaiah, is as but "a polluted garment" (or, as the King James Version expresses it, "as filthy rags") in the sight of God, 64:6. "Not by works done in righteousness, which we did ourselves, but according to His mercy He saved us, through the washing of regeneration and renewing of the Holy Spirit," Titus 3:5. To Paul's assertion that Christ is "all, and in all" in matters of salvation, Col. 3:11, we can add that man is nothing at all as to that work, and has not anything in himself which merits salvation. We are, in fact, nothing but receivers; we never bring any adequate reward to God, and we are always receiving from Him, and shall be unto all eternity. Good works are in no sense the meritorious ground, but rather the fruits and proof of salvation. They are performed not with the purpose of earning salvation, but as an expression of love and gratitude for the salvation which has already been conferred upon us. Good works, done with right motives toward God, are a result of our having been regenerated, not the means of our regeneration. Our part in this system is to praise God, to honor Him by keeping His commandments, and to reflect His glory in all possible ways. And just because salvation is by grace and does not have to be earned by works it is possible even for one who repents on his death bed, or for one like the thief on the cross, to turn to Jesus in the last hour and be saved.

In another connection the present writer has said: "We hold that the law of perfect obedience which was originally given to Adam was permanent, that God has never done anything which would convey the impression that the law was too rigid in its requirements, or too severe in its penalty, or that it stood in need either of abrogation or of derogation. We believe that the requirement for salvation now as originally is perfect obedience, perfect conformity to the will and character of God, that the merits of Christ's obedience are imputed to His people as the only basis of their salvation, and that they enter heaven clothed only with the cloak of His perfect righteousness and utterly destitute of any merit properly their own. Thus grace, *pure grace,* is extended not in lowering the requirements for salvation, but in the substitution of Christ for His people. He took their place before the law and did for them what they could not do for themselves. This Calvinistic principle is fitted in every way to impress upon us the absolute perfection and unchangeable obligation of the law which was originally given to

Adam. It is not relaxed or set aside, but fittingly honored so that its excellence is shown. In behalf of those who are saved, for whom Christ died, and in behalf of those who are subjected to everlasting punishment, the law in its majesty is enforced and executed."—*The Reformed Doctrine of Predestination,* p. 154.

This doctrine of the sufficiency of Christ's work in regard both to His active and passive obedience is beautifully set forth in the Westminster Confession, which declares that "The Lord Jesus, by His perfect obedience and sacrifice of Himself, which He through the eternal Spirit offered up unto God, hath fully satisfied the justice of His Father; hath purchased not only reconciliation, but an everlasting inheritance in the kingdom of heaven, for all those whom the Father had given Him" (Ch. VIII, Sec. 5). And in the Shorter Catechism in answer to the question, "What is justification?" we are told that "Justification is an act of God's free grace, wherein He pardoneth all our sins, and accepteth us as righteous in His sight, only for the righteousness of Christ imputed to us, and received by faith alone."

But while it enables us to understand more clearly and fully the work which Christ has accomplished for us, if we view it as having an active and a passive side, we must not imagine that these two phases can be separated in His life. We cannot even say that His active obedience was accomplished by His life and His passive obedience by His death. For in varying degrees these two works were accomplished simultaneously and concurrently. Throughout all of His life He was perfectly obedient to the moral law in all that He thought and said and did. And in varying degrees every moment of His life on earth involved humiliation or suffering or both,—it involved humiliation beyond our power to comprehend for the King of Glory, the Creator of the universe, the One who is altogether holy and blessed and powerful and rich, to be born a helpless babe, and that in the most humble condition, to subject Himself to the limitations of incarnate man for a period of thirty-three years, to endure the temptations presented by the Devil, to bring His holy and sensitive nature into close association with sinful men so that He would hear their railings and curses and be confronted with their ingratitude and opposition and hatred, to experience fatigue and hunger, and to look forward through all of His public ministry to the most shameful and painful death by crucifixion. And nowhere else was His active obedience so prominently displayed as on the cross, for there in particular as He suffered He also resisted all temptation to doubt God, or hate His enemies, or commit the slightest offense against those who treated Him so shamefully. Throughout His entire life as He actively obeyed He passively endured, and as He passively endured

He actively obeyed. These two aspects of His work, while distinct in nature, were inextricably intertwined in time. Together they secure the wonderful, full salvation which was wrought out vicariously for us.

The Crucifixion on Calvary

Death by crucifixion is, of course, horrible in the extreme. The usual procedure was that the crosspieces would be laid flat on the ground, the person then stretched upon it, and a soldier would drive iron spikes through the hands and feet into the rough wood. Then the cross with its attached victim would be lifted and set in the hole prepared for it. The person was left to writhe in his agony, with the swelling wounds, the parched thirst, the burning fever, until death brought the welcome release. Human ingenuity has never devised greater agony than crucifixion. Yet that is what Christ endured for us.

But not for a minute would we be understood as inferring that we can really fathom the depths of Christ's suffering. We are only given partial information concerning it. His physical suffering was that of a perfectly normal man in crucifixion. Yet that was not all, nor even the most important part, of His suffering. His cry, "My God, my God, why hast thou forsaken me?" indicates a spiritual suffering more intense and more baffling than the physical. We have already seen that the penalty originally inflicted for sin was not merely the separation of the soul from the body, which is physical death, but the separation of the soul from God, which is spiritual death. That Jesus suffered this latter form of the penalty as well as the former is attested by His despairing cry. During those hours that Jesus hung on the cross as the sin-offering for His people that unique spiritual relationship which had existed between His human soul and the Father, and which had so enriched Him during the entire period of His earthly life, was completely withdrawn. No glimpse of Divinity any longer broke in upon Him. God had literally hid His face from Him. His human soul, which in Gethsemane "began to be greatly amazed and sore troubled," was now entirely cut off from all divine enlightenment. Being limited in knowledge and comprehension as all human souls are, utterly distressed by the ordeal through which He was passing, and engaged in this last desperate combat with the Devil and the forces of the evil world which through His entire earthly career had sought untiringly to cause His downfall and to defeat His purpose, His human soul was unable to understand fully this complete abandonment of the righteous soul by God the Father.

Not only was all special grace withdrawn from Him, but also all common grace. No sedative was allowed to dull His pain. Ordinarily those who were sentenced to be crucified were given a stupefying drug, in order that their suffering might be somewhat alleviated. Doubtless the two thieves who were crucified at the same time received that treatment. But Jesus, realizing that such a drug would incapacitate Him for carrying the very burden of suffering for which He had come to that hour and that it would therefore defeat His purpose of redemption, rejected the wine and myrrh and determined to suffer with His senses fully alert. All of His friends forsook Him. Only His enemies remained to taunt. His clothes (also a gift of common grace, clothes being designed since the time of the fall to cover the body and to serve as a restraint on human sin) were removed, leaving Him shamefully exposed to the vulgar rabble. The light, which is one of the greatest gifts of common grace, was denied Him, and for three hours He was left to suffer in the terrifying darkness. Calvary presents a spectacle such as had never been seen before and can never be seen again. For Jesus did not suffer and die passively, as one helplessly submitting to the inevitable, but actively, as one keeping a schedule or as one fulfilling a purpose. Had we been able to have looked within the soul of Christ we would have witnessed the most colossal struggle that the universe has ever known. Far from being the passive sufferer that He appeared to those who witnessed the crucifixion, He was upholding the pillars of the moral universe by rendering full satisfaction to divine justice. For as the sinner's substitute and in his stead Jesus stood before the awful tribunal of God,—before the Judge who abhors sin and burns against it with inexpressible indignation. Justice severe and inexorable was meted out. As He endured the break in the spiritual relationship with the Father He literally descended into hell; for hell is primarily separation from God, a condition the exact opposite of the blessed environment of the divine presence. This does not mean that His soul suffered remorse or any sense of guilt, which is one of the torments of lost souls; for He had no personal sin. Nor does it mean that this condition continued after His death. All was completed on the cross. When the allotted suffering was finished the divine light again broke in upon His soul, and we hear His triumphant cry, "It is finished" (that is, the atonement, God's objective provision for man's salvation, was completed) ; and that was followed almost immediately by the affectionate words, "Father, into thy hands I commend my spirit." Every detail of the account is so presented that we are compelled to recognize the full price of our redemption was paid for by Christ alone, without human assistance of any kind. And thus through the infinite mercy of God and in a manner that shall forever bring glory to His name there was made available a way, the only possible way, through which sinners might be saved.

And after all, does not this Christian doctrine of the atonement stand forth as the only reasonable and logical explanation of the suffering and death of Christ? God has so ordered this world that sin and suffering are inseparably connected. Where there is no sin God cannot under any conditions inflict suffering,—for the simple reason that it would be unjust for Him to punish an innocent person. Christ's suffering can have no other explanation than that it was vicarious, rendered not for Himself but for others. For there One who was sinless and undefiled suffered the extreme of pain and agony and disgrace as though He were the worst of sinners. Unless Christ was acting on behalf of others and as their substitute, God Himself is put under eternal indictment for inflicting such suffering without a cause.

Moreover, if it be denied that Christ's suffering was vicarious and substitutionary, His voluntary acceptance of crucifixion is utterly unreasonable,—in fact it is scandalous, because suicidal. The plain teaching of Scripture is that He accepted this ordeal voluntarily. "I lay down my life for the sheep . . . No one taketh it from me, but I lay it down of myself," John 10:15, 18. Rebuking Peter for His well-intended but misguided use of the sword He said, "Put up the sword into the sheath: the cup which the Father hath given me, shall I not drink it?" John 18:11. Now it is perfectly evident, of course, that no creature, not even a sinless angel, has the right to dispose of his own life. That prerogative belongs only to the Creator to whom he belongs. But Christ did have that right, because He was the King of the universe. Since He had within Himself divine as well as human life He could dispose of Himself without fatal or permanent injury either to Himself or to any other person. When seen in the light of the doctrines of *substitution, satisfaction, sacrifice,* the death of Christ appears as a great divine achievement, a glorious and unapproachable priestly action through which the suffering Messiah offered Himself in order that divine justice might be safeguarded and that sinful man might be reconciled to God. Logic drives us to the conclusion that the death of Christ on the cross was no ordinary death, but a mighty transaction through which God provided redemption for His people.

Unless Christ was what He claimed to be, Deity incarnate giving His life a ransom for many, the Unitarians and Modernists are right in saying that the doctrine of the Atonement is a colossal hoax and that it is ridiculous for anyone to believe that he can obtain salvation through faith in a mere man, a Jew, who was crucified in Palestine nineteen hundred years ago. Either the Christian system is true and we are saved through the supernatural work of Christ as the Bible teaches and as devout people in all ages have believed, or we are left to save ourselves through some humanistic or naturalistic system as skeptics and unbelievers have held.

On the basis of any teaching rightfully calling itself Christian the active and passive obedience of Christ emerges as the only basis of our spiritual and eternal life. Since the demand that sin must be punished was met by Him in His representative capacity, justice was not injured; and since His life of perfect obedience to the moral law was also rendered in His representative capacity, the gift of spiritual cleansing and of eternal life is now conferred upon His people as their right and privilege. He saves them from hell, and establishes them in heaven. There is no blessing in this world or in the next for which they should not give Christ thanks.

5. Christ As Our Ransomer

In numerous places in Scripture Christ's work of redemption is declared to have been accomplished through the payment of a *ransom*. Nowhere is this set forth more clearly than in our Lord's own teaching. "The Son of man came not to be ministered unto, but to minister, and to give His life a ransom for many," said He concerning His own mission, Matt. 20:28. These same words are repeated in Mark 10:45. Paul doubtless had these words in mind when he declared that Christ "gave Himself a ransom for all," I Tim. 2:6. To the Corinthians he wrote, "Ye are not your own; for ye were bought with a price," I Cor. 6:19, 20. The elders from the church at Ephesus were admonished to "feed the church of the Lord which He purchased with His own blood." Acts 20:28. "Christ redeemed us from the curse of the law, having become a curse for us," he wrote to the Galatians, 3:13. In the epistle to Titus he declares that Christ "gave Himself for us, that He might redeem us from all iniquity, and purify unto Himself a people for His own possession, zealous for good works," 2:14. While it is the privilege of a disciple to "lose" his life in the service of his Lord (Matt. 10:39; Luke 9:24), it was the part of the Lord to "give" His life voluntarily for His people (John 10:15; Gal. 2:20).

Closely parallel with this is Peter's teaching: "Ye were redeemed, not with corruptible things, with silver or gold, from your vain manner of life handed down from the fathers; but with precious blood, as of a lamb without blemish and without spot, even the blood of Christ," I Peter 1:18, 19. In his second epistle he warns against those who "bring in destructive heresies, denying even the Master that bought them," 2:1. And in the book of Revelation praise is ascribed to Christ in the words, "Thou wast slain, and didst purchase unto God with thy blood men of every tribe, and tongue, and people, and nation," 5:9.

To "ransom" means specifically to buy back, to deliver by means of purchase; and the kindred expression, to "redeem," means to deliver by payment of a ransom. We are taught that Christ is our Ransomer, our Redeemer, and that He has purchased our redemption at a tremendous cost, the price being His own life. The one pre-eminent service which Jesus came into the world to perform was that of *dying*—giving His life a ransom in behalf of others who themselves deserved to die, in order that they might not have to die. No person can understand the purpose and meaning of the incarnation and crucifixion of Christ until he grasps this central truth, that Jesus came into the world to give Himself a ransom for others. The numerous Scripture references to redemption or to the payment of a ransom invariably imply that redemption has cost something, indeed, that it has cost much. The inability of man to redeem himself or any other man turns precisely on his inability to pay the price which the commission of sin has made mandatory. Christ, and Christ alone, was able to pay the price which would free His people from the curse of sin.

The meaning of the ransom terminology as used in Scripture is set forth by Dr. Benjamin B. Warfield in the following paragraph: "*Lutron,* usually in the plural *lutra,* designates an indemnification, a pecuniary compensation, given in exchange for a cessation of rights over a person or even a thing, *ransom.* It is used for the money given to redeem a field, Lev. 25:24—the life of an ox about to be killed, Ex. 21:30—one's own life in arrest of judicial proceedings, Num. 35:31, 32, or of vengeance, Prov. 6:35—the first born over whom God had claims, Num. 3:46, 48, 51; 18:15, etc. It is ordinarily used of the ransom given for redemption from captivity or slavery, Lev. 19:20; Is. 45:13, etc." (Biblical Doctrines, p. 342).

A present day English writer has set forth the implications of the term very clearly in these words: "I do not merely decide that Christ shall be my Lord. He is my Lord, by right. I was a slave of sin and Satan, and, try as I would, I could not obtain my freedom. I was never a free man, 'I was born in sin and shapen in iniquity.' A slave! And there would I be now, were it not that Christ came and 'bought me with a price.' What follows? 'Ye are not your own.' I am still not free! I have been bought by a new Master! I am a slave, the bond-servant of Christ! He is my Lord, for He has bought me. He does not merely 'demand my soul, my life, my all;' He has bought them, they *are* His. I am His, because He is my Lord, because He owns me, because He has bought me with His own precious blood,"—Dr. D. Martyn Lloyd-Jones.

THOSE RANSOMED MUST BE SET FREE

A ransom, because of its very nature, makes not merely possible but mandatory and certain the release of those for whom it is paid. Justice demands that those for whom it is paid shall be freed from any further obligation. God would be unjust if He demanded the penalty twice over, first from the Substitute and then from the persons themselves. Because of what Christ has done for His people, and because of the covenant that exists between Him and the Father, all of those for whom the ransom was paid must be brought to salvation. Salvation is thus not of works, not through any good deeds done by men, but purely of grace. "If we confess our sins, He is faithful and righteous to forgive us our sins, and to cleanse us from all unrighteousness," I John 1:9—faithful in keeping His promise that if we turn to Him we shall find forgiveness, and righteous in keeping His covenant with Christ who suffered vicariously for His people and purchased for them the regenerating and sanctifying influences of the Holy Spirit. Those who have been given to Christ by the Father invariably receive these influences and are effectively brought to salvation. Under no conditions can they be called upon to pay the debt a second time, nor can these saving influences be withheld from them, and that specifically for the reason that salvation is by the grace of God and not by the works of men. "Who shall lay anything to the charge of God's elect? It is God that justifieth; who is he that condemneth?" Rom. 8:33, 34. "He that believeth hath eternal life," John 6:47. As God's elect we have the assurance that "neither death, nor life, nor angels, nor principalities, nor things present, nor things to come, nor powers, nor height, nor depth, nor any other creature, shall be able to separate us from the love of God, which is in Christ Jesus our Lord," Rom. 8:38, 39.

A striking illustration and a very clear warning as to what it means to lose the idea of ransoming out of Christianity is afforded in present day German religious life. The so-called "higher criticism," more appropriately called "destructive" or "negative criticism," had its origin in that land. Unfortunately, the language employed in the German translation of the New Testament did not express the idea of ransoming, with the result that there has been a strong tendency to de-supernaturalize Christianity and to present it like any other supposedly high grade religion, as merely a religion of deliverance—which deliverance might be accomplished through better morality, enlightenment, altruism, self help, etc. The result is that truly evangelical religion there has been largely dead for three generations; and the leaders of German thought, particularly those in the higher educational circles, turned to humanistic pursuits. "It has been the misfortune of the religious terminology of Germany," said Dr. Warfield a generation ago, "that the words employed by it to represent the great ransoming language of the New Testament are wholly without native implication of purchase . . . The German *erlosen, Erlosung, Erloser,* contain no native suggestion of purchase whatever; and are without any large secular usage in which such an implication is distinctly conveyed. They mean in themselves just deliver, deliverance, Deliverer, and they are employed nowhere, apart from their religious implication, with any constant involvement of the mode in which the deliverance is effected. . . . We may speculate as to what might have been the effect on the course of German religious thought if, from the beginning, some exact reproductions of the Greek words built up around the idea of ransom— such as *loskaufen, Loskaufung, Loskaufer*—had been adopted as their representatives on the pages of the German New Testament, and, consequent to that, in the natural expression of the religious thought and feeling of German Christians. But we can scarcely doubt that it has been gravely injurious to it, that, in point of fact, a loose terminology, importing merely deliverance, has taken the place of the more exact Greek terms, in the expression of religious thought and feeling; and thus the German Christians have been habituated to express their conception of Christ's saving act in language which left wholly unnoticed the central fact that it was an act of purchase." (Biblical Doctrines, pp. 388, 390).

6. The Representative Principle

We have said that at the beginning of the race Adam stood not only for himself but as the federal head and representative of the entire human race which was to follow, and that Christ in His turn in both His active and passive obedience stood for all of those who were to be saved. This representative principle pervades all Scripture, and is the basis for the doctrine of original sin and for the doctrine of redemption. It was, in fact, only because the race as originally created was so constituted that one person could stand as its official and responsible head that Christ, coming at a later time and basing His work on the same principle, could redeem His people. It is as if God had said, If sin is to enter, let it enter by one man, so that righteousness also may enter by one man.

The Scriptures teach that the race is a unit, a family, descended from a common ancestor, and bound together by blood ties. This is in contrast with the order followed in the creation of the angels, for they were created not as a race but independently of each other and all at the same time. Each angel stood his test personally and individually.

In virtue of the vital unity of the human race it was possible for God at the very beginning to enter into a "covenant of works" with the ancestor of the race, in which he, bearing their nature and acting therefore in precisely the same way they would have acted, stood trial for them. This afforded a wonderful opportunity for Adam to secure for himself and for his posterity an inestimable—we may even say, an infinite—blessing. For it was so arranged that if he stood his probation and rendered the perfect obedience which was required (and thereby proved himself a grateful, law-abiding son who could be trusted), eternal life would have been conferred upon him and them. But if he did not stand his probation, but committed sin, the penalty of eternal death would be inflicted not only upon him but equally upon all of his descendants. That covenant involved the most solemn responsibilities. It was freighted with possibilities for infinite good or evil.

As originally created, man was perfect of his kind, possessing a positive inclination toward virtue, yet fallible. He was perfect as the bud is perfect and capable of developing into the flower, or as the acorn is perfect and capable of developing into the oak tree. He was not created as a machine or automaton, but as a free moral agent who might choose evil and plunge himself and everything connected with him into disaster. It is apparently true, as Dr. Fairbairn has said, that "Moral perfection can be attained, but cannot be created; God can make a being capable of moral action, but not a being with all the fruits of moral action garnered within him." Had Adam chosen good, then, by that very action he would have produced moral goodness, and God would have confirmed him (that is, made permanent his character) in that goodness as He has confirmed the holy angels in heaven in their goodness.

In language which is at once childlike and profound the third chapter of Genesis tells us of the fall of the human race. Man had his most fair and favorable chance there in the Garden of Eden; and with his eyes open and in spite of the clearest warning as to what the consequences would be, he chose evil instead of good. The Scriptures assert, and the experience of the race from that hour to this bears witness to the truth of the assertion, that Adam fell and that all of his descendants are born into that same state of moral depravity into which he fell. But they also teach that because of the organic unity of the race it was possible for Christ to enter into a "Covenant of Redemption" with God the Father whereby He should act for His people in precisely the same capacity as Adam had acted for the race, providing, on the one hand, that the penalty for their sin should be laid on Him, and on the other, that the merits of His sinless life and of His suffering should be set to their account.

That the fall of Adam did involve the fall and ruin of the entire human race, and that by a parallel arrangement the righteousness of Christ is similarly imputed to His people, is made clear by the Apostle Paul when he says: "As through one man sin entered into the world, and death through sin; and so death passed unto all men, for that all sinned. . . . Death reigned from Adam until Moses, even over them that had not sinned after the likeness of Adam's transgression, who is a figure of Him that was to come. . . . If by the trespass of the one the many died, much more did the grace of God, and the gift of the grace of the one man, Jesus Christ, abound unto the many. . . . for if, by the trespass of the one, death reigned through the one; much more shall they that receive the abundance of grace and of the gift of righteousness reign in life as through the one, even Jesus Christ. So then as through one trespass the judgment came unto all men to condemnation; even so through one act of righteousness the free gift came unto all men to justification of life. For as through the one man's disobedience the many were made sinners, even so through the obedience of the one shall the many be made righteous," Rom. 5:12-19. And again, "For as in Adam all die, so also in Christ shall all be made alive," I Cor. 15:22. (The meaning here, as the context makes clear, is that as all descended from Adam partake of his sin and die, so also all who by faith are "in Christ" shall be made alive. In the writings of Paul to be "in Christ" means to be vitally connected with Him, to be saved. He repeatedly declares that those who are "in Christ" have been made alive spiritually. Those who are not "in Christ" are still spiritually dead).

In Christian theology there are three separate and distinct acts of imputation. In the first place Adam's sin is imputed to all of us, his children, that is, judicially set to our account so that we are held responsible for it and suffer the consequences of it. This is commonly known as the doctrine of Original Sin. In the second place, and in precisely the same manner, our sin is imputed to Christ so that He suffers the consequences of it. And in the third place Christ's righteousness is imputed to us and secures for us entrance into heaven. We are, of course, no more personally guilty of Adam's sin than Christ is personally guilty of ours, or than we are personally meritorious because of His righteousness. In each case it is a judicial transaction. We receive salvation from Christ in precisely the same way that we receive condemnation and ruin from Adam. In each case the result follows because of the close and official union which exists between the persons involved. To reject any one of these three steps is to reject an essential part of the Christian system.

But while on the basis of the unity of the human race it was possible for man to be redeemed through the work of a substitute, redemption by such means does not seem to have been possible among the fallen angels. We read of "angels that kept not their own principality, but left their proper habitation," and are now "kept in everlasting bonds under darkness unto the judgment of the great day," Jude 6. And the writer of the epistle to the Hebrews, after saying that Christ became incarnate in order that He might perform His redemptive work, adds: "For verily not to angels doth He give help, but He giveth help to the seed of Abraham," 2:16. Since each angel stood his test individually, he is therefore personally and solely responsible for his own condition. But mankind which fell through the act of a representative without personal guilt can be redeemed through the act of a representative without personal merit.

The representative principle is certainly not foreign to our way of life, nor is it difficult to understand. The people of a state act in and through their representatives in the Legislature. If a country has a good president or king, all of the people share the benefits; if a bad president or king, all suffer the consequences. Children are recognized as the rightful and legal heirs of their parents' wealth and good name, and to a considerable extent inherit even their mental and physical characteristics. In a very real sense parents stand representative for, and to a large extent decide the destinies of, their children. If the parents are virtuous, wise and thrifty, the children reap the blessings; if they are immoral, foolish and indolent, the children suffer. In law we have "power of attorney," and the person for whom the attorney acts assumes full legal responsibility for his acts, whether they are beneficial or injurious. In business we have trusteeship. In a thousand ways the well-being of individuals is conditioned by the acts of others, so inwrought is this representative principle in our every day life.

In the following section Dr. Charles Hodge, one of the ablest theologians that America has produced, has given a very clear exposition of this subject:

"This representative principle pervades the whole Scriptures. The imputation of Adam's sin to his posterity is not an isolated fact. It is only an illustration of a general principle which characterizes the dispensations of God from the beginning of the world. God declares Himself to Moses as one who visits the iniquity of the fathers upon the children, and upon the children's children unto the third and to the fourth generation, Ex. 34:6, 7 . . . The curse pronounced on Canaan fell on his posterity. Esau's selling his birthright shut out his descendants from the covenant of promise. The children of Moab and Ammon were excluded from the congregation of the Lord forever, because their ancestors opposed the Israelites when they came out of Egypt. In the case of Dathan and Abiram, as in that of Achan, 'their wives, and their sons, and their little children' perished for the sins of their parents. God said to Eli that the iniquity of his house should not be purged with sacrifice and offering for ever. To David it was said, 'The sword shall never depart from thy house; because thou hast despised me, and hast taken the wife of Uriah the Hittite to be thy wife.' To the disobedient Gehazi it was said: 'The leprosy of Naaman shall cleave unto thee and unto thy seed forever.' The sin of Jeroboam and of the men of his generation determined the destiny of the ten tribes for all time. The imprecation of the Jews, when they demanded the crucifixion of Christ, 'His blood be on us and on our children,' still weighs down the scattered people of Israel . . . This principle runs through the whole Scriptures. When God entered into covenant with Abraham, it was not for himself only but for his posterity. They were bound by all the stipulations of the covenant. They shared its promises and its threatenings, and in hundreds of cases the penalty for disobedience came upon those who had no personal part in the transgressions. Children suffered equally with adults in the judgments, whether famine, pestilence, or war, which came upon the people for their sins. . . . And the Jews to this day are suffering the penalty of the sins of their fathers for their rejection of Him of whom Moses and the prophets spoke. The whole plan of redemption rests on this same principle. Christ is the representative of His people, and on this ground their sins are imputed to Him and His righteousness to them . . . No man who believes the Bible, can shut his eyes to the fact that it everywhere recognizes the representative character of parents, and that the dispensations of God have from the beginning been founded on the principle that the children bear the iniquities of their fathers. This is one of the reasons which infidels assign for rejecting the divine origin of the Scriptures. But infidelity furnishes no relief. History is as full of this doctrine as the Bible is. The punishment of the felon involves his family in his disgrace and misery. The spendthrift and drunkard entail poverty and wretchedness upon all connected with them. There is no nation now existing on the face of the earth, whose condition for weal or woe is not largely determined by the character and conduct of their ancestors . . . The idea of the transfer of guilt or of vicarious punishment lies at the foundation of the expiatory offerings under the Old Testament, and of the great atonement under the new dispensation. To bear sin is, in

Scriptural language, to bear the penalty of sin. The victim bore the sin of the offerer. Hands were imposed upon the head of the animal about to be slaughtered, to express the transfer of guilt. That animal must be free from all defect or blemish to make it the more apparent that its blood was shed not for its own deficiencies but for the sin of another. All this was symbolical and typical . . . And this is what the Scriptures teach concerning the atonement of Christ. He bore our sins; He was a curse for us; He suffered the penalty of the law in our stead. All this proceeds on the ground that the sins of one man can be justly, on some adequate ground, imputed to another."—*Systematic Theology,* II, pp. 198-201.

Strange as it may seem, there are many professing Christians in our day who, while readily acknowledging that our salvation comes from Christ, deny that we inherit any guilt and corruption from Adam. Such a position is, of course, utterly inconsistent, and can have no other effect than to undermine true Christianity. If we accept the doctrine of salvation through Christ we have no right to deny the supplementary and equally Scriptural doctrine of condemnation and ruin through Adam. Unless we are fallen in Adam there is, in fact, no reason why we should be redeemed through Christ. The federal headship of Christ in the covenant of redemption presupposes the federal headship of Adam in the covenant of works. The latter is the necessary basis for the former, and the work and position of Christ in relation to His people can be understood only when it is seen in its true relation to the work of Adam. The Scriptures teach that the principles upon which sin and misery came upon the race through Adam are identical with those upon which righteousness and blessedness come upon the elect through Christ. False views concerning our relation to Adam and the effect that his work has had upon the entire race must inevitably produce false views concerning our relation to Christ and His work of redemption. These two doctrines are strictly parallel, and must stand or fall together. They cannot be separated without destroying the logical consistency of the Christian system.

7. The Extent of the Atonement

One further important question which presents itself in connection with the doctrine of the atonement is this: Did the death of Christ have special reference to particular individuals who had been given to Him by the Father and who were therefore definitely foreknown as His people; or was it intended for the whole race alike, for every individual without distinction or exception? Or in other words, Was the death of Christ designed to render certain the salvation of particular individuals, or was it designed merely to render possible the salvation of all men? These divergent views have usually been discussed under the terms Calvinism and Arminianism,—Calvinists holding that in the intention and secret purpose of God Christ died only for His people, His elect, and that His death had only an incidental reference to others in so far as they are partakers of common grace, while Arminians hold that He died for all men alike.

In the first place it should be perfectly evident that the atonement, having been worked out by God Himself, is His own personal property and that He is absolutely sovereign in the disposal which He chooses to make of it. No limit can be set to its value; and the way is now wide open for Him to forgive, freely and fully, as many as He chooses to call to Himself through the cleansing and saving power of the Holy Spirit. He may save few, many, or all members of the human race as He sees fit. That He does not save all is clearly evident both from the teaching of Scripture and from what we see taking place in the world about us. Just why He does not save all when the sacrifice of Christ is in itself objectively sufficient to save all and He has the power to work mightily in the hearts of all so that they would be saved, we are not able to say. But apparently wiser designs and higher purposes are to be served by allowing some to continue in their self-chosen ways of sin and thus exhibit eternally before men and angels what an awful thing is opposition and rebellion against God. We believe, however, that the merciful and benevolent nature of God implies, and that the Scripture clearly teaches, that in the final analysis the great majority of the human race will be found among the saved.

But as relates to the extent of the atonement, the doctrine of the foreknowledge of God is in itself sufficient to prove that in the plan of God Christ died only for those who are actually saved. For does not God have exact foreknowledge of all things? Is not His ability to predict even the details of history thousands of years in advance based on His foreknowledge? That He does have the foreknowledge is admitted by evangelical Arminians as well as by Calvinists. And since He does have this foreknowledge He could not have sent Christ with the intention of saving those who He positively foreknew would be lost. For as Calvin remarks, "Where would have been the consistency of God's calling to Himself such as He knows will never come?" That a man's accomplishments oftentimes do not measure up to his expectations is due to his lack of foresight or to his lack of ability to accomplish what he purposes. But even a man does not expect what he knows will not be accomplished. If he knows, for instance, that out of a group of thirty persons who might be invited to a banquet a certain twenty will accept and ten will not, then, even though he may still make his invitation broad enough to include the thirty, he expects only the twenty, and his work of preparation is done only on their behalf. Or if he is told that in an adjoining room there are ten chests of gold of which he may have as many as he can carry away at one trip, and his carrying capacity is seven, he does not go into the room expecting to carry away all ten. They do but deceive themselves who, admitting God's foreknowledge, say that Christ died for all men; for what is that but to attribute folly to Him whose ways are perfect? To represent God as earnestly striving to do what he knows He will not do is to represent Him as acting foolishly.

In accordance with this obvious truth the Scriptures teach that Christ died specifically for His people; and nowhere do they teach, either directly or by good and necessary inference that He died for all men alike. Those for whom He died are referred to as "His people," "my people," "the sheep," "the church," "many," or other terms which mean less than the entire human race: e.g., "Thou shalt call His name Jesus; for it is He that shall save *His people* from their sins," Matt. 1:21. "He was cut off out of the land of the living for the transgression of *my people* to whom the stroke was due," Is. 53:8. "I lay down my life for *the sheep*," John 10:15. "The Good Shepherd layeth down His life for *the sheep*," John 10:11. To the unbelieving Jews Jesus said, "Ye believe not, because ye are not of *my sheep*," John 10:26. It was *"the church* of the Lord, which he purchased with His own blood," Acts 20:28. "Christ loved *the church* and gave Himself up for it," Eph. 5:25. "He bare the sin of *many*," Is. 53:12. Christ was "once offered to bear the sins of *many*," Heb. 9:28. "I pray not for the world, but for *those whom thou hast given me; for they are thine,*" John 17:9. The high priest of ancient Israel offered sacrifice, not for the whole world, but only for the penitent children of Israel. And under the symbolism of the bride and the Lamb the book of Revelation portrays Christ's peculiar and electing and discriminating love for His people, 21:2, 9.

Christ's death had special reference to His people is set forth when He is said to have been a *ransom,*—"The Son of man came not to be ministered unto, but to minister, and to give His life a ransom for many," Matt. 20:28. The nature of a ransom is such that when paid and accepted it automatically frees those for whom it was intended. No further obligation can be charged against them. If the death of Christ was a ransom for all men alike, if by His death He purchased all mankind, then the regenerating and cleansing power of the Holy

Spirit which He purchased for them must then be communicated not merely to some but to all alike, and the penalty of eternal punishment cannot be justly inflicted on any. If, as we have said, God is so just that He cannot pardon sin without an atonement, He would certainly be most unjust if He demanded the penalty twice over, once from the Substitute and again from the persons themselves.

The Sovereignty of God

The notion that God has ever striven to accomplish a purpose and has failed, particularly the notion that He can be defeated by the will of puny man, is contradicted by the strong emphasis that the Scriptures place on the sovereignty of God. To cite only a few examples: "He doeth according to His will in the army of heaven, and among the inhabitants of the earth; and none can stay His hand, or say unto Him, What doest thou?," Dan. 4:35. "Ah Lord Jehovah! behold, thou hast made the heavens and the earth by thy great power and by thine outstretched arm; and there is nothing too hard for thee," Jer. 32:17. "Jehovah of hosts hath sworn, saying, Surely, as I have thought, so shall it come to pass; and as I have purposed, so shall it stand. . . . For Jehovah of hosts hath purposed, and who shall annul it? and His hand is stretched out, and who shall turn it back?" Is. 14:24, 27. "I am God, and there is none like me; declaring the end from the beginning, and from ancient times things that are not yet done; saying, My counsel shall stand, and I will do all my pleasure. . . . I have spoken; I will bring it to pass; I have purposed, I will also do it." Is. 46:9-11. "Is anything too hard for Jehovah?" Gen. 18:14. "I know that thou canst do all things, And that no purpose of thine can be restrained," Job 42:2. "Our God is in the heavens: He hath done whatsoever He pleased," Ps. 115:3. "All authority hath been given unto me [Christ] in heaven and on earth," Matt. 28:18. "And He put all things in subjection under His feet, and gave Him to be head over all things to the church," Eph. 1:22. "In whom also we were made a heritage, having been foreordained according to the purpose of Him who worketh all things after the counsel of His will," Eph. 1:11.

Certainly these verses teach that God is the sovereign Ruler of heaven and earth, that the entire course of events is under His providential control, and that nothing does or can occur except by either His decretive or permissive will. Since the atonement was worked out by God Himself we may rest assured that it is therefore fully adequate to accomplish the purpose for which it was intended. That any particular person fails to be saved by it can be for no other reason than that he was not included in the plan of redemption. For if pardon has been purchased for all, then of necessity all would have been saved; for universal redemption means universal salvation.

In another connection the present writer has said: "Shall we not believe that God can convert a sinner when He pleases? Cannot the Almighty, the omnipotent Ruler of the universe, change the characters of the creatures He has made? He changed the water into wine at Cana, and sovereignly converted Saul on the road to Damascus. The leper said, 'Lord, if thou wilt, thou canst make me clean,' and at a word his leprosy was cleansed. God is as able to cleanse the soul as the body, for He created both. We believe that if He chose to do so He could raise up such a flood of Christian ministers, missionaries and teachers of the Word that the world would be converted in a very short time. If He actually purposed to save all men He could, if He chose, send hosts of angels to instruct them and to do supernatural works on the earth. He could Himself work marvelously on the heart of every person so that no one would be lost. Since evil exists only by His permission and within the bounds that He has set for it, He could, if He chose, blot it completely out of existence. His power was shown in the work of the destroying angel who in one night slew all of the first-born of the Egyptians (Ex. 12:29), and in another night slew 185,000 of the Assyrian army (II Kings 19:35). It was shown when the earth opened and swallowed Korah and his rebellious allies (Num. 16:31-33). Ananias and Sapphira were smitten (Acts 5:1-11); King Herod was smitten and died a horrible death (Acts 12:23). God has lost none of His power, and it is highly dishonoring to Him to suppose that He is struggling along with the human race doing the best He can but unable to accomplish His purposes. The Arminian idea which assumes that the serious intentions of God may in some cases be defeated, and that man, who is not only a creature but a sinful creature, can exercise veto power over the plans of Almighty God, is in striking contrast with the Biblical idea of His immeasurable greatness and exaltation by which he is removed from all the weakness of humanity. That the plans of men are not always executed is due to a lack of wisdom or of power; but since God is unlimited in these and all other resources, no unforeseen emergencies can arise, and there is never any occasion for a revision of plans. To suppose that His plans fail and that He strives to no effect, is to reduce Him to the level of His creatures."

While we have not space here for an adequate discussion of the Calvinistic doctrine of Election, we must, however, call attention to the fact that the Scriptures teach that from all eternity the Father gave to the Son a people, the elect, an innumerable multitude, for whom the Son on His part met the requirements of justice at the appointed time. There are, of course, some who, either because they are not acquainted with the Scripture, or because they have never given the matter serious study, deny that there has been any such thing as an election at all. They start at the very word as though it were a spectre just come from the shades and never seen before. Yet, in the New Testament alone, the words *ekletos, ekloga,* and *eklego, elect, election, choose,* are found some forty-seven or forty-eight times. Five times in the seventeenth chapter of John Jesus refers to "those given [Him] by the Father." In writing to the saints at Ephesus Paul declares that God "chose us in Him [Christ] before the foundation of the world [that is, in eternity] . . . having foreordained us unto adoption as sons through Jesus Christ unto Himself, according to the good pleasure of His will," Eph. 1:4, 5. The love which caused God to send Christ into the world to suffer and die was not a general and indiscriminate and ineffectual love of which all persons equally are the objects, but a peculiar, mysterious, infinite love for His elect, His chosen. Any theory which denies this great and precious truth, and which attempts to explain away this redemptive love as general benevolence or philanthropy of which all men alike are the objects, many of whom are allowed to perish, is simply contrary to Scripture.

THE UNIVERSALISTIC PASSAGES

There are, of course, a considerable number of Scripture references which are often quoted to prove that Christ died for all men alike. But none of them definitely teach universal redemption. When in Col. 1:28, for example, Paul refers to his work of "admonishing *every man* and teaching *every man* in all wisdom, that we may present *every man* perfect in Christ," he could not have meant that he expected every man in the world to be made perfect in Christ. Evidently the words "every man" refer to those spoken of in the immediate context, namely, to "His saints" mentioned in verse 26, to whom he says God was pleased to reveal these things. When in Heb. 2:9 we read, "That by the grace of God He should taste of death for *every man,*" the reference evidently is to those mentioned in the immediate context, the "many sons" in verse 10, of whose salvation He is declared to be the Author. The Bible is written in the language of the common people, and we very naturally and very often use such expressions as "every man," "every one," "all," etc., with an implied limitation. When we read the historic words, "England expects *every man* this day to do his duty," we readily understand that Admiral Nelson had in mind not every man throughout the world, nor even every Englishman, but only those who were about to engage on the side of England in the battle of Trafalgar.

In a number of the supposedly universalistic passages in which "all" or "all men" are mentioned, the reference is not to all men individually, but to "all kinds of men," Jews and Gentiles, without reference to nationality, color, or social position, and to women and children as well. In some fifty places throughout the New Testament the words "all" and "every" are used in a limited sense, e.g.: "Ye shall be hated of *all* men for my name's sake," Matt. 10:22. *All* hold John as a prophet," Matt. 21:26. "There went out a decree from Caesar Augustus, that *all the world* should be enrolled . . . and *all* went to enroll themselves, *every one* to his own city," Luke 2:1-3. *"All* men reasoned in their hearts concerning John," Luke 3:15. "Woe unto you, when *all* men shall speak well of you," Luke 6:26. "If we let Him thus alone, *all men* will believe on Him," John 11:48. "And they sold their possessions and goods, and parted them to *all,* according as *any man* had need," Acts 2:45. "My manner of life then from my youth up, know *all* the Jews," Acts 26:4. Ye are our epistle, written in our hearts, known and read of *all* men," II Cor. 3:2. When Jesus said that "Every sin and blasphemy shall be forgiven unto men; but the blasphemy against the Spirit shall not be forgiven," Matt. 12:31, He evidently meant that all kinds of sin when repented of, except blasphemy against the Holy Spirit (which is not repented of), would be forgiven.

In not one of the foregoing instances does the word "all" mean all men without exception living on the earth at the time the words were spoken, much less does it mean all who had lived in the past, together with all who were to live in the future. Clearly the doctrine of universal redemption cannot be based on the words "all" or "every" or the phrase "all men."

Nor does John 3:16 teach universal redemption as is so generally assumed,—"For God so loved the world, that He gave His only begotten Son,—that whosoever believeth on Him should not perish, but have eternal life." In the first place this verse teaches that the redemption which the Jews thought to monopolize is universal as to space. God so loved the *world,* not just a little portion of it, nor one small nation, but the world as a whole, Jews and Gentiles, white and colored, brown and yellow, rich and poor, free and slave, that He gave His only begotten Son for its redemption. And not only the extensity, but the intensity of God's love is made plain by the little word "so",—God *so* loved the world, that He gave His only begotten Son to die for it. Moreover it is the world that is to be redeemed or Christianized. While numerous individuals are lost, in the final analysis the great majority of the human race is to be found among the saved. This verse does not say that God gave His Son that *none* should perish, or that *all* should have eternal life, but that those who believe on Him should be saved,—and from other Scripture we learn that only a portion of those who hear the message do believe, and that those believe only because divine grace causes them to believe: "Except one be born anew (marginal reading: born from above), he cannot see the kingdom of God," John 3:3; "No one can come to me, except the Father that sent me draw him," John 6:44. Nowhere does Scripture either directly assert or imply that Christ died in the stead of all men, or with the purpose of saving all men.

THE WESTMINSTER CONFESSION

Concerning the extent of the atonement and the relative positions of the elect and the non-elect, the Westminster Confession says: "As God hath appointed the elect unto glory, so hath He, by the eternal and most free purpose of His will, foreordained all the means thereunto. Wherefore they who are elected being fallen in Adam, are redeemed by Christ, are effectually called unto faith in Christ by His Spirit working in them in due season; are justified, adopted, sanctified, and kept by His power through faith unto salvation. Neither are any other redeemed by Christ, effectually called, justified, adopted, sanctified, and saved but the elect only." (Ch. III; sec. 6).

This does not mean that any poor sinner who desires salvation is rejected, and the attempt to portray it as doing that is nothing but a gross caricature. All those who sincerely desire salvation will certainly be found among the redeemed. None except the regenerate ever have this desire in the first place. Concerning those in the unregenerate state, the Scriptures declare: "The natural man receiveth not the things of the Spirit of God: for they are foolishness unto him; and he cannot know them, because they are spiritually judged," I Cor. 2:14; "There is none righteous, no, not one; There is none that understandeth. There is none that seeketh after God. . . . There is none that doeth good, no, not so much as one. . . . There is no fear of God before their eyes," Rom. 3:10-18; "The word of the cross is to them that perish foolishness, but unto us who are saved it is the power of God," I Cor. 1:18; "And this is the judgment, that light is come into the world, and men loved the darkness rather than the light; for their works were evil," John 3:19. On the other hand the Scriptures declare concerning the regenerate: "And you did He make alive, when ye were dead through your trespasses and sins," Eph. 2:1; "If any man is in Christ, he is a new creature," II Cor. 5:17; and, "He that heareth my word, and believeth Him that sent me, hath eternal life, and cometh not into judgment, but hath passed out of death into life," John 5:24. We have the unconditional promise of Christ that every one who hungers or thirsts after righteousness "shall be filled," Matt. 5:6. "I will give unto him that is athirst of the fountain of the water of life freely," He declares in Rev. 21:6; and in Rev. 22:17 He again says that "he that will" may "take the water of life freely." It does not detract in the least from these promises when we give God the glory and say that "he that wills" to take the water of life freely has been made willing by a divine operation—that he who thirsts for the water of life has been made thirsty by the Spirit of God—that those who feel the need of salvation and want deliverance through the great Ransom have been made, by sovereign grace and the regenerating power of the Holy Spirit, to feel their need and to desire this great deliverance.

The Atonement Unlimited in Value and Power

When we speak of the atonement as "limited" we do not mean that any limit can be set to its value or power. Its value is determined by the dignity of the person making it; and since Christ suffered as a Divine-human person the value of His atonement is infinite. It is *sufficient* for the salvation of the entire race, and might have saved every member of the race if that had been God's plan; but it is *efficient* only for those to whom it is applied by the Holy Spirit. It is limited only in the sense that it was intended for, and is applied to, particular persons, namely, for and to those who actually are saved. It is indifferently as well adapted to the salvation of one man as to that of another, thus making objectively possible the salvation of all men. But because of subjective difficulties arising out of the inability of fallen men either to see or appreciate the things of God, only those who are regenerated by the Holy Spirit respond to it and are saved. God could change all human hearts by His mighty regenerating and convincing power if He chose to do so. He wrought mightily in the heart of Saul of Tarsus and made him into a new man, as He has wrought mightily in the heart of every other member of this fallen race who has been translated from the kingdom of darkness to the kingdom of light. But for reasons which have not been fully revealed He does not apply this grace to all.

The Gospel is, nevertheless, to be offered to all men, with the assurance that it is exactly adapted to the needs of all men, and that God has decreed that all who place their faith in Christ shall be saved by Him. No man is lost because of any deficiency in the objective atonement, or because God has placed any barrier in His way, but only because of subjective difficulties, specifically, because his own evil disposition and his freely exercised wicked will prevent his believing and accepting that atonement. God's attitude is perhaps best summed up in the parable of the marriage feast and the slighted invitations, where the king sends this message to the invited guests, "I have made ready my dinner; my oxen and my fatlings are killed, and all things are ready: come to the marriage feast," Matt. 22:4.

In reality Arminians do limit the atonement as certainly as do Calvinists. For while Calvinists limit its *extent* in that they say it is not applied to all persons (although they believe that much the greater portion of the human race will eventually be saved), Arminians limit its *power* or inherent value; for they say that in itself it does not save anybody, that in each individual in order to become effective it must be supplemented by faith and evangelical obedience on the part of the person and that each person is sovereign in determining whether or not he will have faith in Christ. Calvinists limit the atonement quantitatively, but not qualitatively; Arminians limit it qualitatively, but not quantitatively. Calvinists believe in an atonement of high value,—and the emphasis which the Scriptures place on the sovereignty and goodness and holiness of God implies that He will apply it very freely and very widely. Arminians believe in an atonement of wide extension,— an atonement reaching to every individual throughout the entire world, although they are compelled to admit that in many instances its effects are not very potent and that great multitudes, paricularly in heathen lands, give very little if any evidence of its effects. The fact of the matter is that Arminians actually place more severe limitations on the atonement than do Calvinists. For when it is made universal its inherent value is destroyed. If it is applied to all men, and if many nevertheless continue in their lost condition, the only possible conclusion is that in itself it does not actually save anybody. According to the Arminian theory the atonement has simply made it possible for all men to co-operate with divine grace by doing meritorious works and thus secure their own salvation,—if they will. But in that system salvation can no longer be said to be by grace, but by grace plus works. The nature of the atonement settles its extent. If it was merely designed to make salvation possible, it had reference to all men. If it effectively secured salvation, it had reference only to certain people, that is, to the elect. As Dr. Charles Hodge has pointed out, "The sin of Adam did not make the condemnation of all men merely possible; it was the ground of their actual condemnation. So the righteousness of Christ did not make the salvation of men merely possible; it secured the actual salvation of those for whom He wrought." And Dr. Warfield says, "The things we have to choose between are an atonement of high value, or an atonement of wide extension. The two cannot go together." The fact of the matter is that the work of Christ cannot be universalized without destroying its substance.

General Benefits Received Through Common Grace

We do not deny, of course, that all mankind does receive many and important blessings because of the work of Christ. The penalty which would have been inflicted because of sin is temporarily postponed. Fallen man in this world remains on a much higher plane than that of the fallen angels who have been abandoned to evil and who are commonly referred to in Scripture as evil spirits or demons. As the Gospel is preached and the plan of redemption is progressively worked out, mankind at large shares many uplifting influences. The forces of evil are kept within bounds, and incomparably higher standards of moral, social and economic life are maintained. Paul could say to the heathen people of Lystra that God "left not Himself without witness, in that He did good and gave you from heaven rains and fruitful seasons, filling your hearts with food and gladness," Acts 14:17. God makes His sun to shine on the evil and the good, and sends rain on the just and the unjust. These are the blessings of common grace. Though designed primarily for the elect, they are shared by all mankind; and since this world is not the place of final rewards and punishments, but the place of discipline and testing and development for the Lord's people, these blessings are oftentimes enjoyed in greater abundance by the non-elect than by the elect. But in themselves they are not sufficient to bring a single soul to salvation. They are on an entirely different plane from the blessings of special grace, which are regeneration, justification, adoption, sanctification and glorification. But in a secondary way the blessings of common grace are designed to serve God's purpose in revealing His glory, manifesting His character, filling the world with beauty and happiness, and in general playing their necessary part in the development of His kingdom. There is, then, a sense in which Christ died for all men, and we do not reply to the Arminian tenet with an unqualified negative. But what we do maintain is that His death had special reference to the elect, that with the accompanying influences of the Holy Spirit which are secured by it, it is effectual for their salvation, and that the effects which are produced in others are only incidental to this one great purpose.

Moreover, we find that there is marked discrimination between the treatment accorded fallen men and that accorded the fallen angels. For while Christ took upon Himself human nature and provided redemption for fallen men, nothing like that has been done for fallen angels. In the Epistle of the Hebrews we read, "Since then the children are sharers in flesh and blood, He also Himself in like manner partook of the same; that through death He might bring to naught him that had the power of death, that is, the Devil; and might deliver all them who through fear of death were all their lifetime subject to bondage. For verily not to angels doth He give help, but He giveth help to the seed of Abraham" (2:14-16).

If the sacrifice of Christ had been intended to effect the salvation of all men indiscriminately instead of the elect only, then undoubtedly the information concerning it would have been transmitted to all men indiscriminately instead of being withheld from two-thirds of the race even at this late date two thousand years after it was accomplished. It is indeed hard to see in what sense redemption can be said to be general or universal when so many people through all the ages have been left in total ignorance concerning it.

Leaving aside the views of unbelief, there are in the final analysis just two views of the atonement which are held by Christians: the Calvinistic and the Arminian. We have presented the Calvinistic view, and we insist that it alone is consistent with Scripture. It sets forth an atonement which is definite and explicit; and its inevitable corollary is a satisfied, because fully triumphant, Saviour, since His work is effective and all those for whom He died are saved. The Arminian view presents an atonement which is indefinite and intangible; and its inevitable corollary is a disappointed, because defeated Saviour, since a large portion of those on whose behalf He died and for whom He hoped do nevertheless perish. The Calvinistic view was taught by Augustine, Wycliffe, Luther, Calvin, Knox, Jonathan Edwards, Whitfield, Spurgeon, Hodge, Kuyper and Warfield; the opposing view by men who in most cases were good and honorable men but who as theologians possessed only a fraction of their ability and understanding. We acknowledge evangelical Arminianism to be Christian, but we believe that it is not in full harmony with Scripture and that it is a compromise toward naturalism and self-salvation. Let us remember that the "Gospel" etymologically is the *good news* of what God has done to save His people, and not merely *good advice* as to what they should do to save themselves. It is the glad tidings, the evangel, that heaven is ours through Him who loved us and gave Himself for us.*

8. Old Testament Ritual and Symbolism

Many people, as they look back at the Old Testament period with its elaborate system of sacrifices, offerings, rituals and ceremonies, are puzzled to know the meaning of such things. We must bear in mind, however, that that was an age of symbolism. The Children of Israel had just been released from Egyptian slavery, and, as is usually the case with slaves, very few of them could either read or write. The Egyptians among whom they had lived were much given to the use of ritualism and pageantry in their own religion, and in fact even their writing was pictorial. So, making allowance for their limitations and adapting the manner of His revelation to their capacity to receive, God graciously gave them the Gospel in picture. By elementary and kindergarten methods a visible representation was provided through which the essentials of the way of salvation were kept constantly before their eyes. This was, of course, not the only message given to them, but was supplementary to, and to some extent explanatory of, that which was given orally and sometimes in writing by the prophets.

The priestly and sacrificial system was designed primarily to center the attention of the people on the coming Messiah, and to teach that there was a way of pardon and access to God. Like shadows of coming events, the sacrifices and rituals of the old system shortened up into definiteness of outline, then vanished completely when the full meridian splendor of the Sun of Righteousness appeared. What our fathers saw only dimly and at a distance we now see in broad daylight. The priesthood and the rituals were thus not the essence of the Church, but only its passing form, and were to be observed only until the One whose coming they foretold had accomplished His work. That the blood of bulls and goats had no power to take away sins, and that the animal sacrifices were only types of the perfect sacrifice which later was to be made on man's behalf, was understood by the enlightened Israelite. It was therefore appointed that such sacrifices and rituals should be repeated daily.

In general conformity with this Dr. A. A. Hodge has said: "The sacrifices of bulls and goats were like token-money, as our paper-promises to pay, accepted at their face-value till the day of settlement. But the sacrifice of Christ was the gold which absolutely extinguished

---

*For a fuller discussion of the doctrine of election and the extent of the atonement, see: "The Reformed Doctrine of Predestination," pp. 83-161, by the present writer.

all debt by its intrinsic value. Hence, when Christ died, the veil that separated man from God was rent from the top to the bottom by supernatural hands. When the real expiation was finished, the whole symbolical system representing it became *functum officio*, and was abolished. Soon after this, the temple was razed to the ground, and the ritual was rendered forever impossible." (Popular Lectures, p. 247).

And John Calvin has this to say concerning the temporary and provisional character of the sacrificial system: "What could be more vain and frivolous than for men to offer the fetid stench arising from the fat of cattle, in order to reconcile themselves to God? or to resort to aspersions of water or of blood, to cleanse themselves from pollution? In short, the whole legal worship, if it be considered in itself, and contain no shadows and figures of correspondent truths, will appear perfectly ridiculous . . . Unless there had been some spiritual design, to which they were directed, the Jews would have labored to no purpose in these observances, as the Gentiles did in their mummeries. Profane men, who have never seriously devoted themselves to the pursuit of piety, have not patience to hear of such various rites; they not only wonder why God should weary His ancient people with such a mass of ceremonies, but they even despise and deride them as puerile and ludicrous. This arises from inattention to the end of the legal figures, from which if these figures be separated, they must be condemned as vain and useless. But the 'pattern,' which is mentioned, shows that God commanded the sacrifices, not with a design to occupy His worshippers in terrestrial exercises, but rather that He might elevate their minds to sublimer objects. This may be likewise evinced by His nature; for as He is a Spirit, He is pleased with none but spiritual worship. Testimonies of this truth may be found in the numerous passages of the Prophets, in which they reprove the stupidity of the Jews for supposing that sacrifices possess any real value in the sight of God. Do they mean to derogate from the law? Not at all; but being true interpreters of it, they designate by this method to direct the eyes of the people to that point from which the multitudes were wandering." (The Institutes, Book II, Ch. 7).

With this background concerning the nature and purpose of the Old Testament sacrifices and rituals we are now ready to ask, What did the ceremonial system of ancient Israel teach concerning the atonement?

Under the Old Testament ritual, atonement for sin was made by the sacrifice of an animal. The animal, whether lamb, bullock or goat, had to be perfect, without spot or blemish of any kind. In the law concerning sacrifices special emphasis was placed on the blood. Concerning it God said: "The life of the flesh is in the blood; and I have given it to you upon the altar to make atonement for your souls: for it is the blood that maketh atonement by reason of the life," Lev. 17:11. The lesson taught was that the life of an innocent holy thing was given to cover the confessed guilt of the erring one. The person who came bringing an animal to be slain thereby confessed himself deserving of death but made petition that God in His mercy would accept instead the life of this his substitute. Sacrifices were offered daily throughout the year, and the penitent sinner could bring his offering at any time. The fundamental element so eloquently symbolized in this ritual was that the life of a holy thing was given to cover the confessed guilt of erring man.

The Day of Atonement

Once each year, on the day of atonement, a special sin-offering was made for the nation of Israel, and the full doctrine was exhibited more fully than was possible in the individual offering. Two he goats were taken from the congregation. Lots were cast to determine which one was to be put to death. When it was slain some of its blood was carried even into the Holy of Holies and sprinkled over the mercy seat. The other goat was not slain. Instead the high priest placed his hands upon its head, confessed over it the sins of the people, symbolically transferring them to it, and then sent it away by the hand of an attendant into the wilderness or solitary place where it would be lost. This goat was to "bear upon him all their iniquities unto a solitary land," Lev. 16:22. In the death of the first goat, which through no fault of its own poured out its soul unto death and thus paid the prescribed penalty for sin, the people were taught that the penalty for their sin was laid on another, on their legal substitute. The animal actually received what the people deserved, that is, death.

Dr. John D. Davis has pointed out that through the ritual connected with the second goat the people were "taught by symbolical act that their sins have been carried away, and removed from the sight and presence of themselves and of Jehovah who dwells in their midst. The two goats together constituted one sin offering. Two were necessary, because of the physical impossibility of setting forth by one goat the two elements to be exhibited. One object was attained. The life of the holy thing was placed before God, and the sin was thereby removed from the camp. God then treated the congregation as without sin; not merely as though He could not see their sin, but as though it were actually removed. It was not only covered and hidden, so that God did not see it; but it was no longer in the camp, it had been removed, never to return. Such was the symbolical teaching. In the full sense, atonement had been secured the sin was expiated, and the sinner was accepted as righteous."

The idea of vicarious and expiatory sacrifice, or in other words, the doctrine of substitution by blood atonement, is woven into the very warp and woof of both the Old and the New Testament. It is set forth with special clearness in the book of Leviticus and in other parts of the priest's code. It is nowhere contradicted, although the prophets gave repeated warnings that the mere performance of the ceremony without a truly penitent heart could avail nothing to the offerer. The priests, who in reality were only types of the great High Priest who was to come, were not permitted to enter the sanctuary without blood; that the faithful might know that only through the sacrifice of the life of another could their lives be spared. And the well-nigh universal prevalence of sacrifice among heathen as well as Jewish people expressed man's consciousness that sin subjects him to the wrath of God, and that that wrath can be turned away only when amends have been made through the forfeiture of life, either his own or that of his legal substitute.

THE TABERNACLE AND ITS RITUAL

In the structure and ritual of the tabernacle there is revealed a most remarkable symbolism, through which the people were given a clearer understanding of the great redemptive truths of the faith. We get some idea of the importance which God attached to the tabernacle and its ritual from the fact that approximately one-third of the book of Exodus, all of Leviticus, and a considerable part of Numbers is devoted to it. Two-thirds of the account of the events at Sinai are also given to this subject. The tabernacle—and later the temple, which was built on the same plan—was designed to teach God's willingness to dwell with His people, and the condition on which this great blessing can be secured. This method of instruction was similar to that with which the Children of Israel had been familiar in Egypt, where every attribute of Deity was represented by some outward form and where, as we have said, even the writing was pictorial.

As the tabernacle was set up, God was in the Holy of Holies, man is outside of the enclosure, and the way is explained step by step as we go from the door back into the holiest of all, to the ark and the mercy seat and the shekinah light which was the visible presence of God. Here the mystery as to how a holy God can dwell with sinful man, and how sinful man is enabled to come into the presence of a holy God, is solved. The tabernacle was a tent, God's tent, pitched at a considerable distance outside the camp,—about two-thirds of a mile. God called the people to Him. But to get to Him they had to come out from the camp. The corresponding truth is that God dwells in Christ, and to get to Him we have to come out from the "world" with its sinful ways and practices. Christ is our tabernacle,—"And the Word became flesh, and dwelt [the Greek says, tabernacled] among us, and we beheld His glory, glory as of the only begotten of the Father, full of grace and truth," John 1:14. Speaking of His body Jesus said, "Destroy this temple, and in three days I will raise it up," John 2:19. The body of Christ is the dwelling place of God. In a somewhat analogous manner God dwelt in the tabernacle, and later in the temple; and thus by a picture visible to all the congregation, to young and old alike, to the literate and the illiterate, great spiritual truths were set forth.

The tabernacle, although comparatively small—it was forty-five feet long, fifteen feet wide and fifteen feet high—was a costly structure, worth about $1,500,000. Unlike most costly churches today, it was not encumbered with debt and mortgage, but was provided through the free will offering of the people who gave so generously that there was more than enough and Moses had to say to them, "Stop!"

Surrounding the tabernacle there was an enclosure or court, seventy-five feet wide and one hundred and fifty feet long, enclosed with pillars and curtains. Thus God's dwelling place is separate, holy, shut off from the rest of the world and from sin. At the front of the court (facing eastward) there is an entrance, the only entrance, with a curtain of blue and scarlet and purple, probably symbolical of the heavenly, the earthly, and the kingly. In a peculiar sense God dwelt within the tabernacle in the Holy of Holies, His presence there being symbolized by the shekinah light.

As we pass through the tri-colored door into the sacred enclosure, very near the entrance and directly before us we find a brazen box or altar, seven and a half feet square and four and a half feet high. It is hollow, made of wood and overlaid with brass. At each corner is a projection or horn, to which the animals for sacrifice might be tied. This is the largest and most prominent piece of furniture in the enclosure. It occupies the foremost place and is very important. No priest could enter the tabernacle except he first placed a sacrifice upon this altar, and the high priest could not go into the Holy of Holies until he had placed his sacrifice there. No teaching could be plainer than this: there can be no access of the sinner to God without an atoning sacrifice. Not only the glory within the veil, but the bread and the light and the privileges of the altar of incense or prayer, were closed until the sacrifice was offered. How forcefully it teaches the lesson that before the sinner can taste of the heavenly bread, or see the heavenly light, or pray acceptably, he must be truly repentant and must avail himself of the atonement God has provided in Christ, the Lamb of God! The tabernacle thus declares that God can be approached only through Calvary. And the great underlying doctrine of the New Testament is that we are accepted only through Christ. The fire on the altar was kindled first from heaven, and was never allowed to go out. As the people journeyed from place to place it was carried in a vessel, symbolizing the perpetuity of the atonement. In a ceaseless rotation the morning sacrifice was followed by the evening sacrifice, and the evening by the morning. The altar was the people's meeting place with God. Even the vilest, if truly repentant, was welcome and could present his offering. In the New Testament "he that will" may come; and we have the promise of Christ that "him that cometh to me I will in no wise cast out," John 6:37.

The animal used in sacrifice was domestic—never the wild animals, but those closely associated with men—without blemish, and perfect of its kind. It was not the sinner's gift—there were other offerings which were presented as gifts—but his representative, his substitute. The man laid his hands on its head and confessed his sin over it, thus signifying the transfer of his guilt to it. It was then slain and its blood sprinkled. The teaching is very clear that the way to fellowship with God for guilty human beings can be found only through an avenue of death. How effectively it testifies to the sinfulness of sin, its fatal consequences, and the need of atonement before God can be approached! Yet it also testifies that God has provided an atonement, a way back to Himself for all who will accept it.

As we proceed from the altar toward the tabernacle we find the laver midway between the altar and the tabernacle. This bowl-shaped structure was filled with water which was used by the priests to wash their hands and feet before they entered the tabernacle for service. As the altar represented justification putting away sin, or pardon, the laver represents sanctification, or the acquiring of holiness,—"without which no man shall see the Lord," Heb. 12:14; "Who shall ascend into the hill of Jehovah? And who shall stand in His holy place? He that hath clean hands, and a pure heart," Ps. 24:3, 4.

Then we come to the Tabernacle, which was a tent within tents. The outer covering was of badger's skin, a strong, stout leather to turn off the rain; the next, of goat's hair, a cloth of which all tents in the east are made; then a ram's skin covering dyed red; and underneath this covering of beauty was the tabernacle, divided into two parts, the holy place and the Holy of Holies, with its ceiling of blue and its walls of purple and scarlet. As we enter the tent we find a single curtain the type of Christ, who is the door. Inside, we find three articles of furniture. On the left hand side is the golden candlestick, with its seven branches, the only source of light since the tabernacle had no windows, and typifying Christ who is the light of the world, the only spiritual light in this world of darkness. On the right hand side stood the table of shewbread, or bread of the presence, as it was called, a table of gold, holding twelve loaves, one for each of the tribes, and representing the communion and fellowship of the soul in the worship of God, just as we have fellowship with our neighbor when we enter his house and sit down as his guest at his table and eat with him,— the bread being a type of Christ, the bread that came down from heaven, upon whom our souls feed and find life, who says, "I am the bread of life." And midway between the candlestick and the table of shewbread stood the altar of incense, a gold-covered box, made of thornwood, with a golden bowl at the top containing the incense which was compounded of four sweet herbs which when burned gave forth a perfumed smoke that was pleasant to inhale, and which was a type of the merits of Christ, upon which our prayers are borne up acceptably before God. The formula for compounding this incense was originally given by God, and any attempt on the part of private individuals to make incense like it was a capital offense. It thus symbolized that nothing but the merits of Christ will avail for our salvation, and that for us to trust to our own good works, or to anything else except Christ's blood and righteousness, is offensive to God and brings death to the soul.

Now we come to the last room in the tabernacle, the Holy of Holies, God's dwelling place among men. It was a cube, which is a symbol of perfection, fifteen feet long, wide, and high. In the description of heaven given in the book of Revelation the city lies four square. This room had no windows, no candle, no light, yet it was the one place in all the world where there was no darkness. For the glory of God shone continually from above the mercy seat,—and of heaven we read, "The city hath no need of the sun, neither of the moon, to shine upon it; for the glory of God did lighten it, and the lamp thereof is the Lamb . . . for there shall be no night there," Rev. 21 :23-25. Into this room no one was ever permitted to enter except the high priest, and he but once a year, and then only after the most solemn service on the day of atonement.

In the Holy of Holies there was but one article of furniture—the ark. This was a small, gold-covered box, forty-five inches long, twenty-seven inches wide, and twenty-seven inches high, with perhaps more resemblance to a cedar chest without a top than to anything else with which we are familiar. In it were kept the two tablets of stone on which were written the Law, that is, the Ten Commandments. Over the ark was the mercy seat, a cover of solid gold, forty-five inches long and twenty-seven inches wide, at each end of which was a golden cherub, facing each other and covering the mercy seat with their wings. These symbolized the presence and unapproachableness of God. The mercy seat was the only seat in the tabernacle, and it was God's seat, the throne of God. It was over the law, thus symbolizing that God's kingdom is founded on holiness. On the day of atonement the high priest took the blood from the sacrifice and sprinkled it seven times over the mercy seat, thus covering or blotting out the law, thereby making atonement first for himself and then for the people. (See Leviticus, Chapter 16). "When God looked down toward His law," says Dr. A. A. Hodge, "on which rests His throne, and which called for the execution of the penalty upon every transgression, His eye rested first on the covering bearing the sacrificial blood; the sins were therefore covered, and God was reconciled." By that ritual we are taught that we can draw near to God, not by our own good works in keeping the law, but only through mercy which forgives the transgressions of the law. Yet while we cannot gain access to God through any righteousness of our own, we must have a hungering and thirsting after righteousness. Had the tables of the law been placed at the threshold instead of in the innermost shrine, we might have thought that we could gain access to God by keeping the law. As actually arranged the teaching is not "keep the law and God will let you in," but "come in and God will give you grace to keep the law." The New Testament statement of the same truth is: "By grace have ye been saved through faith; and that not of yourselves, it is the gift of God; not of works, that no man should glory. For we are His workmanship, created in Christ Jesus for good works, which God afore prepared that we should walk in them," Eph. 2:8-10.

Separating the holy place from the Holy of Holies there was hung, according to the directions given Moses, "a veil of blue, and purple, and scarlet, and fine twined linen; with cherubim the work of the skilful workman," Ex. 26:31. This veil typified the human nature of Christ, adorned with excellent gifts and graces, by which He opened a way for us into heaven, so that Paul says we "have boldness to enter into the holy place by the blood of Jesus, by the way which He dedicated for us, a new and living way, through the veil, that is to say, His flesh," Heb. 10:19, 20. When Christ died on the cross "the veil of the temple was rent in two from the top to the bottom," Matt. 27:51, signifying that God was leaving His temple, and that all legal and ceremonial worship was at an end.

We must notice one more very remarkable phenomenon in the tabernacle: the furniture is arranged in the shape of a cross. The brazen altar is the base, the laver is the stem, the table of shewbread is the right arm, the candlestick is the left arm, the altar of incense is at the center where the shoulders touch, and the ark is the head. This design was hidden by the veil until the hour when Christ died, at which time the rending of the veil, not by human hands but by God himself, laid open the Holy of Holies. Then, standing at the brazen altar and looking toward the ark, the cross stood out clear and distinct.

Thus in the structure and ritual of the tabernacle there is presented the Gospel in picture. The brazen altar, representing Calvary, is at the very entrance; and the blood from this is sprinkled on all things back to the mercy-seat. As the worshipper passes along this wondrous path he beholds the name of Jesus stamped on all he meets. This was the visible representation kept before the people from the time of Moses until the death of Christ. And Christ Himself during His early career, while recognizing the temporary and provisional character of the ceremonial law, rendered it unfailing obedience; for it was abrogated only by His death. The rituals and ceremonies were like the moon shining in the night, not with their own but with reflected or borrowed light, foreshowing the Sun of Righteousness which was soon to appear. And when the reality appeared and accomplished the work to which the types and ceremonies of Judaism had pointed, these latter disappeared, as the petals fall away when the fruit appears, or as the moon and stars fade out when the sun arises.

Christ the Fulfillment of Old Testament Ritual

To us who are privileged to study the Old Testament in the light of the New it is abundantly clear that Christ was the reality toward which the types and rituals pointed. So overwhelming is the evidence that such is usually acknowledged to be the case, even by those who reject its validity. Christ is everywhere presented as our sacrifice. The Old Testament saints looked forward to the same sacrifice as that to which we look back. Their whole system was a build-up for the coming Messiah. Dr. A. H. Strong has observed that "Just as gravitation kept the universe stable, long before it was discovered by man, so the atonement of Christ was inuring to the salvation of men long before they suspected its existence. This light had been shining throughout the ages, but 'the darkness apprehended it not'" (John 1:5). The trail of sacrificial blood that appears just outside the gates of Eden leads unerringly to the cross of Calvary, where "once at the end of the ages hath He been manifested to put away sin by the sacrifice of Himself," Heb. 9:26. In that transaction Christ was at one and the same time the sacrifice and the Priest who offered it. We personally had nothing to offer and no hand or part in the offering—we simply stand aside under guilt and condemnation, helpless and hopeless. Hence the Scriptures declare that "While we were yet weak, in due season Christ died for the ungodly," Rom. 5:6; and again, "While we were enemies, we were reconciled to God through the death of His Son," Rom. 5:10.

We have said that Christ was a priest, specifically, that He was our great High Priest. A priest is one who represents man before the throne of God, one who is able to make a sacrifice to God on man's behalf and who on the basis of that sacrifice can intercede for man. A prophet, by way of distinction, is God's representative, God's spokesman, to man. Christ exercised, of course, not only the office of priest, but also those of prophet and king. Such an arrangement is necessary because sinful man cannot himself come into the presence of God. The Old Testament priests, particularly the high priests, were appointed to serve until the coming of the true Priest. These, however, were not real priests, but only types or shadows of the One who was to come. Christ alone has the qualifications of a real Priest, and is able to mediate with God. And with His coming and the accomplishment of His work the Levitical priesthood, together with all of its sacrifices and rituals, was forever abolished. What they typified, He actually was; and what their sacrifices pointed forward to, He actually accomplished. We look to Christ alone as our true Priest. We therefore reject all merely human and earthly priests, whether in the Roman Catholic Church or in heathen religions, and look upon their continued practice as simply an attempt to usurp divine authority.

That Christ does exercise this office as Priest is the clear teaching of Scripture. "Christ having come a high priest . . . not through the blood of goats and calves, but through His own blood, entered in once for all into the holy place, having obtained eternal. redemption," Heb. 9:11, 12. "Wherefore it behooved Him in all things to be made like unto His brethren, that He might become a merciful and faithful high priest in things pertaining to God, to make propitiation for the sins of the people," Heb. 2:17. He is "a priest forever, after the order of Melchizedek," Heb. 5:6. "But He, because He abideth for ever, Hath His priesthood unchangeable. Wherefore also He is able to save to the uttermost them that draw near unto God through Him, seeing He ever liveth to make intercession for them. For such a high priest became us, holy, guileless, undefiled, separated from sinners, and made higher than the heavens; who needeth not daily, like those high priests, to offer up sacrifices, first for his own sins, and then for the sins of the people: for this He did once for all, when He offered up Himself. For the law appointed men high priests, having infirmity; but the word of the oath, which was after the law, appointeth a Son, perfected for evermore," Heb. 7:24-28. When the whole race was shut out from God by its sin, God was pleased to choose the Israelites as a priestly nation, then to appoint Levi as the priestly tribe, then to appoint the family of Levi as the priestly family, and finally, narrowing down the choice still further, to appoint a succession of individuals from this family as a type of the great High Priest, Jesus Christ.

And that the death of Christ was a sacrifice is no less clearly taught. "But now once at the end of the ages hath He been manifested to put away sin by the sacrifice of Himself," Heb. 9:26. "For our passover also hath been sacrificed, even Christ," I Cor. 5:7. "Behold the Lamb of God, that taketh away the sin of the world," John 1:29. Christ "gave Himself up for us, an offering and a sacrifice to God for an odor of a sweet smell," Eph. 5:2. In instituting the sacrament of the Lord's Supper, Christ set forth His death in sacramental terms, saying of the bread, "This is my body which is given for you," Luke 22:19; and of the wine, "This is my blood of the covenant, which is poured out for many unto remission of sins," Matt. 26:28. His sacrifice paralleled the sin-offering of ancient Israel: "For the bodies of those beasts whose blood is brought into the holy place by the high priest as an offering for sin, are burned without the camp. Wherefore Jesus also, that He might sanctify the people through His own blood, suffered without the gate," Heb. 13:11, 12. "Christ died for our sins according to the Scriptures," I Cor. 15:3. "In whom we have our redemption through His blood," Eph. 1:7.

Even in the Old Testament, in the celebrated prophecy of Isaiah, the vicarious atonement of the coming Messiah is set forth in graphic language: "Surely He hath borne our griefs, and carried our sorrows; yet we did esteem Him stricken, smitten of God, and afflicted. But He was wounded for our transgressions, He was bruised for our iniquities; the chastisement of our peace was upon Him; and with His stripes we are healed. All we like sheep have gone astray; we have turned every one to his own way; and Jehovah hath laid on Him the iniquity of us all. . . . By oppression and judgment He was taken away; and as for His generation, who among them considered that He was cut off out of the land of the living for the transgression of my people to whom the stroke was due? . . . Yet it pleased Jehovah to bruise Him; He hath put Him to grief: when thou shalt make His soul an offering for sin, He shall see His seed, He shall prolong His days, and the pleasure of Jehovah shall prosper in His hand. He shall see of the travail of His soul, and shall be satisfied: by the knowledge of Himself shall my righteous Servant justify many; and He shall bear their iniquities. . . . He bare the sin of many, and made intercession for the transgressors," 53:4-12.

Thus the terms used to describe Christ's death are drawn mainly from the familiar ritual of sacrifice; and from its beginning Christianity, like Judaism, has been a redemptive religion. The Old and the New Testament join together in perfect harmony, the former being prophetic, while the latter is descriptive, of Christ's person and work; and in the development of the Church the transition from the Old to the New was as smooth and natural as is the transition from the bud to the flower. The first century Christians, accustomed as they were to sacrificial worship, could not have understood the Apostles to have taught anything else than that Christ, like the pascal lamb, died in order that their sins might be forgiven and that God might be disposed to look upon them with favor. Add to this the constantly reiterated doctrine that salvation is by grace and not by works and there can be no other reasonable interpretation. But in spite of this the plainest and most unequivocal language, there are some in our day, Unitarians, Modernists, skeptics of different kinds, who, simply because they like something else better and want to claim the support of Jesus for their system, insist on thrusting upon Him some other religion which is essentially different. But taking the New Testament records as our sources of information—and they are almost exclusively the only records which tell anything at all about the person and teaching of Jesus—there can be no doubt that the religion He founded was, in His own mind and in the minds of His closest followers, pre-eminently a redemptive religion.

One of the greatest tragedies of the world has been the inability of the Jews, the very people to whom this glorious revelation was given, to understand the spiritual significance of what they saw. When the veil of the temple was opened it was symbolically taught that God was leaving His temple and that all ceremonial worship was at an end. "Behold, your house is left unto you desolate," said Jesus in anticipation of His death and the end of the old order. Matt. 23:38. In destroying Jesus the Jews not only proved themselves utterly unfit to further administer the things of God, but also (and that without the faintest idea of what they were doing) destroyed the entire Levitical system to which, for commercial and selfish reasons, they were so blindly devoted.

The Apostle Paul speaks of the veil of ignorance, blindness and hardness of heart which keeps the Jews from understanding the spiritual sense and meaning of the law, and from seeing that Christ is the end of the law for righteousness to them that believe: "For unto this very day at the reading of the old covenant the same veil remaineth, it not being revealed to them that it is done away in Christ. But unto this day, whensoever Moses is read, a veil lieth upon their heart." And then he adds, "But whensoever it [or, marginal reading: a man] shall turn to the Lord, the veil is taken away," II Cor. 3:14, 15. How tragic, indeed, is the calamity which has befallen the Jewish people, the very people who were "entrusted with the oracles of God," Rom. 3:2, "of whom is Christ as concerning the flesh," Rom. 9:5. Would that they could see in Him what the humble and spiritually enlightened Simeon saw, the promised Messiah, "A light for revelation to the Gentiles, And *the glory of thy people Israel,*" Luke 2:32.

9. Erroneous Theories of the Atonement

As might have been expected, this great comprehensive doctrine of the atonement which lies at the very heart of the Gospel has not been allowed to go unchallenged. Numerous "theories of the atonement" have emerged from time to time and have been more or less prominent in the Church. Practically all of these with small variations can be included under three main heads: (1) The Moral Influence Theory; (2) The Governmental Theory; and (3) The Mystical Theory.

THE MORAL INFLUENCE THEORY

The most widely held and the most influential of the erroneous theories of the atonement is the moral influence theory. It denies that Christ died to satisfy any principle of divine justice, and holds that His death was designed primarily to impress men with a sense of God's love and thus soften their hearts and lead them to repentance. According to this view the crucifixion was a dramatic exhibition of suffering intended to produce a moral impression in awe-stricken spectators. It represents Christ as suffering for us as a loving father or mother suffers for an ungrateful son or a wayward daughter and with the purpose of moving us so that we will turn and repent. The atonement is then conceived of as directed not toward God, with the purpose of maintaining His justice, but toward man, with the purpose of persuading him to right action. Christ's work on the cross is then made to be an impressive proclamation to the world that God is willing to forgive sin on the sole condition that men turn from it. His suffering and death is explained as merely that of a martyr in the cause of right-eousness, and as the natural consequence of His having taken human nature upon Himself. He is then supposed to have shared in the woes and griefs which human living naturally involves, and His suffering was not an atonement or an expiation in any true sense of the word, but a supreme example of self-sacrifice. And we in turn are to be inspired by His example so that we too become willing to bear our crosses and give our lives in the service of some good cause, perhaps even in martyrdom, and thus work out our own salvation.

The moral influence theory holds that while Christ may have had a great influence in persuading us to walk in the way of the cross, the way of service and self-sacrifice, it is after all our walking in it and not Christ's walking it which really saves us. This means that in the final analysis we are saved by our own efforts, not by Christ's blood. Christ is then not our Saviour in any true sense of the word, but only a friend and example; and the world has had as many saviours as it has had good men and women. It is the same old notion that sinful man can save himself. It is basically the religion of naturalism, decked out in new garments and dishonestly making use of Christian terminology.

This theory rests on the assumption that God is love and only love; and, holding that repentance is the only requirement for forgiveness, it denies the existence of any law which demands that sin shall receive its just punishment. This is really the root of the whole modern assault upon the doctrine of the atonement. Dr. Warfield has very effectively analyzed and exposed this one-sided emphasis on the attribute of love, and we can do no better than to quote his words:

"In the attempt to give effect to the conception of indiscriminate and undiscriminating love as the basal fact of religion, the entire Bib-lical teaching as to atonement has been ruthlessly torn up. If God is love and nothing but love, what possible need can there be of an atone-ment? . . . Well, certainly, God *is* love. But it does not in the least follow that He is nothing but love. God *is* Love: but Love is not God and the formula 'Love' must therefore ever be inadequate to express God. It may well be—for us sinners, lost in our sin and misery but for it, it must be—the crowning revelation of Christianity that God is love. But it is not from the Christian revelation that we have learned to think of God as nothing but love. That God is the Father of all men in a true and important sense, we should not doubt. But the indiscrim-inate benevolencism which has taken captive so much of religious thinking of our time is a conception not native to Christianity, but of distinctly heathen quality. As one reads the pages of popular religious literature, teeming as it is with ill-considered assertions of the general

Fatherhood of God, he has an odd feeling of transportation back into the atmosphere of, say, the decadent heathenism of the fourth and fifth centuries when the gods were dying, and there was left to those who would fain cling to the old ways little beyond a somewhat saddened sense of the *benignitas numinis*. The *benignitas numinis!* How studded the pages of those genial old heathen are with the expression; how suffused their repressed life is with the conviction that the kind Deity that dwells above will surely not be hard on men toiling here below! How shocked they are at the stern righteousness of the Christian's God, who loomed before their startled eyes as He looms before those of the modern poet in no other light than as 'the hard God that dwelt in Jerusalem'! Surely the Great Divinity is too broadly good to mark the peccadillos of poor puny man; surely they are the objects of His compassionate amusement rather than of His fierce reprobation. Like Omar Khayyam's pot, they were convinced, before all things, of their Maker that 'He's a good fellow and 'twill all be well."

"The query cannot help rising to the surface of our minds whether our modern indiscriminate benevolencism goes much deeper than this. Does all this one-sided proclamation of the universal Fatherhood of God import much more than the heathen *benignitas numinis?* When we take those blessed words, 'God is Love,' upon our lips, are we sure we mean to express much more than that we do not. wish to believe that God will hold man to any real account for his sin? Are we, in a word, in these modern days, so much soaring upward toward a more adequate apprehension of the transcendent truth that God is love, as passionately protesting against being ourselves branded and dealt with as wrathdeserving sinners? Assuredly it is impossible to put anything like their real content into these great words, 'God is Love,' save as they are thrown out against the background of those other conceptions of equal loftiness, 'God is Light,' 'God is Righteousness,' 'God is Holiness,' 'God is a consuming fire.' The love of God cannot be apprehended in its length and breadth and height and depth—all of which pass knowledge —save as it is apprehended as the love of a God who turns from the sight of sin with inexpressible abhorrence, and burns against it with unquenchable indignation. The infinitude of His love would be illustrated not by His lavishing of His favor on sinners without requiring an expiation of sin, but by His—through such holiness and through such righteousness as cannot but cry out with infinite abhorrence and indignation—still loving sinners so greatly that He provides a satisfaction for their sin adequate to these tremendous demands. It is the distinguishing characteristic of Christianity, after all, not that it preaches a God of love, but that it preaches a God of conscience. .

And a thoroughly conscientious God, we may be sure, is not a God who can deal with sinners as if they were not sinners. In this fact lies, perhaps, the deepest ground of the necessity of an expiatory atonement.

"And it is in this fact also that there lies the deepest ground of the increasing failure of the modern world to appreciate the necessity of an expiatory atonement. Conscientiousness commends itself only to awakened conscience; and in much of recent theologizing conscience does not seem especially active. Nothing, indeed, is more startling in the structure of recent theories of atonement, than the apparently vanishing sense of sin that underlies them. Surely it is only where the sense of the power of sin has profoundly decayed, that men can fancy that they can at will cast it off from them in a 'revolutionary repentance.' Surely it is only where the sense of the heinousness of sin has practically passed away, that man can imagine that the holy and just God can deal with it lightly. If we have not much to be saved from, why, certainly a very little atonement will suffice for our needs. It is, after all, only the sinner that requires a Saviour. But if we are sinners, and in proportion as we know ourselves to be sinners, and appreciate what it means to be sinners, we will cry out for that Saviour who only after He was perfected by suffering could become the Author of salvation" — *Studies in Theology,* p. 294 f.

The advocates of the moral influence theory are never tired of ridiculing the idea that God must be propitiated. They give no hint of the Scripture doctrine of the subjective effects of sin on the human heart by which it is alienated from God and unable to respond to any appeal of right motives however powerful. They see no impassable gulf between the holy God and sinful man, and, consequently, they see no reason why satisfaction should be made to divine justice. If, as they say, God is continually reaching out His arms from heaven toward man, and the whole difficulty is in inducing men to permit themselves to be pardoned, why, then, of course, there can be no need for an atonement, and in fact the whole idea of atonement is reduced to absurdity. But the Scriptures teach, on the one hand, that the justice of God must be vindicated, and on the other, that an internal action of the Holy Spirit upon the human heart is necessary before man can comprehend spiritual truth, or repent, and that this gift of the Spirit has been purchased for the believer by the sacrifice of Christ. Paul very explicitly grounds the necessity for the atonement, not in the love of God, but in His righteousness or justice, declaring that the ultimate purpose of the atonement was "that He might be just, and the justifier of him that hath faith in Jesus," Rom. 3:26.

The history of the doctrine of the atonement shows how very difficult it is to maintain belief in the Deity of Christ in connection with the moral influence theory. On the basis of this theory the example of a human Christ who, supposedly, is nearer to us, serves as well or even better than a divine Christ. Most modern books on the atonement refuse to impute to man either the sin of Adam or the righteousness of Christ, and so they logically deny both the fall of the race in Adam and the redemption of the race in Christ. They see in Jesus only a great teacher and friend, and consequently their religion tends downward toward the level of humanism.

The far-reaching effect of the moral influence theory and the thoroughness with which it disrupts the whole Christian system has been well stated by Dr. A. H. Strong, who declares that "logically it necessitates a curtailment or surrender of every other characteristic doctrine of Christianity—Inspiration, sin, the Deity of Christ, justification, regeneration, and eternal retribution. It requires surrender of inspiration; for the idea of vicarious and expiatory sacrifice is woven into the very warp and woof of the Old and New Testaments. It requires an abandonment of the Scripture doctrine of sin; for in it all ideas of sin as perversion of nature rendering the sinner unable to save himself, and an objective guilt demanding satisfaction to the divine holiness, is denied. It requires us to give up the Deity of Christ; for if sin is a slight evil, and man can save himself from its penalty and power, then there is no longer need of infinite suffering or an infinite Saviour, and a human Christ is as good as a divine. It requires us to give up the Scripture doctrine of justification, as God's act of declaring the sinner just in the eyes of the law, solely on account of the righteousness and death of Christ to whom he is united by faith; for it cannot permit the counting to man of any other righteousness than his own. It requires a denial of the doctrine of regeneration; for this is no longer the work of God, but the work of the sinner; it is no longer a change of the affections below consciousness, but a self-reforming volition of the sinner himself. It requires a denial of eternal retribution; for this is no longer appropriate to finite transgression of arbitrary law, and to superficial sinning that does not involve [a change in the moral] nature."—Systematic Theology, p. 730.

We readily acknowledge that the surpassing love of God as displayed in the death of Christ on the cross should cause men to forsake their sin and return to God; but the fact of the matter is that this kind of an appeal does not and cannot touch the unregenerate heart. The experience of New England Unitarianism and of present day Modernism makes it perfectly clear that the moral influence theory of the atonement is morally powerless,—and that for the reason that it puts man back on the plane of the so-called natural religions. It takes from Christ His own garment (the garment which the writer of the book of Revelation says is "sprinkled with blood," which has inscribed on it His name, "King of Kings and Lord of Lords," 19:13, 16), and puts on another, divests Him of His glory, and proceeds to proclaim, not the Gospel of the New Testament, but a man-made gospel, which has no power to move sinners to repentance. The convicted sinner knows that he is guilty and polluted, and that he has a debt to be paid to divine justice. And not until he is convinced that Christ has paid that debt for him can he think hopefully of reforming his life.

Furthermore, it should be realized by all that a tragedy gotten up for the transparent purpose of affecting our feelings, having no inherent principle or necessity in itself, necessarily defeats itself and produces only disgust. An unjust punishment is a crime in itself. To hang an innocent man for the good of the community is both a crime and a blunder. Only when the hanging is justified by the ill-desert of the person can it be seen by all the community as either just or necessary.

The moral influence theory furnishes no proper explanation of the suffering and death of Christ, but rather makes absurd if not even criminal His voluntary acceptance of such suffering and death in the very prime of His manhood. Furthermore, if He died simply as a martyr instead of the sin-bearer for His people, it is utterly impossible to explain why in His deepest suffering He was utterly forsaken by the Father.

THE GOVERNMENTAL THEORY

The governmental theory of the atonement holds that because of His absolute sovereignty God is able to relax at will the demands of the law and to forgive men freely without any expiation or sacrifice for sin, but that in order to preserve a fair degree of discipline and respect for law so that men shall not be encouraged to believe that they can commit sin with impunity, He must at the same time give some exhibition of the high estimate which He sets upon the law. The primary purpose in the suffering of Christ then was, not to satisfy any eternal principle of divine justice as the satisfaction view holds, nor to break down man's opposition to God by a manifestation of His love as in the moral influence theory, but to secure man's reformation by inducing in him a horror for sin through the awful spectacle of Christ on the cross. With that spectacle before their eyes men were to be made to understand what a serious thing sin really is, that it will not be allowed to go unpunished, and so induced to maintain respect for divine government even in the face of repeated acts of executive clemency. The governmental theory does not hold that Christ suffered the precise penalty which was originally attached to the law, nor even an equivalent of that penalty, but something much less, which God in His sovereignty is at liberty to accept as a substitute for that penalty. Having given this exhibition of His displeasure with sin, God is now able to offer salvation on much easier terms than those originally announced. Instead of demanding perfect obedience He now demands only faith and a reasonable degree of good works, all of which is, of course, worked out by the person himself. There is, therefore, a vast difference between this theory and the satisfaction view which holds that we are saved solely through the perfect obedience of Christ, which obedience conforms to the high demands which were originally set forth as the condition of salvation.

The element of truth in the governmental theory is that the death of Christ actually is a warning that sin shall not be allowed to go unpunished, and that the orderly government of the universe can continue only as men do have respect for law. But we hold that the primary object of punishment is not to instill devotion to the idea of government, or to an abstract idea of law, but the satisfaction of divine justice, and that righteousness must be done for its own sake, because it is right. No deeply convicted sinner feels that his controversy is with government or law as such, but that he is confronted with an intensely personal problem, that he is polluted and undone, and in antagonism to the purity of a personal God,—"Against thee, thee only, have I sinned," said the truly penitent David when he saw his sin in its true light, Ps. 51:4; and the humble publican cried out, "God, be thou merciful to me a sinner," Luke 18:13.

The governmental theory makes no provision for, and in fact it denies the possibility of, the imputation of the sinner's guilt to Christ or of Christ's righteousness to us. It therefore represents God as unjust in that He punishes an innocent person merely for the sake of the impression that it will make on others. Ill-desert must always go before punishment. Unless the punishment is right and just in itself it can work no good to society. This theory fails to recognize the extreme heinousness of sin, and assumes that sin can be adequately punished with a penalty less than that which God Himself originally set against it. But if that is true and if God in His sovereignty is at liberty to assign whatever value He pleases to every created thing presented to Him, then the blood of bulls and goats could just as well have taken away sins,—the sufferings of Christ were superfluous, and He died in vain. This theory assumes that man has the power to change his moral nature at will and that to accomplish this he needs only to be surrounded by good influences, whereas the Scriptures teach that he needs a complete change of nature, or regeneration, which benefit was purchased for him by Christ and can be made effective only through the power of the Holy Spirit. And finally, the light view of sin which this theory holds fails utterly to show forth the deep love of God for His people; for it has no adequate understanding of the cost involved when God Himself—not a mere man, but God Himself in the person of Christ—took our place on the accursed tree.

The governmental theory is, of course, an inconsistent and unstable theory, and it is held by only a comparatively small number of people. It was invented by a prominent Dutch theologian and jurist of the seventeenth century, Hugo Grotius, who approached the subject from the judicial standpoint. He held that in the forgiveness of sin God is to be regarded primarily as a moral governor or ruler who must act, not according to His emotions or desires, but with a view to the best interests of all of those under His authority. The work of Christ was thus conceived of as purely didactic, and the cross was but a symbol, designed to teach, by way of example, God's hatred for sin.

The governmental theory is sometimes called the "intermediate view." It is not as seriously in error as is the moral influence theory, which conceives of the whole purpose of the atonement as designed to influence man, while this theory acknowledges that it is in part directed toward God in that it is designed to maintain respect for His law. But in principle the two are not essentially different, for each denies any necessity of satisfying divine justice and each holds that the primary design of the cross was to produce an effect in man.

The Mystical Theory

There is one more theory that we must mention, generally known as the "mystical theory." In this theory the human race is looked upon as a mass or unit or organism rather than as individuals, and the seeds of death and corruption which were introduced into the race through the sin of Adam are counteracted and overcome by the principles of life and immortality which Christ is supposed to have introduced into the race through His incarnation. Redemption is regarded as having been accomplished not by anything that Christ taught or did, but by the incarnation in which Deity was infused into or united with humanity. According to some advocates of this theory, in the incarnation, Christ assumed human nature as He found it, that is, fallen human nature, and not only kept it from sinning but purified it by the power of His own divine nature; and men are saved as, by faith, they become partakers of this purified humanity. According to others, the original depravity which the race inherited from Adam was supposed to have been gradually overcome during the earthly life of Jesus until at the time of His death human nature was restored to its original glory and fellowship with God. According to some, humanity is finally to be deified. Redemption is thus conceived of as terminating physically on man in that the transforming essence of Deity was put into the mass of humanity as leaven into a lump of dough. Christ is regarded as having taken into union with Himself not a real and separate human body and soul, but humanity as a generic substance; and the result was a blood brotherhood in which Christ's inner spiritual life was communicated to man, awakening in him the dormant God-consciousness and enabling him to overcome the sensuous world-consciousness.

The mystical theory has never been held by a large number of people, although it has persisted since the early Greek Fathers and has been held by widely separated groups. Its strength lies in the fact that it lays stress on an important truth, namely, the fact that all believers are in a true sense united with Christ and partake of a new nature. But we hold that this union is made effective, not through the incarnation, but through the work of the Holy Spirit, and in individuals rather than in humanity as a mass. This theory is also commendable in that it ascribes redemption to divine grace and emphasizes the importance of holy living.

But there are serious objections against it. In the first place it contradicts the plain teaching of Scripture. It asserts that Christ's suffering and death form no essential part of His redemptive work, while the Scriptures strongly emphasize His suffering and death as the basis for the remission of sin. Nowhere in Scripture are we told that Christ became incarnate in order that He might infuse divine life into humanity. Rather we are told that He assumed human nature in order that in it He might suffer the penalty which was due to His people and thus free them from the obligation which rested upon them.

The mystical theory is essentially pantheistic in its tendency. Its assertion that divine life was infused into the human in order to purify and lift the human to the divine breaks down the fundamental distinction between God and man, and leaves the way open for a pantheistic interpretation of life. Its logical corollary is that ultimately the entire human race which has lived since the time of Christ will be transformed and restored to holiness and God.

It leaves unexplained the redemption of the saints who died before the time of Christ, since the subjective and somewhat mechanical process through which redemption is supposed to have been accomplished could not have affected them. Some of its advocates have gone so far as to say that there was no salvation before the time of Christ and that all of the patriarchs perished.

In concluding this study we should observe that each of the erroneous views errs by defect. Each substitutes for the chief aim of the atonement one which is subordinate and incidental. But at no time in the history of the Church has any one of these been able to displace the doctrine of "satisfaction," either in the creeds or in the hearts of believers. In the final analysis no one of them makes any provision for the satisfaction of divine justice, and therefore offers nothing that can honestly be called an atonement. The burden of the apostolic preaching was not that Christ's death was designed primarily to move men by a transcendant display of God's love, nor that it was designed to induce respect for some general or abstract principle of law, nor that all mankind was to be reunited to God by some mysterious union of the divine and human, but rather that He "was delivered up for our trespasses and was raised for our justification" (Rom. 4:25). Very few earnest Christians can ever be persuaded to believe that the life and death of Christ was only "a liturgical service, a chant and a dirge, to move the world's mind; a pageant with a moral."

Neither the moral influence nor the governmental nor the mystical theory finds any support in the sacrificial system of ancient Israel. In no instance is there the slightest indication that any Old Testament sacrifice was ever designed to produce a moral influence on the offerer, or to teach a general respect for law or government, or to illustrate the infusion of the divine nature into the human. Always the immediate and primary end sought in sacrifice was *forgiveness;* and the effect is said to be "to make atonement for sin," Lev. 4:20, 26, 31; 6:30; II Chr. 29:24.

The fact of the matter is that the satisfaction view sets forth much more profoundly and effectively the elements of truth which each of these theories embraces, while at the same time it refutes and excludes their erroneous elements. In revealing to us the infinite love of God for His people and showing at what great cost our redemption was purchased it far excels the moral influence theory in producing in us the particular moral effect which that theory was designed to produce, while at the same time it avoids the error of assuming that the sufferings of Christ were designed primarily to influence men rather than to satisfy divine justice. In revealing to us the true nature of the law of

God as a transcript of the divine nature, which therefore is perfect and holy and immutable, it far excels the governmental theory in producing respect for that law, while it avoids the errors of assuming that punishment laid on an innocent person can of itself produce a good reaction in human society. And in revealing to us how we are legally and representatively united with Christ so that our sin and punishment becomes His while His righteousness and inheritance and glory becomes ours, it far excels the mystical theory in portraying the true nature of our union with Him, while it avoids the error of assuming that sinful human nature is cleansed by an infusion of divine life such as that theory supposes to have occurred at the incarnation.

Conclusion

Quite often we hear it said that it makes little difference what "theory" of the atonement we hold. The fact of the matter is that it makes all the difference in the world. If when we contemplate the cross of Christ we see there the eternal Son of God who loved us and gave Himself for us, who assumed the curse and bought us with His own most precious blood, we shall have the supernatural Christian faith which is set forth in the Scriptures. But if in the suffering of Christ we see only a noble example of self-sacrifice which we in turn are to emulate as well as we can and so work out our own salvation, we shall have only a man-made naturalistic religion such as has deluded so many multitudes down through the ages.

With so much of the world in confusion and men's souls so sorely tried as they are today, this certainly is no time to talk of bloodless atonement. The truly penitent soul, conscious of the burden of sin and guilt, cries out for redemption and refuses to be satisfied with anything else. Others may build on the sands of human speculation if they wish. We are convinced that Christ's death is the only means of salvation, and that where it is unknown or neglected or rejected the soul perishes. The distinction is indeed vital. It is the most momentous that can confront any person.

That the doctrine of the atonement has been neglected and obscured in our day is very evident. Only rarely do we hear a sermon or see an article printed on it. Yet it is the very heart of the Christian message and without it the Gospel is powerless. The minister who neglects it either because of a lack of spiritual experience or because of intellectual difficulties associated with it, becomes hesitant and ineffective or eccentric and sensational,—and that for the very simple reason that his message will then be seriously lacking either in spiritual depth or in intellectual background. In either case it cannot be taken seriously by either minister or hearers. No doubt much of the lack of spiritual power and warmth so frequently charged against the religious life of our day is due in large measure to the neglect of this cardinal truth in so many churches. We do not mean to imply that it has been lost from the hearts of the Christian community. For, as Dr. Warfield has said, "It is in terms of the substitutive atonement that the humble Christian everywhere still expresses the grounds of his hope of salvation. It is in its terms that the earnest evangelist everywhere still presses the claims of Christ upon the awakened hearer. It has not even been lost from the forum of theological discussion. It still commands powerful advocates wherever a vital Christianity enters academic circles ; and, as a rule, the more profound the thinker the more clear is the note he strikes in its proclamation and defense."—*Studies in Theology*, p. 287.

While the satisfaction view was in substance the view held by the Church from the earliest days, it was not analyzed and set forth in systematic form until the eleventh century, when Anselm, Archbishop of Canterbury, set it forth in his epoch-making book, *Cur Deus Homo*. Since that time it has been an essential part of the creeds and doctrines of all Christian churches, Catholic and Protestant.

At the time of the Reformation the Protestant theologians put the strongest emphasis on the doctrine of the atonement. Calvin in particular in his *Insitutes* worked it out broadly in all of its implications. The result was a dynamic and evangelistic faith. A return to that emphasis probably would do more to re-vitalize the Church and to restore its evangelistic zeal than anything else that could possibly be done. The hierarchy of the Roman Catholic Church has been quick to realize that their main hold on the minds and hearts of the plain people through all the centuries has been the Mass, which is the visible re-enactment, by the use of symbols, of the suffering and death of Christ. Even the pagan religions, with their elaborate temple services and systems of sacrifice, are witnesses to the fact that something more than a lovely system of ethics or a winsome example of fine behaviour is needed to lift the burden of sin from the human soul.

The doctrine of the atonement thus emerges as a vital doctrine in the Christian system. On no other basis than that of Christ's redemptive work is any one warranted in calling himself a Christian. In all other systems one's entire relation with Christ, the ground of His acceptance with God and therefore the entire nature of his religious life, is different. The validity of Christianity as a God-given supernatural system of redemption from sin is bound up with the truth or falsity of its distinctive doctrine of the atonement. We are living in a day when many things pass for "Christianity." But Christianity has a fixed and definite doctrinal content as certainly as Mormonism, Mohammedanism, and Christian Science have their fixed and definite doctrinal contents. At a minimum Christianity involves (1) acknowledgment of one's sin; (2) sorrow for that sin; and (3) trust in Christ as one's only Redeemer from sin. The doctrinal content of Christianity has been fixed by Christ, either personally or through His Apostles, and has been unchangeably recorded in the Bible. For any one to call himself a Christian only because it is popular to do so, or because he approves of the general moral or social life that is found in a Christian community, is as dishonest and unethical as it would be for him to call himself a Mormon or a Mohammedan only because he likes certain outward features in one of those systems. We are not at liberty to call anything "Christianity" unless it conforms to the system of doctrine that was established by Christ Himself.